Routledge Library Editions

A KEY TO RICARDO

ECONOMICS

HISTORY OF ECONOMIC THOUGHT
In 23 Volumes

I	A Select Bibliography of Modern Economic Theory	*Batson*
II	Early British Economics	*Beer*
III	Nassau Senior	*Bowley*
IV	The Theory of Marginal Value	*Birck*
V	Ricardo and the Theory of Value Distribution and Growth	*Caravale & Tosato*
VI	Productive Labour and Effective Demand	*Coontz*
VII	London Essays in Economics	*Gregory & Dalton*
VIII	Capitalism and the Historians	*Hayek*
IX	The Origins of Scientific Economics	*Letwin*
X	The Individual in Society	*Macfie*
XI	Essays on Hayek	*Machlup*
XII	The Economics of Physiocracy	*Meek*
XIII	Karl Marx	*Mehring*
XIV	Marx's Critique of Political Economy I	*Oakley*
XV	Marx's Critique of Political Economy II	*Oakley*
XVI	J R McCulloch	*O'Brien*
XVII	A Key to Ricardo	*St Clair*
XVIII	Roads to Freedom	*Streissler*
XIX	Economics in the Twentieth Century	*Suranyi-Unger*
XX	Elements of Pure Economics	*Walras*
XXI	The Common Sense of Political Economy I	*Wicksteed*
XXII	The Common Sense of Political Economy II	*Wicksteed*
XXIII	Social Economics	*von Wieser*

A KEY TO RICARDO

OSWALD ST CLAIR

Routledge
Taylor & Francis Group
LONDON AND NEW YORK

First published in 1957

Reprinted in 2003 by
Routledge
2 Park Square, Milton Park, Abingdon, Oxon OX14 4RN
or
270 Madison Avenue, New York, NY 10016

First issued in paperback 2010

Routledge is an imprint of the Taylor & Francis Group

British Library Cataloguing in Publication Data
A CIP catalogue record for this book
is available from the British Library

A Key to Ricardo
ISBN 978-0-415-31337-7 (hbk)
ISBN 978-0-415-60728-5 (pbk)

Miniset: History of Economic Thought

Series: Routledge Library Editions – Economics

A KEY TO RICARDO

OSWALD ST. CLAIR

A KEY TO RICARDO

London

Routledge & Kegan Paul

First published 1957

Broadway House, Carter Lane, E.C.4

Contents

Foreword

RICARDO is one of the most imposing figures in the history of economic thought, yet at times his writings are among the most obscure. Often he wrote the simplest and plainest English, but he wrote also many passages which contain riddles and apparent inconsistencies. In this book, Mr. Oswald St. Clair attempts to trace, simplify and clarify Ricardo's ideas on the principal topics on which he wrote. A valuable service has thus been performed for students and scholars. The recently published ten-volume Cambridge edition of the works of Ricardo, edited with great care, learning and insight by Piero Sraffa and M. H. Dobb,[1] began to appear just as Mr. St. Clair's work was in process of completion. But the publication of the Cambridge volumes enhances the value of the present contribution. The student who is in a position to do so may well read Mr. St. Clair's 'Key' with the ten-volume edition at hand. There are page references throughout to this edition as well as to the original publications.

Mr. St. Clair, like Ricardo himself, is not a professional economist. He is a retired business man. As a youth, he entered the profession of insurance because, he says, he thought it would give him leisure for the indulgence of his love for literature and art. The controversy between Ruskin and J. S. Mill caught his attention, and his interest in the classical economists, and economics generally, dates from his study of the latter's *Political Economy*. He has published two other books on economic topics: *Low Wages and No Wages*, 1908; and *The Physiology of Credit and Money*, 1919.

On his retirement—at the age of sixty-eight—the author, who is now eighty-seven, decided to write an elementary introduction to the theory of value. It was in the course of planning this work

[1] *The Works and Correspondence of David Ricardo*, edited by Piero Sraffa and M. H. Dobb, 10 volumes, Cambridge at the University Press, from the Royal Economic Society, 1951–5.

that he perceived the need for a *key* to Ricardo. He saw that students would be greatly assisted by a work which firstly dissected and explained the somewhat cryptic passages which occur in Ricardo's writings, and secondly considered the reasoning by which he was sometimes led to apparently erroneous conclusions. It is a virtue of Mr. St. Clair's treatment that he does *not* try to interpret Ricardo in the light of modern economic theory or to apply the teachings of the great economist to the problems of the modern world. To deal fairly with the classical economists, we must see them in the light of their contemporaries and the world that they knew. But the relevance of the Ricardian contribution to the present age and its thinking is obvious.

Teachers of economics and those who lecture on the history of economic thought will, I believe, find Mr. St. Clair's book invaluable, even though they may not, on all points, accept the author's conclusions.

W. H. HUTT

Professor of Commerce,
University of Cape Town.

Preface

In undertaking this study of 'Ricardo's Book of Headaches' (as I have heard it called) I had in mind principally the Home Student. Ricardo's *Principles of Political Economy and Taxation* is written in very simple English; but while easy to read, it is by no means always easy to understand. The late Professor Cannan called it a 'happy hunting-ground to the false interpreter'. The book, in fact, teems with baffling conundrums. My aim has been to analyse every difficult passage in a manner which would save the Home Student much despairing puzzlement and expenditure of precious time. For this task I felt that I had one qualification not possessed by professional economists, namely, a considerable degree of obtuseness; it seemed to me that if I could make Ricardo's meaning perfectly clear to myself, it would necessarily be perfectly clear to the average reader. I hope that in this I have not flattered myself unduly.

De Quincey, a great admirer of Ricardo, attributed his obscurity to profundity of thought. It is natural, said the author of the *Opium Eater*, that a man of brilliant intellect should express himself in elliptical language, difficult for less gifted persons to follow; those who dig up Truth from the mine where it lies hidden, he said, are seldom fitted to be also the labourers of the Mint who shape the precious metal for general circulation. Hence the need for 'popularisation' such as I have attempted in this book.

Another authority, however, writing about the same time, took a different view of 'the occasional obscurity which clouds Mr. Ricardo's writings'. 'His language', said Samuel Bailey, 'is uncommonly precise and perspicuous, and the construction of his periods is simple and compact. . . . The defect has a deeper source, and is to be traced . . . to an original perplexity and confusion in some fundamental ideas, from which he was never able to extricate himself. Although Mr. Ricardo possessed remarkable logical powers, he seems to have been less gifted with analytical subtilty.'

These divergent views are carefully examined in the present work, and the reader will form his own opinion.

While my primary object has been to smooth the path for those who wish to study Ricardo in the original, I have also endeavoured to write a book which may be found readable (I would like to say enjoyable) even by those who have never had the time, or perhaps the wish, to make a study of Political Economy, but who would nevertheless welcome an opportunity to acquire 'without tears' some acquaintance with the economic problems which shook the world in Ricardo's day, and are shaking it a good deal more at the present time.

And lastly, I am not without hope that even professional economists will find this work useful, partly as a textbook which they can recommend to their pupils, and partly as a sort of Dictionary of Ricardo's Sayings which will enable them to put their hand readily upon any passage of Ricardo's that they desire to quote when lecturing to their students.

References

In this book the quotations from Ricardo's *Principles* and other writings are very numerous; to save space, the location of each passage quoted is indicated very briefly. In the case of pamphlets, speeches, letters and miscellaneous jottings, the reference is in this form—(vol. 3, p. 174). This indicatesthat the passage cited will be found on page 174 of volume 3 in the excellent collected edition of Ricardo's *Works and Correspondence* recently published by the Cambridge University Press, under the editorship of Piero Sraffa, with the collaboration of M. H. Dobb.

In the case of Ricardo's *Principles of Political Economy and Taxation* (which forms volume 1 of the collected edition), I have thought it necessary to refer also to pages in the cheap popular edition which is included in the well-known Everyman's Library. This double reference is given thus—page 64(110); or it may be given thus—(64/110); in both cases the reference is to Ricardo's *Principles*, and in both cases the first figure refers to the page in the 'Everyman's' edition and the second figure to the page in volume 1 of Sraffa's collected edition.

In my quotations I have not always adhered rigidly to the original punctuation.

There are also many quotations from the *Principles of Political Economy* by Ricardo's friend T. R. Malthus, author of the famous *Essay on the Principle of Population*. In each case I have quoted the page in the first edition, which is the one Ricardo had before him, and also the corresponding page in the second edition, published long after Ricardo's death. The greater part of the first edition is reproduced in the *Notes on Malthus*, which forms volume 2 of Sraffa's edition, where the reader will have no trouble in checking my quotations, as the numbering of Malthus' pages is given in the margin.

I

General Outline

ADAM SMITH began his world-famous masterpiece, *An Inquiry into the Nature and Causes of the Wealth of Nations*, with the following words:

> The annual labour of every nation is the fund which originally supplies it with all the necessaries and conveniences of life which it annually consumes, and which consist always either in the immediate produce of that labour, or in what is purchased with that produce from other nations. According therefore as this produce, or what is purchased with it, bears a greater or smaller proportion to the number of those who are to consume it, the nation will be better or worse supplied with all the necessaries and conveniences for which it has occasion.

These words relate only to the aggregate production of wealth by the community. Ricardo approached the subject from a different standpoint. A nation with a large production 'per head' can scarcely be called happy if most of the wealth goes into the hands of a few, while large numbers receive very little. Before the publication of his *Principles*, Ricardo had already written to his friend Malthus:

> I wish much to see a regular and connected statement of your opinions on what I deem the most difficult and perhaps the most important topic of Political Economy, namely, the progress of a country in wealth, and the laws by which the increasing produce is distributed (vol. 7, p. 24).

Four years later, after he had himself attempted to deal with this difficult problem, he again wrote to Malthus:

> Political Economy, you think, is an enquiry into the nature and causes of wealth; I think it should rather be called an enquiry into

the laws which determine the division of the produce of industry amongst the classes who concur in its formation (vol. 8, p. 278).

In the Preface to the first edition of his *Principles* (1817) he explained the purpose of his investigation as follows:

> The produce of the earth—all that is derived from its surface by the united application of labour, machinery, and capital, is divided among three classes of the community, namely, the proprietor of the land, the owner of the stock or capital necessary for its cultivation, and the labourers by whose industry it is cultivated. But in different stages of society the proportions of the whole produce of the earth which will be allotted to each of these classes, under the names of rent, profit, and wages, will be essentially different; depending mainly on the actual fertility of the soil, on the accumulation of capital and population, and on the skill, ingenuity, and instruments employed in agriculture. To determine the laws which regulate this distribution is the principal problem in Political Economy; much as the science has been improved by the writings of Turgot, Stuart, Smith, Say, Sismondi, and others, they afford very little satisfactory information respecting the natural course of rent, profit, and wages.

Ricardo, then, set himself to work, not merely to show what are the 'laws' which determine the proportions in which the nation's annual produce is shared amongst those concerned in its production, but also to indicate the course which this distribution will take in the future, as a result of those laws. His words, quoted above, might seem to suggest that he had in view mainly, if not exclusively, an agricultural country; but he purports to deal with all categories of production, and to show what governs the proportions in which the product, whether from the field, the mine, or the factory, is shared among the different classes of the community. In Ricardo's view, the conditions governing agricultural production dominated the entire economic situation; but still more, I think, they dominated his own thought and outlook in explaining economic phenomena—so much so that, in framing his theory of rent, he puts forward an explanation based upon the cost of agricultural produce, but does not seem even conscious that he has left the enormous aggregate of urban rents totally unexplained.

Rent, he tells us, arises when the need of mankind for food and raw materials drives them to cultivate land which requires more capital and labour to obtain the same quantity of produce.

The worse the land, the more labour and capital will be required to obtain a given quantity of produce; in other words, the cost of the product rises, and therefore its price or value rises. The lands of better grade, of course, continue to produce at the same expenditure of labour as before, but their owners benefit by the rise in the value of the product. If the farmer on the least fertile land earns a profit (and he would not farm if he did not), then the cultivator of superior land earns still more, or would earn still more but for the fact that the difference (i.e. the excess over the ordinary rate of profit) is taken by the landlord as rent.

This, then, gives us the first answer to the tripartite question as to how the whole produce of the earth is allotted among the three classes entitled to participate, namely the proprietor of the land, the owner of the capital, and the labourer. It tells us how the landlord's share of the produce is determined; but Ricardo sought something more, namely, to foresee what conditions will be brought about in the course of time as a necessary consequence of this 'law' of distribution. With the increase of population, he held, mankind is driven to cultivate less and less fertile land. He not only held that this increasing difficulty in raising food would operate in the future, but he also believed that, as an historical fact, it had so operated in the past. He states, but without quoting his authority, that the poorest land under cultivation in his day was much inferior to the poorest land cultivated three hundred years earlier (142/217); and he regards it as certain that the new lands which will have to be brought into cultivation in three hundred years from now, if population continues to grow, will be much less productive than any cultivated at the present time. Agricultural produce will therefore rise continuously in price.

And this carries with it as a necessary consequence that the landlords, although contributing nothing in the way of work or personal sacrifice, will nevertheless receive an ever-increasing portion of the wealth annually created by the community. The only cultivator from whom they take nothing is the cultivator of the poorest land actually cultivated, and he pays no rent because the sale of his produce does not yield anything in excess of the amount required to pay the wages of labour and the ordinary remuneration of capital. Ricardo held that in every country there is some cultivated land that pays no rent.[1] In every country there is likely to be land of various grades or qualities. There will be some so poor that it is not possible to make a living out of it, and there will be some out of which the cultivator can just make a living if he has no rent to pay; that is to say, there will be some land capable of producing just sufficient to yield the ordinary wages of labour and the ordinary remuneration of capital: and so long as there is any such land available, rent free, it is almost certain to be cultivated, for capital is ever on the look-out for an opportunity to make a profit.

But where, it may be asked, shall we find landlords so obliging as to allow capitalists to occupy and use their land rent free? To this there are several answers. It may happen in new countries that a certain quantity of land can be had for nothing. Where all the land is already appropriated, a farm of fifty acres that is rented to a tenant may contain only forty-five acres of land good enough to yield a rent; in that case the rent is really paid for the forty-five acres, yet the farmer may cultivate the other five if he can just make the ordinary profit out of them. Or the owner of land not good enough to produce rent may possibly cultivate it himself, since he will thereby find an employment for his capital and an opportunity to make the ordinary rate of profit. In one form or another, scattered over the country, there may exist portions of land which will thus be brought under cultivation if the price of produce is sufficiently high to yield ordinary wages and profit, but which it would not pay to cultivate if the cost of cultivation rose or if the price of produce fell.

The landlords, then, receive no rent from the marginal lands (the lands that just cover the cost of cultivation), but they receive rent from all lands of a quality superior to this; and when cultivation is from time to time extended to lands of lower grade, more and more lands become rent-bearing, and all rents rise in proportion to the difference between their quality and that of the lowest

[1] In his pamphlet *On Protection to Agriculture* (vol. 4, p. 240) Ricardo says: 'I am myself fully persuaded that a large quantity of corn is raised in every country, for the privilege of raising which no rent whatever is paid.' In his *Principles* (219/328) he remarks: 'I believe that as yet in every country, from the rudest to the most refined, there is land of such a quality that it cannot yield a produce more than sufficiently valuable to replace the stock employed upon it, together with the profits ordinary and usual in that country.' Stock of course here means capital.

grade that it pays to cultivate. So long as only two qualities of land are cultivated, A and B, which we will suppose respectively produce 40 and 35 bushels of corn per acre for the same expenditure, the landlords will receive as rent what A produces in excess of B; for if the farmer of B (paying no rent) is satisfied with a return of 35 bushels, then the farmer of the A land must also be satisfied with 35 bushels, and the other 5 must be rendered to the landlord. When three grades of land are cultivated, A (40), B (35), and C (30), the same argument applies; those who farm A and B lands must be content with the same return that satisfies the farmer of the marginal land C, namely, 30 bushels per acre, and the excess produced by A and B (10 bushels in the one case, 5 bushels in the other) belongs to the owner of the land. When twenty different qualities of land are cultivated, the landlords will receive as rent all that is produced by the first nineteen grades in excess of what is produced by the twentieth grade. The payment of rent, in short, puts all the farmers on the same footing; for all farmers it reduces the rate of profit to the same level. Thus, as time goes by and the population increases, food becomes dearer and dearer, and with the rise in its price some land which before paid no rent commences to pay rent, while upon all the lands already paying rent those rents are increased. There for the moment we may leave the landlords while we turn to consider the prospects of the labourers and capitalists under Ricardo's law of distribution.

Since the marginal farmers (those who cultivate the poorest land) pay no rent, the annual produce of land, labour and capital is in their case divided amongst two classes only, namely, the farmers who supply the necessary capital and the labourers who do the work. Thus we eliminate rent from our problem, which resolves itself into the question, what determines the proportions in which the product is divided between labour and capital; or in other words, what determines the rate of wages paid for labour and the rate of profit upon capital? Seeing that in this case wages and profit make up the whole amount of the product, it follows that the larger the proportion that goes to the one, the smaller must be the proportion remaining for the other. Although this appears to be a mere arithmetical truism, it forms one of Ricardo's principal tenets; profits rise if wages fall, and fall if wages rise. The rate of wages determines the rate of profit, and therefore, if we can learn what determines the rate of wages we shall at the same time learn what determines the rate of profit.

Now the rate of wages, according to Ricardo, is determined by the cost of subsistence. The continuous growth of population keeps the supply of labour constantly increasing, and competition for employment keeps the rate of wages down to the lowest level compatible with the survival of the labouring class. Since, then, the quantity of product (food and other necessaries) given to the labourer cannot be reduced, it follows that it is the quantity of product received by the capitalist that must be diminished when less fertile land is cultivated. The labourer receives no more than before, but what he receives constitutes a larger proportion of the product, and what remains for the capitalist is a smaller proportion. And since the cultivators of the good lands, after paying their rent, are in no better position than the marginal farmers, the fall in the rate of profit is common to all.

We must consider this in more detail. Generally speaking, at any particular time prices in the market are governed by the ratio between supply and demand. This, which applies to commodities, also applies to the price paid for labour. But Ricardo always refused to accept the ratio between supply and demand as a final explanation of price. We must ask, what causes the ratio to be what it is? The demand for labour, he thinks, comes mainly from capital; it comes, that is to say, from the capitalists, who are the principal employers of labour. To understand what determines the rate of wages we must consider what governs the supply of capital, and what governs the supply of labour.

Capitalists, of course, are not the only people who employ labour. As Adam Smith pointed out, a man pays his domestic servants from his income, not from his capital. But Ricardo's intention, announced in his Preface, was to examine how the annual product is divided among the three classes responsible for its production; in what manner each class spends the share that it receives is a different matter. He was well aware that soldiers and other 'unproductive labourers' are paid for their services from other people's incomes (see his 26th chapter), but he apparently did not consider that this invalidated the general proposition that the rate of wages is determined by the ratio between capital and the supply of labour.

In this he was merely accepting what appears to have been the common doctrine in his day. Professor Cannan[1] quotes from the first edition of Mrs. Marcet's *Conversations on Political Economy* as follows:

> CAROLINE: What is it that determines the rate of wages?
>
> MRS. B.: It depends upon the proportion which capital bears to the labouring part of the population of the country.
>
> CAROLINE: Or in other words, on the proportion which subsistence bears to the number of people to be maintained by it?
>
> MRS. B.: Yes.

As Mrs. Marcet was not an original thinker, but a populariser, her book, published in 1816, may be regarded, says Palgrave's Dictionary, as showing 'what were the accepted doctrines just before Ricardo's *Principles* appeared'.

Not merely does this doctrine imply that capital is practically the only fund from which wages are paid, but it also appears to imply that capital consists exclusively, or almost exclusively, of a fund for the maintenance of labourers.[2] Perhaps the habit of regarding agriculture as the main industry of the country was responsible for this. Up to Adam Smith's time England had been, except when the harvest was poor, an exporter, not an importer, of corn. When *The Wealth of Nations* appeared the 'Industrial Revolution' had scarcely begun. Weaving and spinning were still cottage industries. Etymologically, the word *manufacture* means handicraft, and it still meant handicraft in Smith's day, not production by machinery. Forty years later when Ricardo wrote, this, to be sure, had already changed. Steam had been harnessed to machinery by the genius of James Watt, and machinery in consequence rapidly developed, factories sprang up, the quantity of fixed capital employed in industry increased enormously. But the minds of the men who write books are often more filled with what they have read than with what they have observed, and much of what they read has generally been produced by an earlier generation. Ricardo's French contemporary, Say, was himself a manufacturer, and could check what he read by his own experience; but Ricardo, now retired and a country gentleman

[1] E. Cannan, *Theories of Production and Distribution*, page 242.

[2] Lord Lauderdale, however, writing in 1804, seems to have stressed the part played by fixed capital in supplanting or supplementing labour (Palgrave's Dictionary).

interested in farming, had passed his life on the Stock Exchange, dealing mostly in Government stocks, and probably had little direct knowledge of industrial conditions, and therefore fell easily into the habit of regarding agriculture as typical of industry in general.

In a purely agricultural country fixed capital is comparatively small, or at all events was so in Ricardo's day, when farming implements were still for the most part of a very simple character. The farmer's main use for capital was to provide a fund for the maintenance of his workers; and as the land only yields its harvest once a year, it was necessary for him to begin the year with a stock of food (a wages fund) sufficient to maintain his labourers for twelve months. Whatever changes Ricardo made in his book, he never departed from this assumption that the capitalist begins the year with a capital or wages fund sufficient to maintain his employees for a period of twelve months.

Since Ricardo's day the conditions of the food problem have been greatly altered by the fact that we are able to obtain supplies from two hemispheres with their alternating seasons, and also by the fact that more meat is eaten, while the development of transport and refrigeration makes it possible for inland districts to enjoy abundance of fish. But a hundred years ago, when the bulk of the population (the poor) lived upon corn and little else, the assumption that the quantity stored in the granaries after the harvest determined the condition of the people for the ensuing twelve months was not an unnatural one, if the community was thought of as an isolated unit. The stock, large or small, had to suffice for the whole body of wage-earners, whether employed in agriculture, manufacture, or commerce. Hence, as 'Mrs. B.' remarked, the rate of wages depended on the proportion that capital bore to the labouring part of the population, all wage-earners being *labourers* in the broad sense given to the word in economics. If the stock of food held by the capitalists at the beginning of the year was large in proportion to the number of labourers, the latter and their families would be well fed; if the stock was small compared with the number of labourers they would necessarily have to get along as best they could on a meagre diet, since they could not have what did not exist.

The doctrine that the rate of wages depends upon the size of the population compared with the quantity of capital carries with it another tenet, namely, that the size of the population depends upon the quantity of capital. The population cannot exceed the number that can be supported by the current supply of food; it cannot grow more quickly than the quantity of capital grows. On the other hand the population will never be less than the number that can subsist on the quantity of food provided. This is due to the philoprogenitive habits of the people. 'Men, like all other animals,' Adam Smith had said, 'naturally multiply in proportion to the means of their subsistence.'[1] Both men and the other animals *tend* to increase at a faster rate than this; what prevents the population increasing faster is the fact that those for whom food cannot be found necessarily die of under-nourishment or actual starvation. But let capital increase—let the size of the food supply be augmented—and there will quickly be a corresponding increase of population.

It follows from this doctrine that wages will never rise for long above that low level which suffices to provide the labouring class with the bare necessaries of existence. If the capitalists save and add to their fund for the support of productive labour, wages may rise for a time, but the labouring class quickly responds with an increase in the number of labourers, which brings the wage down again to the subsistence level. Ricardo, it is true, sometimes tells us that wages are not usually as low as this in England; nevertheless, his reasoning seems more often than not to be based on the assumption that the labourer has no margin whatever for even the simplest luxuries. He assumes wages to be at a level so low that any reduction would result in a decline in the numbers of the population; he assumes them to be so low that if the price of bread rises, money wages must necessarily be increased, or starvation will reduce the supply of labour; and if a tax is levied on wages, the employer must either pay that tax or raise the wages of his workmen, who otherwise could not pay it without trenching on the minimum required for continued existence. The constant tendency of the labour supply to exceed the supply of capital keeps wages down to this minimum.

Thus in our enquiry into the distribution of the wealth annually produced by the country we have now discovered the laws that determine the landlord's share and the labourer's share. We have at the same time discovered what determines the share of the

[1] *Wealth of Nations*, Bk. I, chap. II, beginning of Part I.

capitalist, since, in the case of the marginal farmer, he receives what is left after wages have been paid, while the tenants who pay rent are in the same position after they have paid both rent and wages.

Hence, in Ricardo's view, the rate of profit declines progressively with the extension of cultivation to less and less fertile land. Although the product diminishes, the farmer must still supply each labourer with the same minimum quantity of subsistence, but that fixed quantity now forms a larger proportion of the product, and what remains to the farmer is both a smaller proportion of the product and a smaller quantity of product.

How and when will this continuous fall in the rate of profit be halted? Food cannot be produced without capital, for the labourers must be supplied with subsistence while waiting for their labour to bear fruit, and it is not to be supposed that capital will be forthcoming for the cultivation of additional land if the quantity of corn obtainable will only just replace what the labourers have consumed while producing it. 'No one accumulates', says Ricardo, 'but with a view to make his accumulation productive' (73/122), that is, productive of profit. Ricardo does not speculate to what minimum the rate of profit may fall before extinguishing the incentive to further accumulation, but he does tell us that accumulation will cease long before the rate of profit has sunk to zero. And when accumulation ceases the growth of population must also cease (71/120).

So now we have the full account of the laws which decide the proportions in which the wealth annually produced by the land, labour and capital of the country is shared among the owners of these three productive agents. The prospect is not bright, except for the landlords. The most numerous class of the community, the labourers, already condemned to see a proportion of their offspring carried off each year by the inadequacy of the food supply, will in the course of time, if they do not revise their multiplication table, find themselves in the position that starvation will destroy all their children in excess of the minimum which suffices to keep the population stationary. As for the capitalists, individually they may be wealthy because one person may own a large quantity of capital, but the rate of profit upon their capital will be reduced to a level too low to tempt further accumulation. Only the lucky landlords have a bright future to look forward to, as they thrive on other people's misfortunes. The dearer bread becomes, the higher rents will be. Ricardo does not hold the landlords responsible for this;[1] if food becomes dearer, it is not their doing; it is due to the niggardliness of nature,[2] which has only furnished mankind with a limited quantity of first-class land. But although Ricardo does not blame the landlords for receiving rents on an increasing scale, he was strongly opposed to the attempts of the landed gentry to keep up the price of food, and so keep up rents, by imposing prohibitive duties on the importation of corn from other countries where it could be produced more cheaply.

Here I can imagine the reader reflecting that if this is a correct account of Ricardo's teaching, he seems to have had in mind a purely agricultural country, since the progress of manufacturing industry has been characterised by increase instead of decrease of product for the same quantity of cost.

Ricardo, however, as already remarked, held that his law of distribution applied to all industry. 'In all countries and all times', he says, 'profits depend on the quantity of labour requisite to provide necessaries for the labourers on that land or with that capital which yields no rent' (76/126). If the price of food rises, labourers in every branch of industry will require higher money wages, and therefore profits fall in manufacture and commerce as well as in agriculture. While it is true, that, owing to inventions, improvements of technique, and the economies of mass production, falling rather than rising cost is a feature of manufacture, manufacturers reap no advantage from this. Competition compels them to reduce the price of the product when its cost of production falls; it is the consumer who benefits by a lower price, not the manufacturer by a higher profit.

That there can be only one rate of profit in all branches of industry is one of Ricardo's principal tenets; and that there is only one rate of wages is an assumption that underlies all his reasoning.[3] If more profit could be made in one industry than another, capital

[1] Ricardo was a landlord himself, and delighted in possession. That he was one of the best landlords was testified by Malthus in his *Principles* (page 238 in first edition; page 216 in second edition).

[2] Adam Smith said that Nature labours for man; but man must pay a price for Nature's gifts, and, says Ricardo, 'in proportion as she becomes niggardly in her gifts she exacts a greater price for her work' (footnote, 39/76).

[3] The one exceptional occasion when Ricardo recognised different rates of pay for different kinds of labour will be discussed in a later chapter.

would flow into the more profitable industry and desert the less profitable; if wages were higher in one occupation than another, labourers would leave the low-paid and flock to the well-paid employment. Hence all industries are on the same footing; in agriculture, rent reduces all profit to the level of the marginal farmer's, and in other branches of industry the same result is brought about by competition.

Thus the law of diminishing returns from the land dominates the economic position, and governs the fortunes of all classes. The labourers, owing to their lack of restraint in propagation, are destined to remain perpetually poor. The capitalists may increase their capital, but owing to the continually rising price of the labourer's food the rate of profit upon capital must continually fall. The landlords alone will grow fat, for every extention of cultivation to inferior land brings to them an increase of rent. The law of diminishing returns will only cease to operate when it becomes impossible to cultivate land of a lower grade because it will not yield sufficient to replace the expense of cultivation together with a small profit for the capitalist who made the advances. When that day arrives, not only population, but also rents and the rate of profit on capital will reach a stationary state.

Ricardo's reputation as a prophet has suffered from the fact that up to the present the white man's world has made no visible approach to the state of things he anticipated. Facilities for obtaining food have increased, not diminished, yet population in some countries has come to a standstill; and we have seen governments offering rewards and encouragements to large families. In England, it is true, a Royal Commission in 1949 expressed itself in favour of familiarising the poorer classes with contraceptive devices, but this was designed rather to improve the quality than to limit the size of the population.[1]

From these facts, however, it would be wrong to infer that the law of diminishing returns can be ruled out as non-existent. Ricardo himself recognised that the operation of diminishing returns, and the consequent tendency of profit to fall, 'is happily checked at repeated intervals by the improvements in machinery connected with the production of necessaries, as well as by discoveries in the science of agriculture' (71/121). He also recognised

[1] I have not read the Commission's Report; I gathered its purport from the newspapers.

the possibility of new and fertile tracts of land being found and made accessible. So far from supposing that England was already inescapably shackled with a rising cost of living, he insisted that she had only to remove the restrictions upon the importation of cheap corn and there need be no rise of wages and no fall of profit (vol. 2, p. 222). But the world, taken as a whole, cannot import supplies from any other quarter, and sooner or later diminishing returns must make it increasingly difficult and finally impossible to feed a growing population. Sooner or later, then, the stationary state must be reached.

Was it of such a world-climax that Ricardo was thinking when he pictured the stationary state of page 71(120), or did he suppose that a single country or a single race might reach this position before the rest of the world? In a later chapter he discusses the unemployment and distress liable to follow the return of peace after a long war (such as that which had recently ended with the fall of Napoleon), and he remarks:

> Man from youth grows to manhood, then decays and dies; but this is not the progress of nations. When arrived to a state of the greatest vigour, their further advance may indeed be arrested, but their natural tendency is to continue for ages to sustain undiminished their wealth and their population (177/265).

The reference to 'arrested' progress might seem to indicate that a single country may reach, and before now has reached, the stationary state described on page 71(120) while in other countries the position was different; it appears more likely, however, that in this *obiter dictum* Ricardo was not thinking of diminishing returns or the stationary state, but was merely emphasising his point that the normal course of economic development is not altered, but merely interrupted, by war. When peace returns, and industry has had time to get back into the old channels, rents, profits and wages will resume their 'natural course'.

This feeling of confidence in the permanence of the economic structure evolved by the white races was not peculiar to Ricardo. The idea that war was a mere interruption to orderly progress—a remnant of former savagery which was gradually dying out—coloured the outlook of all Western peoples throughout the nineteenth century. Germany alone preached war for aggrandisement; it was the well-fed Germans only who clamoured for 'more room to live'. The general confidence in the continuance of the established order was not shaken until 1914, and even then it recovered from the shock, for was not the turmoil into which Europe was then plunged a 'war to end war' and establish perpetual peace? But men's faith in perpetual peace has again been shaken, not so much by the outbreak of fresh war in 1939 as by the conditions that have followed that war. I do not refer to the internal dissensions, threatening chaos rather than betterment, by which the Western nations are at present torn; past experience leaves room to hope that, given time, common sense will again prevail; but there is another peril which, given time, may overwhelm everything the white peoples have achieved by centuries of endeavour. The white races are, after all, only a section of the world's population; there is a still larger section which has never dreamed of restricting its propagation, and is now less than ever likely to accept the suggestion that it is only by restricting its numbers that it can hope to improve its conditions of living. Today all 'rights' are being questioned, and all boundaries seem in danger of being trodden underfoot, sooner or later, by hungry multitudes bent on enlarging their feeding ground. If Germany, which was supposed to be highly civilised, could adopt a ruthless policy of aggression, it would certainly be unwise to count on a kindlier attitude on the part of more backward nations. Although these backward nations evince little disposition to adopt the culture of the West, some of them have shown a remarkable capacity to absorb its knowledge, and to use, and even produce, its most powerful weapons. Some day these weapons may be turned against the West, and Ricardo's fear that the comforts and refinements of civilised life will be overwhelmed by a flood of population may be justified at the expense of his assumption that rents and profits will always follow their 'natural course'.

But in this book we are not concerned with Ricardo as a prophet. Our object in the following pages is to study his theory of value, and his doctrines regarding prices, profits, wages and rent. It seemed right, however, to give this preliminary sketch, because it shows what he had in mind when he penned his Preface, and what coloured his whole outlook; and this, perhaps, may help us to understand and piece together his various arguments, which are not developed in a very orderly or systematic manner. Sir E. C. K. Gonner recommends the student to start with chapter one, then go on to number twenty, on again to number twenty-eight, then back to twenty-seven, and from there back to four, forward once more to thirty, then back again to number two, and so on.[1] The method I have followed in these pages is to take Ricardo's doctrines one by one, collecting the material from any part of the book where I could find it, and, whenever it seemed helpful, quoting from other writings from his pen. The various doctrines or assumptions associated with Ricardo's name, which will have to be examined in the following pages, may be briefly summarised as follows:

(1) The object of industry is to produce things that are desired, and which cannot be obtained without labour. Things that no one desires will have no value; but neither will they be produced.

(2) Neither desire nor utility is capable of explaining the relative values of those commodities which can be multiplied indefinitely by human labour. The clue to their relative values or prices is to be found in their relative costs of production. What costs two days' labour is worth twice as much as what costs one day's labour; but the labour bestowed on the production of tools, etc., must be taken into account.

(3) In the case of commodities which can be multiplied indefinitely, but only at the expense of an increasing quantity of labour, their value or price depends upon the quantity of labour required to produce that part of the supply which costs most labour to produce.

(4) Instances of No. 3 are food and other products of the soil. The most fertile and most favourably situated lands are naturally the first to be cultivated. When population increases men are necessarily driven to cultivate less and less fertile land, or more distant land, and therefore each addition to the supply is secured at the expense of an increased quantity of labour. As the selling price in the same market is the same for all producers, it is necessarily the cost of the most expensive part that regulates the price of the whole. This gives rise to rent on those lands which can produce more cheaply than the poorest land under cultivation.

(5) Where there is free competition the rate of profit, or the remuneration of capital, tends to be the same in all employments, subject to some allowance for particular advantages or drawbacks

[1] See Gonner's Introduction to his edition of Ricardo's *Principles*, 1891 (reprinted 1929).

which may attach to certain employments. If profits were higher in one employment than another, capital would flow into the one and quit the other as quickly as possible.

(6) Where there is free competition wages, or the remuneration of hired labour, also tend to be the same in all employments, subject to minor qualifications. As in the case of capital, if wages were higher in some employments than others, labour would quite the ill-requited and flow into the well-requited employment.

(7) While the market price of labour, like that of commodities, may rise or fall with varying conditions of demand and supply, it tends in the long run to be no more than is required to keep up the supply of labourers. For if labour is relatively scarce and the labourer is paid more than sufficient for his needs, the usual result is an increase of population, and therefore an increased supply of labour, which reduces wages to the bare cost of living.

(8) Wages cannot increase without diminishing profits, nor profits without diminishing wages. The joint product of labour and capital being divided between the labourer and the capitalist, if the one has a larger share, the other must have a smaller share. As the cost of living rises (see 4), money wages have to be increased to enable the labourer to live (see 7). Accordingly, the surplus which constitutes profit is diminished.

(9) Thus, owing to the diminishing returns obtainable on the marginal land cultivated, the money wages of the labourer rise without his being any better off, the profits of the capitalist fall owing to the rise of wages, and the only person who benefits by the rise in the price of food is the idle landlord, whose rents continue always to increase.

2

Prices in the long run are determined by the Cost of Production

If two articles are commonly exchanged for one another, or are both sold in the market at the same price, they are said to be of equal value. If a pound of one commodity exchanges for two pounds of another, the first is said to be twice as valuable as the second.

The economist is concerned to explain the ratio in which various goods exchange for one another, or what comes to the same thing, the different prices at which they are sold. The only distinction between price and value, according to one of Ricardo's dicta, is that when we compare goods with money we speak of their price; when we compare them with one another we speak of their respective values, or relative values.[1] Market price and market value mean the same thing. If a tax of a halfpenny is placed on a penny box of matches, the price or value of a box of matches is raised by 50 per cent. Before the tax, two boxes of matches were worth two penny pencils; after the tax, two boxes of matches are worth three pencils.

What governs the ratio of exchange? Ricardo's starting point is the statement by Adam Smith that 'the real price of everything, what everything really costs to the man who wants to acquire it, is the toil and trouble of acquiring it. . . . Labour was the first price, the original purchase-money that was paid for all things.'[2] Adam Smith adds that among a primitive people 'it is natural that what is usually the produce of two days' or two hours' labour,

[1] See vol. 4, p. 60, and vol. 7, p. 297.
[2] *Wealth of Nations*, chap. 5, 2nd paragraph.

should be worth double of what is usually the produce of one day's or one hour's labour'.[1]

Ricardo tells us that this, which was true in the beginning, is still true today, and underlies all the phenomena of modern industry and commerce. Properly understood, he thinks it will be found that the ratio in which goods exchange for one another in the market is determined by the respective quantities of labour required for their production.

The leading European economist in Ricardo's day was the Frenchman, Jean-Baptiste Say, who maintained that utility is the basis of value. This notion Ricardo repudiates on his first page. In his opening paragraph he says:

> Water and air are abundantly useful; they are indeed indispensable to existence, yet under ordinary circumstances nothing can be obtained in exchange for them. Gold, on the contrary, though of little use compared with air or water, will exchange for a great quantity of other goods. Utility then is not the measure of exchangeable value, although it is absolutely essential to it.

The last sentence evidently means that, although nothing has a value unless it is useful, the value is not in proportion to the utility. If one thing is more useful than another, it is not on that account more valuable, i.e. it does not necessarily fetch a higher price. If one thing is twice as valuable as another (i.e. is sold at double the price), it does not follow that it is twice as useful. Prices, in short, are not in proportion to utility; the ratio in which commodities exchange for one another, or the value of a commodity in exchange, 'depends on the relative quantity of labour which is necessary for its production'.[2]

But the labour spent on producing an article will not give it value if it is something that nobody wants; utility is 'absolutely essential'. Ricardo states right at the outset:

> If a commodity were in no way useful—in other words, if it could in no way contribute to our gratification—it would be destitute of exchangeable value, however scarce it might be, or whatever quantity of labour might be necessary to procure it.

[1] *Wealth of Nations*, chap. 6, 1st paragraph. Ricardo quotes both these sayings (page 6(12–13)), but the reference he gives is only correct for the first one.

[2] See heading to Ricardo's first chapter.

This caution, expressed at the very beginning of Ricardo's first chapter, must never be lost sight of. He does not repeat the warning, and the reader who allows himself to forget it will be very liable to misinterpret Ricardo's theories as to cost and value.

Ricardo goes on to say:

> There are some commodities the value of which is determined by their scarcity alone. No labour can increase the quantity of such goods, and therefore their value cannot be lowered by an increased supply. Some rare statues and pictures, scarce books and coins, wines of a peculiar quality, which can be made only from grapes grown on a particular soil, of which there is a very limited quantity, are all of this description. Their value is wholly independent of the quantity of labour originally necessary to produce them, and varies with the varying wealth and inclinations of those who are desirous to possess them (6/12).

Although Ricardo commences this paragraph with the statement that in this category of goods value is determined by scarcity alone, the quantity of value is said in the last sentence to depend on the varying wealth and inclinations of those who desire to possess them, i.e. on the strength of demand. The enormous increases that have taken place in the values of some old pictures, books, etc., during the past hundred years have been due rather to growth of demand than to diminution of supply. The fact is 'scarcity' is a relative term, and in this connection really indicates the relationship of supply to demand. Ricardo's statement practically amounts to this, that the prices of the articles here referred to are determined by demand and supply alone, the quantity of labour originally bestowed upon their production having no bearing whatever on the price.[1]

[1] Similar conditions apply when goods are 'scarce' owing to a monopolist restricting output. 'When a commodity is at a monopoly price, it is at the very highest price at which the consumers are willing to purchase it. . . . The exchangeable value therefore of a commodity which is at a monopoly price is nowhere regulated by the cost of production' (164/249). In his opening statement Ricardo follows Adam Smith, who said: 'The price of monopoly is upon every occasion the highest which can be got', or 'which can be squeezed out of the buyers' (*Wealth of Nations*, chap. 7, 27th paragraph). This, however, is not correct, as it may often pay the monopolist better to sell a larger quantity at a lower price.

Having mentioned this class of goods, however, Ricardo dismisses it as unimportant. Such commodities, he says,

> form a very small part of the mass of commodities daily exchanged in the market. By far the greatest part of those goods which are the objects of desire are procured by labour; and they may be multiplied, not in one country alone, but in many, almost without any assignable limit, if we are disposed to bestow the labour necessary to obtain them.

The last dozen words constitute Ricardo's clue to the problem of value for goods of this kind. The labour necessary to obtain them is the price that must be paid for most of the things required to satisfy our daily wants. While some of our wants are more important than others, and some commodities more useful than others, the price of a commodity does not depend upon the importance of the want that it ministers to, but upon the quantity of labour necessary to produce it. If gold has a high value in exchange and air no value at all, it is not because our need for gold is great and our need for air unimportant—which is indeed the reverse of the fact—but because much work is required to obtain gold, whereas an unlimited supply of air is at the disposal of everyone without any effort at all.

> When I give 2000 times more cloth for a pound of gold than I give for a pound of iron [he says], does it prove that I attach 2000 times more utility to gold than I do to iron? Certainly not; it proves only . . . that the cost of production of gold is 2000 times greater than the cost of production of iron. If the cost of production of the two metals were the same I should give the same price for them; but if utility were the measure of value it is probable I should give more for the iron (188/283).

Hence, as stated in the heading on his first page, 'the value of a commodity, or the quantity of any other commodity for which it will exchange, depends on the relative quantity of labour which is necessary for its production'. And it follows, as stated on page 7(13), that 'every increase of the quantity of labour must augment the value of that commodity on which it is exercised, as every diminution must lower it'.

The word 'must' is perhaps rather startling. The sentence, taken by itself, seems to mean that any given quantity of labour necessarily results in a value proportionate to its quantity. It is in reading a dictum such as this that one needs to bear in mind Ricardo's identification of value and price, and his warning that nothing has value, whatever the quantity of labour necessary to procure it, unless it 'contributes to our gratification'. To say that one thing costs more labour than another is to say that the producer pays a higher price to obtain it; and if he is producing for another he will not pay this higher price unless he has been promised, or has reason to expect, that he will be compensated for this higher cost.

That labour does not confer value upon anything if it does not confer utility upon it, holds good not only of the first dose of labour, but of all subsequent doses. If one day's labour creates a utility that has value, a second day's labour will not add to the value unless it adds to the utility. Supposing that one day's labour creates a knife that will cut butter, two days' labour one that will cut bread, three days' one that will sharpen a stick, and six days' one that you can shave with, the ratio of value according to Ricardo's doctrine will be 1 : 2 : 3 : 6. This is the ratio of their cost, but no one will say that it is the ratio of their usefulness. Would anyone maintain, for instance, that a knife sharp enough to cut wood is only 50 per cent more useful than one that will cut nothing tougher than bread?—would anyone contend that to be able to remove one's whiskers is twice as important to human happiness as being able to cut bread and carve wood? It is not the ratio of utility that determines the quantity of value, but the quantity of labour required for production, and if the making of a razor necessitates six times as much labour as is required to make a butter knife, its price, or value in exchange, will be six times as great. Another day's labour would not necessarily add to the value, but if it did not, the producers would soon discover the fact and would be guided accordingly. Labour will not be expended in producing things that have no utility; additional labour will not be bestowed upon a commodity if it makes no addition to its utility.[1]

Ricardo feels justified therefore in asserting that every increase

[1] In ordinary speech we distinguish between things that are useful and things that are ornamental or beautiful. The reader unacquainted with economics must remember that in that science everything that 'contributes to our gratification' is said to possess utility. The mere fact that there is a demand for it shows that somebody has a 'use' for it.

in the quantity of labour must augment the value of that commodity on which it is exercised. If it costs twice as much labour to produce A as to produce B, its price or value in the market must be twice as great, otherwise it will not pay to produce it, and it will not be produced. If the cost of producing A rises to treble that of B, then the price at which it sells will be treble, or the supply will stop. If on the other hand a way is discovered of producing A with less labour, its price or value will infallibly fall—'every diminution' in the quantity of labour 'must lower it'. Owing to competition, you cannot keep up the price of an article after its cost of production has fallen.

Having warned the reader that a product cannot have value if it does not contribute to our gratification, that is to say if no one wants it, he seldom mentions demand; but he does so occasionally. On page 262(385) he says: 'A commodity is not supplied merely because it can be produced, but because there is a demand for it.' On page 279(409) he writes: 'In the usual and ordinary course of things, the demand for commodities precedes their supply.' To his friend Trower he wrote: 'No commodity is raised unless there is a demand for it. If it were raised without a demand, it would sink in value, and not afford the price necessary to remunerate the labour bestowed upon it', etc. (vol. 8, p. 235).

Ricardo, then, did not overlook demand; nor did he overlook that an increase of demand may cause price to rise for a time when there is no increase whatever in the cost of production. 'Whenever a commodity is required in greater abundance than before', he tells us, 'its relative value rises' (60/104). But increase of price leads to increased production, and increased production causes price to fall again. If there has been no increase in the cost of production, the price will revert to its former level; if the cost of production has changed, the new price will conform to the new cost; in either case, after the adjustment of supply to demand, the commodity will once more exchange for other articles in the ratio of their relative costs of production (103/163).

Ricardo, then, did not devote a great deal of attention to demand, because he did not believe that it exercises anything more than a temporary influence upon price in the case of those commodities which 'can be increased in quantity by the exertion of human industry, and on the production of which competition operates without restraint' (6/12). The law of supply and demand was adequate to explain the prices of old pictures, rare books and scarce wines; but in Ricardo's opinion it offered no clue to the determination of price in the case of those articles which could be multiplied almost without assignable limit. If demand increased before supply, no doubt there would be competition on the part of demanders for a time; but only until supply could be brought up to the same level (260/382), when the competition would once more be on the part of the suppliers, each anxious to secure as large a share of the market as he could. Thus competition on the part of suppliers would always take command of the situation in the long run, and suppliers would undercut one another until selling-price again coincided with cost of production, and there was no more advantage to be gained by producing one thing than another. Relative prices would then once more be in proportion to relative costs. This then is why Ricardo does not speak of demand; it is because he thinks demand, although essential, has little permanent influence upon price. In a letter to Malthus, he refers as follows to the theory of J.-B. Say:

> He certainly has not a correct notion of what is meant by value when he contends that a commodity is valuable in proportion to its utility. This would be true if buyers only regulated the value of commodities; then indeed we might expect that all men would be willing to give a price for things in proportion to the estimation in which they held them; but the fact appears to me to be that the buyers have the least in the world to do in regulating price; it is all done by the competition of the sellers, and however the buyers might be really willing to give more for iron than for gold, they could not, because the supply would be regulated by the cost of production, and therefore gold would inevitably be in the proportion which it now is to iron, although it probably is by all mankind considered as the less useful metal (vol. 8, p. 276).

And again in the following month he writes to Malthus:

> I shall not dispute another proposition in your letter. 'No wealth', you say, 'can exist [1] unless the demand or the estimation in which the commodity is held exceeds the cost of production.' I have never disputed this. I do not dispute either the influence of demand on the price of corn or on the price of all other things; but supply follows close at its heels and soon takes the power of regulating price in his own hands, and in regulating it, he is determined by cost of production (vol. 8, p. 302).

[1] I.e. it cannot exist because it will not be produced.

3

Modifications of the doctrine that Value is in proportion to the Quantity of Labour

THE first chapter of Ricardo's book is divided into several sections. The heading of the first section states that the value of a commodity, or the quantity of any other commodity for which it will exchange, depends on the quantity of labour necessary for its production. He proceeds in subsequent sections to introduce certain modifications of this doctrine. We will defer consideration of section 2 until our next chapter and proceed at once to section 3, which is headed as follows: 'Not only the labour applied immediately to commodities affect [*sic*] their value, but the labour also which is bestowed on the implements, tools, and buildings, with which such labour is assisted' (13/22). This, to be sure, is not a modification, but merely an amplification. If it takes a man one hundred days to dig a pit, and the spade he uses took him six days to make, then the labour involved in creating the pit is not 100 but 106 days. This, however, is assuming that by the time the hole is finished the spade is completely worn out. If with the same spade the man can dig two pits of the same size in 200 days, then the total labour of digging these two pits is 206 days, and the cost of one pit is only 103 days' labour. Thus the cost of the product includes part, but part only, of the cost of making the tool. We cannot just add the labour of making the spade to the labour spent in digging, but must ascertain how much of the 'accumulated labour'[1] embodied in the spade has been 'transferred to' and 'realised in' (13/23) the product.

[1] 'Fixed capital, or accumulated labour' (21/34). 'Labour and capital (that is, accumulated labour)' (280/410).

Let me give this doctine in Ricardo's own words; he says:

> If we suppose the occupations of the society extended, that some provide canoes and tackle necessary for fishing, others the seed and rude machinery first used in agriculture, still the same principle would hold true, that the exchangeable value of the commodities produced would be in proportion to the labour bestowed on their production; not their immediate production only, but on all those implements or machines required to give effect to the particular labour to which they are applied.
>
> If we look to a state of society in which greater improvements have been made, and in which arts and commerce flourish, we shall still find that commodities vary in value conformably with this principle; in estimating the exchangeable value of stockings, for example, we shall find that their value, comparatively with other things, depends on the total quantity of labour necessary to manufacture them and bring them to market. First, there is the labour necessary to cultivate the land on which the raw cotton is grown; secondly, the labour of conveying the cotton to the country where the stockings are to be manufactured, which includes a portion of the labour bestowed in building the ship in which it is conveyed, and which is charged in the freight of the goods; thirdly, the labour of the spinner and weaver; fourthly, a portion of the labour of the engineer, smith, and carpenter, who erected the buildings and machinery by the help of which they are made; fifthly, the labour of the retail dealer, and of many others whom it is unnecessary further to particularise. The aggregate sum of these various kinds of labour determines the quantity of other things for which these stockings will exchange, while the same consideration of the various quantities of labour which have been bestowed on those other things will equally govern the portion of them which will be given for the stockings (14/24).
>
> But in every state of society the tools, implements, buildings, and machinery employed in different trades may be of various degrees of durability, and may require different portions of labour to produce them. . . . There is, however, a vast difference in the time for which these different capitals will endure; a steam engine will last longer than a ship, etc. (18/30–31).
>
> Of the durable implement only a small portion of its value would be transferred to the commodity; a much greater portion of the value of the less durable implement would be realised in the commodity which it contributed to produce (13/23).

This, as above remarked, is merely an elaboration or development of the doctrine that relative values are in proportion to the quantities of labour by which the various commodities are produced. To estimate the quantity of labour realised in a stocking we must consider not merely the immediate labour of the stocking-maker, but 'the total quantity of labour necessary in various forms, from first to last, to produce it and bring it to market' (37/72).

Was Ricardo, then, under the impression that goods are sold in the market at a price that covers only the labour realised in them? Not at all. There was never any hesitation on his part in recognising that the price of every article produced by labour in conjunction with capital must include a profit for the owner of the capital as well as a wage for the labourer. In his *Notes on Malthus* (vol. 2, p. 42) he writes: 'By cost of production I invariably mean wages and profits.' If the capitalist advances £1000 as wages during the year, he expects at the end of that period to receive more than £1000; and if he pays £500 for a machine that will last for five years, he expects during those five years, or at all events by the end of that period, to receive back the whole amount advanced plus a profit. If the capitalist received no profit he would have no inducement to employ his capital himself, or to allow others to make use of it. He would not risk his wealth, or forego the immediate enjoyment of it, if the most that he could hope for were that it would be returned to him undiminished. Capital will not offer its services in the market without remuneration any more than labourers will offer their services without wages.

But the rate of profit that is thus entitled to rank as a necessary cost in production is only that minimum which suffices to attract the quantity of capital required. Where there is free competition, the rate of profit in each industry must be as high as in others, else capital will not stay in that industry, but will remove to those which make a better return. And similarly, if the return in one industry is higher than the average, more capital will flow into that industry and the rate will be brought down to the general level. Hence there is a common market rate of profit. 'In cost of production', says Ricardo (vol. 2, p. 369), 'I always include profits at their current rate.' In his *Principles* he says: 'The real and ultimate regulator of the relative value of any two commodities is the cost of their production' (231/344). 'It is the cost of production which must ultimately regulate the price of commodities' (260/382). And in the *Notes on Malthus* (vol. 2, p. 38) we have this: 'Price will be finally regulated by the competition of sellers—it will settle at or about its natural price; that price which, as Adam Smith observes, is necessary to give the current rate of wages to the workmen and the current rate of profits to the capitalist.' In the footnote on page 30(47) of his *Principles* Ricardo observes: 'Mr. Malthus appears to think that it is a part of my doctrine that the cost and value of a thing should be the same; it is, if he means by *cost*, cost of production including profits.'

Thus the dictum that the ratio in which commodities exchange for one another is determined by the relative quantities of labour 'realised in' them is virtually withdrawn, and replaced by the proposition that value is proportionate to the cost of production, which includes the remuneration of capital as well as of labour. Ricardo calls this a mere 'modification', and we may agree that it would not invalidate the original proposition as to relative values if the quantity of capital always bore the same proportion to the quantity of labour, which is what Ricardo assumes in the last paragraph of section 6 of his first chapter. But he himself demonstrates that this is not the case. One capitalist who employs 100 men may have very little expense beyond the wages he pays them, while another employing the same number of men may operate with a large quantity of machinery and extensive buildings which have cost him many thousands of pounds. In the first case the price of the product must yield to the capitalist a profit on the wages he has advanced, but in the second case the capitalist must be rewarded not merely with a profit on the wages he has advanced, but also with a profit in proportion to the size of the fixed capital he has employed. Ricardo himself points this out, and furnishes examples to illustrate the difference in the cost of production. These I shall refer to presently, but before doing so there is another point to be noted.

Ricardo's ardent disciple, J. R. McCulloch, 'more Ricardian than Ricardo',[1] refused to admit that the inclusion of profits as well as wages in the cost of production can be considered as modifying the doctrine that labour is the only cost of production. Since capital is accumulated labour, 'the profits of capital', he says, 'are only another name for the wages of accumulated labour'.[2] Here McCulloch commits an error of which Ricardo was not

[1] Halevy's *Philosophical Radicalism*, page 343 in English edition.

[2] McCulloch's *Principles of Pol. Econ.*, Part 3, section 6, 3rd paragraph.

guilty. If we suppose a spade to represent the accumulated labour of six days, we may argue that a job which 'wastes' or uses up half the life of the spade transfers to and realises in the product one half of the labour that created the spade. The pit is not the product of 100 days, but of 103 days' labour. The purchaser of the product must restore to the owner of the spade the quantity of 'capital or accumulated labour' of which it has been robbed. In other words, the price of the product must include a charge for the wear and tear, or depreciation, of the tools used in making it; each article that is produced must contribute towards a sinking-fund which will replace the capital-good by the time it is worn out. But this is not profit; this is mere replacement of capital; and Ricardo, as already said, recognised that the cost of production includes profit as well as wages, for no man will embark his capital in industry if the most that he can expect is that his capital will remain undiminished. He risks his wealth in industry for the sake of making a profit on it. Whether he spends fifteen shillings on a spade or £1500 on a machine, he must year by year receive a profit on that capital sum, while the capital itself must be kept intact by a sinking-fund which receives each year an accretion equivalent to the depreciation which the capital-good has suffered.

Ricardo himself, in his first two editions, illustrated the difference between sinking-fund and profit by an imaginary example in which the cost of the product, so far from being made up of labour only, comes pretty near to consisting of profit only. 'Suppose', he said, 'that an engine is made which will last for a hundred years and that its value is £20,000. Suppose too that this machine, without any labour whatever, could produce a certain quantity of commodities annually, and that profits were 10 per cent; the whole value of the goods produced would be annually £2000 2*s.* 11*d.*[1] Each year the capitalist sells his product for £2000 2*s.* 11*d*, of which £2000 consists purely of profit. Not more than 2*s.* 11*d.* can be regarded as replacing the cost or wages of 'accumulated labour'. This small sum paid annually and compounded at 10 per cent, in fact, not only replaces the labour consumed in the production of the machine, but also the profit which the maker of the machine included in his price. The machine itself, on its hundredth birthday, falls to bits like the Wonderful One-hoss Shay in O. W. Holmes' *Breakfast Table*, but the capitalist

[1] Page 34 in first edition; see vol. 1, p. 59.

who bought it and set it to work still has his £20,000 intact after enjoying 10 per cent profit on that amount for one hundred years.[1]

The reader, however, will look in vain through the pages of Ricardo's third edition for any trace of the imaginary machine which produces commodities without any assistance from labour. Nor will he find any reference to a sinking-fund. In all Ricardo's arithmetical illustrations (most of which I have brought together in Table A below) he will find the cost of production represented as consisting only of profit on capital and the wages of current labour. In none of them will he find any reference to depreciation of fixed capital. Ricardo, however, did not ignore depreciation, but in his third edition he adopted a different method of dealing with it. His method is to assume that each capitalist who produces commodities with labour and fixed capital employs sufficient labour to keep the fixed capital always as good as new, thus avoiding depreciation. Here are Ricardo's own words:

> If fixed capital be not of a durable nature it will require a great quantity of labour annually to keep it in its original state of efficiency; but the labour so bestowed may be considered as really expended on the commodity manufactured, which must bear a value in proportion to such labour. If I had a machine worth £20,000 which with very little labour was efficient to the production of commodities, and if the wear and tear of such machine were of trifling amount, and the general rate of profit 10 per cent, I should not require much more than £2000 to be added to the price of the goods on account of the employment of my machine; but if the wear and tear of the machine were great, if the quantity of labour requisite to keep it in an efficient state were that of fifty men annually, I should require an additional

---

[1] No machine, of course, is likely to last for 100 years, especially without attention, but other forms of fixed capital may do so. A bridge or a granite dock, McCulloch remarks, 'will probably last for five hundred or a thousand years' (*Principles of Pol. Econ.*, last paragraph of section 2 in Part 3). Nor is the idea of a machine that will produce goods without assistance so very fanciful if we accept the view of McCulloch—a capitalist, he suggests, might secure and plant a sapling at a total cost of one shilling, and at the end of one hundred years he (or his descendant) might find himself in possession of a tree worth £25 or £50—'A tree', he says, 'is at once a piece of timber, and a machine for manufacturing timber' (*Prin. of Pol. Econ.*, last paragraph but six in section 6 of Part 3).

> price for my goods equal to that which would be obtained by any other manufacturer who employed fifty men in the manufacture of other goods, and who used no machinery at all (24/39).

In substance, Ricardo's teaching here is much the same as in his first two editions. Many will prefer a separate item for the depreciation of fixed capital, because this is in fact the method actually adopted by business men in calculating the cost of their production. The stocking-maker employs men to keep his machinery in running order, but he does not have a separate workshop where another set of men are building fresh machinery to be ready by the time the existing plant is worn out. But while this is true of the individual capitalist, Ricardo as an economist is concerned with industry as a whole; and taking industry as a whole, it is a fact that while some machines are actually depreciating day by day, other machines are day by day being produced. The gradual creation of new capital goods is simultaneous with the gradual destruction of old capital goods, and the total is not lessened. In some cases, indeed, the capitalist does actually employ his own men to replace his capital, and keep it always 'new'. A railway company, for instance, keeps its permanent way always new, and even improving. Engines and carriages cannot be kept perpetually new in this way, but the owners of the railway may have their own workshops where carriages and engines are fabricated, and they may have on their pay-roll engineers and mechanics constantly engaged in this work. But whether or not capital goods are produced by the same people who will make use of them, the fact remains that, taking industry as a whole, the depreciation that occurs day by day is made good day by day, and concrete capital as well as money capital remains intact.

In the following figures, which are taken from Ricardo's pages, he assumes that 'the capitalist's capital is every year put into its original state of efficiency' (265/388). There is no separate item for depreciation because there is no depreciation; the capital is maintained always 'new' by current labour, and the remuneration of the labourers so engaged is included in the wages 'expended on the commodity manufactured' (24/39).

These figures illustrate Ricardo's doctrine that the cost of production consists of two things only, namely, the remuneration of labour and the remuneration of capital. There is no charge for

TABLE A

	Capital	Cost and Value of Product	
First pair (20/32)			
(1) Circulating	£5000	Wages	£5000
Fixed	—	Profit 10 per cent	500
Total	£5000	Product sold for	£5500
(2) Circulating	£5000	Wages	£5000
Fixed	5500	Profit 10 per cent	1050
Total	£10,500	Product sold for	£6050
Second pair (134/207)			
(3) Circulating	£2000	Wages	£2000
Fixed	8000	Profit 20 per cent	2000 [1]
Total	£10,000	Product sold for	£4000
(4) Circulating	£8000	Wages	£8000
Fixed	2000	Profit 20 per cent	2000
Total	£10,000	Product sold for	£10,000
Third pair (265/388)			
(5) Circulating	£13,000	Wages	£13,000
Fixed	7000	Profit 10 per cent	2000
Total	£20,000	Product sold for	£15,000
(6) Circulating	£5500	Wages	£5500
Fixed	14,500	Profit 10 per cent	2000
Total	£20,000	Product sold for	£7500

raw materials;[2] these are supplied by Nature free of charge, but the cost of procuring them must be paid for, and it consists of wages and profit. The figures also show that the relative values of products are not by any means in proportion to the quantity of

[1] To illustrate my present point I have brought together three pairs of figures, but the reader must remember that there is no connection between one pair and another. The figures in each pair are employed by Ricardo merely to illustrate an argument and no significance attaches to the fact that in one part of his book he assumes the current rate of profit to be 20 per cent while in another he assumes it to be 10 per cent.

[2] Ricardo's exclusion of payments to the owners of land from cost of production will be discussed in later chapters.

labour or wages. In reference to the first pair in Table A Ricardo says:

> Here, then, are capitalists employing precisely the same quantity of labour annually on the production of their commodities, and yet the goods they produce differ in value on account of the different quantities of fixed capital, or accumulated labour, employed by each respectively (21/34).

None of the figures in Table A give any support whatever to Ricardo's original proposition that value is in proportion to the quantity of labour. They illustrate the proposition that price is in proportion to the quantity of cost including profit, but they certainly do not suggest that there is any uniformity in the ratio between wages and profit, or between wages and total cost, for in No. 1 wages represent ten-elevenths of the cost, in No. 2 about five-sixths, in No. 3 one-half, in No. 4 four-fifths, in No. 5 thirteen-fifteenths, and in No. 6 eleven-fifteenths. What the figures indicate is that the price or value is identical with the total cost, which is made up of wages at the current rate and profit at the current rate.

But Ricardo has other 'modifications' to make. After telling us (21/34) that goods produced by the same quantity of labour will differ in value if different quantities of capital are used in their production, he goes on to say that goods produced by the same quantity of capital will differ in value if the capital is engaged for a longer period in one case than the other. On page 23(37) he writes: 'It is hardly necessary to say that commodities which have the same quantity of labour bestowed on their production will differ in exchangeable value if they cannot be brought to market in the same time.' If capitalist No. 1 has produced corn he expects to sell it after the harvest for £5500; but if he has produced wine he may have to keep it for a further twelve months before it is fit to drink. Thus his capital of £5000, together with his first year's profit of £500, remains tied up for a second year, and at the end of that year he expects to sell his product for £6050 (like capitalist No. 2), which will give him £500 on one year's investment of £5000 plus £550 on one year's investment of £5500.[1]

[1] McCulloch, as already remarked, was more Ricardian than Ricardo; he was so enamoured of the idea that value is derived from labour only that (as pointed out by Halevy) he attributed the enhanced value of wine matured in the cellar to labour, i.e. Nature's labour. What is capital but 'accumulated

This is not the end of Ricardo's 'modifications', but before we proceed to the next one let us refresh our memory of his proposition as it was first stated. The heading of the first section of the first chapter reads: 'The value of a commodity, or the quantity of any other commodity for which it will exchange, depends on the relative quantity of labour which is necessary for its production, and not on the greater or less compensation which is paid for that labour.' The modification we now have to consider concerns the statement that the rate of wages (the greater or less compensation paid to the labourers) has no influence upon relative values.

By this Ricardo does not mean, of course, that if one capitalist employs ten men at £1 a week each, while another employs ten men at 25*s*., the cost of what is produced will be the same in both cases. He assumes that, although this difference in wages might occur in two different countries, it cannot occur in one and the same country, where competition will make the rate the same for all labourers. But the rate may alter in the course of time, and the meaning of his proposition is that if articles Y and Z are of the same value when both employers pay 20*s*. a week, their values will still be equal when both employers pay 25*s*. a week.

It is this proposition that is now modified. Ricardo does not abandon the assumption that all labourers are paid at the same rate, but he admits that even under these circumstances a rise or fall in the general rate of wages will alter the ratio in which some goods exchange for others, owing to the different proportions in which labour is combined with capital; he even tells us that the price of some goods will fall in consequence of the rise of wages.

labour', and what is profit but the wages of accumulated labour? 'Mr. Ricardo was inclined to modify his grand principle that the exchangeable value of commodities depended on the quantity of labour required for their production, so far as to allow that the additional exchangeable value that is sometimes given to commodities by keeping them after they have been purchased or produced, until they become fit to be used, was not to be considered as the effect of labour', but McCulloch, 'notwithstanding the hesitation I cannot but feel in differing from so great an authority', can see no good reason for making this concession. His view is, as I have mentioned in a previous note, that if you spend a shilling in planting an acorn, and after a hundred years you get a piece of timber worth perhaps £30, you may call this increase *profit*, but in reality it is the wages of the acorn's labour during this long period (McCulloch's *Principles of Pol. Econ.*, Part 3, section 6, 30th, 33rd and 34th paragraphs). For Ricardo's criticism of this doctrine see his letter to McCulloch, vol. 9, p. 358.

Stripped of its paradox, as Malthus pointed out,[1] this statement means that as prices are made up of wages and profits, the decrease of profit may exceed the increase of wages, and so lead to a diminution of price. If the reader will glance back at Table A he will see that in every case the cost of production is made up of profits and wages. The entire value of the product is divided between master and men; if the latter receive more as wages, the less will be left for the employer as profit. Referring to capitalists No. 1 (a farmer) and No. 2 (a manufacturer), Ricardo writes as follows on page 21(35):

> There can be no rise in the value of labour without a fall of profits. If the corn is to be divided between the farmer and the labourer, the larger the proportion that is given to the latter the less will remain for the former. So if cloth or cotton goods be divided between the workman and his employer, the larger the proportion given to the former the less remains for the latter. Suppose then, that owing to a rise of wages, profits fall from 10 to 9 per cent, instead of adding £550 to the common price of their goods (to £5500) for the profits on their fixed capital, the manufacturers would add only 9 per cent on that sum, or £495, consequently the price would be £5995 instead of £6050. As the corn would continue to sell for £5500, the manufactured goods in which more fixed capital was employed would fall relatively to corn or to any other goods in which a less portion of fixed capital entered.

Let us tabulate these figures:

TABLE B

	Before wages rise. *Profit* 10%	*After wages rise.* *Profit* 9%
Wages	£5000	£5050
Profit on Wages	500	450 [2]
Price of Product No. 1	£5500	£5500
Add profit on Fixed Capital	550	495
Price of Product No. 2	£6050	£5995

[1] See Malthus' *Principles of Pol. Econ.*, page 91 in first edition, page 88 in second edition. Malthus uses the epithet 'paradoxical', but his remarks refer to certain passages in Ricardo's second edition, which he altered in the third edition.

[2] Profit of course should be based upon £5050, not £5000. On page 69(117) Ricardo mentions the need for adjustment, but he neglects it for simplicity.

Thus does Ricardo justify the paradox that the price of cloth has fallen because wages have risen.

The reader will note that, according to these figures, the price of corn is not affected by the rise of wages; a rise of wages, says Ricardo (31/48), 'does not, except in some instances, produce the effect of raising price, but has a great effect in lowering profits'. The corn is divided between the labourers and the capitalist, and if the labourers receive a larger share, the capitalist's share must be smaller than before. The total quantity of product to be divided is not altered; the alteration is in the proportions in which it is shared by those who have produced it. If the farmer pays an additional £50 to his labourers, there remains £50 less for profit. But there is a notable difference between the farmer and the manufacturer. The farmer's loss of profit is identical in amount with what the labourers have gained, but the manufacturer's loss of profit exceeds the additional amount he has paid in wages. Not only does he, like the farmer, obtain a smaller profit on his wages-fund, he also receives a smaller profit on his fixed capital. The reason why a rise of £50 in wages causes the farmer's profit to fall from 10 per cent to 9 per cent is that £50, which is 1 per cent of wages, is also 1 per cent of his capital. This is not so with the manufacturer: nevertheless, his profit must also fall to 9 per cent, because there cannot be two rates of profit, one for agriculture and another for manufacture, one for wages-fund and another for fixed capital. Whatever differences may exist for a time will soon be flattened out by the tendency of capital to leave less remunerative for more remunerative employments. Hence, while the farmer's product still sells for the same price as before, the manufacturer's product falls in price.[1] On page 22(35) Ricardo sums up the position as follows:

> The degree of alteration in the relative value of goods, on account of a rise or fall of labour, would depend on the proportion which the fixed capital bore to the whole capital employed. All commodities

[1] What seems extraordinary is Ricardo's assumption here that the farmer's capital consists entirely of wages-fund, for in his chapter on Profits he assumes that the farmer employs a capital of £3000 while his wages bill is no more than £240 (68/116). Thus the farmer's capital is twelve times as great as the amount paid in wages; the proportion of total capital to wages is larger than is assumed in the case of any of the manufacturers represented in our Table A. On page 21(35) the farmer arrives at the amount of his profit by

which are produced by very valuable machinery, or in very valuable buildings, or which require a great length of time before they can be brought to market, would fall in relative value, while all those which were chiefly produced by labour, or which would be speedily brought to market, would rise in relative value.

While Ricardo never hesitates to admit 'modifications', the trouble is that he seldom gives them much weight. An eminent French writer observed: 'It is a fact that Ricardo constantly tends to minimise the influence of disturbing factors.'[1] We have a good instance of this in connection with the remarks we have just been considering. After showing that a rise of wages would affect the ratio of exchange, Ricardo proceeds as follows:

> The reader, however, should remark that this cause of the variation of commodities is comparatively slight in its effects. With such a rise of wages as should occasion a fall of one per cent in profits, goods produced under the circumstances I have supposed vary in relative value only one per cent; they fall, with so great a fall of profits, from £6050 to £5995. The greatest effects which could be produced on the relative prices of these goods from a rise of wages could not exceed 6 or 7 per cent; for profits could not, probably, under any circumstances, admit of a greater general and permanent depression than to that amount (22/35).

By this he apparently means that if the rate of profit fell from 10 per cent to 3 per cent the manufacturer's price would fall from £6050 to about £5665, which is a comparatively small drop to result from such a drastic cut in profits. But had Ricardo been intent on showing how much, instead of how little, this reduction in the rate of profit might affect the price he would have chosen a case where fixed capital bore a large proportion to wages; he might (since he was fond of illustrating a theoretical principle by 'strong cases')[2] have brought forward the illustration he himself

deducting wages from the price he receives for his product, while the manufacturer arrives at his price by adding profit at the current rate to the amount paid in wages. On pages 68 and 69(116 and 117) this distinction disappears. Both farmer and manufacturer employ much capital besides their wages-fund, yet Ricardo still holds that if £7 is added to wages the profit of the capitalist will be £7 less, and if wages rise by £34 5*s*. the diminution of profit will be £34 5*s*., neither more nor less. Ricardo's views as to the manner in which prices and profits are affected by a rise of wages will be further considered in our ninth chapter.

[1] Halevy's *Growth of Philosophical Radicalism*, page 324 in the English translation.

[2] See his letter to Malthus, vol. 8, p. 184.

gave in his first edition where he imagined goods to be produced by machinery requiring scarcely any labour at all for its attendance and upkeep. In connection with this hypothetical machine he said that if the rate of profit fell from 10 per cent to 3 per cent the price of the product would fall from £2000 2*s.* 11*d.* to £632 16*s.* 7*d.*, and he added: 'By a rise in the price of labour then, under 7 per cent, which has no effect on the prices of commodities wholly produced by labour, a fall of no less than 68 per cent is effected on those commodities wholly produced by machinery.'[1] This machine which requires no labour at all is certainly an extreme case; but it is scarcely more incredible than the assumption at the other extreme that some commodities are produced and brought to market without any fixed capital, which is what Ricardo imagines in No. 1 of Table A.

The dictum on page 22(36), as I have said, is an example of what Halevy calls Ricardo's tendency to minimise disturbing factors. Perhaps this might be put more strongly, for when Ricardo comes to the conclusion that a 'modification' is almost negligible, he is apt to neglect it altogether. Thus, having persuaded himself that 'it would be incorrect to attach too much importance' to the influence of a rise of wages and fall of profit, he proceeds to say:

> In the subsequent part of this work, though I shall occasionally refer to this cause of variation, I shall consider all the great variations which take place in the relative value of commodities, to be produced by the greater or less quantity of labour which may be required from time to time to produce them (23/36).

If we follow Ricardo's reasoning step by step, we find that he begins by selecting an example in which the quantity of fixed capital is comparatively small, and on the strength of this comes to the conclusion that a change in the rate of wages does not much affect the price of the product; he then decides that under these circumstances a change in the rate of wages may be disregarded entirely when discussing 'great variations' in relative value; his next step is to neglect change in the rate of wages for *all* variations, whether large or small, and to regard the quantity of labour only as affecting the price, as will be seen in the following remarks:

Page 64(110): We have seen, too, that all manufactured

[1] First edition, p. 36; p. 59 in Sraffa's, vol. 1.

commodities rise and fall in price in proportion as more or less labour becomes necessary to their production.

Page 69(118): In all cases commodities rise because more labour is expended on them, and not because the labour which is expended on them is at a higher value.

Page 182(273): Everything rises or falls in value in proportion to the facility or difficulty of producing it, or in other words, in proportion to the quantity of labour employed on its production.

Page 183(275): That commodity is alone invariable [in value] which at all times requires the same sacrifice of toil and labour to produce it.

Ricardo's statement on page 23(36) that he will consider all great variations in relative values as due to variations in the quantity of labour required for production must be carefully noted, because it means that he intends to ignore the 'modifications' which he has been at pains to set before the reader. And another thing to be noted is that, in practice, he applies to *differences* of value the same disregard of modifications that he applies to *changes* of value. We can understand to some extent his dwelling on changes in the quantity of labour in the case of natural products which rise in price when it becomes necessary to resort to less and less fertile land. But if it were true that the natural price of corn 'never varies unless a different quantity of labour becomes necessary to production' (203/304), it would not follow that the difference in the value of a salmon and an optical instrument corresponds with the difference in the quantity of labour employed on their 'production'.

In the first heading of his first chapter Ricardo tells us that the value of a commodity, or the quantity of any other commodity for which it will exchange, depends on the relative quantity of labour necessary for its production. In the same chapter he qualifies this by a number of modifications; by pushing these qualifications into the background as unimportant, he practically reverts to the original unqualified statement. In correspondence with his friends he defended his attitude. 'I am more convinced than ever', he wrote to McCulloch in 1819, 'that the great regulator of value is the quantity of labour required to produce the commodity valued. There are many modifications which must be admitted into this doctrine, from the circumstance of the unequal times that commodities require to be brought to market, but this does not invalidate the doctrine itself' (vol. 8, p. 142). In his *Notes on Malthus*, 1820, he wrote: 'The real value of a commodity, I think, means the same thing as its cost of production, and the relative cost of production of two commodities is nearly in Proportion to the quantity of labour from first to last respectively bestowed upon them' (vol. 2, p. 35). Malthus wrote to Ricardo: 'You assert that with few exceptions the quantity of labour employed on commodities determines the rate at which they will exchange for each other. This is a *proposition*, and one that is not well founded' (vol. 8, p. 261). Ricardo replied: 'I acknowledge that it is not rigidly true, but I say that it is the nearest approximation to truth, as a rule for measuring relative value, of any I have ever heard' (vol. 8, p. 279). In 1821 he wrote to his friend Trower: 'Exchangeable value is regulated by positive value, and therefore is regulated by the quantity of labour expended' (vol. 9, pp. 1 and 2). In 1822 Ricardo wrote to Say: 'I have always contended that commodities are valuable in proportion to the quantity of labour bestowed upon them' (vol. 9, p. 169).

It thus appears that Ricardo's list of modifications made little impression upon himself. Neither his disciple McCulloch, nor that other disciple, James Mill, saw anything in them to disturb his faith in labour as the determinant of value. This seems strange, because when all Ricardo's modifications are taken into account, scarcely anything appears to remain of the original proposition that relative values are in proportion to the relative quantities of labour; the doctrine, in fact, is so whittled down that it amounts to no more than this:

> If men employed no machinery in production, but labour only, and were all the same length of time before they brought their commodities to market, the exchangeable value of their goods would be precisely in proportion to the quantity of labour employed. If they employed fixed capital of the same value and of the same durability, then too the value of the commodities produced would be the same, and they would vary with the greater or less quantity of labour employed on their production.

Should the reader ask me who said this?—my reply is that these are Ricardo's own words (19/32). Each sentence begins with 'If', and as Touchstone observes in *As You Like It*, there is 'much virtue in If'. But Ricardo seems to attach no significance whatever to his 'If'. After marshalling the various reasons why relative values are not in proportion to the relative quantities of labour, he sweeps them all into the waste-paper basket, and without either 'if' or 'nearly' or 'approximately', he reaffirms (29/46) his original proposition that value is in proportion to the quantity of labour:

> It is necessary for me also to remark that I have not said because one commodity has so much labour bestowed upon it as will cost £1000, and another so much as will cost £2000, that therefore one would be of the value of £1000 and the other of the value of £2000; but I have said that their value will be to each other as two to one, and that in those proportions they will be exchanged. It is of no importance to the truth of this doctrine whether one of these commodities sells for £1100 and the other for £2200, or one for £1500 and the other for £3000; into that question I do not at present inquire; I affirm only that their relative values will be governed by the relative quantities of labour bestowed on their production (29/46).

This disregard of the 'modifications' was not shared by Ricardo's critics. A contemporary economist, Colonel Torrens, expressed the view that Ricardo's 'modifications' amounted, not to a mere qualification, but to a positive refutation of the doctrine that value is in proportion to the quantity of labour (vol. 4, p. 317). But Ricardo did not alter his opinion; I quoted just now his statement that he was 'more convinced than ever'; and in fact, the paragraph I have quoted from page 29(46) did not appear in Ricardo's first two editions, but was inserted for the first time in his third edition,[1] apparently to emphasise that it would be a mistake to attach 'too much importance' to the modifications he had enumerated. In this paragraph, it is true, he recognises that profits as well as wages form part of the cost of production; but he makes what, in view of his modifications, is the strange assumption that capital and labour are always combined in the same proportion. As Malthus remarked: 'Mr. Ricardo often uses the terms *quantity of labour* and *quantity of labour and capital* to express the same thing.'[2] Ricardo, in fact, never seems able to rid himself entirely for long of the notion that capital consists only of a fund for the

[1] The original draft of this paragraph will be found in the *Notes on Malthus*, written in 1820 (vol. 2, p. 34). For Malthus' comments on this paragraph, see the second edition of his *Principles*, page 93.

[2] Malthus' *Principles*, second edition, page 295.

maintenance of labour. Although he now and then lifts the curtain on the role played by fixed capital, his conception of capital as a wages-fund seems always to return and intrude itself with the same persistency that baffled the efforts of Mr. Dick to keep King Charles' head out of his manuscript. While value is sometimes said to be in proportion to the total cost of production (which may include a tax), it is more often said to be in proportion to the quantity of labour—'it must be said, too', remarks the Austrian economist Boehm-Bawerk, 'that he is much more interested and cordial in his exposition of this latter principle than in that of its capitalist modification'.[1] Ricardo's earliest notions of Political Economy were derived from Adam Smith, whose dictum that, in a primitive society, the quantity of labour required to produce various commodities determined their relative values,[2] captured Ricardo's imagination and became the basis upon which his theory was built. He thought he saw in this principle the key or clue to all the intricacies and complexities of modern industry and commerce, and he took Adam Smith to task for deserting this fundamental principle—'as if', he wrote in his first edition, 'when profits and rent were to be paid, they would have some influence on the relative value of commodities independent of the mere quantity of labour that was necessary to their production'.[3]

It is true that Ricardo withdrew these words in his third edition; but he did not expunge the remark that Adam Smith 'was bound in consistency to maintain that all things became more or less valuable in proportion as more or less labour was bestowed on their production' (7/13), and he inserted the new and uncompromising paragraph on page 29(46). A fundamental principle is not to be obscured by 'disturbing factors'; modifications are followed by minimisations, and leave no more trace than water on a duck's back. When machinery is brought into the picture, what Ricardo sees is not an addition to capital but a diminution of labour: machinery 'saves labour' (22/36), it 'abridges labour'

[1] *Capital and Interest*, page 95 in Smart's translation (1890).

[2] *Wealth of Nations*, Book 1, chap. 6, 1st paragraph (quoted by Ricardo on page 6(13), although in all three of his editions he wrongly gives the reference as chap. 5).

[3] Page 16 in first edition (see footnote, vol. 1, p. 23). This dig at Smith was left standing in the second edition, but apparently by oversight, for on page 31 of that edition, and again on page 39, he distinguishes between the 'early stages of society' and later stages.

(46/86), and therefore reduces the cost of production. Thus on page 182(273) Ricardo writes:

> Suppose with a given capital, the labour of a certain number of men produced 1000 pair of stockings, and that by inventions in machinery, the same number of men can produce 2000 pair . . . then the value of the 2000 pair of stockings . . . will be neither more nor less than that of the 1000 pair of stockings before the introduction of machinery; for they will be the produce of the same quantity of labour.

It is clear that the price of a pair of stockings has fallen because the cost of its production has diminished. But in concluding that the price will now be exactly half, Ricardo ignores the fact that capital has been increased by the addition of a machine, and the capitalist must have a profit on his fixed capital as well as on his circulating capital. If the cost of the machine is small, and the increase of output large, then indeed the fall in the price of stockings may be very nearly, though not quite, in the same proportion as the diminution in the quantity of labour embodied in each pair. We may imagine that the hosier, like the capitalist who heads the list in our Table A, was able in the beginning to produce goods without employing any fixed capital; we may assume that he paid £900 in wages and produced 1000 pairs of stockings which he sold for £1000, or 20 shillings a pair, thus making a profit of £100. We may also imagine that for the modest sum of £900 he is able to buy a machine which will double his output. We arrive at his price as follows:

Wages	£900
Profit on £900	100
Profit on Fixed Capital	100
Price of Product	£1100

Two thousand pairs of stockings being produced at this price, the quantity of direct labour embodied in each pair is half what it was before, and the price, which was formerly twenty shillings, is now eleven shillings, which is a fall of nearly, but not quite, 50 per cent.

But in this case we have minified the influence of fixed capital by assuming the quantity employed to be small compared with the quantity of labour. It is just as likely to happen that the hosier, by expending £9000 on machinery, is able with the same quantity of labour to turn out 8000 or perhaps 20,000 pairs of stockings—

for, as Ricardo wrote to Malthus, 'no law can be laid down respecting quantity' (vol. 8, p. 278). Whatever may be the quantity, the price of the total product will be as follows:

Wages	£900
Profit on £900	100
Profit on £9000	1000
Price of Product	£2000

Although the total cost has doubled, the product has more than doubled, and the price of stockings has accordingly fallen. But the price of a pair of stockings has not diminished in the same proportion as the quantity of direct labour 'embodied' in it. If the product is now 8000 pairs, the quantity of labour in each pair is only one-eighth of what it was in the beginning; but the price has only fallen to one-fourth; it has fallen from twenty shillings to five shillings. If the quantity produced with the aid of the machine is 20,000, the quantity of labour in each pair is no more than one-twentieth; the price, however, is one-tenth, or two shillings.

Sometimes Ricardo says that price is in proportion to the quantity of labour, at other times he says it is in proportion to the cost of production, which includes the remuneration of fixed as well as circulating capital; as remarked by Boehm-Bawerk, his leaning is towards the former expression. To Malthus he wrote: 'Cost of production is, with some deviations, in proportion to labour employed. My commodity and your commodity are both worth £1000—they will therefore probably have the same quantity of labour realised in each' (vol. 8, p. 279). If the reader will glance back at our Table A, he will see that of the six arithmetical illustrations found in Ricardo's *Principles*, all except the first are 'deviations' from this rule. The one that does not deviate is that in which it is assumed that goods are produced without any assistance from fixed capital, and I think we may fairly describe this class of goods as non-existent. Moreover, Ricardo's theory that goods exchange for one another in proportion to the quantity of labour embodied in them, assumes that all labour is of the same quality and all remunerated at the same rate, which I think may also be described as a non-existent state of things. And this may serve to remind us that we have not yet dealt with the 'modification' in Ricardo's section 2, but have reserved it for our next chapter.

4

Different Qualities of Labour

In the last chapter we reserved for separate discussion section 2 of Ricardo's first chapter, in which the most important 'modification' of all is recognised, namely, the fact that not all labour is of the same quality, and not all remunerated at the same rate. If one employer pays £1000 in wages, and another £2000, we cannot assume, as Ricardo does in the last paragraph of section 6, that the *quantities* of labour employed are in that proportion.

Yet this is Ricardo's assumption, not only in chapter 1, but throughout his book. In the arithmetical examples which he inserts from time to time to illustrate his arguments (see Table A in our last chapter) the labour-cost always appears as a sum paid in wages; but the reader is expected to understand that if two capitalists pay the same amount in wages, it is because they employ the same quantity of labour (see capitalists 1 and 2 in the table—each of whom, Ricardo states, employs 100 men); and if the wages bill of one capitalist is £2000 and that of another £8000 (capitalists 3 and 4) it indicates that the latter employs four times as many men as the former. This is not stated by Ricardo in each individual case, but it is always and everywhere his assumption; always and everywhere, that is to say, except in section 2, where he admits that different qualities of labour receive different rates of pay. But this 'modification' is no sooner introduced than it is minimised, and then consigned to the waste-paper basket, never to be mentioned again. It is buried—quietly, without any fuss, and without any monument to keep its memory green.

But we cannot acquiesce in this stealthy burial; the modification is too important for that. It is not so much a modification as a complete refutation of the doctrine that value is in proportion to the quantity of labour.

The modifications reviewed in the last chapter, as was there remarked, practically reduce Ricardo's proposition to this: 'If men employed no machinery in production, but labour only, and were all the same length of time before they brought their commodities to market, the exchangeable value of their goods would be precisely in proportion to the quantity of labour employed' (his own admission, (19/32)). But even this conclusion is seen to be erroneous when we take into account the fact that what one man produces in a day may be larger in quantity or better in quality than what another man produces.

It may be reasonable to suppose that in a primitive society, among a nation of hunters,[1] all men are equally skilled, or equally unskilled, both in the making of weapons and in the use of them; it may be reasonable to assume that what one man can secure in a day, any other can secure in a day; and that what is produced by one man in two days will usually exchange for what two men produce in one day. But it is quite obvious that this condition no longer prevails when one man earns £1 a week, another £2, and a third perhaps £5, perhaps £100. Hence, while it may or may not be true that the price of commodities is in proportion to their cost of production, it is obviously not true that either their prices or their cost of production is always in proportion to the quantity of labour expended on them. Even if we discarded all the 'modifications' brought about by the use of fixed capital, and supposed commodities to be produced by 'labour only', it would still not be true that their 'exchangeable value . . . would be precisely in proportion to the quantity of labour employed' (19/32).

Even Ricardo's faithful disciple, McCulloch, found it impossible to swallow the assumption that all labour is of the same quality and all remunerated at the same rate. This says something for McCulloch's common sense; but his method of justifying Ricardo says little for his logic. His suggestion amounts to this, that if one labourer earns £1 a week and another £2, the latter must be regarded as two labourers. Here are his own words:

> In stating that the quantity of labour required to produce commodities is at once the only determining principle and measure of their real, and generally speaking also of their exchangeable value, it is taken for granted, of course, that all sorts of labour are reduced to the same common standard of intensity.[2]

[1] See first paragraph in Adam Smith's sixth chapter.

[2] McCulloch's *Principles of Pol. Econ.*, Part 3, section 1. McCulloch himself

J.-B. Say, the French economist, another of Ricardo's friends (but not, like McCulloch, a disciple), found the same difficulty. He could make neither head nor tail of Ricardo's doctrine that value is in proportion to the quantity of labour unless Ricardo meant by this, in proportion to the amount paid for labour. Ricardo hastened to inform Say that this was *not* what he meant. 'I do not say that it is the value of labour which regulates the value of commodities, for that is an opinion I do all in my power to overthrow; but I say that it is the comparative quantity of labour necessary to the production of commodities which regulates their relative value.'[1]

In other words, Ricardo's theory of value is based on the assumption that there is only one quality of labour and one rate of wages. If we were dealing with the question of felling trees and sawing them into planks we might possibly be willing to accept McCulloch's view that if one man could accomplish twice as much as another it would not be unreasonable to reckon his labour as the labour of two men. We might regard man-power as a unit of measurement in the sense that horse-power is a unit of measurement. But Say's idea (in common with that of most people) was that there are many different qualities of labour; many different kinds and qualities of skill, natural or acquired; that these differences result in the wages of the carpenter and joiner being different from those of the lumberman who felled the trees, those of the surgeon being different from those of the butcher. He could not see any sense in assuming that the price or value of a commodity was in proportion to the quantity of labour, without regard to the different qualities of labour and the different amounts of money it is necessary to pay in wages. Neither quantity of labour nor cost of production will explain why a barrister earns £100 in a week while a bricklayer's wage is not a tenth part of that

found a disciple in Karl Marx, who says: 'Skilled labour counts only as intensified, or rather multiplied, simple labour, so that a smaller quantity of skilled labour is equal to a larger quantity of simple labour. Experience shows that skilled labour can always be reduced in this way to the terms of simple labour' (*Capital*, chap. 1, section 2 (page 13 in *Everyman* edition).

[1] Vol. 8, p. 149. The remark of Say's to which Ricardo refers is apparently that on p. 9, vol. 2, of Say's fourth edition, that 'ce n'est pas la valeur des services productifs qui fonde la valeur des produits, ainsi que l'ont avancé quelques auteurs'. Ricardo's differences with Say will be discussed in a later chapter.

amount. To the current labour of the lawyer you may add the 'accumulated labour' of his student days—you may add the cost of his education;[1] but if you take all his toil and all his earnings, from first to last, and do the same with the bricklayer, you will not find that the two men earned equal pay for equal quantities of labour. A *prima donna* may, in her day, receive fifty times as much as a coal-miner, but it would be difficult to show that she had crammed into her lifetime fifty times as much hard work. As for the notion that the rewards are practically equalised by the greater agreeableness of the miner's work, the less said about that the better.[2]

We may conclude that these ideas did not occur to McCulloch. If they occurred to Ricardo, he must have rejected them. He does, indeed, in a footnote on page 12(21) quote Adam Smith's remark that there may be more labour in an hour's hard work than in two hours' easy business;[3] but he does not attempt to build on this. He tells us that a working jeweller is paid more for his work than a common labourer, but he does not suggest that the jeweller does more or harder work than the common labourer, nor does he refer to the accumulated labour of the jeweller's apprenticeship. He apparently admits, without reservation, that in this instance two equal quantities of labour produce different values, and the admission seems to destroy entirely the doctrine that relative values are in proportion to the relative quantities of labour.

How does Ricardo extricate himself from this dilemma? He does so in a rather curious way. Although he does not employ the above-mentioned idea of Smith's as a way out of his difficulty, he makes use of another passage in *The Wealth of Nations*, namely the last paragraph of chapter 10, where Smith observes that the proportion between the rates of wages in different employments, once fixed, seems seldom to vary. Ricardo's argument in section 2 runs as follows:

> In speaking, however, of labour being the foundation of all value,

---

[1] See *Wealth of Nations*, Bk. 1, chap. 10, Part 1, 6th and 9th paragraphs. For a passing reference by Ricardo to the cost of education as influencing future remuneration, see vol. 2, p. 226.

[2] For Smith's remarks, see Bk. 1, chap. 10, Part 1, paragraphs 2, 3 and 4.

[3] In all three editions Ricardo gives the reference to *The Wealth of Nations* as Bk. 1, chap. 10, but it should be chap. 5 (4th paragraph).

and the relative quantity of labour as almost [1] exclusively determining the relative value of commodities, I must not be supposed to be inattentive to the different qualities of labour, and the difficulty of comparing an hour's or a day's labour in one employment with the same duration of labour in another. The estimation in which different qualities of labour are held comes soon to be adjusted in the market with sufficient precision for all practical purposes, and depends much on the comparative skill of the labourer and intensity of the labour performed. The scale, when once formed, is liable to little variation. If a day's labour of a working jeweller be more valuable than a day's labour of a common labourer, it has long ago been adjusted and placed in its proper position in the scale of value.

In comparing, therefore, the value of the same commodity at different periods of time, the consideration of the comparative skill and intensity of labour required for that particular commodity needs scarcely be attended to, as it operates equally at both periods. One description of labour at one time is compared with the same description of labour at another; if a tenth, a fifth, or a fourth has been added or taken away, an effect proportioned to the cause will be produced on the relative value of the commodity.

If a piece of cloth be now of the value of two pieces of linen, and if, in ten years hence, the ordinary value of a piece of cloth should be four pieces of linen, we may safely conclude that either more labour is required to make the cloth, or less to make the linen, or that both causes have operated.

As the enquiry to which I wish to draw the reader's attention relates to the effect of the variations in the relative value of commodities, and not in their absolute value, it will be of little importance to examine into the comparative degree of estimation in which the different kinds of human labour are held. We may fairly conclude that whatever inequality there might originally have been in them, whatever the ingenuity, skill, or time necessary for the acquirement of one species of manual dexterity more than another, it continues nearly the same from one generation to another; or at least that the variation is very inconsiderable from year to year, and therefore can have little effect for short periods, on the relative value of commodities.

To understand Ricardo's attitude here, we must bear in mind the object he had in view when he sat down to write his book. As explained in our first chapter (and in his own Preface), he sought to elucidate the principles that govern the distribution of the

[1] Even this 'almost' was not inserted until his third edition.

nation's annual commodity income among the different classes of the community. He was interested, not so much in past or present distribution, as in the modifications this distribution would undergo in the future as a consequence of the law of diminishing returns. With increase of population there will be an increase of demand for commodities. If a ten per cent addition to the quantity of labour bestowed on production would result in a ten per cent addition to the supply of commodities, there would be no rise in prices; but in the case of food and raw materials an addition of ten per cent to the supply requires more than a ten per cent addition to the quantity of labour employed on production. Food and raw materials rise in price, and the cause of this increased price is the increased quantity of labour required for production.

In this rise in the relative value of natural products Ricardo sees an economic force that gradually changes the distribution of the national income—puts more money into the pockets of the landlords and reduces the rate of profit on capital. He was, therefore, not so much interested in prices as in the trend of prices; it was not to the ratio of exchange itself, but to alterations in the ratio of exchange, and the effect of these alterations, that he 'wished to draw the reader's attention'. But while we are thus invited to focus our attention upon what causes relative values to change, we cannot allow our notice to be diverted from the fact that in section 2 Ricardo contradicts the statement made in the heading to his first section, that the rate of the labourer's remuneration has no influence on the ratio in which goods exchange for one another. But unfortunately, he has no sooner brought forward this modification than he turns his back on it. Everywhere, except in section 2, he assumes that price is in proportion to the quantity of labour. Section 2, in fact, seems to be inserted, not for the purpose of modifying this doctrine, but in the hope of persuading us that no modification is necessary. He could not refuse to acknowledge, what every office-boy knew, that different qualities of labour are differently rewarded; but while the fact is bowed in at one door, it is bowed out at another. He minimises its importance by asserting that it does not affect variations of value, and then eliminates it from the discussion. The admission that there are different qualities of labour, selling at different prices, is not formally withdrawn, but it disappears from his pages, whisked away by what amounts to a feat of literary prestidigitation; less politely perhaps, we might describe section 2 as a red herring drawn across the path. The 'reader's attention' is diverted from *quality*, and thereafter it is quietly assumed that *quantity* only is what counts. This is the assumption in section 4 when he says that if men employed no machinery, but labour only, the value would be 'precisely, in proportion to the quantity of labour' (19/32), and again in the last words of section 6 when he 'affirms only' that relative values are always in proportion to the relative quantities of labour. Whether Ricardo discusses relative values, or variations in relative values, his language is always the same, as we saw in the last chapter. Was Ricardo not conscious of any flaw in his reasoning? Among the passages there quoted was his remark: 'My commodity and your commodity are both worth £1000—they will therefore probably have the same quantity of labour realised in each.' This is followed immediately by what seems a confession: 'But the doctrine is less liable to objections when employed, not to measure the whole absolute value of the commodities compared, but the variations which from time to time take place in relative value' (vol. 8, p. 279). Yet in the following year he writes to his friend Trower: 'Exchangeable value is regulated by positive value, and therefore is regulated by the quantity of labour expended.'[1] Thus in defence of his favourite theory[2] Ricardo is content to ignore all 'disturbing factors'—not merely differences in the quality of labour, but also differences in the quantity of capital employed, and differences in the time for which the capital is tied up.

In subsequent chapters Ricardo occasionally refers to the fact that all capital is not 'wages-fund'; that all labour is not of the same quality, on the other hand, is a fact of which he appears scarcely conscious after greeting it with Hail and Farewell in section 2. I say scarcely conscious, not totally unconscious, for on page 100(159) he refers to 'wages of the lowest kind', and there are similar expressions on pages 140 and 143 (215 and 220). But this implied recognition of different rates of pay is only momentary; it is taken over from Adam Smith without being mentally absorbed by Ricardo, who in fact, as I shall show later (in chapter 8), ignores it at the same moment that he refers to it. His chapter on Wages from end to end seems to take for granted that there is

[1] Vol. 9, pp. 1 and 2. Trower, like Ricardo, was a retired stockbroker turned country gentleman. He was a cousin of Sydney Smith's.

[2] See Boehm-Bawerk's remark, quoted in our last chapter (page 41).

only one quality of labour and only one scale of pay for those who are neither capitalists nor landlords. The high emoluments often earned by architects, engineers, chemists, inventors, experts of all descriptions, seem to be left entirely out of the picture. Yet the remuneration of this highly paid labour forms part of the cost of production, and must enter more largely into some products than others, and must therefore affect the ratio in which they exchange for one another.

The fact is Ricardo made a capital error when he decided that differences in the quality of labour could be neglected. This would have been an error on his part even if he had been content to apply his ruling (as in section 2) to *variations* of price only. To illustrate this, let us suppose that there are three qualities of labour, respectively paid £1, £2, and £5 per week. Just as labour and capital may be combined in different proportions, so different qualities of labour may be combined in different proportions, as assumed in the following table:

TABLE C

A			B		
50 men at £1		£50	88 men at £1		£88
50 men at £2		100	10 men at £2		20
1 man at £5		5	3 men at £5		15
101 men	Total Wages	£155	101 men	Total Wages	£123

We assume that in case A and case B the product is the same both in quantity and quality. We assume, too, that in both cases the same number of men is employed, and that there has been no alteration in the scale of pay for different grades of labour. But the employer has discovered a better combination of the different grades of labour. By employing more skilled labour at the top he is enabled to reduce the number of semi-skilled men, and to substitute labour of a cheaper grade. The result is a fall of £32 in the cost of production. While there is no reduction in the rate of wages paid for each class of labour, there is an increase of profit; or if competition compels a reduction in the selling price of the commodity, the 'variation' in its value is due to a diminution in the total cost of production and not to a diminution in the quantity of labour employed.

5

Production of Equal Values at Unequal Costs

WE have now examined all the 'modifications' by which in his first chapter Ricardo qualifies the doctrine that the ratio in which commodities exchange for one another is determined by the relative quantities of labour required for their production. We saw in our last chapter that one fact admitted by him, namely, that different prices are paid for different qualities of labour, is really quite irreconcilable with this doctrine, and that Ricardo makes no attempt to reconcile it. What he tries to do is to get rid of it; or hide it. He diverts our attention while he quietly pushes the family skeleton back into its cupboard, and smoothly proceeds to enlarge upon other modifications of a less disturbing nature.[1] The mention of fixed capital leads to the admission that value is not precisely in proportion to the quantity of labour; but this, he says, makes little difference, for profit on capital forms a comparatively small part of price. If the reader will turn back to Table A he will see that halving or doubling the quantity of profit will not, in five of the six cases quoted, affect price to anything like the same extent as halving or doubling the quantity of labour. Where capital and labour are combined in different proportions, Ricardo is content to claim (vol. 2, p. 35) that 'the relative cost of production of two commodities is nearly in proportion to the quantity of labour'. He is even willing to amend the text of his *Principles* by withdrawing the statement in the first and second editions that relative value depends exclusively on the quantity of labour expended on each, and to substitute depends 'almost

[1] Ricardo's attitude towards disturbing factors contrasts with that of Herbert Spencer, whose idea of tragedy (Huxley said) was a beautiful theory knocked on the head by a hard fact.

exclusively' (11/20). But he attaches so little importance to these corrections that he apparently regards it as a matter of indifference whether we say that value is proportionate to the quantity of labour, to the quantity of labour and capital, or to the quantity of cost. The first, as Boehm-Bawerk remarked, was his favourite expression, but the last I think more accurately represents his real doctrine.

If there was thus a certain ambiguity in Ricardo's definition of his own doctrine, he was at all events perfectly clear in his refusal to accept the view of his opponents that price is regulated by the law of Supply and Demand. In his *Principles* (231/344) he said: 'The real and ultimate regulator of the relative value of any two commodities is the cost of their production, and not the respective quantities which may be produced, nor the competition amongst the purchasers.' Competition amongst the purchasers may raise the price temporarily, just as an excessive supply in the market may cause it to fall temporarily; but—

> It is the cost of production which must ultimately regulate the price of commodities, and not, as has been often said, the proportion between the supply and demand. The proportion between supply and demand may, indeed, for a time, affect the market value of a commodity until it is supplied in greater or less abundance, according as the demand may have increased or diminished; but this effect will be only of temporary duration (260/382).

Thus demand is not credited with anything more than a passing influence on price. Variations in the ratio of demand to supply will cause prices to fluctuate; but these fluctuations are always round about the cost of production, to which the price always tends to return. In the long run, the rule holds good that equal costs produce equal values.

Unfortunately for this theory the most important of all commodities, food, is notoriously produced at a great variety of costs without any difference of value resulting from this fact. Wheat of the same quality will sell for the same price though produced at very different costs. One farmer will produce with ten men as much corn as another can produce with twelve, but their products, if of the same quality, will sell at the same price. This is true of all descriptions of raw materials, be it cotton or coal, iron or rubber. Not only is value not in proportion to the quantity of labour; it is not in proportion to the total cost. In short, equal values are produced at unequal costs and with unequal quantities of labour. How then can the quantity of labour, or the quantity of cost, be said to regulate the price?

Faced with this difficulty, Ricardo's doctrine undergoes yet another 'considerable modification'—a modification which, this time, is neither minimised nor evaded, but is incorporated in his teaching, of which it becomes a leading feature. His attitude in chapter 1 was that equality of cost and value held good despite all modifications; in chapter 2 the terms of the proposition are changed to fit the new facts brought into view. In the following paragraph on page 37(73) his doctrine assumes its final shape:

> The exchangeable value of all commodities, whether they be manufactured, or the produce of the mines, or the produce of land, is always regulated, not by the less quantity of labour that will suffice for their production under circumstances highly favourable, and exclusively enjoyed by those who have peculiar facilities of production; but by the greater quantity of labour necessarily bestowed on their production by those who have no such facilities; by those who continue to produce them under the most unfavourable circumstances; meaning, by the most unfavourable circumstances, the most unfavourable under which the quantity of produce required renders it necessary to carry on the production.

Those who prefer a briefer statement will find one on page 246(363), where he says: 'I have endeavoured to show that the real value of a commodity is regulated, not by the accidental advantages which may be enjoyed by some of its producers, but by the real difficulties encountered by that producer who is least favoured.' The least favoured producer is what we should now call the marginal producer.

Now this proposition appears to be very different from the one with which we started. It was then assumed that equal costs produce equal values; it is now stated that equal values are often produced at unequal costs. It was originally assumed that all capitalists make the same rate of profit, whereas it is now implied that some make a higher rate than others; for their costs are less, while they obtain the same price as those whose costs are higher. The new form the doctrine has taken admits, what seemed formerly to be denied, that many a sack of coals, many a bag of wheat, and perhaps many a shirt or pair of shoes,[1] is sold at a price which does not correspond with its cost of production and is not governed by the quantity of labour 'realised in it'. The quantity of labour that determines the price of the article you purchase is not the quantity actually bestowed upon it, nor is it the average quantity required for production, or the quantity 'bestowed' by the majority of producers; it is the quantity found necessary by the 'least favoured' producer. It is only the marginal producer, in fact, who sells his product for what it cost him to produce. The marginal producer may be responsible for nine-tenths of the supply, or on the other hand he may supply only one-tenth or one-hundredth of the quantity consumed; nevertheless, in Ricardo's view, it is the marginal producer's cost of production that 'determines' the price that will be received by all producers and paid by all consumers.

In what sense can the marginal producer's cost be said to determine the price? Let us consider this question, using for this purpose Ricardo's own presentation of the position. On page 222(331) he writes:

> After Adam Smith has declared that there are some mines which can only be worked by the owners, as they will afford only sufficient to defray the expense of working, together with the ordinary profits of the capital employed,[2] we should expect that he would admit that it was these particular mines which regulated the price of the produce from all mines. If the old mines are insufficient to supply the quantity of coal required the price of coal will rise, and will continue

[1] So far as I can recall, the paragraph on page 37(73) is the only passage in Ricardo's writings where he assumes that the production of equal values at unequal costs occurs in manufacture as well as in agriculture and mining. Everywhere else his assumption appears to be that in manufacture the cost of production is, at any one time, the same for all producers. On page 165(250), for instance, he makes this distinction between agriculture and manufacture: 'One portion of capital employed in agriculture regulates the price of corn, namely that portion which pays no rent; whereas in the production of manufactured commodities every portion of capital is employed with the same results, and as no portion pays rent, every portion is equally a regulator of price.' Thus, if we produce a million quarters of wheat, the cost of producing the last thousand may be twice as great as the cost of producing the first thousand; but if a million hats are produced, the cost of the last thousand will be precisely the same as the cost of the first thousand (see vol. 2, p. 47).

[2] *The Wealth of Nations*, Bk. 1, chap. 11, Part 2, 13th paragraph.

rising till the owner of a new and inferior mine finds that he can obtain the usual profits of stock[1] by working his mine. If his mine be tolerably fertile, the rise will not be great before it becomes his interest so to employ his capital; but if it be not tolerably fertile, it is evident that the price must continue to rise till it will afford him the means of paying his expenses, and obtaining the ordinary profits of stock. It appears, then, that it is always the least fertile mine which regulates the price of coal.

That all the coal will sell at the same price if it is all of the same quality, is not disputed. The question is whether the marginal producer's cost regulates the price, or whether it is the price prevailing in the market that determines the maximum cost of production that can be profitably incurred. When Ricardo says that it is the least fertile mine that regulates the price of coal, he means the least fertile mine that is actually worked, but the reason it is worked is that the market price is sufficiently high to cover its cost of production. It was not the cost of production on the least fertile mine that raised the price to this level; on Ricardo's own showing, it was the increase of demand that caused the price to rise, and it is the rise in the price that permits the less fertile mine to be worked at a profit.

Nevertheless, Ricardo's contention on page 37(73) and elsewhere is that it is the marginal producer's cost that regulates the price. If all lands and all mines were equally fertile, increase of demand would not cause a permanent rise of price. There might be a temporary rise, until supply was adjusted to demand, but in the long run, owing to the competition of producers, the price would always be brought back to the level which yields only the ordinary rate of profit. Consumers have the least in the world to do with the fixing of price.[2] However high may be the price they would be willing to pay, the competition of producers keeps the price down to the cost of production. This competition operates even though all mines and all lands are not of the same degree of fertility; cost of production still governs the price, but in this case it is the cost of producing on the least fertile land or from the least fertile mine that forms the rock bottom below which competition will not reduce the price.[3]

[1] Profits of stock means the same as profits on capital.

[2] Vol. 8, p. 276 (quoted at end of our second chapter, page 23).

[3] See Ricardo's argument on pages 71(120) and 103(163) of his *Principles*.

Let us examine this view, first on the assumption that the best mine not yet brought into use is a good deal less fertile than the least favoured one at present in operation; and second, on the assumption that the difference of fertility is very small.

For simplicity we will suppose that there are only two mines, one producing coal at a cost of five shillings a ton, and another, not yet tapped, which is capable of producing coal at a cost of ten shillings a ton. The owner of the first mine practically enjoys a monopoly so long as he keeps his price below ten shillings. He is under no compulsion to sell his coal for what it costs to produce; he can, without fear of competition, raise the price to nine shillings or nine and sixpence. But high price is unfavourable to a large sale, and it may pay him better to sell a larger quantity at a lower price. With the growth of demand, however, he may presently find that he can get ten shillings a ton for all that he can produce, while if he could produce more he could sell it at the same price. The supply being now less than the demand, the price is likely to rise above ten shillings; but it will not remain above ten shillings, for at that price the owner of the second mine is able to make the ordinary rate of profit, and he accordingly enters the field as a competitor.[1] The owner of mine No. 2 cannot afford to sell for less than ten shillings and the owner of mine No. 1 cannot charge a higher price than his competitor; hence Ricardo's conclusion that the marginal producer's cost is what determines the price.

But is there any reason to suppose that in the long run the market price will continue to coincide with the marginal producer's cost of production? If the demand goes on increasing as it did when only one mine was in operation, the history of the second mine will be the same as that of the first. The price, instead of remaining at ten shillings, may rise to eleven, twelve, or more, with the result that the second or marginal mine yields rent as well as ordinary profit. Price and cost of production will not be again brought into harmony unless the pressure of demand

[1] A coal mine and a seam of coal, of course, are not the same thing. For simplicity we assume that the various mines are already in existence and ready to commence production as soon as a remunerative price can be obtained for the product. Ricardo habitually ignores the preliminary expenses which must be undertaken before inferior resources can be brought into play.

raises the price so high that it becomes profitable to work a third mine whose cost of production we assume to be still higher. And if in this way price and marginal cost of production again correspond, it is not because increased cost has forced the price up, but because increase of price has made it possible to earn the ordinary rate of profit while working at a higher cost. But we cannot assume that in the long run price and cost will coincide. The tendency of rising price is to check the growth of demand; it may even halt it altogether. And there appears no reason to assume that this will occur at the precise moment when price and marginal cost are identical. If a certain quantity of coal can be sold at thirteen shillings a ton, and any attempt to raise the price above that level results in a shrinkage of demand, then the third mine will never be brought into action if it cannot produce at a less cost than fifteen shillings, and the second mine will remain the marginal mine, although yielding rent as well as profit.

Let us now turn to the alternative assumption, namely, that the difference in the 'fertility' of the various mines is but slight, and that, whatever may be the current price of coal, there is always another miner able and willing to increase the supply as soon as the price rises by a fractional amount. In this case, of course, the price can never exceed the marginal producer's cost by more than a fraction, because as soon as it exceeds his cost by a fraction he ceases to be the marginal producer, and the title descends to another producer whose cost of production is only a fraction higher. In this way the price is kept in harmony with the marginal cost—or rather, the marginal cost is kept in harmony with the price. If price and cost are not at all times 'precisely' the same, they will at all events be 'almost', or 'nearly', or 'approximately' the same.

By assuming, however, that there is very little difference between the fertility of the poorest mine in operation and that of the best not yet in operation, we do not alter the principle illustrated by the 'strong' case given above; we merely narrow the extent by which the selling price can exceed marginal cost, and shorten the time required for the new cost to catch up to the new price. Nor do we betray this principle if we admit that in practice production at higher cost may sometimes precede the rise of price. 'No commodity is raised unless there is a demand for it,' says Ricardo (vol. 8, p. 235), but production takes place in anticipation of demand, and the producer who observes that demand is steadily increasing will not hesitate to incur a higher immediate expense in production if he is satisfied that by the time he is ready to sell his product the price will have reached a level which will compensate him for his higher costs and yield him the ordinary rate of profit. But the rise of cost is not what causes the rise of price. If coal cannot be obtained from mine No. 3 at a less cost than fifteen shillings a ton, it is logical to conclude that when the price rises to fifteen shillings mine No. 3 will commence producing; we reverse cause and consequence if we say that when mine No. 3 commences to produce coal the price will rise to fifteen shillings. Yet the latter was Ricardo's favourite expression; we shall see many instances of this in our next chapter.

6

The Theory of Rent

RENT is a direct result of the fact that equal values are sometimes produced at unequal costs. A given expenditure of capital and labour will, on one piece of land, produce twice as much corn as on another, but if all the corn is of the same quality, it will all fetch the same price per bushel in the market. The rent of the first piece of land will be higher than the rent of the second, but this will make no difference to the price at which the farmers sell their corn. 'Rent', says Ricardo, 'does not and cannot enter in the least degree as a component part of its price' (41/77). 'Corn', he remarks on page 38(74), 'is not high because a rent is paid, but a rent is paid because corn is high; and it has been justly observed that no reduction would take place in the price of corn although landlords should forego the whole of their rent. Such a measure would only enable some farmers to live like gentlemen.'

Ricardo made no clain to originality here. When he said 'it has been justly observed', he was thinking of his friend Malthus,[1] but the remark was much older than either he or Malthus knew. It had been made nearly forty years earlier by James Anderson, a Scottish writer on agricultural subjects, who is now acknowledged as the real father of what has been sometimes called Ricardo's theory of rent.

According to Anderson (writing in 1777, the year after the publication of *The Wealth of Nations*), in every country there is a variety of soils, differing considerably from one another in point of fertility. If there is enough first-class land to supply all the corn required by the people, the price will be low; but if the needed

[1] To whom Ricardo attributed the remark in his pamphlet on the *Low Price of Corn*, vol. 4, p. 22.

quantity cannot be supplied without cultivating lands of the second, third and fourth qualities, the price must be high enough to yield a profit to the man who cultivates the fourth quality. It may be that on the poorest land thus brought under the plough the expense of cultivation will be equal to the value of the whole produce; if so, says Anderson, the utmost avarice of the proprietor will be unable to extort a rent. On the other hand, the owners of the better lands, which produce the same quantity of corn at less expense, will have no difficulty in obtaining rents proportioned to the profit that can be made out of them, because the farmers, knowing they can live just as well upon such soils though paying these rents, as they could upon the poorest land without paying rent, would be equally willing to take one or the other. Moreover, if the owners of the good lands patriotically decided to reduce rents, the consumer of grain would not benefit, for there would be no reduction in the price; the fourth quality of land must still be cultivated, and the price must still be sufficient to remunerate those who cultivate it. The only result of the landlord's quixotry, says Anderson, would be to enrich certain farmers.

Such was the reasoning of Anderson in 1777, and as the language of Ricardo, forty years later, was almost precisely similar, one might imagine that he wrote with Anderson's pamphlet before his eyes. But it seems unlikely that he had ever seen or heard of it. Anderson's theory appears to have attracted no attention from economists at the time of its publication. It seems even to have escaped the notice of Adam Smith, a fellow Scot, or else Smith attached no importance to it, for it is not referred to in any edition of *The Wealth of Nations*.[1] The subject was not of general interest, and the pamphlet was forgotten.

Forty years later, however, when Ricardo wrote, the times had much changed. The French Revolution had occurred, and had been followed by a long period of war, during which the price of bread

[1] Adam Smith perhaps regarded the theory as nothing new, but merely an elaboration of what he himself taught. He can hardly have been ignorant of Anderson's writings, for although Anderson wrote as a practical farmer, he was a writer of sufficient distinction to be honoured by the University of Aberdeen with the degree of LL.D. Moreover, Smith knew him, but perhaps found him prosey, for we are told that he went to sleep while Anderson was reading a paper before a Society to which they both belonged (Rae's *Life* of Smith, 1895, page 421).

had risen. Whereas in Smith's day £3 a quarter was practically a maximum price for wheat, it afterwards became practically a minimum to which the price seldom fell. Upon more than one occasion it rose above £6. While the people complained of high prices, and the farmers of high rents, the landlords grumbled at the high rates for the relief of the poor. Rents, wages, Corn laws, Poor laws, inflated currency, all were subjects of hot discussion both before and after the battle of Waterloo.

Moreover, in 1798 a cheerful young clergyman had sent a shiver down the spines of rich and poor alike by proclaiming that population naturally increases in a geometrical ratio (1–2–4–8–16), while the food supply can be increased at most in an arithmetical ratio (1–2–3–4–5),[1] the result being, as every schoolboy can see at a glance, that there is no possibility of rearing all the children that are born, and many of them must necessarily perish every year from starvation—which is Nature's way of adapting demand to supply. The theory was not new, to be sure, but Malthus' pithy way of putting it was new. The arithmetical and geometrical catchwords caught the popular imagination, and made the 'principle of population' a matter of sudden interest to everybody.

The arithmetical formula for the increase of food did not, of course, pretend to be scientifically exact. Malthus, in fact, pronounced it an over-sanguine estimate—it is 'certainly far beyond the truth', he said (page 22). The increase will, in reality, be at a diminishing rate. In a new country, such as America then was, it had been found possible to double the population in twenty-five years, because it had been possible to double the annual production of food in that period; but it does not follow that an addition of the same magnitude can be made to the annual production of food in the next twenty-five years; and certainly in an old country such as England this could not happen. 'When acre has been added to acre, till all the fertile land is occupied,' said Malthus, 'the yearly increase of food will depend upon the amelioration of the land already in possession; and even this moderate stream will be gradually diminishing' (page 107). Again, 'There is no person with the smallest knowledge of land but would say that it was

[1] Page 14 in the first edition of the *Essay on the Principle of Population.* My quotations are taken from the reprint issued by the Royal Economic Society in 1926.

impossible that the average produce of the country could be increased during the second twenty-five years by a quantity equal to what it at present yields' (page 188). In his second edition (1803) Malthus wrote:

> The improvement of the barren parts would be a work of time and labour; and it must be evident to those who have the slightest acquaintance with agricultural subjects, that in proportion as cultivation extended, the additions that could yearly be made to the former average produce, must be gradually and regularly diminishing.[1]

Thus the 'law' of diminishing returns, which was unknown to Adam Smith,[2] and not accepted by Anderson,[3] must be regarded as the offspring of Malthus' brain. That Ricardo had adopted it not later than 1810 we may gather from one of his Notes of that year, in which he says: 'This opinion is founded on the decreasing power of the land to produce in proportion to the labour and capital employed on it' (vol. 3, p. 287). At that time Ricardo had no personal acquaintance with Malthus; they met in the following year and soon became close friends. Malthus, in 1805, had been appointed Professor of History and Political Economy at the newly founded East India College at Haileybury, and as such he had to lecture on Rent. In 1815 he published a couple of pamphlets in one of which he defined the rent of land as 'that portion of the value of the whole produce which remains to the owner after all the outgoings belonging to its cultivation, of whatever kind have been paid, including the profits of the capital employed, estimated according to the usual and ordinary rate of profits of agricultural stock at the time being'.

[1] I quote here from the reprint of select chapters issued by Messrs. Macmillan in 1895, page 84.

[2] Smith did not believe that corn was dearer in his day than in earlier times; see *Wealth of Nations*, Bk. 1, chap. 11, 28th paragraph in the section headed 'First Period'. His only allusion to diminishing returns or increasing costs is, I think, the following: 'A market which, from requiring only one thousand, comes to require annually ten thousand ton of fish, can seldom be supplied without employing more than ten times the quantity of labour which had before been sufficient to supply it' (Bk. 1, chap. 11, 15th paragraph in the section headed 'Third Sort').

[3] Anderson thought that owing to the advance of science, agriculture had become more productive instead of less. See Cannan's *Theories of Production and Distribution*, 1893, page 145.

Ricardo accepted this definition,[1] but on some points he differed from Malthus, to whom he wrote: 'I will try, if I have a little leisure, to put my thoughts on this subject on paper' (vol. 6, p. 173). As a matter of fact, although Ricardo up to this time (1815) had published nothing apart from his contributions to the Bullion controversy, he and Malthus had been discussing economic questions ever since they became acquainted, and Ricardo had almost completed a pamphlet expounding his views on Profit. All he had to do, apparently, was to add some 'Remarks on Mr. Malthus' two last publications', and his brochure followed almost immediately on the heels of Malthus' publications.[2] This was his celebrated *Essay on the Influence of a Low Price of Corn on the Profits of Stock*. In this essay we find the substance of Ricardo's subsequent teaching. It was James Mill (the historian of India, and father of the more famous John Stuart Mill) who persuaded Ricardo to develop his views more at length in a book, the result being *The Principles of Political Economy and Taxation*, published in 1817, and it is with the theory of Rent as expounded in that volume that we have now to deal.

In adopting the teaching of Malthus both as regards diminishing returns and rent, Ricardo made those two doctrines the basis of his theory as to the distribution of wealth among the three classes of the community, labourers, capitalists, and landlords. What in the hands of Anderson had been a mere demonstration that price determines rent, not rent price, became in Ricardo's pages a principle which illuminates the past and enables us to peer into the future. Rents, Ricardo thought, have increased, are increasing, and will continue to increase. It was necessary for him, however, to reconcile this principle with his own doctrine that value is determined by the cost of production; the manner in which he met this difficulty has already been explained in our last chapter. 'The value of corn', he said, 'is regulated by the quantity of labour bestowed on its production on that quality of land,

[1] See vol. 4, p. 10; also in his *Principles* (274/401).

[2] In the short interval between the pamphlets of Malthus and Ricardo appeared another pamphlet from the pen of an anonymous 'Fellow of University College, Oxford'. Ricardo had not seen this when he wrote his own pamphlet. The writer, Edward West, was a young Barrister (afterwards a Judge in India); he introduced himself to Ricardo, who, however, respected his desire for anonymity when referring to his work in the Preface to his *Principles*.

or with that portion of capital, which pays no rent' (38/74)—'That corn which is produced by the greatest quantity of labour is the regulator of the price of corn' (40/77). This notion colours Ricardo's exposition of the theory of rent from start to finish. Let us follow him step by step.

Ricardo starts with the assumption that in every country 'the most fertile and most favourably situated land will be first cultivated' (37/72)—a convenient hypothesis for the purpose of theoretical exposition, but quite incorrect as a matter of history—a fact emphasised by later writers such as H. C. Carey.[1] The first-comers, selecting the best land, are able to produce 100 quarters of corn with a given quantity of capital and labour (35/70). Those who arrive on the scene after all the best land has been appropriated must content themselves with the second-best, which, it may be supposed, for the same outlay of capital and labour, will only produce 90 quarters of corn. Thus rent comes into existence; there is a difference of ten quarters in the return obtainable for the same expenditure of capital and labour. 'Whether the proprietor of the land, or any other person, cultivated No. 1, these ten quarters would equally constitute rent . . . for rent is always the difference between the produce obtained by the employment of two equal quantities of capital and labour' (36/71). The result of this position is that when only second-best land is to be had free, the newcomer will get the same return for his labour and capital whether he cultivates second-best land which yields him 90 quarters, or hires a piece of first-class land, paying the owner 10 quarters and retaining 90 quarters for himself.[2]

[1] It was also pointed out in Ricardo's own time. Only two years before Ricardo published his *Principles*, Arthur Young (no mean authority) had expressed the opinion that owing to the progress of science some of the last land brought under cultivation was now among the most fertile and valuable; see Cannan's *Theories of Production*, page 321. Anderson appears to have been of the same opinion. Cannan also quotes, page 167, a speech made in the House of Commons by Matthias Attwood in 1822 (see vol. 5, p. 163).

[2] By becoming owner of the second-class land the newcomer would benefit by any future appreciation in its value; he would also be owner of any improvements which he made, whereas if he made them as a tenant they would revert to the landlord at the expiration of the lease. Moreover, in comparing purchase with hire we must take into account 'the advantages of the former in the shape of influence, enjoyment, and amusement' which attach to the ownership of land (vol. 9, p. 88); see also his reference to 'the security and respectability which attends the employment of capital on land' (vol.

Proceeding a step further, Ricardo invites us to suppose the best and second-best qualities of land all taken up, with the result that fresh arrivals must content themselves with third-grade land, which only yields 80 quarters for the same quantity of labour and capital. That being so, the second-class land enjoys an advantage or rent of ten quarters, while at the same time the rent of first-class land rises to 20 quarters, for it is always the poorest land cultivated that furnishes the basis for the calculation of rent upon lands of better quality.

All this is a revival of Anderson's teaching, but with this difference, that while in his hands the theory was purely static, it has now assumed a dynamic complexion; it pictures a continuous process by which, as population increases, cultivation is extended to less and less fertile soils, in consequences of which rents have necessarily risen in the past, and must inevitably continue rising until population reaches the limit that the earth can carry. If cultivation at length reaches that quality of land which only yields 10 quarters of corn for the same quantity of labour and capital that on the best land yields 100 quarters, then the owner of the best land will take 90 quarters as rent, the owner of the second-best 80 quarters, and on all qualities, from best to worst, all that the farmer and his men will have for division between them, to cover both profit and wages, will be 10 quarters. Whether cultivation will be extended as far as this, however, depends upon what proportion of the 10 quarters is absorbed in wages. It depends, that is to say, upon whether the labourers are able, on this quality of land, to produce a surplus over and above what is required for their subsistence.

> As soon as wages should be equal . . . to the whole receipts of the farmer, there must be an end of accumulation [1] [says Ricardo] for no capital can then yield any profit whatever. . . . Long indeed before this period the very low rate of profits will have arrested all accumulation, and almost the whole produce of the country, after paying the labourers, will be the property of the owners of land, and the receivers of tithes and taxes (71/120).

All land that is cultivated, then, must yield profit as well as

4, p. 38). These, however, are details which do not affect the principle illustrated.

[1] I.e. accumulation of capital.

wages, for it cannot be cultivated without the aid of capital;[1] but not all cultivated land yields rent.

> I believe that as yet in every country, from the rudest to the most refined [says Ricardo (219/328)], there is land of such a quality that it cannot yield a produce more than sufficiently valuable to replace the stock [2] employed upon it, together with the profits ordinary and usual in that country. In America we all know that this is the case, and yet no one maintains that the principles which regulate rent are different in that country and in Europe.[3]

In support of his contention Ricardo might have referred to Adam Smith's observation that there is many a coal-mine in Scotland so poor that no one would pay a rent for it, yet it is worked by its owner because it affords him the means of earning the current rate of profit on his capital.[4] And Anderson no doubt had in mind many a small patch of oats in the Scottish highlands when he remarked on the inability of the landlord to squeeze any rent out of the cultivator.

But there is more than this to be said in support of Ricardo's view. Even if we suppose every acre of land in the country to be leased to a rent-paying tenant, yet the fact is that most farms, or at any rate most large ones, embrace more than one quality of soil, and some portions of the farmer's holding may be such as

[1] If there were unappropriated land which could be cultivated rent free by anyone who chose to make the attempt, yet it could not be done without capital, i.e. tools and a supply of necessaries to support the labourer until the harvest. If the labourer himself possessed this amount of capital, and could produce each year just sufficient to repeat the operation in the following year, this would not show that capital produces no profit; what it would show is that the producer, who is both labourer and capitalist, is obliged to consume both wages and profit in order to survive. Karl Marx' practice of confining the meaning of *capital* to large accumulations in the hands of 'exploiters' appears more likely to obscure than to clarify reasoning.

[2] Stock, i.e. capital.

[3] In view of the last sentence, it is rather curious to find Ricardo writing to Trower: 'In America I should think that there was no land for which a rent was not paid, but that is to be attributed to their particular institutions. The government is proprietor of all uncultivated lands in the interior of the country, which it is ready to sell, and daily sells, at the moderate price of 2 dollars per acre. Rent, then, must amount in every part of America to the interest which 2 dollars would make, per acre, at the least; but this fact makes no difference in the principle, as you seem to be fully aware' (vol. 7, p. 297).

[4] *Wealth of Nations*, Bk. 1, chap. 11, 13th paragraph in Part 2.

would not be worth a rent. In that case, the rent paid by the farmer is in fact paid for the good land only; in reality he pays nothing for the poor parts; they are thrown in because they cannot be thrown out. Nevertheless, these lands being in his possession, the farmer may find that by cultivating them he can make the ordinary rate of profit upon the capital required for working them. Neither these particular patches of land, nor the capital employed in working them, yields any rent; their product is sold at a price which covers no more than the current rate of wages and the current rate of profit.

But even this does not exhaust Ricardo's defence. So far, we have referred only to the application of capital to land too poor to yield a rent; there is also the application of capital to a more intensive cultivation of land that is already yielding a rent. While we regard Malthus as the author of the doctrine of diminishing returns so far as it relates to the extension of cultivation to poorer land, the oldest, and in some respects the most important, form of the doctrine relates to the dwindling returns yielded by successive doses of capital on the same land. This doctrine was formulated by the great Frenchman, Turgot, in 1768, eight years before *The Wealth of Nations* was published, and when Malthus was only two years old. I quote the English translation given by Cannan:[1]

> Seed thrown on a soil naturally fertile, but totally unprepared, would be an advance almost entirely lost. If tilled once the produce will be greater; tilling it a second, a third time, might not merely double and treble, but quadruple or decuple the produce, which will thus augment in a much larger proportion than the advances increase, and that up to a certain point, at which the produce will be as great as possible compared with the advances. Past this point, if the advances be still increased, the produce will still increase, but less, and always less and less, until the fecundity of the earth being exhausted, and art unable to add anything further, an addition to the advances will add nothing whatever to the produce.

Thus there are two forms in which the agriculturist encounters the law of diminishing returns. If he seeks to increase his output by intensive cultivation, he finds that after a certain point each fresh dose of labour and capital yields a smaller addition to the product; if he turns to new land, it will generally be land of

[1] *Theories of Production*, 1893, page 148.

inferior quality which will require more expense to obtain the same quantity of product. Both forms of the law are recognised by Ricardo.[1] On page 36(71) he said: 'It often, and indeed commonly, happens that before . . . the inferior lands are cultivated, capital can be employed more productively on those lands which are already in cultivation. . . . Rent is always the difference between the produce obtained by the employment of two equal quantities of capital and labour.' On a later page he wrote: 'Rent, it should be remembered, is the difference between the produce obtained by equal portions of labour and capital employed on land of the same or different qualities' (98/157). Hence, when Ricardo's critics tell him that all land pays rent, he replies that this is no proof that all corn yields a rent, for when cultivation is intensified on good land there comes a point when the additional corn produced returns to the capitalist no more than the capital advanced plus the ordinary rate of profit. In the last pamphlet that he published Ricardo wrote: 'I am myself fully persuaded that a large quantity of corn is raised in every country, for the privilege of raising which no rent whatever is paid.'[2]

If, then, we criticise Ricardo's statement that 'the price of corn is regulated by the quantity of labour necessary to produce it with that portion of capital which pays no rent' (64/110), it is not because we object to the assumption that some corn is raised on land, or with capital, that pays no rent, but because we do not believe that it is the marginal producer's cost that regulates the price in the market, but think, on the contrary, that it is the price in the market that determines the maximum cost that any producer can profitably incur. In support of this view we may quote Ricardo's own remarks on page 220(328):

> If a farmer agrees for land on a lease of seven or fourteen years he may propose to employ on it a capital of £10,000, knowing that at the existing price of grain and raw produce he can replace that part of his stock[3] which he is obliged to expend, pay his rent, and obtain the general rate of profit. He will not employ £11,000 unless

---

[1] And of course by Malthus as early as 1798; see the passage quoted from his *Essay* earlier in this chapter (page 62).

[2] Vol. 4, p. 240. See Ricardo's complaint to Mill that his critics, Malthus and Say, ignored this point (vol. 7, p. 372). See also the footnote he inserted in the third edition of his *Principles* (282/413).

[3] Stock, i.e. capital.

> the last £1000 can be employed so productively as to afford him the usual profits of stock. In his calculation whether he shall employ it or not, he considers only whether the price of raw produce is sufficient to replace his expenses and profits, for he knows that he shall have no additional rent to pay.

Now here it is made perfectly clear that the additional £1000 is employed because the price of corn in the market is such as to leave the producer the ordinary rate of profit after paying all his expenses; there is no suggestion that it is the expenses that regulate the price. It is perfectly clear that the rent paid by the tenant does not depend in any way upon whether he employs £10,000 or £11,000. If he pays a rent of £300, it is because his capital earns £300 in excess of 'the general rate of profit', and because, it is to be assumed, any other farmer could earn the same excess with the same piece of land. The very poorest land under cultivation will yield a rent to its owner if it enables the cultivator to earn more than 'the general rate of profits'. Yet according to Ricardo, no land yields rent until poorer land is cultivated. On page 35(70) he says:

> When, in the progress of society, land of the second degree of fertility is taken into cultivation, rent immediately commences on that of the first quality, and the amount of that rent will depend on the difference in the quality of these two portions of land.

On page 37(72) he writes:

> Rent invariably proceeds from the employment of an additional quantity of labour with a proportionally less return. . . . When land of an inferior quality is taken into cultivation, the exchangeable value of raw produce will rise, because more labour is required to produce it.

On page 38(74) we have this:

> It is true that, on the best land, the same produce would still be obtained with the same labour as before, but its value would be enhanced in consequence of the diminished returns obtained by those who employed fresh labour and stock on the less fertile land.[1]

Ricardo's books, pamphlets, notes, and letters bristle with similar statements. The farmer pays rent to his landlord, he tells

[1] This last remark appears nearly, if not quite, absurd, for the cultivation of additional land must increase the supply and thereby tend to lower, not enhance, the price of the commodity.

Malthus, 'only because lands of a poorer quality are taken into cultivation' (vol. 7, p. 283). In an earlier letter to the same correspondent he said: 'In the case of the Scotch farmers who made such large profits on their capital during the latter part of their leases, they appear to me to have been enjoying rent, arising . . . from poorer land being taken into cultivation' (vol. 6, p. 177). To another friend, Trower, he wrote that if a piece of land is so poor that it can produce no more than is necessary for the subsistence of the labourers, 'there can neither be surplus produce to afford profit or rent. If it should be even enough to afford a trifling profit, there could be no rent, because no worse land could be taken into cultivation' (vol. 7, p. 234).

In his *Principles* (281/412) he wrote: 'Nothing can raise rent but a demand for new land of an inferior quality . . .'; to which he added the following footnote:

> It is not necessary to state on every occasion, but it must be always understood, that the same results will follow, as far as regards the price of raw produce, and the rise of rents, whether an additional capital of a given amount be employed on new land for which no rent is paid, or on land already in cultivation, if the produce obtained from both be precisely the same in quantity.

Such continued to be Ricardo's teaching till the end; in the *Notes on Malthus*, written shortly before he published his last edition, he wrote: 'That rents would rise when we ceased importing corn is precisely what would be expected—poorer soils would be taken into cultivation, which never fails to raise rent' (vol. 2, pp. 149, 150): 'I have uniformly contended that one of the main causes of rent is the employment of an additional capital on the old land without as large a return as from the capital before employed' (vol. 2, p. 170). Such reasoning would seem to imply that the farmer who works his land with a capital of £10,000 might have to pay no rent; but if he employs £11,000, then he will immediately have to pay rent—he will be called upon to pay rent, not because he earns a high profit on £10,000, but because he earns a lower profit upon £1000![1]

Perhaps I shall be told that this is merely Ricardo's way of

[1] Compare the eighth paragraph in Ricardo's second chapter. Ricardo's error in making resort to inferior land the cause instead of the consequence of rise in price was pointed out in 1831 by Richard Jones (see Dr. W. A. Scott's *Development of Economics*, page 136).

putting things; that either from a Puckish delight in startling people or from a sober design to make his readers think, he preferred paradox to straightforward statement. When, for example, he said that a rise of wages will cause some prices to fall, what he meant was (as we saw in an earlier chapter) that if wages rise, profits fall, and the net result may be a reduction of price. The truth of the proposition becomes evident when we know the reasoning on which it is based. This explanation of Ricardo's obscurities was adopted by De Quincey (of *Opium Eater* fame), who was one of Ricardo's earliest and most ardent admirers. Writing in 1824, the year after Ricardo's death, he said there are two possible explanations of obscurity in a writer; one is 'the writer's own perplexity of thought', while the other (Ricardo's) is

> elliptical obscurity, arising, I mean, out of the frequent ellipsis or suppression of some of the links in a long chain of thought. These are often involuntarily suppressed by profound thinkers, from the disgust which they naturally feel at overlaying a subject with superfluous explanations. So far from seeing too dimly, as in the case of perplexed obscurity, their defect is the very reverse; they see too clearly, and fancy that others see as clearly as themselves.[1]

The use of this kind of ellipsis is not confined to profound thinkers. It would be impossible to develop an argument, point

[1] *Dialogues of the Three Templars on Political Economy*, page 182 of volume 4 in the Collected Edition of De Quincey's Works, 1862. De Quincey outdoes McCulloch in his partisanship, which perhaps explains, but can hardly excuse, the remark at once ridiculous and vile—'Mr. Malthus, every part of whose writings since the year 1816, I am assured, have had one origin—jealousy of Mr. Ricardo.' As for De Quincey's praise of Ricardo's 'inexorable consistency in the use of words', this certainly indicates '*trop de zèle*'. A single instance will suffice—Ricardo's use of the word Rent. As pointed out by Professor Cannan in his *Theories of Production*, page 195, Ricardo defines rent at the beginning of his second chapter as 'that portion of the produce of the earth which is paid to the landlord for the use of the original and indestructible powers of the soil', whilst in the very next chapter he says—'Mines, as well as land, generally pay a rent to their owner' (46/85), thus ignoring the fact that what the lessee of a mine or quarry pays for is not the right to use the indestructible powers of the soil, but the right to carry off almost all the value of the property, so that a mining lease is more like a purchase on the instalment plan with a stipulation for the return of empty bottles. Ricardo did not overlook this, but it is characteristic of his unmethodical way of writing that his remarks on this point are not to be found in his chapter on mining rents but in his chapter on agricultural rents (34/68).

by point, if at each stage it were necessary to recapitulate, in the manner of the House-that-Jack-built, all the arguments by which the previous stage had been reached. Ricardo therefore only follows the ordinary course when, having arrived at one conclusion, he uses it as a stepping-stone to the next. The trouble in his case is not that he assumes without mention what has been previously proved, but that he sometimes assumes what has been neither proved nor mentioned, or makes an erroneous application of what has been proved through forgetting the conditions under which it was true.

When Ricardo set out, in his second chapter, to tackle the problem of rent, what he carried forward in his mind from the first chapter was the conclusion that it is not demand, but cost of production that regulates price. What he failed to keep in mind was that this conclusion was based on the assumption that cost of production is uniform for all producers and all quantities of product, with the result that increase of demand cannot cause a permanent rise of price, because the supply can be increased by competitors to the same extent that demand increases, and this without any rise in the cost of production per unit.

But the moment you assume that the desired addition to supply cannot be provided at the same cost of production, the conditions upon which this conclusion was based disappear. If one man can produce at five shillings while no other can produce at less than ten shillings, the first producer has no competitor so long as the price remains below ten shillings. And when the price, owing to growth of demand (not growth of cost), rises to ten shillings, we are not justified in assuming that it will stay there unless we also assume that at this price the supply can be increased by competing producers in the same proportion that demand increases.

Ricardo forgets that it is competition of producers that keeps the price down; what he carries is his mind in his own interpretation of the situation, namely, that it is the cost of production that determines price, and with this idea in mind he proceeds to attribute to an increase or decrease of marginal cost the same consequences as he had shown would follow an increase or decrease of cost where the cost is the same for all producers. On page 98(156) he writes:

> Having in a former part of this work established, I hope satisfactorily, the principle that the price of corn is regulated by the cost

> of its production on that land exclusively, or rather with that capital exclusively, which pays no rent, it will follow that whatever may increase the cost of production will increase the price; whatever may reduce it will lower the price.

Here he gives us cause and effect; rise of cost (marginal cost in this case) is the cause, rise of price the consequence. Ricardo does not seem to perceive that by interpreting cost of production to mean the cost of the least-favoured producer only, instead of a cost common to all producers, he has lost the basis on which he rested his conclusion that cost regulates price.

Happily, we have no occasion to complain that owing to the employment of ellipsis Ricardo has left us in the dark as to the 'long chain of reasoning' by which he reaches this conclusion. It is fully set forth on page 71(119), as follows:

> It should be recollected that prices always vary in the market, and in the first instance, through the comparative state of demand and supply. Although cloth could be furnished at 40*s*. per yard, and give the usual profits of stock, it may rise to 60 or 80*s*. from a general change of fashion, or from any other cause which should suddenly and unexpectedly increase the demand or diminish the supply of it. The makers of cloth will for a time have unusual profits, but capital will naturally flow to that manufacture, till the supply and demand are again at their fair level, when the price of cloth will again sink to 40*s*., its natural or necessary price. In the same manner, with every increased demand for corn, it may rise so high as to afford more than the general profits to the farmer. If there be plenty of fertile land, the price of corn will again fall to its former standard, after the requisite quantity of capital has been employed in producing it, and profits will be as before; but if there be not plenty of fertile land—if, to produce this additional quantity more than the usual quantity of capital and labour be required—corn will not fall to its former level. Its natural price will be raised . . .[1]

Thus although the higher cost of production applies only to the additional quantity required, Ricardo represents corn as being on the same footing as cloth, with regard to which his assumption is that the cost of production is the same for all producers—if it rises or falls for one, it rises or falls for all. He makes it clear why

[1] I cut my quotation short at this point because Ricardo's next words bring in another aspect of his teaching, which can be better discussed when we deal with Profits.

the additional quantity of corn cannot be supplied at the old price, but he does not explain why the old producers, whose cost of production has not risen, now receive a higher price than before. If Ricardo were accused of an ellipsis, he might reply that he had omitted nothing except what is known to every reader, that, there can be only one price for the same commodity. True, there will be only one price; but these equal values are produced at unequal costs, and the inference seems plain that a sufficient explanation of price is not to be found in the cost of production.

Ricardo's mistake is in ignoring the influence of demand. It is demand, he admits, that causes price to rise 'in the first instance', but he appears to think that as soon as supply has overtaken demand, demand can be eliminated as an influence on price. The consumers are satisfied, and therefore no longer compete. True, they cease pushing the price up, but they remain the prop that keeps it up. It was owing to the pressure of demand that price rose, and it is owing to the incompressibility of demand that price remains at a level that permits the marginal producer to make the ordinary rate of profit and yields to other producers more than the ordinary rate.

As a matter of fact, while Ricardo constantly belittles the influence of demand, and seeks to establish cost of production as the sole determinant of price, the influence of demand is frequently found lurking in his pronouncements, apparently unrecognised by himself. The excerpt quoted just now from page 35(70) of his *Principles* began: 'When, in the progress of society, land of the second degree', etc., what is implied by 'the progress of society' but growth, including growth in the effective demand for corn, which leads to a rise of price, and makes it worth while to cultivate inferior land? A later reference to the progress of society specifically mentions growth of population—'the increase of population, and the necessity of cultivating, at an increased charge, land of an inferior quality, which always causes a rise in the value of corn' (vol. 4, p. 235). What is meant by the *necessity* of cultivating poorer land? He does not mean that the law requires the farmers to supply everybody with sufficient food, regardless of the cost of production. We shall see what he has to say on this point in following chapters. Meanwhile I have quoted his statement that the farmer is under no necessity to increase the supply of corn, and will not invest an additional £1000 unless he has good reason to expect that he can sell his product at a price that will yield the ordinary rate of profit (220/328). On page 98(156), after stating that whatever may increase the cost of production will increase the price, Ricardo continues: 'The necessity of cultivating poorer land, or of obtaining a less return with a given additional capital on land already in cultivation, will inevitably raise the exchangeable value of raw produce.' What does the necessity of cultivating poorer land mean? As above remarked, if the law made it obligatory on every farmer to contribute his quota to the full amount required to feed the entire population, he would indeed be under the necessity of cultivating inferior land if he could not otherwise produce the amount required. But the farmer is under no such necessity, and in fact does not engage in the cultivation of inferior land until the pressure of demand has raised the market price to a figure which will make such cultivation profitable. The omission of any reference to the part played by demand is to be attributed perhaps to Ricardo's habit of 'ellipsis' which De Quincey thought so excusable; but to attribute rise of price to the cultivation of inferior land instead of attributing the cultivation of inferior land to the rise of price (caused by increase of demand), seems to be reversing cause and effect.

Perhaps it will be said that while it is wrong to represent the rise of price as caused by the rise of cost, yet Ricardo is justified in regarding the marginal cost of production as what *regulates* the price. Let us suppose that the growth of demand has raised the price of wheat from 100*s.* per quarter to 105*s.* When the supply has been increased by the marginal producer the price perhaps falls to 104*s.*; thus it is the marginal producer who finally regulates the price. But Ricardo's conclusion on page 71(120) goes further than this; he takes for granted that 'the price obtained by the producer of additional corn, like the price obtained by the producer of additional cloth, will be identical with his cost of production, whereas the fact might be that his cost of production was 103*s.*, whilst the pressure of demand enabled him to sell all he could produce at 104*s.*, and this without fear of being undersold if no fresh competitor could grow corn at a less cost than 105*s.* a quarter.

What pins the price of cloth down to the cost of production is not the producer's own cost, but the fact that additional supplies can be produced at the same cost by competitors who will undercut him if he charges more. Either Ricardo overlooks this when he assumes that the marginal producer of corn always sells at a price which only just yields the current rate of profit, or else his conclusion is subject to the tacit assumption that the quality of land cultivated by the marginal producer exists in such 'plenty' (and free of rent) that if the marginal producer fixes a price in excess of his cost of production he will soon be faced with competition from fresh producers who can produce at the same cost as himself.

There is thus an essential incompatibility between the conception of diminishing returns, or increasing cost for successive additions to supply, and the doctrine that price necessarily corresponds with marginal cost. On the other hand, as pointed out in our last chapter, if successive increases of cost are so gradual, so slight, as to be almost imperceptible, rise of marginal cost may follow rise of price almost as closely as cart follows horse. In other words, if the price cannot rise above the marginal producer's cost by more than a fraction without provoking competition from another producer whose cost of production is scarcely higher, then it will be true that price will never for long exceed marginal cost by more than a fraction. The smaller the difference is assumed to be between the fertility of the marginal land and that of the next best land—in other words, the further we get from assuming increase of cost and the closer we approach to assuming uniformity of cost—the nearer we get to the proposition that price is regulated by the cost of production. It is interesting, therefore, to enquire whether Ricardo did, in fact, regard agriculture as an industry in which the costs of production rise, not by noticeable steps, but by a slope so gentle that the marginal producer's cost never will differ by more than a fraction from the sale price.[1]

This, to be sure, is not the state of things depicted by Ricardo on page 35(70). There he represents the facilities for production as diminishing at an alarming pace. For a given amount of labour and capital the land first cultivated yields 100 quarters of corn, the next best only 90 quarters, and the third best only 80. But these figures, of course, are adopted merely for the purpose of illustration; the differences of yield are exaggerated to give the reader an

[1] The picture here presented of course takes no account of the fact that the new land may require a considerable expenditure of time, labour and capital before it is brought to a state of efficient production.

easy grasp of the principle of diminishing returns. The actual assumption which Ricardo's line of argument implies, according to his Editor, Sir E. C. K. Gonner,[1] is that cultivable land consists of units indefinitely small, each successive unit brought under cultivation being a shade less fertile than the preceding one.[2] I am glad to have such high authority for this view, else I should hardly have dared to put the position so strongly. I imagine that the ghost of Ricardo, if it visits the Earth to keep abreast of modern criticism,[3] must have been considerably startled on reading Gonner's statement; for did not Ricardo more than once admit the supposition that there might be 'abundance' (55/98) or 'plenty' (71/120) of fertile land, or land 'of the same fertility' (103/163); and did he not declare in a note on page 26(41) that in a new country 'it may be as easy to provide for the seventh, eighth, and ninth million of men as for the second, third, and fourth'? Ricardo, then, did not imagine that there are no two units of land which have the same degree of fertility. New tracts of fertile land are sometimes discovered, he tells us.[4] Nevertheless, in the long run, and subject to these interruptions, the curve is a descending one. 'With every increase of capital and population', says Ricardo (270/395), 'food will generally rise, on account of its being more difficult to produce.' Generally, then, though not always, the additional supply of food is obtained at a higher cost, and according to Ricardo, the price always corresponds with, or fluctuates around, the marginal producer's cost of production. This conclusion, as already pointed out, can only be true if the marginal producer is threatened with competition the moment his price exceeds his cost of production by a fraction, and such

[1] See appendix B to Gonner's edition of Ricardo's *Principles*.

[2] It is not likely that Ricardo foresaw the modern application to Economics of the mathematical conception of infinitesimal increases or decreases. He seems, in his method of expounding the theory of rent, to have been largely influenced by West, and West very definitely visualised diminishing fertility as continuous and gradual from first to last. Not only does he represent the second £100 of capital as returning less than the first £100, and the third less than the second, but also the second £10 as returning less than the first £10, and the third £10 less than the second. See Cannan's *Theories of Production*, pages 317/319.

[3] Ricardo's somewhat patronising friend, Jeremy Bentham, would have given years of his life to be able to revisit the Earth at intervals after death to watch the progress the world was making as a result of his teaching.

[4] Page 8(15). See also vol. 4, p. 235.

competition can only be possible if there is always land available for cultivation by a competitor at the same cost, or at a cost which is only a shade higher than on the worst land already cultivated at a profit.

In closing this chapter, I should point out that in expounding the theory of rent Ricardo makes no attempt to deal with urban rents. It would be quite impossible to explain the value of land in great cities and their suburbs while leaving out the influence of demand. Even in the case of agricultural rents Ricardo himself said: 'Land, like everything else, rises or falls in proportion to the demand for it' (vol. 6, pp. 293–4), but many of his statements on the subject of rent are quite inapplicable to land in commercial and residential areas; for instance, the statement in his *Principles* (281/412): 'Nothing can raise rent but a demand for new land of an inferior quality, or some cause which shall occasion an alteration in the relative fertility of the land already under cultivation.' Perhaps Ricardo regarded himself as relieved of the necessity of explaining why a house in the West End of London commands a higher rent than a similar house in Whitechapel by the fact that his enquiry was concerned with the proportions in which the annual product of land, labour and capital is divided in the first instance among those directly concerned in its production, and was *not* concerned with the subsequent modifications of this distribution which result from the manner in which the receivers of rent and profits spend their respective incomes.

7

Ricardo and the Wages Fund

According to Ricardo, the marginal producer pays no rent, and the whole product is divided between himself and his labourers. If the labourers get a large share, the capitalist must be content with a small share. 'The proportion which might be paid for wages', says Ricardo, 'is of the utmost importance in the question of profits; for it must at once be seen that profits would be high or low exactly in proportion as wages were low or high' (16/27).

If, then, we can ascertain what determines the rate of wages, we at the same time learn what determines the rate of profit.

Ricardo's chapter on Wages (chapter 5) commences with the following remarks:

> Labour, like all other things which are purchased and sold, and which may be increased or diminished in quantity, has its natural and its market price. The natural price of labour is that price which is necessary to enable the labourers, one with another, to subsist and to perpetuate their race, without either increase or diminution. . . . The market price of labour is the price which is really paid for it, from the natural operation of the proportion of the supply to the demand. . . . However much the market price of labour may deviate from its natural price, it has, like commodities, a tendency to conform to it (52–3/93–4).

We will leave to the next chapter the consideration of what Ricardo understands by the natural price of labour, confining ourselves at present to his remarks on the market price. This price, he says, like the price of corn or iron, is decided by the proportion of supply to demand. In this connection it is necessary to bear in mind that Ricardo recognises only one price for labour. He not only likens it to a commodity, but he treats it as a commodity of which there is only one quality and for which there is only one price in the market. The price of corn is so much a quarter, the price of iron so much a ton, and the price of labour so much per man. The market price is high when the supply is small compared with the demand, and low when, compared with the demand, the supply is large.[1]

What constitutes the demand for labour? It is the offer of wages for work; and here again there is something to be noted, that the only work that Ricardo appears to have in mind in framing his theory of wages is the work of producing commodities. The nation lives on what it produces; that part of the annual product which is allotted to the labourers employed in its production is called wages; Ricardo's statement in his Preface that the produce annually obtained from the earth 'by the united application of labour, machinery, and capital, is divided among three classes of the community, namely, the proprietor of the land, the owner of the stock or capital necessary for its cultivation, and the labourers by whose industry it is cultivated', can only mean that, if we ignore the share enjoyed by the landlords, the entire product is divided between the capitalists who employ the labourers in producing it, and the labourers who are thus employed by the capitalists. There are no other employers and no other labourers entitled to share in the product. It is true that in his 26th chapter Ricardo refers to the employment of soldiers, etc., but he makes no reference to them in his chapter on wages, and appears to frame his theory of wages on the assumption that the existence of these 'unproductive' labourers can be ignored. The chapter on wages is not the only one in which it is assumed that the capitalists are the only employers of labour. Chapter 16 deals with taxes on wages, and begins as follows:

> Taxes on wages will raise wages,[2] and therefore will diminish the rate of the profits of stock. . . . Towards a tax on wages . . . neither the stockholder, the landlord, nor any other class but the employers of labour will contribute. A tax on wages is wholly a tax on profits.

[1] For Ricardo's decision to treat all labour as of one quality, see section 2 of his first chapter.

[2] We shall see in our next chapter that Ricardo assumed all labourers to be so poor that they cannot pay taxes, hence if such a tax is levied on wages the employer must either pay it himself or give the labourer a higher money wage to enable him to pay it; in either case it reduces profit.

The labourer being too poor to pay a tax, it must come out of the employer's profit. The only persons who make profits are the capitalists; landlords may enjoy rents, and stockholders may receive interest, but apparently neither of them is thought of as employing labour, and neither of them therefore contributes anything towards a tax on wages.

If, then, we repeat our question, what constitutes the demand for labour?—the answer is that it is the offer made by the capitalists to pay wages in exchange for work; or to put it in another form, it is the offer of goods at present ready for consumption in exchange for the production of other goods for consumption hereafter. As remarked in our first chapter, none of us, whether labourers, capitalists, or landlords, can exist on the corn that is still in the ground or ripening on the stalk. Our present wants can only be met out of commodities already in existence. Although the labourer is paid only for work done, what he receives is not part of what he is at present producing. Ricardo speaks of the farmer dividing the corn between himself and the labourers (21/35), but as a matter of fact, when the corn is gathered in after a whole year's toil, the labourer is no longer entitled to a share of it. He has been paid for his labour week by week as the work proceeded; his wages were paid to him out of capital held by the farmer for this very purpose; they were paid out of corn brought forward from the previous harvest; and part of the present harvest will again be carried forward by the capitalist as a fund for the sustenance of the labourers while preparing the next harvest.

As remarked above, the labourer is not alone in being dependent upon existing stocks for the satisfaction of present wants. Where his position differs from that of the capitalist is in the fact that he possesses no stock, or not more than sufficient to last for a few days, whereas the capitalists hold large stocks of all kinds, including vast quantities of food and necessaries, far exceeding their own needs or powers of consumption; stocks which in fact they have produced, or caused to be produced, for the express purpose of supporting labourers while engaged in fresh production. These stocks of 'working-class goods' constitute the real 'fund for the maintenance of labour'; they constitute what at a later date came to be called 'the wages fund'.[1] Although wages are commonly

[1] We shall find it convenient to use the expression 'wages fund', but the reader will, I hope, bear in mind that it is not used by Ricardo.

paid in money, the distribution of money only serves as a convenient method of distributing the real commodity wages fund.

The fact that we can only consume at present what has already been produced lies at the root of the 'wages fund' theory. It may be that next year, as a result of our present efforts, stocks will be larger, and that consumption will then be possible on a more generous scale; but this prospect will not enable us to consume at present more than at present exists. The quantity of commodities that each man can receive for his present work depends on the size of the present stock and the number of men amongst whom it is to be divided. But in calculating the amount that can be distributed week by week we must take into account the question how long the stock must be made to last—how long it will be before a new supply will be available.

If we have a spring of water that yields 1000 gallons a day, we can distribute for consumption 1000 gallons a day. But if we are dealing with a crop that can only be harvested once a year, then the quantity in hand after the harvest, be it large or small, must be made to last until the next harvest. It is here we get at the heart of the wages-fund theory.

In Ricardo's day the labourer lived mainly on corn, and Ricardo reckoned that half his wage was spent on this commodity (58/103). Forty years earlier Adam Smith had said: 'The money price of labour . . . seems to be everywhere accommodated . . . to the ordinary or average price' of corn.[1] In saying 'everywhere', Smith does not mean all over the globe; although a Scot, he does not mean Scotland, where, he tells us, 'the common people' are fed on oatmeal; nor Ireland, where the food of the poor is potatoes;[2] still less is he referring to the labourers in Asiatic countries, whose food is rice, of which, under favourable conditions of soil and

[1] *Wealth of Nations*, Bk. 1, chap. 5, 16th paragraph, but see chap. 8, 30th paragraph, and Bk. 4, chap. 5, 12th paragraph.

[2] Ibid., chap. 11 (last paragraph but one in Part 1). Smith says: 'The common people in Scotland, who are fed on oatmeal, are in general neither so strong nor so handsome as the same rank of people in England, who are fed with wheaten bread. . . . But it seems to be otherwise with potatoes. The chairmen, porters, and coal-heavers in London, and those unfortunate women who live by prostitution, the strongest men and the most beautiful women perhaps in the British dominions, are said to be, the greater part of them, from the lowest rank of people in Ireland, who are generally fed with this root.'

climate, three or four crops can be obtained in the year. He is referring to English labourers, 'who are fed with wheaten bread'. The conditions that he depicts are represented by Ricardo and Malthus as still prevailing when they wrote. Now wheat, oats, and potatoes are all annual crops, and each year's product must be made to last for twelve months. In this connection it must be borne in mind that the Southern Hemisphere had not then become a granary for the Northern Hemisphere, thus halving the interval between crops. As a matter of fact, the wages-fund theory is based on the conception of a self-contained country, and does not take importation into account.[1]

Thus the corn held by the capitalists in their barns and warehouses constituted practically the only supply of food available for the labourers until the next harvest. Demands for higher wages, backed by strikes or combinations, could not increase the stock of food available for consumption during the current year; riots, accompanied by rick-burning, the burning of barns and the destruction of machinery, would diminish, but could not augment, the existing fund. An increase of money wages would only raise the price of food; it would not increase the supply of food available for present distribution. Such was the view widely held in Ricardo's day (and for long afterwards, largely as a result of Ricardo's adoption of it). Ricardo did not originate this theory; he took it over from Malthus.[2] In his *Essay on Population* Malthus said:

> It may at first appear strange, but I believe it is true, that I cannot by means of money raise a poor man and enable him to live much better than he did before. . . . If I only give him money, supposing the produce of the country to remain the same, I give him a title to a larger share of that produce than formerly, which share he cannot receive without diminishing the shares of others.[3]

---

[1] One trouble in reading Ricardo is that sometimes his arguments are based on the unexpressed assumption that the community is an isolated one, while at other times he takes into account imports and exports.

[2] See Malthus' *Essay on Population*, pages 79 and 205–6 in the reprint of the first edition. Toynbee said: 'Malthus was the founder of that doctrine of wages which, under the name of the wages-fund theory, was accepted for fifty years in England' (*The Industrial Revolution*, 1st paragraph in 11th section).

[3] These remarks, which appear on page 79 of the first edition, will be found in the last edition in the 6th paragraph of chap. 5, Bk. 3. Malthus does not express himself well, since he begins by saying that he cannot help a poor

So far, then, as wages consist of food, the quantity that the labouring classes can receive during the current year is fixed and unalterable. But in a cold climate there are other things besides food that are indispensable to existence, such as clothes, blankets, shelter. Was it assumed that these also are an annual crop? Professor Cannan quotes[1] the following from Ricardo's friend and disciple, James Mill:[2]

> The year is assumed in Political Economy as the period which includes a revolving circle of production and consumption. No period does so exactly. Some articles are produced and consumed in a period much less than a year. In others the circle is greater than a year. It is necessary for the ends of discourse that some period should be assumed as including this circle. The period of a year is the most convenient. It corresponds with one great class of productions, those derived from the cultivation of the ground. And it is easy when we have obtained forms of expression which correspond accurately to this assumption, to modify them in practice to the case of those commodities the circle of whose production and consumption is either greater or less than the standard to which our general propositions are conformed.

Thus the assumption that goods of every description constitute an annual crop was recognised as a fiction, and was adopted only to simplify reasoning; but Mill made a curious slip in saying that in the case of corn it is literally true that the period of one year covers both production and consumption. The essence of the theory is that since production occupies a whole year, consumption cannot take place until the following year.[3] For 'convenience'

man, and then shows that he can help a poor man, though only at the expense of other poor men. Cannan remarks that this view of wages was adopted and endorsed by a Committee of the House of Commons in 1817 (see *Theories of Production*, pages 44/45).

[1] *Theories of Production*, page 97.

[2] James Mill described himself and McCulloch as Ricardo's 'only two genuine disciples' (see his letter to McCulloch of 19th Sept., 1823 (vol. 9, p. 391)).

[3] Mill expressed his meaning better in his second edition when he said that 'the whole of what is annually produced is annually consumed, or what is produced in one year is consumed in the next' (Cannan's *Theories of Production*, page 96). See also Sismondi's *Nouveaux Principes* (page 113 in the 1951 reprint): 'We do nothing, after all, but exchange the total of the year's production against the total of the previous year's production'. Malthus quoted and commented on this remark in his *Principles* (page 420 in first edition, page 366 in second).

it was assumed that all products were on the same footing—milk and meat and fish as well as corn, shoes and clothes and candles and chairs as well as food stuffs; which explains what Cannan called Ricardo's 'absurd assumption . . . that no goods are sold till the end of the year',[1] and also explains Ricardo's assumption that 'each year the capitalist begins his operations by having food and necessaries in his possession' sufficient to support his labourers for one year (265/388). What the labourers consume this year is what was produced last year, and what they are producing this year will not be available for consumption until next year.

The demand for labour, then, or the offer of present food and necessaries in exchange for future products, comes from the capitalists; and the rate of wages during the current year depends upon the size of the wages fund thus brought forward by the capitalists from the previous year and the number of labourers amongst whom it is to be divided. In this connection let me quote again from Mill:

> Universally we may affirm, other things remaining the same, that if the ratio which capital and population bear to one another remains the same, wages will remain the same; if the ratio which capital bears to population increases, wages will rise; if the ratio which population bears to capital increases, wages will fall.[2]

It will be observed that the ratio upon which the rate of wages depends is not stated to be the ratio between the total amount paid by the capitalists to their employees and the number of men they employ (which would be a mere truism); it is represented as a ratio between capital and the entire population. Thus all capital is regarded as wages fund, and it is to this fund, and to this fund only, that the 'population' [3] must look for the means of subsistence.

But it is with Ricardo that we are concerned, not his disciple, so let us turn to what Ricardo himself says. On page 41(78) he writes: 'Population regulates itself by the funds which are to employ it, and therefore always increases or diminishes with the increase or diminution of capital.' On page 54(95–6) he tells us

[1] *Theories of Production*, page 94.

[2] Quoted by Cannan in his *Theories of Production*, page 260.

[3] Landlords and capitalists are apparently not included under the heading of 'population', perhaps because their number is regarded as negligible.

that 'in proportion to the increase of capital will be the increase in the demand for labour . . . with every improvement of society, with every increase in its capital, the market wages of labour will rise'.[1] On page 103(163) he observes: 'An accumulation of capital naturally produces an increased competition among the employers of labour, and a consequent rise in its price.' On page 194(292) he tells us that 'when the funds for the maintenance of labour increase much more rapidly than population—wages will then be high and profits low'; the reference to profits plainly shows that by 'the funds for the maintenance of labour' he means capital. Thus Ricardo appears to subscribe to the doctrine that the whole nation (excepting always those fortunate people who live on income from property) are dependent for food and necessaries upon the wages fund employed by the capitalists in their business.

Not only does Ricardo treat capital as the only source of wages, but he appears in these extracts to regard capital as consisting exclusively of a fund for the maintenance of labour; otherwise, how could he say that every increase of capital will raise wages, and that the increase in the demand for labour is in proportion to the increase of capital? Yet Ricardo was well aware that there is much capital in the form of machinery and plant, even if he sometimes appears to forget it. On page 53(95) he tells us that 'Capital is that part of the wealth of a country which is employed in production, and consists of food, clothing, tools, raw materials, machinery, etc., necessary to give effect to labour.' On page 95(151–2) he refers to shipping, docks, and canals as capital. Both these passages appeared in his first edition, and in that edition, as we saw in an earlier chapter, he went so far as to imagine a machine that would produce goods without any help from labour. Nevertheless, there was a tendency on his part, which he never completely overcame, to think of capital as consisting only of a fund for the support of labourers [2]—a tendency which was coupled with another tendency to think of agriculture as typical of

[1] In December, 1819, Ricardo is reported as saying in the House of Commons that 'the proportion of the capital to population regulated the amount of wages, and, to augment them, it was important to increase the capital of the country' (vol. 5, p. 32).

[2] Adam Smith had said: 'Almost the whole capital of every country is annually distributed among the inferior ranks of people as the wages of productive labour' (Bk. 5, chap. 2). But Ricardo had no love for such qualifications as *almost*.

all forms of industry. Both these tendencies are conspicuous in the Preface to his first edition (which he never modified), and we may note here (what was pointed out by Cannan) that he there refers to the produce of the Earth as being obtained 'by the united application of labour, machinery, and capital'—as though capital were one thing and machinery another—as though, in short, capital did not include machinery, but consisted only of a fund for the maintenance of labour.[1]

In his last edition Ricardo made many corrections, mainly as a result, I think, of his perusal of the book published by Malthus in 1820. As early as 1798 Malthus had included in his famous *Essay* a chapter on the 'Probable Error of Dr. Adam Smith in representing every increase of the revenue or stock of a society as an increase in the Funds for the maintenance of Labour'.[2] Ricardo must have read this chapter, but paid little attention to it. In the same year that Ricardo published his *Principles* (1817) one John Barton issued a pamphlet in which he maintained that 'the demand for labour depends on the increase of circulating and not of fixed capital'.[3] If Ricardo read this at the time, he attached no importance to it, for it is not mentioned in his second edition. It was not until he had been rudely shaken up by Malthus' *Principles of Political Economy* (in which Barton's 'ingenious pamphlet' is mentioned)[4] that Ricardo realised the necessity of amending some of his dicta, if not some of his doctrines. He recognised that he had been too sweeping when he said that 'in proportion to the increase of capital will be the increase in the demand for labour' (54/95), and when he said that population 'always increases or diminishes with the increase or diminution of capital' (41/78). These dicta, to be sure, remain unaltered in Ricardo's third edition; perhaps they were already printed before he added a footnote to a later chapter (270/395) quoting Barton with approval.[5]

[1] It is possible that the word *machinery* was inserted by Mill, whom Mr. Sraffa credits with taking a hand in the composition of the Preface.

[2] Chap. 16 in first edition. It now figures as chap. 13 of Bk. 3.

[3] Page 17 in the reprint of Barton's pamphlet, edited by J. H. Hollander.

[4] Page 261 in first edition. In the corresponding page of the second edition (234) alterations have been made, and the reference to Barton appears to have dropped out.

[5] Ricardo criticised Mill for not having altered his language; he wrote him: 'You say in this chapter that the demand for labour and the power of employing it will be in proportion to the increase of capital. I believe I have said the

In a sense, Ricardo's acceptance of Barton's contention does not represent a new departure. As already remarked, he had all along recognised that some capital consists of buildings and machinery, and that wages are paid out of circulating capital. On page 22 of the first edition he had said that buildings and machinery may form a large part of the brewer's capital, while a shoemaker's capital may consist chiefly of a fund for the payment of wages. In his second edition he amplified this (page 21) by pointing out that even in the case of two circulating capitals, that of the farmer might be tied up for a whole year, while the baker who buys wheat 'can get it ground into flour, sell it as bread to his customers, and have his capital free to renew the same, or commence any other, employment in a week'.[1] In the arithmetical examples brought together in Table A of our third chapter it is only in the first example that the entire capital is represented as expended in the support of labour. In the third and fourth examples we have two capitalists, each employing a capital of £10,000, but while one spends £8000 annually in wages, the other's fund for the support of labour is no more than £2000. Here we have two equal capitals, but instead of the quantity of employment being in proportion to the quantity of capital, the quantity of labour employed by one capital is only a quarter of the quantity employed by the other. It is difficult to discern here that 'inexorable consistency' which De Quincey so much admired in Ricardo. The fact is, Ricardo was prone to think in compartments; it was part of his logical method to isolate the point under discussion, and in his references to the brewer and the shoemaker, the farmer and the baker, he was investigating only the degrees of 'durability' in different forms of capital, and, far from drawing a sharp line of distinction between fixed and circulating capital, his aim was to show that there is no such line, and that the difference is merely one of degree.

Although in his third edition Ricardo may be said to withdraw his contention that population increases or decreases with every increase or decrease of capital, he did not re-model his book, but

---

same, and it may be perhaps right to say so in an elementary book, although it is not strictly correct. The power of employing labour depends on the increase of a particular part of capital, not on the increase of the whole capital' (vol. 9, p. 127).

[1] For these references to Ricardo's first and second edition, see Sraffa's vol. 1, p. 52, and footnote, p. 53.

only patched it; and even the patching is 'patchy'—to the bewilderment of the student, the old statements on pages 41(78) and 54(95) are left standing, and there is not even a footnote referring the reader to the correction made in the footnote on page 270.

But while Ricardo did not re-write his book, he inserted a new chapter, and in it we find the following revised presentation of the wages-fund theory:

> A capitalist, we will suppose, employs a capital of the value of £20,000, and that he carries on the joint business of a farmer and a manufacturer of necessaries. We will further suppose that £7000 of this capital is invested in fixed capital, viz. in buildings, implements, etc., etc., and that the remaining £13,000 is employed as circulating capital in the support of labour. Let us suppose, too, that profits are 10 per cent, and consequently that the capitalist's capital is every year put into its original state of efficiency and yields a profit of £2000.
>
> Each year the capitalist begins his operations by having food and necessaries in his possession of the value of £13,000, all of which he sells in the course of the year to his own workmen for that sum of money, and during the same period he pays them the like amount of money for wages;[1] at the end of the year they replace in his possession food and necessaries of the value of £15,000, £2000 of which he consumes himself, or disposes of as may best suit his pleasure and gratification (264/388).[2]

Here a sharp line of distinction is drawn between fixed and circulating capital, although the statement is left standing on page 19(31) that a 'line of demarcation cannot be accurately drawn'. It is now made plain that the quantity of labour employed is in proportion, not to the total capital, but to the circulating capital.[3] Despite what he said on page 19(31) of the baker's capital returning to him once a week, Ricardo retains the old wages-fund

[1] As there is no mention of either capitalist or labourers commencing the year with a stock of money to serve as a shuttle in these exchanges, we must suppose the 'money' to consist of some form of I.O.U.s issued by the capitalist.

[2] This is example 5 in our Table A. The sixth example will be dealt with in a later chapter.

[3] As Cannan remarks, circulating capital 'is conceived as consisting entirely of amounts paid by the employer in wages'—'he has numerous examples in which the circulating capital of an employer is the amount he pays in wages in a year' (*Theories of Production*, page 93).

assumption that what can be consumed during the current year is limited to what was brought forward at the beginning of the year, no part of the current year's product being ready for consumption until next year.

Let us consider this in the light of the late Professor Cannan's remark that 'Ricardo's arguments always require the absurd assumption, not only that no goods are sold till the end of the year, but also that all the wages are paid at the beginning of the year'.[1] These two things are part and parcel of the same assumption. If we assume, 'for the ends of discourse' (to use Mill's expression), that what is produced in one year will not be ready for consumption until the next, it follows necessarily that at the beginning of each year the capitalist (or capitalists as a body) must hold a twelve-month stock of food and other necessaries for the support of the labourers during the current year. Ricardo's remarks on page 265(388) make it clear that he did not suppose that the whole of this fund was handed over to the labourers at the beginning of the year. The capitalist begins the year with £7000 worth of fixed capital and £13,000 of circulating capital; the latter may consist partly of food and partly of raw materials (see page 193/291) both of which, during the current year, will be gradually converted into, or replaced by, the product which will be ready for sale at the end of the year, when the capitalist will get back the £20,000 with which he began the year, plus a year's profit. If we assume that not only corn, but all products, constitute a crop that is gathered in once a year, then we must also assume that the capitalists as a body begin the year by holding a stock of goods sufficient to meet the needs of the community for twelve months, and that, during the current year, more cannot be consumed than was thus brought forward at the beginning of the year.

This assumption, as we have seen, led Malthus to say that by giving the labourers more money you would not enable them to live any better than before. This dictum obviously takes for granted that the community is a self-contained and isolated one, which cannot supplement its consumption during the current year by importing from abroad. Such a self-contained and self-supporting community is what Ricardo depicts on page 265(388). He did not suppose that any individual capitalist begins the year by having in his cupboard sufficient food and necessaries for twelve

[1] *Theories of Production*, page 94.

months. The capitalist on page 265 is the embodiment or epitome of capitalists in the aggregate; he and his men make up a miniature world which produces annually all that it consumes and consumes annually all that it produces. In making the capitalist both farmer and manufacturer, Ricardo presumably intended to typify all industry, both extractive and constructive. Mother Earth is the source from which materials are obtained; the extraction of these materials is part of that process of 'production' which is assumed to be carried from start to finish within a period of twelve months. Hence, although Ricardo on page 53(95) mentions raw materials as one form of capital, neither the capitalist on page 265 nor any other capitalist in our Table A begins the year with a stock of raw materials. Circulating capital, when the year begins, and again when the year ends, consists entirely of a fund or stock of goods ready for immediate consumption, but a stock which must be made to last for twelve months. Week by week during the current year these goods will be purchased by consumers, and if a stock-taking took place in the middle of the year it would be found that one half of the goods brought forward at the beginning of the year had been sold to consumers, and their place taken by raw materials, or materials partly worked up with a view to next year's consumption. It is only at the beginning of the year, before 'production' has commenced, and at the end of the year, after 'production' is completed, that circulating capital consists entirely of goods ready for consumption.

But while Ricardo accepted the view that this year's consumption is necessarily limited to the quantity of goods brought forward at the beginning of the year, he did not accept the dictum of Malthus that you cannot by giving the labourers more money enable them to live any better than before.

To understand this view we have to recollect that what the capitalist brings forward at the beginning of the year is the whole of last year's product. If the reader will glance again at the passage quoted from page 265(388) he will see that the capitalist ends the year with a product worth £15,000; he begins the following year, therefore, by having in his possession, not merely £13,000 worth of goods which he intends to distribute as wages, but also £2000 worth of goods which he will consume himself 'or dispose of as may best suit his pleasure and gratification'. If it is his pleasure to spend only £1500 during the current year on the purchase of goods for consumption by himself and his family, and to add £500 to his wages fund, the result will be that the labourers, instead of consuming thirteen-fifteenths, or twenty-six thirtieths, of last year's product, will be enabled to consume twenty-seven thirtieths. Total consumption cannot exceed last year's product, but the labourers may be given a larger share of it.

When Ricardo tells us (64/110) that at the end of the year the capitalist divides the whole value of the product 'into two portions only; one constitutes the profits of stock, the other the wages of labour', it is not a physical division that he has in mind, but a book-keeping division; it is not the goods produced during the year, but their value, that he separates or distinguishes into two parts. The labourers, in fact, have already received their share of the product in the shape of wages paid to them week by week during the period of production. The whole product therefore belongs to the capitalist; he has expended £13,000 and in exchange obtained a product worth £15,000. It is this value that he divides or distinguishes into two portions, one representing the replacement of his capital, while the other, the surplus, constitutes income or profit. There is no physical division; after the capitalist has taken stock and ascertained his profit, the goods 'divided' remain where they were, in the shops and warehouses, awaiting sale to consumers. Not until the goods are sold week by week to consumers is there an actual distribution or apportionment of the goods between wage-earners and profit-makers, and the proportions in which they are then shared between labourers and capitalists respectively will be altered, as already observed, if the capitalist, either at the beginning of the year or at some later period of the year, decides to transfer part of his unexercised consuming power to his labourers.

Thus it cannot be said that at the beginning of the year a definite portion of the product brought forward is ear-marked for consumption by capitalists and another portion by labourers, as the wages-fund theory takes for granted. Nevertheless, many of the articles produced last year and now offered for sale will be of a kind or quality that only wealthy people can afford to buy. Such articles might be pointed to as 'destined' for consumption by the wealthy, while other articles might be of a kind or quality that none but people with small incomes would be likely to buy, and these might be classified as wage-fund goods or subsistence-goods.

But the wages fund, in its most rigid form, exaggerates this distinction; it seems almost to assume that labourers and capitalists are two different kinds of animal, as unlike as cats and cattle, the one unable to subsist upon what the other thrives on. It seems to be taken for granted that capitalists never spend any portion of their money incomes upon food and necessaries, and that goods of this description are all destined for consumption by the labourers; it seems on the other hand to be assumed that what the capitalists buy with their profits consists predominantly of such things as carriages, pianos, carpets, cigars, perfumes, and other luxuries which, even if given to the labourers, would not enable them to rear larger families.

While the wages-fund theory exaggerates in assuming this sharp line of demarcation between wage goods and profit goods, Ricardo goes to the opposite extreme when on page 265(388) he assumes that the only product of his little community consists of food and necessaries. In this picture not only is there no physical separation of last year's product into two distinct stocks, earmarked for two different destinations, but there is not even a physical difference in the nature of the goods available for consumption by labourers and capitalists. Profit as well as wages fund consists of food and necessaries, and the capitalist has only to write a cheque transferring a portion of his profit to his wages fund and, contrary to the dictum of Malthus, the labourers will immediately enjoy an increased supply of food and necessaries.

It would be wrong, however, to suppose that this was Ricardo's doctrine. The assumption on page 265(388) that the product consists only of food and necessaries was, it seems likely, adopted merely for simplicity. Ricardo knew quite well that some part of the product brought forward from last year would consist of other things, and he did not suppose that by writing a cheque the capitalist could increase the quantity of food and necessaries available for consumption during the current year. What he did suppose is made plain in many places. For instance, on page 277(406) he writes:

> It is by giving the workman[1] more money . . . that his situation is improved. . . . He will in all probability employ a portion of his

[1] The third edition reads 'workmen', which is obviously a misprint. The first two editions read 'workman'.

> increased wages in furnishing himself abundantly with food and necessaries, but with the remainder he may, if it pleases him, purchase any commodities that may contribute to his enjoyments—chairs, tables and hardware; or better clothes, sugar and tobacco.

His friend Trower, having assumed that the labourer is not a consumer of luxuries, Ricardo replies:

> If he is not, must we not impute it to his poverty? Give him the means, and do you think he wants the inclination? Will he not improve his house and furniture, his clothing, and that of his wife and children—will he not purchase more fuel, and indulge himself in the enjoyment of better beer, tea, tobacco and snuff? (vol. 8, p. 275).

Thus good clothes, sugar, tea, tobacco and snuff are not earmarked or strictly reserved for the use of capitalists; instead of profit goods being separated from wage goods by an unbridgeable gulf, there is a neutral zone where both rich and poor go shopping, the rich buying as much as they want and the poor as much as they can.

Neither in money nor in goods, then, is the wages fund regarded by Ricardo as a quantity rigidly fixed at the beginning of the year. But the assumption is retained that the goods that can be consumed this year by the community as a whole are only those that were produced last year (the community is regarded as self-contained, with neither exportation nor importation). By giving the labourer more money you will enable him (if prices have not altered) to obtain a larger share of last year's product; but if the quantity of food and necessaries brought forward from last year is only sufficient to maintain a million people, an increase of money wages will not enable a larger number to be supported. The capitalist may add £200 to his capital, Ricardo tells us, by reducing his consumption by £200 (79/131); but when Ricardo said on page 41(78) that population always increases with the increase of capital, he cannot have been thinking of either money or fixed capital; the capital he was thinking of must have been a stock of food and necessaries for the maintenance of labourers. And it must have been of such an accumulated stock that he was thinking when he said (192/289): 'If the funds for the maintenance of labour were doubled, trebled, or quadrupled, there would not long be any difficulty in procuring the requisite number of hands to be employed by those funds.' Two, three, or four times the population could not be maintained until two, three, or four times as much food was available annually for consumption. On page 53(95) Ricardo described capital as consisting of 'food, clothing, raw materials, machinery, etc.' and then went on to say: 'Capital may increase in quantity . . . an addition may be made to the food and clothing of a country.' Thus, despite the complex nature of capital, 'increase of capital' presents itself to his mind first or foremost as an increase in the stock of food and necessaries for the support of labour. Nature provides raw material; everything else is created by labour. 'If I had food and necessaries at my disposal, I should not be long in want of workmen' (194/292). It is the offer of food and necessaries that constitutes the demand for labour; it is food and necessaries that constitute the means of employing labour. On the previous page he tells us that if a man came into possession of £10,000 which he wished to make productive, his first care would be to obtain a supply of 'food, clothing, and raw material which might set new labourers to work'. Writing to Trower, he put the position in this way—a man 'wants to increase his possessions, and it can be done only by having the power to employ more people; must not his first step be to provide necessaries for such additional number of people?' (vol. 8, p. 257). Always and everywhere his assumption is that the capitalist begins the year with a supply of food and necessaries for the labourers he intends to employ. It is goods, not money—food and necessaries, not luxuries—that constitute circulating capital or wages fund, and it is only an increase of foods of the kind upon which the human animal can be supported that permits the natural tendency of population to increase, to become effective. On page 197(295) Ricardo quotes, with apparent approval, Adam Smith's remark that 'the number of workmen increases with the increasing quantity of food'.[1]

These sayings seem to indicate that while increase of food and increase of population keep close together, the increase of food necessarily comes first. Under these circumstances Malthus must, I think, have counted on Ricardo's acquiescence when he said that however much the annual production of food might increase, the supply would never for long exceed the demand, on account of the power 'peculiar to the necessaries of life . . . to raise up a number of demanders in proportion to the quantity of necessaries

[1] *Wealth of Nations*, Bk. 1, chap. 11 (7th paragraph in Part 2).

produced'.[1] This seems to be only another way of putting Adam Smith's dictum that mankind always increases up to the limit that the supply of food makes possible. But Ricardo did not let this pass. His mind was always particularly alert in controversy. To him, argument was the spice of life, and to floor his friend Malthus gave him, I venture to think, a particular pleasure. Moreover, he loved paradox. He must therefore have experienced a threefold thrill when he wrote: 'It is not the abundance of necessaries which raises up demanders, but the abundance of demanders which raises up necessaries.' [2] More corn, Ricardo argued, will not be produced until the price has risen; the price will not rise until the demand has increased; and there will be no increase of demand until population has increased. To grow more food before there are more mouths to be fed, would be suicidal on the part of the farmer. 'What motive', Ricardo asks (278/407), 'can a farmer have to produce more corn than is actually demanded, when the consequence would be a depression of its market price below its natural price, and consequently a privation to him of a portion of his profits, by reducing them below the general rate?'[3]

What, then, actually occurs, according to Ricardo? The successive steps by which an increase of capital brings about an increase of population and food are as follows. First, the capitalist decides to increase his circulating capital by saving. He cuts down his own consumption by £200 (or whatever the amount may be), and transfers this additional purchasing power to the labourers. The labourers perhaps spend the money on tobacco, snuff, better beer or better clothes. 'The increased wages', says Ricardo (103/163), 'are not always immediately expended on food, but are first made to contribute to the other enjoyments of the labourer. His improved condition, however, induces and enables him to marry, and then the demand for food for the support of his family naturally supersedes that of those other enjoyments on which his wages were temporarily expended.'[4] And again (278/407) he

[1] These words from Malthus' *Inquiry into the Nature and Progress of Rent* (1815) are quoted by Ricardo, page 274(400).

[2] Page 560 in Ricardo's first edition. Ricardo altered the paragraph in his second edition, but the wording of the first edition is quoted in a footnote on page 405 of Sraffa's vol. 1.

[3] See also Ricardo's correspondence with Trower, vol. 8, pp. 235 and 255.

[4] The same succession of events is described on page 205(305) and pages 277–8(406–7).

writes: 'So great are the delights of domestic society that, in practice, it is invariably found that an increase of population follows the amended condition of the labourer; and it is only because it does so that . . . a new and increased demand arises for food. This demand, then, is the effect of an increase of capital and population, but not the cause.'

That increase of demand and rise of price must precede increase of supply is a sound proposition if additional supply cannot be obtained except at a higher cost (which is Ricardo's usual assumption in the case of food); but it is not so sound if increase of supply is brought about by advances in science, labour-saving inventions, or the opening up of new tracts of fertile land. Larger harvests at reduced cost may result in supply exceeding demand, and agriculture may suffer a period of depression with profits below the general level; the point made by Malthus is that, since men like other animals increase up to the limit of subsistence, the greater abundance of food will bring about in due course a corresponding abundance of demanders. Population increases, not because capitalists have surrendered part of their consuming power to the labourers, but because food has become cheaper and more abundant, and the labourers can therefore, on the same money wage, rear a larger number of children than before.

But would the labourers receive the same money wage if the cost of food and necessaries fell? In a letter that Ricardo wrote to Malthus he appears to think that if goods became cheaper and more abundant in consequence of greater facility of production, the labourers would not benefit unless the capitalists took steps to increase their capital. He wrote:

> It appears to me that if, instead of four, ten measures could be produced by a day's labour, no rise would take place in wages—no greater portion of corn, cloth, or cotton would be given to the labourer—unless a portion of the increased produce were employed as capital; and then the rise in wages would be in proportion to the new demand for labour, and not at all in proportion to the increase in the quantity of commodities produced. This increase would be exclusively enjoyed by the owner of the stock, and if he consumed in his family the whole increased produce, without augmenting his capital, wages would remain stationary, and not be in any way affected by the increased facility of production (vol. 6, p. 227).

While we can imagine things happening in this way if the capitalist begins the year with a fixed quantity of food and necessaries which he hands out in weekly instalments to his labourers, it is not the state of things depicted by Ricardo himself under a system of money wages. On page 9(16) of his *Principles* his assumption is that if there is a fall in the price of food and necessaries the labourer will be able to buy more goods, and rear more children, and it is not until the number of labourers has increased that money wages fall. 'It is probable', says Ricardo, 'his wages would in no long time be adjusted by the effects of competition, and the stimulus to population, to the new value of the necessaries on which they were expended.'

If the capitalist, who has been in the habit of paying £13,000 annually in wages, continues to pay the same amount after food and necessaries have fallen in price, would Ricardo say that his capital has increased? One might think he would do so, for on page 53(95) he says: 'Capital . . . consists of food, clothing, tools, raw materials, machinery, etc.' and he adds:

> Capital may increase without its value increasing, and even while its value is actually diminishing; not only may an addition be made to the food and clothing of a country, but the addition may be made by the aid of machinery without any increase, and even with an absolute diminution in the proportional quantity of labour required to produce them. The quantity of capital may increase while neither the whole together, nor any part of it singly, will have a greater value than before, but may actually have a less.

This seems to be the very case we are considering; while the *value* of the capital remains stationary at £13,000, the quantity of capital increases.

But Ricardo has no sooner laid it down that the quantity of capital may increase without its value increasing than he proceeds to tell us that 'the market rate of wages will rise, for in proportion to the increase of capital will be the increase in the demand for labour'. The labourer, he says on the next page, 'will receive increased money wages without having to pay any increased price, and perhaps even a diminished price, for the commodities which he and his family consume'. But if the capitalist is to give his labourers more money, will he not require a larger money wages fund? If he now pays £14,000 in wages instead of £13,000, is there not an addition to the value as well as to the quantity of his capital?

The fact seems to be that although Ricardo from time to time makes a passing reference to discoveries and inventions as resulting in the multiplication and cheapening of commodities, the idea usually present in his mind is that if wealth and population continuously increase, it is because capitalists continuously save and add to their capital. Improvements in technique increase the product, but the whole product belongs to the capitalist, and (as set forth in his letter to Malthus quoted above) if the capitalist retains the increase of product for his own consumption, it will have no effect on wages or population. But when, in the normal course of things, the capitalist saves £200 and adds it to his capital (79/131), he not only increases the quantity and value of his capital, but he increases the demand for labour. The labourers receive more money, and are enabled to increase their demand for food and necessaries; and what Ricardo is concerned to point out on pages 53–4(95–6) is that when money wages rise the labourer benefits, 'but not much' if there is a rise in the price of food or necessaries, whereas, if food and necessaries have fallen in price 'the condition of the labourer will be very greatly improved'. And later on he tells us (266/390) that it is particularly during a period of falling costs that the capitalists are likely to make large savings, for they 'have increased means of saving—increased facility of transferring revenue into capital'. It is this transfer of consuming-power from the capitalist to the labourers, and not a fall in the price of food, that always figures in Ricardo's mind as the cause of increasing population.

Before we close this chapter we must consider the demand for labour from another point of view. In the *Notes on Malthus* (vol. 2, pp. 264–5) Ricardo claims that he has always 'recognised' that the market rate of wages is regulated by 'the relative amount of population to capital'. Thus if capital is £13,000 and the number of labourers is 130, each gets £100 a year. If the capital increases or the number of labourers diminishes, wages will be higher; if the number of labourers increases or the quantity of capital shrinks, wages will be lower; if both capital and population increase in the same proportion, wages will remain the same. This is the wages-fund theory, and it is the theory expounded in Ricardo's chapter on wages.

But the fact is that the capitalist who employs a certain number of men with his capital of £13,000 is almost certain to spend some of his £2000 profit upon personal service. Part will be paid to actors and singers who amuse his leisure, part to cooks and parlour maids who assist his wife to run the home, part to doctors who attend his family, part to teachers for his children. Some of his income, too, will be taken from him by the Government to employ soldiers, policemen, and civil servants. Capital, then, is not the only fund that creates a demand for labour. There might be an increase in the demand for personal services while the quantity of capital remained stationary.

In his letter to Malthus (vol. 6, p. 227, quoted above) Ricardo argues that if Industry becomes more productive the capitalist is faced with the choice between increasing his capital or increasing his personal consumption. He appears to overlook that if the capitalist decides to reserve the whole additional product for his own 'pleasure and gratification' (265/388–9) the result is likely to be an increase in the demand for personal services as well as for commodities. The rich would derive little enjoyment from the possession of large houses if they had to do all the housework themselves, or from the ownership of carriages and horses if they had to wash down the former and groom the latter. Hence growth of profit as well as growth of capital—or growth of profit without growth of capital—is likely to result in an increased demand for labour. In short, as Adam Smith said, 'the demand for those who live by wages' increases with the increase of capital and income.[1]

As mentioned at the beginning of this chapter, Ricardo was well aware that profit, or surplus, is largely expended on personal services, and he devoted his 26th chapter to this subject. But the strange thing is that in framing his theory of wages in chapter 5 he entirely ignores the demand for personal services. Although in that chapter he purports to expound 'the laws by which wages are regulated, and by which the happiness of far the greatest part of every community is governed' (61/105), he dwells exclusively on the ratio between population and capital. There is, he says, a minimum or natural rate below which the labourer's wage cannot sink without threatening to extinguish the supply of labour; this is to be studied in our next chapter. Apart from this, the rate of wages is determined by supply and demand, and the only demand recognised in the chapter on wages is the demand made by capital. 'In proportion to the increase of capital will be the increase in the

[1] *Wealth of Nations*, Bk. 1, chap. 8 (21st paragraph).

demand for labour. . . . With every increase in its capital the market wages of labour will rise' (54/95–6). On page 57(101) he writes:

> In the natural advance of society, the wages of labour will have a tendency to fall, as far as they are regulated by supply and demand; for the supply of labourers will continue to increase at the same rate, whilst the demand for them will increase at a slower rate. If, for instance, wages were regulated by a yearly increase of capital at the rate of 2 per cent, they would fall when it accumulated only at the rate of 1½ per cent. They would fall still lower when it increased only at the rate of 1 or ½ per cent, and would continue to do so until the capital became stationary, when wages also would become stationary, and be only sufficient to keep up the numbers of the actual population.

The younger Mill, who had a kindly recollection of his father's friend Ricardo, always sought to give as reasonable a complexion as possible to the latter's doctrines, and although he could not accept the quantity theory of wages in this form, he thought the theory could be defended if the wages fund were defined as including both the amounts advanced by capitalists to 'productive' workers (who must replace what they receive with a profit) and the amounts paid by consumers out of income for personal services.[1] Apparently he did not recognise that his own presentation of the doctrine reduced it to a mere arithmetical truism, void of significance,[2] whereas the theory as expounded by Ricardo and others implied (what was very important, if true) that the only way in which the demand for labour could be increased and the condition of the labourer improved was by the capitalists restricting their immediate enjoyments and adding to their capital.

A more effective defence of this doctrine would have been as follows. If the capitalist cuts down his consumption of commodities in order to employ labour in personal services the increase in the quantity of wages distributed is for the current year only, whereas if he transfers £200 to his circulating capital the amount is likely to remain there as a permanent addition to the wages

[1] J. S. Mill's *Principles of Political Economy*, opening paragraph in chap. 11, Book 2.

[2] It 'merely amounts to saying that the quotient will be such as the dividend and divisor determine', said J. E. Cairnes (*Some Leading Principles of* P.E., Part 2, chap. 1, 5th section). Mill subsequently gave up the wages-fund theory.

fund.[1] True the capitalist might continue year after year to spend £200 of his profit upon services instead of commodities, but this would not have the same effect as an annual addition of £200 to his circulating capital, the vital difference between the two cases being that the labourers employed by capital produce commodities while those employed in rendering services do not. And it is only by increasing the total quantity of food and necessaries annually produced that any large increase of population is made possible. However much we may modify the proportion in which the annual product is shared between labourers and capitalist, there can be no doubling, trebling, quadrupling of the population unless the quantity of the annual product is increased. If the quantity of food and necessaries remains stationary, a progressive increase in the number of labourers employed upon personal services will make the situation worse instead of better. It is therefore the demand for labour made by capital, not the demand made by consumers of personal services, that permits population, food and necessaries, and general wealth, to increase.[2] This, then, explains the dictum that population 'increases or diminishes with the increase or diminution of capital' (page 41), although it hardly justifies the other dictum that 'in proportion to the increase of capital will be the increase in the demand for labour' (page 54). On this point Ricardo himself came to take a different view, but he did not express it in his chapter on wages, and it will be better to leave our discussion of it[3] until we come to consider the new chapter that Ricardo inserted in his final edition.

[1] This was pointed out by Adam Smith; see *Wealth of Nations*, Bk. 2, chap. 3, 19th paragraph.

[2] This is substantially Adam Smith's teaching; see the third paragraph in his Introduction and the subsequent development of the theme in chap. 3 of Book 2.

[3] See 13th chapter in the present work.

8

The Natural Price of Labour

In our last chapter we examined Ricardo's statement (53/94) that the market price of labour depends on the proportion of the supply to the demand, or as James Mill put it, on the proportion of population to capital. But in the same paragraph Ricardo declared that the market price of labour has, like that of commodities, a tendency to conform to the natural price. Let us now turn our attention to this point. We will begin by asking what he meant by the natural price of labour.

The term 'natural price' is taken from *The Wealth of Nations*. What Adam Smith means by 'the natural rate of wages' and 'the natural rate of profit' he explains in the opening paragraph of his seventh chapter:

> There is in every society or neighbourhood an ordinary or average rate both of wages and profit in every different employment of labour and stock. This rate is naturally regulated, as I shall show hereafter, partly by the general circumstances of the society, their riches or poverty, their advancing, stationary, or declining condition; and partly by the particular nature of each employment.

Thus the natural rate of wages, or the natural rate of profit, is simply the ordinary or average rate current in the market at the time. For capital there may be several different rates, according to the risk involved in different kinds of investment, or the facility with which capital can be withdrawn if so desired. For labour there will be a number of different rates, depending not merely on the different degrees of danger or unpleasantness involved in different employments, but also on the different degrees of skill required. For each class of employment there is, Smith considers, an ordinary or average rate prevailing in the market at any particular time.

But this is not Ricardo's definition of natural price. He adopts Smith's term, but (as in the case of fixed and circulating capital) twists it to a meaning of his own. 'By natural price', he says in the *Notes on Malthus* (vol. 2, p. 227), 'I do not mean the usual price, but such a price as is necessary to supply constantly a given demand.' In the same *Notes* (vol. 2, p. 46) he says: 'Natural price is only another name for cost of production.' What is the cost of 'producing' a labourer? In his *Principles* (52/93) Ricardo says: 'The natural price of labour is that price which is necessary to enable the labourers, one with another, to subsist, and to perpetuate their race without either increase or diminution.' Thus, expressed in commodities, the natural price, or cost of production, is the quantity of food, clothing, etc., necessary to enable the labourers as a class to continue in existence and to bring up a sufficient number of children to maintain a stationary supply of labour; in terms of money it is the wage required to enable the labourers to purchase this quantity of goods at current market prices.

Thus the ordinary or average rate of wages current in the market, which is what Adam Smith calls the natural rate, is not the natural rate according to Ricardo's definition. If the usual and ordinary rate of wages exceeds what is necessary to maintain a stationary supply of labour, it is above the natural rate, and the consequence, as in the case of commodities, will be an increase of supply. So long as capital (i.e. wages fund) continues to increase, population and therefore the supply of labour will continue to increase; but if capital ceases to increase—if the demand for labour ceases to grow—then wages must sooner or later settle at the natural rate, as would be the case with commodities. Ricardo describes the position on page 53(94) as follows:

> However much the market price of labour may deviate from its natural price, it has, like commodities, a tendency to conform to it.
>
> It is when the market price of labour exceeds its natural price that the condition of the labourer is flourishing and happy, that he has it in his power to command a greater proportion of the necessaries and enjoyments of life, and therefore to rear a healthy and numerous family. When, however, by the encouragement which high wages give to the increase of population, the number of labourers is increased, wages again fall to their natural price, and indeed from a reaction sometimes fall below it.[1]

[1] See also 103–4/163–4.

When the market price of labour is below its natural price, the condition of the labourers is most wretched; then poverty deprives them of those comforts which custom renders absolute necessaries. It is only after their privations have reduced their number, or the demand for labour has increased, that the market price of labour will rise to its natural price, and that the labourer will have the moderate comforts which the natural rate of wages will afford (53/94).

Ricardo, it will be observed, assumes that the natural wage includes 'moderate comforts', or 'those comforts which custom renders absolute necessaries'. On page 54(96) he writes:

It is not to be understood that the natural price of labour, estimated even in food and necessaries, is absolutely fixed and constant. It varies at different times in the same country, and very materially differs in different countries. It essentially depends on the habits and customs of the people. An English labourer would consider his wages under their natural rate, and too scanty to support a family, if they enabled him to purchase no other food than potatoes, and to live in no better habitation than a mud cabin.

Different races have different ideas as to what are necessaries. The Irish peasant is content with potatoes and a mud cabin,[1] the Scotch peasant lives on oatmeal;[2] but, says Malthus, 'the labourers of the South of England are so accustomed to eat fine wheaten bread that they will suffer themselves to be half-starved before they will submit to live like the Scotch peasants'.[3]

[1] Cobbett always speaks with contempt of the potato, 'especially when carried cold to the field in a bag'. See *Rural Rides*, vol. 1, p. 178, and vol. 2, pp. 40 and 280, in *Everyman* edition. While agreeing with Cobbett as to cold potatoes, I cannot share his regret that Raleigh was not 'hanged' before instead of after importing the plant. (Raleigh, as a matter of fact, was beheaded; but not for importing potatoes.)

[2] 'Oats—A grain which in England is generally given to horses, but in Scotland supports the people'.—Johnson's Dictionary, 1755. The Scots were sore at this; many years later (1783) Johnson acknowledged to Boswell: 'Why, I own that by my definition of Oats I meant to vex them.' Boswell's national pride was soothed when he found the people of Johnson's own City of Lichfield eating oat-cakes.

[3] *Essay on Population*, page 132 in reprint of first edition. In *The Village Labourer* J. L. and B. Hammond tell us that the labourers declared that brown bread ' disordered their bowels'. 'The poorer the labourer grew', they say, 'the more stubbornly did he insist on wheaten bread' (page 100 in 1924 edition). Pitt, however, declared in 1795 that although formerly corn was 'almost the only food of the labourer', it was now supplied by cheaper sub-

> Custom [said Adam Smith] has rendered leather shoes a necessary of life in England. The poorest creditable person of either sex would be ashamed to appear in public without them. In Scotland custom has rendered them a necessary of life to the lowest order of men; but not to the same order of women, who may, without any discredit, walk about bare-footed.[1]

If we may believe the French economist, J.-B. Say, beer was regarded as a necessary in England; the French beggar, he said, asks for bread, but the English beggar's appeal is for beer.[2] In India or China the labourer will bring up a family if he can provide them with rice, but the English labourer, says Ricardo, would consider his wages too scanty to marry on if matrimony meant living on potatoes. 'The labourer who earns eighteenpence a day,' says Malthus, 'and lives with some degree of comfort as a single man, will hesitate a little before he divides that pittance among four or five which seems to be but just sufficient for one.'[3]

---

stitutions' (see page 559 in *English Economic History*, published in 1914 by G. Bell and Sons). The Hammonds, in *The Skilled Labourer* (page 288) quote the *Manchester Mercury* as referring to potatoes in 1812 as 'that indispensable part of the sustenance of the poor'.

[1] *Wealth of Nations*, Bk. 5, chap. 2, article 4, 3rd paragraph in section headed 'Taxes upon consumable commodities'. Readers of Scott will recall that when Jeanie Deans set out on her heroic journey from Edinburgh to London she found it necessary when she crossed the Border to don shoes and stockings to avoid provoking unfavourable notice. When Ricardo visited Italy in 1822 he received the impression that the Italian beggar could do without shoes, but regarded an umbrella as indispensable (vol. 10, p. 298).

[2] Say's *Traité d'Économic Politique*, vol. 2, p. 114, in fourth edition. C. R. Prinsep, who translated this work into English in 1821, appears sceptical. Adam Smith seems to have hesitated whether to regard beer as a necessary. Cannan points out that in the first edition of *The Wealth of Nations* beer was classified as a necessary in Bk. 4, chap. 2, and as a luxury in Bk. 5, chap. 2, but in the second edition it disappeared from the list of necessaries. The Hammonds (page 105 in *The Village Labourer*) quote the Rev. B. Davies as saying in 1795: 'Time was when *small beer* was reckoned one of the necessaries of life, even in poor families.'

[3] *Essay on Population*, 1798, page 67 of reprint. Adam Smith said: Eighteenpence a day may be reckoned the common price of labour in London and its neighbourhood. At a few miles distance it falls to fourteen and fifteen pence' (Bk. 1, chap. 8, 31st paragraph). He wrote in 1776. In 1791 Hannah More, in a letter to Wilberforce, reports the ordinary wage in Somerset to be a shilling a day. Ricardo (1817) usually assumes the wage to be about £24 a year. Cobbett often refers to wages of 8*s*. or 9*s*. a week; and as late as

Thus in the view of Ricardo, and also of Malthus, it is in every country the labourers themselves who determine what their standard of living shall be.[1] The market price of labour is regulated by supply and demand. The quantity of capital, or wages fund, constitutes the demand; but the labourers control the supply of labour and thereby control its price in the market. It is an error to suppose that the capitalists fix the rate of wages, and pin the labourers down to poverty, for the capitalists are perpetually exerting themselves to increase their capital, and every such increase must result in a rise of wages if the number of labourers remains unaltered. Thus the labourers frequently have an improved standard of living offered to them, and it depends upon themselves whether wages 'continue permanently high' (278/406), or whether, by increasing their numbers, the labourers bring the wage down again to the natural rate. Experience shows, thinks Ricardo, that they always do the latter. When capital increases, the labourer may for a time enjoy some addition to his comforts—more sugar, more tobacco, better clothes; he may hesitate a little before giving up these luxuries; but, says Ricardo, 'so great are the delights of domestic society that, in practice, it is invariably found that an increase of population follows the amended condition of the labourer' (278/406–7).

> It generally happens, indeed [he tells us] that when a stimulus has been given to population, an effect is produced beyond what the case requires; the population may be, and generally is, so much increased as . . . to bear a greater proportion to the funds for maintaining labourers than before the increase of capital. In this case . . . wages will be below their natural level, and will continue so till the usual proportion between the supply and demand has been restored (103/164).

Here, then, we have a see-saw movement, with the natural wage as the pivot. 'Experience demonstrates', says Ricardo, 'that capital and population alternately take the lead' (vol. 4, p. 23). Each

---

1848 J. S. Mill mentions that in some agricultural countries labourers with large families were still earning eight or nine shillings a week 'when in full employment'. See his *Principles*, Bk. 2, chap. 11, section 6.

[1] In his *Principles* Malthus said of the labourers: 'They are really the arbiters of their own destiny; and what others can do for them is like the dust of the balance compared with what they can do for themselves' (page 306 in first edition; page 279 in second edition).

increase of capital results in an increase of wages, and each increase of wages is followed by an increase of population, which brings the wage down again. While, however, this suggests an oscillatory or pendulum movement, Ricardo does not rule out the possibility that under exceptional circumstances the market rate of wages may continue for a considerable time to be above the natural rate. 'The agreement of the market and natural prices of all commodities', he says, 'depends at all times on the facility with which the supply can be increased or diminished. In the case of labour, as well as many other things, this effect cannot, under some circumstances, be speedily produced' (125–6/196). When the fund for the maintenance of labour is augmented, there will not be an immediate addition to the number of labourers, for 'you cannot increase their number in one or two years when there is an increase of capital' (105/165). On page 53(94) Ricardo writes:

> Notwithstanding the tendency of wages, to conform to their natural rate, their market rate may, in an improving society, for an indefinite period, be constantly above it; for no sooner may the impulse which an increased capital gives to a new demand for labour be obeyed, than another increase of capital may produce the same effect; and thus, if the increase of capital be gradual and constant, the demand for labour may give a continued stimulus to an increase of people.

Again, on page 55(98) he says:

> It has been calculated that under favourable circumstances population may be doubled in twenty-five years;[1] but under the same favourable circumstances the whole capital of a country might possibly be doubled in a shorter period. In that case, wages during the whole period would have a tendency to rise, because the demand for labour would increase still faster than the supply.

These remarks, however, apply only to new countries, such as America then was, where population is small and land abundant. In old and thickly inhabited countries, where the soil has been cultivated for many centuries, the position is very different. The passage quoted above continues as follows:

> In new settlements . . . it is probable that capital has a tendency

[1] 'In the United States of America . . . the population has been found to double itself in twenty-five years'—Malthus' *Essay on Population*, 1798, page 20 in reprint.

> to increase faster than mankind [but] in proportion as these countries become populous, and land of a worse quality is taken into cultivation, the tendency to an increase of capital diminishes. . . . Although then it is probable that, under the most favourable circumstances, the power of production is still greater than that of population, it will not long continue so; for the land being limited in quantity, and differing in quality, with every increased portion of capital employed on it there will be a decreased rate of production, whilst the power of population continues always the same. [In short] in long settled countries . . . the population increases faster than the funds required for its support (55–6/98–9).

It was with England and other long settled countries that Ricardo was mainly concerned. In such countries, he considered, the law of diminishing returns had been in operation for centuries, and as it was not accompanied by any law of diminishing birth-rate, the result was that more children were born each year than the number for which it was possible to provide subsistence. This tendency of population to increase faster than the means for its support had been noted by philosophers long before the doctrine of diminishing returns had been born or thought of; but Malthus, with his catch phrase of the arithmetical and geometrical rates of progression, was the first to capture the ear of the public. His scientific-looking formula made him famous, but not popular. Simple folk clung to the comfortable notion that 'God never sends mouths without sending meat'.[1] The contrary proposition, that Nature's way of balancing the supply of meat and the number of mouths is to remove the excess population by starvation (what Malthus calls the 'positive check') struck people as impious, particularly when coming from a young clergyman, and by none was Malthus more vigorously denounced than by Cobbett. That great master of prose never tired of pillorying 'the monster Malthus' for his 'infamous and really diabolical assertion' that 'man has a natural propensity to breed faster than food can be raised for the increase'. Cobbett was a good hater, and he hated no one more heartily than 'beastly Malthus' and 'his nasty disciples'—'blasphemers who contend that God has implanted in man a principle

[1] See Cobbett's *Advice to Young Men*, paragraph 99. This proverb is akin to that other comfortable saying, 'God tempers the wind to the shorn lamb'. In Australia I have known thousands of sheep to perish in a cold snap after shearing.

that leads him to starvation'.[1] But the very heat with which the battle was waged served to draw attention to the doctrine, and it gained adherents. In a sentence, corrugated with commas, James Mill summed up the position as follows:

> Though no part of the doctrine of Mr. Malthus has been left uncontested, it is now, among thinking men, pretty generally allowed that, excepting certain favourable situations, as in new countries, where there is unoccupied land of sufficient productiveness, which may be placed under cultivation as fast as men are multiplied, a greater number of human beings is produced than there is food to support. This, it is understood, is the habitual condition of human nature.[2]

What particularly roused Cobbett's ire was that Malthus, a clergyman, and his wealthy disciples, should expect from the poor a self-restraint which they did not exercise themselves. 'Malthus does not seem to see any harm', he wrote, 'in parsons having large families; it is the working population, those who raise the food and the clothing, that he and Scarlett want to put a stop to the breeding of'.[3] Malthus himself had but three children, of whom only two survived him,[4] but it is true enough that large families

[1] These expressions of Cobbett's will be found in his *Rural Rides*, pages 37, 52, 53, 182, vol. 2 in *Everyman* edition. Ricardo was one of the 'nasty disciples' whom Cobbett hated as much as he hated Malthus himself. Some of his remarks concerning Ricardo are quoted in Sraffa's footnote on page 41 of vol. 5. Ricardo's early death did not appease Cobbett's wrath. Jogging along in the neighbourhood of Minchinhampton Cobbett pulled up his horse to admire a beautiful property. 'Whose beautiful place is that?' he asked of a countryman who was passing. The reply was—'One Squire Ricardo I think they call him, but the old gentleman is dead, and . . .' The hated name was too much for Cobbett—'God damn the old gentleman, and the young one too, said I, and giving my horse a blow instead of a word, on I went down the hill' (*Rural Rides*, vol. 2, p. 103).

[2] Quoted in Bain's *Life of James Mill*, pages 257/8. According to Harriet Martineau, the historian Hallam said of Malthus' arithmetical and geometrical ratio: 'There is no one who could question it that might not as well dispute the multiplication table.' As for the monster Malthus, she says: 'All that I know is that a more simple-minded, virtuous man, full of domestic affections, than Mr. Malthus, could not be found in all England'; he is also 'one of the serenest, and most cheerful men that society can produce' (pages 209, 210, 211, in vol. 1 of her *Autobiography*, 2nd edition).

[3] *Rural Rides*, vol. 2, p. 81. Scarlett was a Member of Parliament interested in Poor Law reform; subsequently became Lord Abinger.

[4] Karl Marx seems to have thought that Malthus was a celibate; see *Capital*, page 680 in *Everyman* edition.

were then far more common among the well-to-do than they are today. King George III and his royal spouse presented a grateful nation with fifteen Princes and Princesses. Ricardo himself was one of seventeen children (for list, see vol. 10, pp. 54–61), but his own offspring numbered no more than eight. His friend Mill had nine children; but another friend, Maria Edgeworth (author of the delightful *Castle Rackrent*), was one of nineteen (one father, four mothers). Her compatriot, Lord Edward Fitzgerald, the Irish rebel (or patriot), was one of twenty-two (all by the same mother, but two of them by her second husband). Ricardo's contemporary, Dr. Bathurst, Bishop of Norwich, was one of thirty-six children (one father, assisted by two wives). It might well seem to Cobbett, therefore, that the alleged impossibility of supplying food was merely a pretext in a class war which aimed at reserving philoprogenitive indulgence as a privilege of the rich. No doubt Ricardo and Malthus thought rich families too few in number to exercise any appreciable influence on the ratio between the quantity of food and the quantity of population. The position was different if the masses multiplied recklessly. In a footnote on page 62(107) Ricardo criticises Pitt for saying in the House of Commons (1796) that the poor man who enriched his country with a number of children had a claim on the community for assistance. If the poor were thus encouraged to have children, whether they could support them or not, the result must be each year an addition to the population out of all proportion to the addition that could be made to the food supply. Parliament had no more power than Canute to repeal the laws of nature, and while it might tax the rich to feed the poor, it would not thereby increase the quantity of food available. Practically all the corn actually produced, Ricardo and Malthus thought, is already distributed among the wage-earners;[1] depriving the rich of their comforts would not make corn more abundant. But even if some increase of supply could be brought about in this manner,[2] it would not improve the

[1] Adam Smith had said: 'Almost the whole capital of every country is annually distributed among the inferior ranks of people, as the wages of productive labour. Secondly, a great part of the revenue arising from both the rent of land and the profits of stock is annually distributed among the same rank, in the wages and maintenance of menial servants and other unproductive labourers' (*Wealth of Nations*, Bk. 5, chap. 2, article 4, 43rd paragraph in the section headed 'Taxes upon Consumable Commodities').

[2] For instance, by ladies ceasing to powder their hair. In Mrs. Marcet's

condition of the poor, for every increase of the food supply is invariably followed by an increase in the population—Cobbett himself reports, for the information of Parson Malthus and his 'tribe', that when nuts are plentiful on the wayside, there follows an increase in the birth-rate among vagrants.[1]

So far, then, from giving a pat on the back to the labourer who has enriched his country with a family that he cannot support, Ricardo and Malthus reserve their praises for the labourer who 'hesitates a little' before marrying on eighteenpence a day. 'It is a truth which admits not a doubt', says Ricardo (61/106), 'that the comforts and well-being of the poor cannot be permanently secured without some regard on their part, or some effort on the part of the legislature, to regulate the increase of their numbers, and to render less frequent among them early and improvident marriages.' What the legislature might do, according to Malthus, is to make it compulsory on every clergyman, when publishing the banns of a projected marriage, to follow it up with a public warning to the amorous pair that should they bring into the world children whom they cannot support, they must expect no assistance from the parish.[2] If the labourers fail to exercise what Malthus calls the prudential or *preventive* check on over-population, then they must be prepared to see the excess population removed by Nature's *positive* check—death from misery and starvation. Barbarous and blasphemous doctrine according to Cobbett, but Cobbett's own testimony is that the poor will continue to propagate though reduced to living on wayside nuts; he says nothing of their hesitating a little. Such, Ricardo feared, always had been and always would be the habits of the poor. The testimony of Adam

Conversations, third edition (1819), I find the following observations by 'Mrs. B.': 'Hair-powder we may consider as a kind of granary for the preservation of wheat, for though the powder would not, unless in cases of very great urgency, be converted into food, the quantity of corn annually grown for the purpose of making hair-powder would, during a moderate scarcity, find its way more readily to the baker's than to the perfumer's shop.' Mrs. B.'s conclusion may be questioned.

[1] *Rural Rides*, page 221, vol. 1 in *Everyman* edition.

[2] *Essay on Population*, Bk. 4, chap. 8, 5th paragraph (page 430 in 8th edition). J. S. Mill quotes a report that 'in Norway no one can marry without showing to the satisfaction of the clergyman that he is permanently settled in such a manner as to offer a fair prospect that he can maintain a family' (*Principles*, Bk. 2, chap. 11, sec. 4).

Smith when Ricardo was a child was that it is the scantiness of subsistence alone that limits the multiplication of the common people, 'and it can do so in no other way than by destroying a great part of the children which their fruitful marriages produce';[1] and the testimony of J. S. Mill twenty-five years after Ricardo's death was to the same effect—'I much doubt', he says, 'if the generality of agricultural labourers practise any prudential restraint whatever. They generally marry as early, and have as many children to a marriage, as they would or could do if they were settlers in the United States.'[2]

It is not, then, the preventive check, but the positive check that keeps down the number of labourers, and under these circumstances Ricardo saw no prospect of any permanent improvement in the condition of the working classes. A more hopeful view might seem to be indicated by his remark in the *Notes on Malthus* (vol. 2, p. 115) that 'it is not difficult to conceive' that with better education and improved habits the labourer's condition might be improved; but although this is 'conceivable', the very Note in which the remark is made begins by saying that 'population is found to increase invariably with the means of providing for it'. In his *Principles* he said (as already remarked) that although an improvement in the labourer's condition 'might be the consequence of high wages', yet 'in practice it is invariably found that an increase of population follows the amended condition of the labourer' (278/407). 'It generally happens indeed' (103/164) that population increases so much that wages fall below the natural rate. 'No point is better established', he says, 'than that the supply of labourers will always ultimately be in proportion to the means of supporting them' (194/292).

Not only does Ricardo see no prospect of a permanent improvement in the condition of the labouring class, he sees a more or less continuous deterioration. 'In the natural advance of society', he says (57/101), 'the wages of labour will have a tendency to fall, as far as they are regulated by supply and demand; for the supply of labourers will continue to increase at the same rate whilst the demand for them'—i.e. capital or wages fund—'will increase at a slower rate.' What has a tendency to fall is the commodity wage, not the money wage. When diminishing returns make food dearer,

[1] *Wealth of Nations*, Bk. 1, chap. 8, 39th paragraph.

[2] Mill's *Principles*, Bk. 2, chap. 11, section 3.

money wages must increase, 'but they would not rise sufficiently to enable the labourer to purchase as many comforts and necessaries as he did before the rise in the price of those commodities' (57/101). 'Even with the above increase of wages, his situation would be comparatively worse' (59/104). He repeats this on page 75(125–6). 'Each labourer would receive more money wages; but the condition of the labourer, as we have already shown, would be worse, inasmuch as he would be able to command a less quantity of the produce of the country . . . When poor lands are taken into cultivation . . . each man may, and probably will, have a less absolute quantity.'

At what date in the world's history, or in the history of England, this downward trend of commodity wages first began, Ricardo does not tell us;[1] that it had, in his opinion, been going on for at least three hundred years, may be inferred from his statement on page 142(217) that 'the lands which are now taken into cultivation are much inferior to the lands in cultivation three centuries ago'. That being so, one might have supposed that whatever the comforts enjoyed by labourers in the reign of Henry VIII, they would have since much diminished, or disappeared entirely, under the pressure of increasing population and diminishing returns. But he not only tells us on page 53(94) that the natural wage includes 'moderate comforts', but follows this up on page 55(97) with the remark that 'many of the conveniences now enjoyed in an English cottage would have been thought luxuries at an earlier period of our history'.

This survival of comforts as part of the natural wage seems to call for some explanation. If Ricardo had said that the *market* rate of wages in his day permitted the labourer to enjoy some luxuries unknown to his ancestors, it would have called for no comment; for on page 53(94) he had admitted that despite the downward trend of wages, repeated increases of capital will sometimes keep the market rate of wages for long periods above the natural rate; and what is more, he informs us later in the same chapter (63/108) that England had been enjoying just such a period of prosperity —it had, he said, been passing through 'a period of progressive

[1] Ricardo always seems to assume that there was once a Golden Age, when the land yielded abundance for very little effort. This assumption was well dealt with by Dr. Chalmers in chap. 1, paragraph 5, of his work *On Political Economy* (1832).

prosperity, when funds for the maintenance of labour have regularly increased, and when an increase of population would be naturally called for'. On page 95(151) he refers to this in more detail; he writes:

> Notwithstanding the immense expenditure of the English government during the last twenty years,[1] there can be little doubt but that the increased production on the part of the people has more than compensated for it. The national capital has not merely been unimpaired, it has been greatly increased, and the annual revenue of the people, even after the payment of their taxes, is probably greater at the present time than at any former period of our history. For the proof of this, we might refer to the increase of population—to the extension of agriculture—to the building of docks—to the opening of numerous canals, as well as to many other expensive undertakings; all denoting an increase both of capital and of annual production.[2]

With capital thus rapidly increasing, wages according to Ricardo's doctrine would be above the natural rate; hence his remark on page 55(97) with regard to the comforts 'now enjoyed' by the labourer does not appear very logical—as evidence that the natural rate of wages includes moderate comforts he points to the luxuries to be found in the English cottage at a time when wages are above the natural rate.

If in the south of England the natural rate of wages affords the labourer such a 'luxury' diet as white bread it is, according to Malthus, because the labourers will suffer themselves and their families to be half-starved rather than submit to a coarser diet; and if the married labourer, when wages are at the natural rate, can furnish himself with beer and tobacco we must suppose it is for the same reason, namely, that when he receives his wage his first care is to provide himself with these indispensable luxuries, while his wife and children have to survive as best they can upon what is left after these deductions.

The poverty and distress of the labouring class were much

[1] A period of war, ending at Waterloo, 1815.

[2] Malthus also bears witness to 'that rapid and astonishing increase in the value of the national wealth which has taken place during the last thirty or forty years' (*Principles of Political Economy*, 1820, page 422 in first edition; page 368 in second edition).

deplored by Ricardo and Malthus, but they thought that no one could help them if they did not help themselves. 'The friends of humanity', wrote Ricardo, 'cannot but wish that in all countries the labouring classes should have a taste for comforts and enjoyments. . . . There cannot be a better security against a superabundant population.' We may be quite certain Ricardo did not mean by this that the friends of humanity would rejoice if the labourers half-starved their children in order that they might indulge their taste for 'more tobacco, better clothes'. What he and Malthus wanted to see was a diminution in the number of births (the preventive check to over-population), and Ricardo's meaning is that if the labourers developed a more pronounced taste for comforts and enjoyments, the labourer who already hesitates a little before marrying on eighteenpence a day might be unwilling to marry on less than two shillings or half a crown. Both Ricardo and Malthus appear to have thought that the way, and the only way, to secure a slower growth in the quantity of labour, and a better standard of living, was by putting a stop to 'early and improvident marriages'.

Neither Ricardo nor Malthus, however, expected that the labourers would listen to their advice. Although Ricardo suggests that the English labourer would shrink from marriage if it imperilled his allowance of white bread, his real doctrine is that after hesitating a little the labourer invariably succumbs to the delights of domestic society, and it is left entirely to Nature's positive check to see that population is proportioned to the quantity of white flour available. Owing to the saving habits of the capitalist class the wages fund increases from time to time, and wages rise; but an increase in the number of labourers always follows, and wages fall again. 'However much the market price of labour may deviate from its natural price, it has, like commodities, a tendency to conform to it' (53/94). The market rate oscillates about but never diverges far or for long from the natural rate; and the natural rate is the wage that just suffices to keep the population stationary.

This, of course, is not what Adam Smith understood by the natural rate. According to his definition (quoted at the beginning of this chapter) the natural rate in an advancing society will be different from that in a stationary society. This was also the opinion of Malthus. When, in 1820, Ricardo opened his friend's newly published volume of *Principles*, he found the following criticism:

> Mr. Ricardo has defined the natural price of labour to be that price which is necessary to enable the labourers one with another to subsist, and to perpetuate their race, without either increase or diminution. This price I should really be disposed to call a most unnatural price; because in a natural state of things, that is, without great impediments to the progress of wealth and population, such a price could not generally occur for hundreds of years. But if this price be really rare, and, in an ordinary state of things, at so great a distance in point of time, it must evidently lead to great errors to consider the market-prices of labour as only temporary deviations above and below that fixed price to which they will very soon return.[1]

This criticism appears to be justified. Ricardo's own teaching is that capital is constantly increasing, and that every increase of capital is followed by an increase of population. On page 71(120) he tells us that capital and population will not cease to grow until the only land left uncultivated is such as cannot be made to yield a profit; and this is not likely to happen, says Malthus, for hundreds of years. If, pending the arrival of this stationary condition, there is a more or less continuous increase of capital and population, it can scarcely be correct to say that there is a tendency for wages to settle at a rate that prevents increase of population.

To be consistent, Ricardo should have said that what tends to remain stationary, or to re-establish itself if disturbed by a rise or fall of wages, is not the quantity of population but the standard of living. The labourer whose wage is increased may for a time indulge in tobacco, or beer, or fine clothes; but he marries, and must soon bid farewell to these luxuries in order to provide food and clothing for children. Thus the old pinched standard of living returns, although there has been no increase in the number of labourers participating in the wages fund. Ricardo appears seldom to pay any attention to this point. His language usually seems to imply that every addition to population is an addition to the supply of labour. No doubt it is, 'in the long run'.[2] But, said

[1] Malthus' *Principles*, first edition, page 247. In the second edition the wording is slightly altered, page 223. For Ricardo's comments on this passage, see page 227 in vol. 2.

[2] 'The increase of labour is the increase of mankind; of population,' said J. S. Mill, *Principles*, Bk. 1, chap. 10, section 2.

Malthus, 'it is obvious that from the very nature of population, and the time required to bring full-grown labourers into the market, a sudden increase of capital cannot effect a proportionate supply of labour in less than sixteen or eighteen years'.[1] Ricardo recognised this, of course; on page 105(165) he said that you cannot increase the number of men 'in one or two years when there is an increase of capital'. But his tendency is to neglect this lag. Sometimes he appears to treat increase of population and increase in the number of labourers as equivalent expressions, as, for instance, when he says 'a small supply of labour, or a trifling increase in the population, will soon reduce the market price to the . . . natural price of labour' (54/96). Sixteen or eighteen years cannot be called 'soon'.

Both Malthus and Ricardo, as already remarked, appear to think that if a rise of wages causes the population to increase it is because it encourages early marriage. Both argue as though an increase of population could only be brought about by an increase in the number of births, which appears inconsistent with their assumption that in old countries the number of births is at all times in excess of the number for whom food can be provided. The progenitive powers and inclinations of the poor do not require the stimulus of high wages; the testimony of Cobbett is that children are born even though their parents have nothing to eat but wayside nuts, and Adam Smith tells us that poverty 'seems even to be favourable to generation. A half-starved Highland woman frequently bears more than twenty children, while a pampered fine lady is often incapable of bearing any, and is generally exhausted by two or three.'[2] As George Dawson said: 'Amongst the mysteries of nature is this one, that where means are small, brats are many.'[3] And (for what it may be worth) we have it on the authority of Mr. Jaggers (in *Great Expectations*) that the children of the poor are 'generated in great numbers for certain destruction'. Poverty, then, does not prevent propagation; what it

[1] Page 307 in first edition of Malthus' *Principles*. The same paragraph slightly modified will be found on page 280 in the second edition. Neither Ricardo nor Malthus takes into account the child-labour which was such a disgrace to that period—little children working like slaves twelve hours a day, terrified little boys suffocated in chimneys.

[2] *Wealth of Nations*, Bk. 1, chap. 8, 37th paragraph.

[3] *Biographical Lectures*, edited by George St. Clair, page, 184 (Kegan Paul Trench and Co., 1886).

prevents is the rearing of the children to healthy manhood.[1] If a rise of wages enables the married labourer to carry on a more successful fight with Nature's 'positive check', some of his already half-grown children who would otherwise have fallen by the way may be enabled to reach maturity, and it may not be necessary to wait 'sixteen or eighteen years' for the increase in wages to result in an increased supply of labour. Ricardo would have done better to stick to his dictum on page 53(94) that when the labourer is well paid he is able 'to rear a healthy and numerous family'.

Let us now take stock of the situation so far as we have gone. Despite occasional references to comforts and conveniences to be found in the modern cottage, Ricardo habitually thinks of the labourer's wage as affording him nothing beyond necessaries. The additions made year after year to the wages fund fail to produce any improvement in the labourer's standard of living because 'in long-settled countries . . . population increases faster than the funds required for its support' (56/99). That is to say, population *tends* to outrun subsistence, but of course cannot do so; Nature's 'positive check' prevents it. For the married labourer, life is one continuous struggle to keep the wolf from the cottage door in the shape of periodical visits from the undertaker. Money wages are never for long high enough to provide anything in excess of food, clothing, and shelter. When money wages rise permanently it is because, owing to the law of diminishing returns, the cost of subsistence has risen; if the cost of subsistence falls, there will be a corresponding fall of money wages. This is Ricardo's doctrine from end to end of his book. 'The only adequate and permanent cause for the rise of wages is the increasing difficulty of providing food and necessaries for the increasing number of workmen' (197/296). It is 'absolutely certain' that wages will rise if the price of corn rises (64/111).[2] 'It is impossible to conceive that the money

[1] 'Poverty, though it does not prevent the generation, is extremely unfavourable to the rearing of children. . . . It is not uncommon, I have been frequently told, in the Highlands of Scotland for a mother who has borne twenty children, not to have two alive'—*The Wealth of Nations*, Bk. 1, chap. 8, 38th paragraph.

[2] This emphatic statement, to be sure, appears to be qualified shortly afterwards when he says that profits 'are lowered by a rise in the price of raw produce, if it be accompanied by a rise of wages' (67/115). The logical interpretation of this 'if' seems to be that the price of raw produce may sometimes rise without causing money wages to rise, and his footnote suggests that a

price of wages[1] should remain stationary with a gradually increasing price of necessaries' (70/118). 'We have seen in treating on Wages that they invariably rise with a rise in the price of raw produce' (68/116). The labourer's money wages rise 'to enable him to live just as well and no better than before' (58/103). On the other hand, if the cost of producing the labourer's clothes should fall 'it is probable his wages would in no long time be adjusted by the effects of competition, and the stimulus to population, to the new value of the necessaries on which they were expended' (9/16). 'Diminish the cost of subsistence of men, by diminishing the natural price of the food and clothing by which life is sustained, and wages will ultimately fall' (260/382). 'It has been one of the objects of this work to show that with every fall in the real value of necessaries' (i.e. in their cost of production) 'the wages of labour would fall' (287/420).

And since the labourer has no margin above the bare cost of living, it follows that he cannot pay any taxes unless his wage is raised to enable him to do so—or rather, it follows that if part of his wage is taken in taxes he will have less to spend on food and necessaries, with the result that, owing to deficient nourishment, the number of labourers will diminish, and wages will automatically rise. 'Taxes on wages', says Ricardo (140/215), 'will raise wages. . . . We have already seen that a tax on necessaries will raise their prices, and will be followed by a rise of wages.' Since labourers cannot pay taxes, 'a tax on wages is wholly a tax on profits'. This does not mean that capitalists are the only tax-payers, for landlords also can pay taxes;

---

temporary rise in the price of corn due to a bad season will not cause a rise of wages. In the *Notes on Malthus* (vol. 2, p. 265) he quotes the above words as evidence that he had recognised that wages might rise from some other cause than a rise in the price of corn—they will rise temporarily if an addition is made to the wages fund.

[1] This curious expression occurred several times in Ricardo's first edition, but now survives only in the above passage and on page 103(163). Presumably he had in mind his own dictum in his pamphlet on an *Economical Currency* (vol. 4, p. 60) that when speaking of the value of anything *in money* the correct word to use is *price*. Malthus used the expression 'price of wages' in a letter to Ricardo dated 23rd April, 1815 (vol. 6, p. 223). See Sraffa's Introduction to vol. 1, p. li. On page 269(394) Ricardo refers to 'the value of wages', which should either be the *rate* of wages or the value or price of *labour*.

but not labourers. On page 234(347) we have the following statement:

> The whole produce of the land and labour of every country is divided into three portions;[1] of these, one portion is devoted to wages, another to profits, and the other to rent. It is from the last two portions only that any deductions can be made for taxes or for savings; the former,[2] if moderate, constituting always the necessary expenses of production.

It is true that, in revising his book for its third edition, Ricardo introduced at this point a footnote reading as follows:

> Perhaps this is expressed too strongly, as more is generally allotted to the labourer under the name of wages, than the absolutely necessary expenses of production. In that case a part of the net produce of the country is received by the labourer, and may be saved or expended by him; or it may enable him to contribute to the defence of the country.

It would be a great mistake, I think, to interpret this as meaning that Ricardo intended to withdraw any of the arguments or conclusions set forth in his text. He is emphatic that it is only from what he calls the nation's 'net real income' that taxes can be paid. There was no alteration of his view in this respect.[3] Where he had expressed himself 'too strongly' was in his assumption that no portion whatever of this net real income finds its way into the pockets of wage-earners. The footnote acknowledges that what is given to the labourer 'under the name of wages' may be a little above the indispensable minimum necessary for subsistence. Hence, instead of representing the whole of the net real income as going into the pockets of landlords and capitalists, he should have said that *practically* the whole of it does so. That is the full extent of this modification. His theory remains what it was from the beginning. It continues to be based on the assumption that those

[1] Compare with the opening statement in his Preface.

[2] I.e. wages.

[3] I confess that I do not understand what Ricardo meant by the following remark with which he concludes his 'Advertisement' to the third edition of his *Principles*: 'I have endeavoured to show that the ability to pay taxes depends, not on the gross money value of the mass of commodities, nor on the net money value of the revenues of capitalists and landlords, but on the money value of each man's revenue, compared to the money value of the commodities which he usually consumes.'

who have nothing to live on except what they earn by their toil must look to the wages fund of the capitalists for the means of subsistence, and the never-ceasing competition for a share of this fund which arises from the never-ceasing growth of the population, prevents wages ever remaining for long above the indispensable minimum necessary for subsistence.[1]

Ricardo's assumption that all labour is remunerated at the same rate differs widely from the teaching of Adam Smith, who said, as we saw at the beginning of this chapter, that the interplay of supply and demand in the market determines the ordinary rate of wages for each different kind of employment.[2] The tailor is not paid the same wage as the weaver, nor the blacksmith the same as the collier.[3] Some workmen, Smith tells us, can afford to visit a puppet-show, or to pay taxes, or even to keep a servant.[4] Nature's positive check, which Ricardo assumes to operate among all classes of labour, operates, according to Smith, only amongst the

[1] In distinguishing the nation's total income into rents, profits and wages, Ricardo treats rent as remuneration for the use of land, and he similarly treats profit as remuneration for the use of capital. Not only may landlords be idlers without any loss of income, but capitalists are in the same position. In both cases the income figures as an income derived from ownership of property. Profit is always assumed to be strictly in proportion to the quantity of capital employed (see Table A in our third chapter). If the owner of the capital himself plays any part in productive industry, it is confined to deciding from time to time in which branch of industry his capital shall be employed.

So convinced was Ricardo that it is only owners of property who can pay anything (or anything substantial) in the way of taxes that he based on this assumption his scheme (which he often mentioned in Parliament) for repayment of the National Debt by a levy on property. He sought to convince his fellow property-owners that they would be just as well off after the levy as before. His argument, as I understand it, was this. When the Government borrow £20,000 at 5 per cent, it is the property-owner who lends them the money and receives the annual interest of £1000; it is the property-owner who must pay the Government £1000 every year in taxes to enable them to pay the interest. The property-owner would be just as well off if the debt and the interest and the tax were all wiped out (see Ricardo's essay on the Funding System, vol. 4, p. 187). Incidentally, the fact that professional men with large incomes from personal exertion would be quite capable of contributing to the tax, but would escape it if they were not property-owners, is admitted by Ricardo on page 188; but he only mentions the point to minify its importance.

[2] See also 4th paragraph in chap. 5 of *The Wealth of Nations*, and the elaborate discussion in chap. 10.

[3] Ibid., chap. 10, 2nd paragraph in Part 1.

[4] Ibid., Bk. 2, chap. 3, 7th paragraph.

poorest: 'In civilised society', he says, 'it is only among the inferior ranks of people that the scantiness of subsistence can set limits to the further multiplication of the human species.'[1]

But (apart from section 2 in his first chapter) Ricardo does not recognise different classes of labour;[2] he treats capital as a mass all of which earns the same rate of profit, and labour as another mass all of which is paid the same rate of wages. The capitalist and the labourer share the product as a mass of value (64/110), and while the proportions in which the value is divided between each unit of capital and each unit of labour may be different at one period from what they are at another, they are not different in one employment from another. Now whatever may be said for this view in the case of capital, it is obviously far from true that all kinds and qualities of labour can be had in the market at the same price. How did Ricardo come to adopt so false an assumption? It may be that when he started out to frame a theory of wages he adopted this simplified assumption tentatively 'for the ends of discourse', as James Mill put it. John Mill, the son, who was still in his teens when Ricardo died, later on defended this method of approach as follows:

> Under the head of wages are to be considered, first, the causes which determine or influence the wages of labour generally, and secondly, the differences which exist between the wages of different employments. It is convenient to keep these two classes of consideration separate; and in discussing the law of wages, to proceed in the first instance as if there were no other kind of labour than common unskilled labour of the average degree of hardness and disagreeableness.[3]

It may have been in this way that Ricardo was originally led to adopt the assumption that all labour is of the same quality and all remunerated at the same rate; and it may be that, overlooking the

[1] *The Wealth of Nations*, Bk. 1, chap. 8, 39th paragraph. In his *Essay on Population* (page 71, first edition) Malthus adopted this with a modification: 'The positive check to population . . . is confined chiefly, though not perhaps solely, to the lowest orders of society.'

[2] Unless in the following sense: 'There are, as you observe, two classes of labourers, the single and the married. . . . We must suppose then that the single men receive more than their wants require' (vol. 7, p. 133). 'The single man amongst the labouring class may bear, and often does bear, his portion of taxation' (vol. 8, p. 172).

[3] J. S. Mill's *Principles*, Bk. 2, chap. 11, 1st paragraph.

fictitious nature of the assumption, he proceeded to build upon it the conclusion that goods produced by equal quantities of labour will have equal value and will sell at the same price. But if he did not discover his error before sitting down to write his book, he became aware of it very soon after, for in the second section of his first chapter he acknowledges that the working jeweller is paid at one rate and the agricultural labourer at another. Did he not recognise that this reduced to nonsense the proposition that goods produced by equal quantities of labour will sell at the same price? Whether he did or not, the fact is that in section 2 of his first chapter his recognition of differences in the rate of pay is accompanied by an announcement of his intention to ignore them, and a curtain of silence thereafter conceals the troublesome factor.

But curiously enough this curtain of silence is unaccountably lifted for a moment in two of his chapters on taxation. On page 140(215), in a chapter dealing with Taxes on Wages, he has occasion to quote a passage from Adam Smith which commences with the words: 'The wages of the inferior classes of workmen.' This expression implies that there are higher and lower grades of labour. Ricardo does not comment on this at the time, but the distinction made by Smith must have been in his mind when, three pages later, he wrote as follows:

> Suppose the circumstances of the country to be such that the lowest labourers are not only called upon to continue their race, but to increase it; their wages would be regulated accordingly. Can they multiply in the degree required if a tax takes from them a part of their wages, and reduces them to bare necessaries? (143/220).

Here, then, he appears to accept the view that there is more than one rate of wages, and that the wages of 'the lowest labourers' may be raised while in the higher ranks of labour wages remain unaltered. How could Ricardo make such an admission as this, and yet continue to maintain that the value of products is in proportion to the quantity of labour employed upon them, and is not affected by 'the greater or less compensation which is paid for that labour' (see heading of first chapter)? If one article is produced by a week's labour for which the capitalist pays ten shillings, and another by a week's labour for which he pays forty shillings, it is obvious that he cannot sell them both at the same price and make (as Ricardo assumes) the same rate of profit on his outlay in both cases. If goods sell for what they cost to produce, the ratio in which they exchange for one another cannot be in proportion to the quantity of labour unless the 'compensation' paid for that labour is at the same rate in both cases; and the relative values or costs cannot be unaffected if the rate of wages changes in one case and not in the other. It must surely have been in an unguarded moment that Ricardo allowed some imp of mischief to bring back into his pages the idea of different rates of pay which he had so neatly disposed of in section 2 of his first chapter.

I have said that differences in the rate of wages are recognised in two of Ricardo's chapters on taxation; the other is the chapter on Taxes on Raw Produce. On page 100(159) he writes:

> A tax, however, on raw produce, and on the necessaries of the labourer, would have another effect—it would raise wages. From the effect of the principle of population on the increase of mankind, wages of the lowest kind never continue much above that rate which nature and habit demand for the support of the labourers. This class is never able to bear any considerable proportion of taxation; and consequently, if they had to pay 8*s.* per quarter in addition for wheat, and in some smaller proportion for other necessaries, they would not be able to subsist on the same wages as before, and to keep up the race of labourers. Wages would inevitably and necessarily rise; and in proportion as they rose, profits would fall.

What are we to think of Ricardo's logic here? On page 58(103) he estimates that to perpetuate the race undiminished the labourer and his family require as food three quarters of wheat per annum. A tax of eight shillings on each quarter would therefore add twenty-four shillings a year, or about sixpence a week, to his cost of living. Ricardo's inference in the above paragraph appears to be that because the lowest-paid labourer cannot pay this tax, therefore all wages would rise. That he assumes the rise of wages will be general is made plain by his statements that a tax on wages is wholly a tax on profits (140/215), and that none but landlords and capitalists can pay taxes (234/347–8). Moreover, it does not appear very logical to infer that because the labourer is unable to bear 'any considerable proportion of taxation' he will therefore pay no tax at all. On page 154(235) Ricardo writes: 'Dr. Smith uniformly, and I think justly, contends that the labouring classes cannot materially contribute to the burdens of the state. A tax on necessaries, or on wages, will therefore be shifted from the poor to the rich.' Thus the whole tax falls on the rich because the poor, or some of the poor, cannot pay much of it! This is not Smith's reasoning, for Smith said that although the individual labourer cannot materially contribute to taxation, yet so great is the number of labourers that their total contribution might be considerable.[1]

Perhaps it will be suggested that there is nothing illogical in assuming that all wages will rise when the minimum rate rises, if we bear in mind the dictum of Adam Smith (behind which Ricardo sheltered in section 2 of chapter 1), that the various scales of pay tend to keep the same ratio to one another at all times. But it is not possible to explain Ricardo's reasoning on page 100(159) in this way. His conclusion is not that if the lowest wage rises by 5 per cent, all wages will rise by 5 per cent; his contention is that if the cost of living is increased by sixpence a week every labourer's wage will be increased by sixpence a week. 'The labourers, it is agreed, would be recompensed for the tax', is what he says on page 146(223). The additional sixpence a week would enable every labourer to live as well as, but no better than, before (58/103), whereas if the labourer whose wage was forty shillings received an additional 5 per cent, or two shillings, when his cost of living had only risen by sixpence, he would be able to live better than before, which could hardly be called mere 'compensation' or mere 'shifting' of the tax from the poor to the rich.

Ricardo's conclusion that all wages will rise by sixpence a week if the cost of food rises by sixpence a week requires the assumption (which appears to have been ever present in his mind, whatever admissions he may make at odd moments) that there is only one rate of wages, and this rate so low that the number of labourers will diminish if there is any reduction in the wage. To admit that there are different scales of pay is virtually to abandon this tenet, and with it the tenet that price is in proportion to the quantity of labour; and as Ricardo had no intention of abandoning these doctrines we might suppose that the reference on page 100(159) to 'wages of the lowest kind' was a mere slip or oversight were it not that on page 143(220), as we have seen, he again refers to 'the lowest labourers' in a paragraph which he carefully revised for his third edition.

And this passage on page 143 affords another puzzle. Ricardo, as we have seen, accepted the wages-fund theory. He represents

[1] *Wealth of Nations*, Bk. 2, chap. 3, 7th paragraph.

the capitalists as beginning each year with a supply of food and necessaries for distribution as wages; each labourer receives an equal share, and whether he fares well or ill depends upon the number of labourers and the size of the pool that is shared amongst them. This pool or fund is increased from time to time; it is not increased because the labourers require more money, but because the capitalists every year make fresh savings and add to their capital. If population increases more rapidly than capital, wages fall, and the condition of the labourer deteriorates. Nature's positive check is always at work, and the number of labourers automatically adjusts itself to the size of the fund. But on page 143(219) this doctrine seems to be practically reversed. Ricardo is anxious to prove that a tax on wages raises wages, and he says:

> Nothing is more common than to see hats or malt rise when taxed; they rise because the requisite supply would not be afforded if they did not rise; so with labour, when wages are taxed its price rises, because if it did not, the requisite population would not be kept up.

This does not give one the idea of a fixed wages fund to which the quantity of population must adapt itself as best it can. On the contrary, the impression it conveys is that the capitalists require a certain quantity of labour, and are not to be balked in obtaining what they want by a mere rise in price. If they cannot obtain the quantity they require at the old price, they will offer more; if a tax threatens to diminish their supply, they will compensate the labourer rather than allow their supply to be diminished. Instead of population being called upon to adjust itself to a given wages fund, it is the wages fund that will be increased in order that the 'requisite population', or supply of labour, may be kept up. 'In proportion to the work to be done will be the demand for those who are to do it.'[1]

There seems to be something hazy about Ricardo's thought in regard to wages. The idea that if an employer cannot get as much labour as he requires at a low price, he will offer a higher price, is reasonable enough, but it is not consistent with Ricardo's teaching on the subject of wages. According to his theory, if employers increase their capital from time to time it is not because they think

[1] This remark seems appropriate here; it seems strangely out of place on page 54(95).

the condition of the labourers needs raising; nor because the labourers are clamouring for better pay; it is because, whatever may be the condition of the labouring class, the aim of every capitalist is to increase his capital, and therefore every year he endeavours to make some addition to his savings. There is nothing in Ricardo's theory of wages to suggest that if a tax is imposed on the labourer's wages, or on his food, the employer will promptly compensate him by giving him more money. On the contrary, the theory implies that if a tax is deducted from the labourer's wage, he will have to get along as best he can with a reduced standard of living until privation and suffering have diminished the number of labourers participating in the wages fund, thereby causing a rise in the rate per man. Ricardo is prepared to be told, but not prepared to agree, 'that there would be a considerable interval between the rise in the price of corn and the rise of wages, during which much distress would be experienced by the labourer' (101/160). He recognises that the number of labourers cannot be reduced quickly, like the supply of hats (105/165), but he has a habit of belittling or minifying the importance of intervals that interrupt or delay the operation of long-term trends, and he remarks that some people 'seem to have conceded too readily that . . . a rise in the price of necessaries will be very slowly succeeded by a rise . . . of wages' (102/161). To prove that there would be no considerable period of distress[1] he brings forward the following remarkable argument (105/166):

> A tax on corn does not necessarily diminish the quantity of corn, it only raises its money price; it does not necessarily diminish the demand compared with the supply of labour; why should it diminish the portion paid to the labourer? Suppose it true that it did diminish the quantity given to the labourer, in other words, that it did not raise his money wages in the same proportion as the tax raised the price of the corn which he consumed; would not the supply of corn exceed the demand?—would it not fall in price? and would not the labourer thus obtain his usual portion? In such cases, indeed, capital would be withdrawn from agriculture; for if the price were not increased by the whole amount of the tax, agricultural profits would

[1] Ricardo does not seem to recognise that, according to his theory, there is *always* distress in the labourer's home except when wages are *above* what he calls the natural rate, since it is only the insufficient nourishment of children that keeps the population down to a stationary condition.

> be lower than the general level of profits, and capital would seek a more advantageous employment. In regard then to a tax on raw produce, which is the point under discussion, it appears to me that no interval which could bear oppressively on the labourer would elapse between the rise in the price of raw produce and the rise in the wages of the labourers.

Ricardo's first suggestion here is that if wages did not rise when the price of corn was increased, the farmers would recognise that much of their crop would be left on their hands unsold, and would therefore hasten to reduce the price to its former level. This hardly seems a reason for assuming that wages would rise promptly, but rather the reverse.

His next suggestion is that if wages did not rise, and the farmers had to sell their corn at the old price, less corn would be produced next year. Ricardo's opening statement was that a tax on corn does not necessarily diminish the supply, but only raises its money price;[1] but here he shows that a rise in the money price will cause a diminished demand, and the diminished demand will be followed by a diminished production. And when this rise of price and reduced production occurs, the labourers must suffer a period of distress which will last until their numbers have decreased and caused wages to rise.[2]

To make any sense of Ricardo's argument in this passage we must suppose him to mean that when corn rises in price the capitalists will foresee that if they do not raise wages the supply of labour will diminish, and as this will not suit them, they will make

[1] 'Nothing is to me so little important as the fall and rise of commodities in money' (vol. 9, p. 83).

[2] In his *Wages and Capital*, page 177, Professor Taussig commented as follows on the above argument of Ricardo's: 'It is not easy to make out by what process Ricardo thought that the tax on food would raise its price. His language in this chapter usually implies that the effect would be immediate; and certainly he thinks that, if this happened, money wages would rise immediately. But it is more in accord with his general mode of reasoning, and with the drift of this passage, to interpret him as concluding that the price of food would not rise at once. The first incidence of the tax is on agricultural profits; then comes a withdrawal of agricultural capital, a diminution of the supply of food; and so a rise in price. How, after this, "no interval which could bear oppressively on the labourer would elapse between the rise in the price of raw produce and the rise in the wages of the labourer", it is difficult to see. Apparently money wages can then rise only in consequence of a decline in population; a process which in fact must bear very oppressively.'

up their minds to raise wages promptly. But if this is what he had in mind, it is entirely inconsistent with his theory of the automatic regulation of wages through the instrumentality of Nature's positive check.

On page 144(220) Ricardo brings forward a different kind of argument to show that when labour is taxed 'there is no necessary diminution in the demand for labour'. His argument here is that—

> the fund raised by the tax is employed by the Government in maintaining labourers, unproductive indeed, but still labourers.[1] If [the price of] labour were not to rise when wages are taxed, there would be a great increase in the competition for labour, because the owners of capital, who would have nothing to pay towards such a tax, would have the same funds for employing labour, whilst the Government who received the tax would have an additional fund for the same purpose. Government and people then become competitors, and the consequence of their competition is a rise in the price of labour. The same number of men only will be employed, but they will be employed at additional wages.

Ricardo's idea appears to be this. If the capitalists have a wages fund of £1,000,000, which employs 40,000 men (£25 a year each), and the government decides to spend £40,000 in wages for additional soldiers or police, the total amount paid to the wage-earners will be increased to £1,040,000; which, as there is no increase in the available supply of labourers, will have the effect of raising wages from £25 to £26. The government obtains the £40,000 by taxing every wage-earner £1, but as each man now receives £1 more than before, his net wage remains £25.

Here Ricardo's conclusion that the labourer will be promptly compensated for the tax is arrived at in a more logical manner than on page 105(166). Whether the rise of wages will fully compensate him for the tax, however, is not altogether clear. We must suppose, I think, that if some of the labourers are withdrawn from productive industry, and employed on unproductive services, there will be a diminution in the product. If the wage-earners have the same amount of money to spend as before, and the capitalists

[1] The reader will note that this reference to unproductive labourers, as well as the reference to labour of different grades already quoted, occurs in a chapter discussing taxation, not in his chapter on wages, where the existence of unproductive labourers (those who receive payment for personal services) is entirely ignored.

still have the same money income, prices must rise when the product to be divided amongst wage-earners and capitalists is diminished. If the tax had been placed on profit, thereby diminishing the spending power of the capitalists without interfering with that of the wage-earners, we might perhaps assume that the diminution of product would be entirely a diminution in the production of luxuries.

It will be noted that Ricardo's conclusion on page 144(220) that the tax on wages will be promptly compensated, is based as he himself points out on the assumption that the tax collected from the labourers is expended by the government on the employment of labour; in the next paragraph he remarks: 'If when the tax were levied, Government at once exported the produce of it as a subsidy to a foreign State, and if therefore these funds were devoted to the maintenance of foreign, and not of English labourers, such as soldiers, sailors, etc., etc., then indeed there would be a diminished demand for labour, and wages might not increase, although they were taxed'—which is a notable qualification of the dictum on page 140(215) that 'Taxes on wages will raise wages'.

But why does Ricardo say that wages *might* not rise, which implies that they might. In a letter to Ricardo, McCulloch imagined just such a case as Ricardo postulates:

> Suppose Ireland is obliged to remit a subsidy of 10 millions to Russia, and that there are two methods of raising it—a duty on potatoes and a duty on claret and coaches. If the first be adopted it is plain that wages will not rise in proportion to the duty; for as the subsidy is to be remitted to a foreign country, it cannot enable the government to employ more labour, and as the number of labourers will remain the same, and the demand for their labour is not increased, they must continue to suffer the extreme of misery until the pressure of famine or the slackened operation of the principle of population shall have equalised the supply and demand.[1]

If the tax were levied on claret and coaches it would fall on the rich; there might be a reduced production and consumption of these luxuries, but the labourers would still obtain their food (potatoes) at the old price and in the same abundance.

Ricardo himself, in the paragraph last referred to, suggests that when the government wanted to employ unproductive labourers

[1] Vol. 8, p. 189. Ricardo's reply, page 195, does not appear to me very clear.

they might tax the capitalists instead of the wage-earners; but the strange thing is that instead of assuming, as he usually does, that the tax will fall on profits, he supposes it in this case to fall on circulating capital: 'If the tax had been laid at once on the people of capital, their fund for the maintenance of labour would have been diminished in the very same degree that the fund of the government for that purpose had been increased' (144/221). Surely Ricardo cannot have meant that if the government imposed the same tax for a second year there would be another reduction of circulating capital, and if the tax were repeated for a third and fourth year (as it might be in the case of a long war) the process of taxing circulating capital out of existence would be continued?[1] Why, then, does Ricardo depart from his usual teaching? He tells us on page 234(347) that all taxes are paid from rents or profits. It is true that on pages 94 and 95(150 and 151) he tells us that taxes fall either on capital or revenue; and in the passage with which we are now dealing he says (145/222) that taxes 'commonly either diminish capital or retard its accumulation'. But I think these passages only mean that if taxation is excessive there is a danger that capital may be encroached upon. No man can spend more than his income, no country can consume more than it produces, without encroaching on capital. If the government takes so much of your income that you cannot keep your house in proper repair, if your carpets and clothes wear out faster than you can replace them, and your stock of crockery is from time to time diminished by breakages which you are unable to make good, then you are living partly on your capital. The industrialist is in a similar situation if heavy taxes prevent his providing for depreciation. When he sells his product he normally devotes part of his receipts to the re-employment of labour, but if a heavy demand from the tax-gatherer prevents his employing the same number of men as before, his circulating capital is diminished. But I do not think Ricardo meant to go further than this. In one of his *Notes on Blake* (vol. 4, p. 339) he says: 'There can be no doubt that a nation may make great inroads on its capital', but he probably means it *might* or *could* make such inroads, for he adds: 'In point of fact, it never does, because public extravagance is met by private frugality and savings.'

[1] Blake (1823) refers to this 'conversion of capital into revenue' and devotes himself to its *reductio ad absurdum*. See vol. 4, pp. 338 and 339.

It would be wrong, I think, to close this chapter without some notice of the conditions prevailing at the time when Ricardo launched his theory of wages upon the world. His pages contain little reflection of what those conditions were. In one respect his picture is faithful enough; he did not exaggerate the poverty of the lowest class of labour. On the other hand, his statements that it is 'absolutely certain' that wages will rise if the price of corn rises (64/111), that wages 'invariably rise with the rise in the price of raw produce' (68/116), and that it is inconceivable that wages should remain stationary 'with a gradually increasing price of necessaries' (70/118), must have struck his contemporaries as very strange in view of the actual conditions with which their daily life made them familiar. He was no doubt justified in saying that 'the necessity which the labourer would be under of paying an increased price for such necessaries would oblige him to demand more wages' (70/118); but in those days there were no trade unions,[1] and according to Ricardo's own theory the only way in which the labourers could make their demand effective was by allowing privation to thin their ranks.

So little, in fact, did wages keep pace with the rising price of corn that in 1795 Whitbread introduced a Bill into Parliament with the object of compelling employers to raise money wages when the price of corn rose. The condition of the agricultural labourer, which had once been happy, had sunk to a state of misery, because money wages had remained pretty much the same as they were in the early part of the century, namely, a shilling or eighteenpence a day,[2] while the price of wheat had risen from twenty-two shillings a quarter to eighty shillings or more.[3]

Whitbread's proposal was rejected by Parliament. Nevertheless, something had to be done if wholesale starvation was to be avoided, and the local authorities, who were responsible for relieving the poor, dealt with the matter in their own way. Under

[1] The only instance of anything at all resembling a workers' trade union that I know of in the eighteenth century was that of domestic servants in London in early Georgian days. 'It was said that while no servants in Europe were so highly paid or so well fed as the English, none were so insolent, uncertain or nomadic . . . Servants had their clubs, and their societies for maintaining each other when out of place' (Lecky's *England in the Eighteenth Century*, vol. 2, pp. 218/219 in the 1913 edition).

[2] Thorold Rogers, *Six Centuries of Work and Wages*, eighth edition, page 404. [3] Ibid., page 407.

an old Act of Elizabeth the Justices of the Peace had the power to fix the rate of wages in each district;[1] but the practice had fallen into disuse, except in the case of the silk-weavers of Spitalfields, who had their own special Act. The manner in which the Justices dealt with the situation is described by Thorold Rogers as follows:

> On May 6th, 1795, a meeting of the Berkshire magistrates was held at Speenhamland . . . when it was unanimously affirmed that the state of the poor required larger assistance than had been given them generally. The meeting also decided that it was not expedient for the magistrates to grant that assistance by regulating wages according to the statute of Elizabeth, but that the magistrates should earnestly recommend the farmers and others to increase the pay of their labourers according to the price of provisions. They thereupon put out a scale, in which they calculated what should be the wages of workmen, according to the rise or fall in the price of bread. . . . Thus when the gallon loaf should cost a shilling, they reckoned that the labourer should receive, either by his own earnings or by an allowance from the poor rates, three shillings weekly for himself and one shilling and sixpence for each of his family, and that with the rise of every penny in the loaf, he should receive an additional threepence for himself and one penny for each of his family.[2]

This decision of the Berkshire Justices did not, of course, oblige other counties to follow suit; but as a matter of fact it was such a boon to have a fixed rule to go by, that most of them did so. Thus a practice was introduced by which, if the wages of the labourer were insufficient to enable him to maintain a subsistence standard for his family, whether large or small, the amount would be made up to him by a Poor Law grant.

The result of this system was what might have been expected. With every child a source of additional income to the labourer, Nature's positive check was set at defiance, and the increase of population was 'beyond what the case required'. The Poor Rates grew alarmingly. The number of children was not the only cause of this. The earnest recommendation of the Justices that farmers

[1] As a matter of fact, Elizabeth's Act only gave the Justices power to fix the maximum rate; it was an Act of James I that gave them the power to fix a minimum rate. See *The Village Labourer*, by J. L. and B. Hammond, page 109 in 1924 edition.

[2] *Six Centuries of Work and Wages*, page 408 in the eighth edition.

and others should raise wages when prices rose, does not appear to have touched the hearts or consciences of the employers; on the contrary, when they found that the community was prepared to make good any deficiency in wages, too many of them seized the opportunity to lower instead of raising them. It became a widespread practice to treat the Poor Law allowance as a regular part of the labourer's subsistence. The conscientious employer had to follow the example of the less conscientious, or see his products undersold in the market; and if a labourer protested that he could not live on what he received, it was pointed out to him that he would not benefit by an increase of wage because his Poor Law allowance would be correspondingly reduced.[1] Under this system, particularly when trade was bad, wages fell almost to vanishing point. In 1817 Brougham declared in Parliament that the wages of cotton-weavers, which in 1802 were 13*s.* 10*d.* a week, had fallen in 1806 to 10*s.* 6*d.*, in 1812 to 6*s.* 4*d.*, and in 1816 to 5*s.* 2*d.*; while in 1817 they had sunk to 4*s.* 3½*d.*, 'from which', said Brougham, 'when the usual expenses paid by the workpeople for the loom were deducted, there remained no more than 3*s.* 3*d.* to support human life for seven days'.[2]

Yet it was in this very year, 1817, that Ricardo said that it is 'absolutely certain' that wages will rise if the price of corn rises, and that it is 'impossible to conceive' that money wages should not rise when there is a rise in the price of necessaries; it was in this very year that he referred to the 'moderate comforts' enjoyed by the labourer and the 'conveniences' to be found in the modern cottage. Such being his aloofness from his surroundings, it is not surprising that when, a year or two later, he entered Parliament, Brougham said that he argued like a man dropped from another planet.[3]

A critic much later than Lord Brougham said of Ricardo that he legislated for Saturn. Economists, of course, do not legislate, any more than the Lord Chief Justice legislates. They endeavour, like a Judge, to discover and interpret the law. They have not the Judge's power to compel compliance with it, but they may, and as good citizens should, point out the consequences of disregarding it. This is what Ricardo endeavoured to do. In composing his *Principles* he pictured to himself a community in which economic

[1] J. L. and B. Hammond, *The Skilled Labourer*, page 92 in second edition.
[2] Smart's *Economic Annals* (1801–1820), page 595. [3] Ibid., page 733.

laws were allowed free play, without interference from either Parliament or Justices of the Peace. Under *laissez-faire*, wages, profits, prices, all find their 'natural' level. 'The price of labour will express clearly the wants of the society respecting population; it will be just sufficient to support the population which at that time the state of the funds for the maintenance of labourers requires' (143/219). While the competition of the labourers for a share of the wages fund keeps wages down, the competition of capitalists for a share of the labour supply tends to keep them up. Capital, however, would cease to accumulate if wages threatened to extinguish profit. 'The farmer and manufacturer can no more live without profit than the labourer without wages' (73/122). But profit must not be limited to what the capitalists need for the upkeep of their own families. If profit is too small the capitalists will be unable or unwilling to save; capital will cease to grow, and population will be brought to a standstill (71/120). If capitalists can spare nothing for the needs of others, then hospitals and almshouses can no longer be provided for the helpless, the aged, the crippled, and the blind. Moreover it is to rents and profits that the community must look for the support of all 'unproductive' labourers, and these include not merely soldiers and sailors to defend the country from aggression, and police and civil servants to preserve order and assure good government; they include also the painters, sculptors, musicians, composers, poets, novelists, philosophers, and many others whose labours give dignity to life and raise man above the level of the beasts (chap. 26; see also vol. 2, p. 211).

Such is the position under a system of *laissez-faire*. That system admittedly relies upon self-interest as the motive force in industry; nevertheless, it was defended by Adam Smith (a man certainly not biassed in favour of landlords or capitalists) as a more efficient promotor of human welfare than any system that relied solely on benevolence.[1] And the system may be said to have received the blessing of the Church, or at all events the blessing of a clergyman, Malthus, who wrote:

> the substitution of benevolence for self-love as the moving principle of society, instead of producing the happy effects which might be expected from so fair a name, would cause the same pressure of want

[1] *Wealth of Nations*, chap. 2, 2nd paragraph.

to be felt by the whole of society which is now felt only by a part. It is to the established administration of property, and to the apparently narrow principle of self-love, that we are indebted for all the noblest exertions of human genius, all the finer and more delicate emotions of the soul, for everything, indeed, that distinguishes the civilised from the savage state.[1]

Ricardo endorsed this teaching. Like Malthus, he regarded the Poor Rate as a diversion of rents and profits from their proper employment to the well-meant and ill-considered purpose of ameliorating the condition of the labourer—ill-considered and futile because the object in view will always be defeated by the labourer's incurable habit of multiplying up to the limit of his power; ill-considered, too, because while ineffective for the purpose in view, it brings misery on the community. In the last paragraph of his chapter on wages he says:

> If by law every human being wanting support could be sure to obtain it, and obtain it in such a degree as to make life tolerably comfortable, theory would lead us to expect that all other taxes together would be light compared with the single one of poor rates. The principle of gravitation is not more certain than the tendency of such laws to change wealth and power into misery and weakness; to call away the exertions of labour from every object except that of providing mere subsistence; to confound all intellectual distinction; to busy the mind continually in supplying the body's wants; until at last all classes should be infected with the plague of universal poverty.

To his friend Trower Ricardo writes: 'These rates are a yawning gulf in which all that is valuable will be ultimately swallowed' (vol. 7, p. 135). 'No scheme for the amendment of the Poor Laws', he says in his *Principles* (68/107), 'merits the least attention which has not their abolition for its ultimate object.' Despite the miserable condition of the labouring classes in 1817, as described by Brougham, Ricardo's view was that 'like all other contracts, wages should be left to the fair and free competition of the market, and should never be controlled by the interference of the legislature' (61/105). Consistently with this attitude, almost the last act of Ricardo's public life was to vote in Parliament for the repeal of the Law whereby the wages of the silk-weavers of Spitalfields were still fixed by the Magistrates at a figure which gave them a reasonable standard of living and made them the envy of the

[1] *Essay on Population*, page 286 in reprint of first edition.

rate-assisted labourers in other parts of the country (vol. 5, p. 292 and p. 308).

Since Ricardo recognised (chap. 26) that much 'unproductive' labour is supported out of rents and profits, and since he regarded Poor Law allowances, paid out of rents and profits, as likely to bring about an alarming increase in the population, it is surprising that he should have laid it down as an economic law (41/78) that population is regulated by the quantity of capital (i.e. by the capitalists' wages fund). What further remarks he had to make on this subject after reading the *Principles* of Malthus in 1820 will be discussed in a later chapter.

9

The Natural Tendency of Profits is to Fall

RICARDO'S Preface states that the whole produce of the Earth is divided amongst the owners of the land, the owners of capital, and the labourers upon whom devolves the work of current production. He sets out to study what determines the proportions in which these three classes share the product. These proportions change with the increase of population. A fundamental assumption of Ricardo's is that the most fertile land and the richest mines are the first to be exploited; with a growing population it becomes necessary to resort to less and less fruitful sources of supply, with the result that each equal addition to supply requires for its production a greater expenditure of labour and capital. To produce 180 quarters of wheat upon inferior land will require more labour and more capital than was required to produce that quantity upon the better land already in cultivation; or to put it in another way, the same quantity of labour and capital that produces 180 quarters on the better land will perhaps only yield 160 quarters on the inferior land now taken into cultivation.

How does this affect the proportions in which the product is divided between the different classes entitled to share it?

No land can be cultivated without labour. The wages of the labourer, therefore, are a first charge upon the product, and in fact are necessarily advanced to him while at work on the long job of production; hence when the harvest is gathered in, it is only that part of the product which exceeds the amount thus advanced that is available as profit on the farmer's capital. Now it is another fundamental assumption of Ricardo's that the labourer's wage may be regarded as the minimum necessary to keep the supply of labour in existence. If the labourers cannot survive on less than six quarters of corn each per annum, then they must each have this six quarters of corn, whether the total product is 180 or 160. Hence if the product is now 20 quarters less than formerly, it is the farmer's profit which will be reduced by that amount; he cannot look to the labourer to share the loss.

This must not be understood to mean that wages are never at any time above the irreducible minimum. When capitalists add to their capital the first result is a rise of wages; wages for a time are above what Ricardo calls the natural rate, and the labourers can indulge in a few simple luxuries; but owing to their incurable habit of multiplication it will not be long before the increase in the number of labourers overtakes the increase of the wages fund, and the rate of wages will be back at the irreducible minimum. And there is another point to be noted. Although Ricardo holds that the labourer's commodity wage is not capable of any substantial reduction without being followed by a reduction in the supply of labour, this does not imply that because the labourer received 6 quarters of corn when he produced 18, he will still require 6 quarters when he only produces 16 quarters; he may be able to live just as well as before on $5\frac{2}{3}$ quarters. The reason for this is explained by Ricardo on page 58(103). He regards the labourer's wage as practically divisible into two portions, one of which is employed in the purchase of food and the other in the purchase of such things as clothing, shelter, candles, etc. He reckons that the labourer requires three quarters of corn for food; hence when corn is at £4 a quarter he requires £12 for food and £12 for other necessaries. If corn becomes dearer he will require more than £12 for food, but he may not require more than £12 for the purchase of other necessaries, for the law of diminishing returns which has raised the price of corn may not have caused any rise in the price of other things.

Ricardo takes this into account in the figures which he furnishes on page 68(116) to illustrate the changes brought about by the law of diminishing returns. To give precision and clearness to his argument he expresses values in money. He is aware, as he tells us on page 29(46), that money made of gold varies in value like other things, but for the purpose of illustrating changes of value he asks the reader to imagine that we have a money which is free from this disadvantage. In examining his table of figures, then, we are to assume that we have a money which reflects changes in the value of other things as accurately as a yardstick, which has the same length today as it had a hundred years ago, measures changes in the length of other things with which it is compared.

The reader will bear in mind Ricardo's doctrine that the value of each commodity is determined by the quantity of labour and capital required for its production. If, then, the labour of ten men supported for a year by a certain quantity of capital produces 180 quarters of wheat, and if we assume that the value of this product is £720, then the value of each quarter is $\frac{1}{180}$th of this, or £4. If the same quantity of capital and labour could produce 200 quarters the value would still be £720 and the value of each quarter would be $\frac{1}{200}$th of this. If on the other hand this quantity of capital and labour can produce no more than 160 quarters, the value of the whole product will still be £720, and the value of each quarter will be £4 10*s*.

Ricardo starts off with the assumption that in the first instance there is plenty of first-class land free to anybody who has the capital to cultivate it, and the farmer accordingly has no rent to pay. He will require the labour of ten men and must give them 6 quarters of corn each for sustenance. He obtains a product of 180 quarters worth £720, of which £240 goes to the labourers to enable them to buy 60 quarters of corn, and £480 remains in the farmer's hands as profit.

When all the best land has been taken into cultivation, and the newcomer has to cultivate inferior land which yields only 160 quarters for the same expenditure of capital and labour, he also obtains £720 for his product, which means that the price per quarter rises to £4 10*s*. The labourer requires the same quantity of food and other necessaries as before, but 5·66 quarters instead of the former 6 quarters will enable him to live as well as before. Wages, then, absorb £255, and the farmer is left with a reduced profit of £465.

When inferior land is cultivated the better land of course continues in cultivation, and continues to yield 180 quarters for the same quantity of labour and capital. Ricardo assumes that there can be only one rate of wages, one rate of profit, and one price for wheat. If the labourers on the inferior land receive £255 as wages and the farmer £465 as profit, the farmer and his men on the better land will do the same; but the 180 quarters of wheat grown on the better land, selling now at £4 10*s*. per quarter, will yield £810. The product on the better land exceeds that on the inferior by 20 quarters, and this or its equivalent value £90 must be given to the owner of the land as rent. The landlord will see to this as soon as his tenant's lease expires, for if the tenant is not content with the same profit as the farmer of the marginal land the landlord will find another farmer on the look-out for land on which he can employ his capital at the current rate of profit. If later on it becomes necessary to cultivate land that only yields 150 quarters for the same labour and capital, the smaller product will still be worth £720; the price per quarter will rise to £4 16*s*., wages upon all qualities of land will rise to £264, and the profits of all farmers will fall to £456. Each time the margin of cultivation is extended to poorer land the rate of profit falls, but the landlords gain. The land that returns 160 quarters now pays a rent of 10 quarters, for by that amount the product exceeds the product of the poorest land cultivated; and for this reason the land that yields 180 quarters must now surrender 30 quarters to the landlord. 'Whatever cause may drive capital to inferior land', says Ricardo, 'must elevate rent on the superior land' (276/403). The landlord in fact gains in two ways. Not only does the owner of the best land now see his share of the product increase from 20 to 30 quarters, but the value of each quarter is higher than before; while the farmer's profit has fallen from £465 to £456 (a decrease of £9), the landlord's rent has risen from £90 to £144 (a gain of £54).[1]

Ricardo's doctrine that the tendency of profits is to fall is set forth on page 71(120) as follows:

> The natural tendency of profits then is to fall; for in the progress of society and wealth the additional quantity of food required is obtained by the sacrifice of more and more labour. This tendency, this gravitation as it were of profits, is happily checked at repeated intervals by the improvements in machinery connected with the

[1] Ricardo himself points this out (vol. 4, pp. 18 and 20). In view of the increase of rent being so much greater than the decrease of profit it seems strange that Ricardo should immediately follow up his remark as follows: 'Rent then is in all cases a portion of the profits previously obtained on the land.' Later, in his *Notes on Malthus* we have: 'There is no rent which did not at one time constitute profits' (vol. 2, p. 157). I think, too, Ricardo must have overlooked that if a hitherto untapped source of supply is discovered it may be so rich as to afford both rent and profit. Moreover, a piece of waste land never before used for any purpose whatever may yield a rent when the land is wanted for a railway siding or as a site for a factory. But Ricardo never takes into account land required for any but agricultural or pastoral purposes.

production of necessaries, as well as by discoveries in the science of agriculture which enable us to relinquish a portion of labour before required, and therefore to lower the price of the prime necessary of the labourer. The rise in the price of necessaries and in the wages of labour is however limited, for as soon as wages should be equal (as in the case formerly stated) to £720, the whole receipts of the farmer, there must be an end of accumulation; for no capital can then yield any profit whatever, and no additional labour can be demanded, and consequently population will have reached its highest point. Long indeed before this period the very low rate of profits will have arrested all accumulation, and almost the whole produce of the country, after paying the labourers, will be the property of the owners of land and the receivers of tithes and taxes.

Thus, in Ricardo's view, as time goes by and less and less fertile land is taken into cultivation, more and more of the product passes into the hands of the landlords, and less and less remains in the hands of the capitalists as profit.

The farmers, however, are not the only capitalists whose rate of profit falls when it becomes necessary to cultivate less fertile land. The increased price of food, which compels farmers to raise the money wages of their labourers, will necessitate the same rise in the wages of labour employed in other industries, and it is always the rise of wages that causes profit to fall. If wages were higher in one industry than another, labourers would remove from the ill-paid to the better-paid industry; if profits were higher in one trade than another, capital would flow from the less to the more remunerative employment. 'In one and the same country', says Ricardo (81/134), 'profits are, generally speaking, always on the same level; or differ only as the employment of capital may be more or less secure and agreeable.'[1]

In 1814 Ricardo had not yet studied the subject of Rent; but he had thought a good deal about Profit, and had come to the conclusion that since there can be only one rate of profit, that rate must necessarily be the rate obtainable in agriculture. The farmer's product is food. A portion of that product—sufficient for the needs of existence—must necessarily be given to the labourers who produce it. It is only to the surplus yielded by the land in excess of the labourers' subsistence that the farmer can look for a

[1] Ricardo also recognises these slight differences of profit on page 49(90). He took the idea from Adam Smith, whom he quotes (vol. 4, p. 12).

profit on his capital, and when less and less fertile land is cultivated this surplus becomes smaller and smaller. The manufacturers are affected in the same way as the farmers. When the price of corn rises all labourers require higher wages in order to live as well as, and no better than, before. 'In short', said Ricardo, writing to his friend Trower in March 1814, 'it is the profits of the farmer which regulate the profits of all other trades.' This was his own conviction, but he told Trower—'Mr. Malthus does not agree. He thinks that the arena for the employment of capital may increase, and consequently profits and interest may rise, although there should be no new facilities, either by importation or by improved tillage, for the production of food—that the profits of the farmer no more regulate the profits of other trades than the profits of other trades regulate the profits of the farmer' (vol. 6, p. 104). A year later, in March 1815, Ricardo wrote to Malthus: 'It is by the rise of the price of corn that all other profits are regulated to agricultural profits. If the price of corn remained low, money wages would not rise, and general profits could not fall' (vol. 6, p. 194). By this time Ricardo had published his essay on Profits, in which he said: 'Profits of stock fall because land equally fertile cannot be obtained, and through the whole progress of society, profits are regulated by the difficulty or facility of procuring food' (vol. 4, footnote, p. 13). A few pages later we read: 'The general profits of stock depend wholly on the profits of the last portion of capital employed on the land' (vol. 4, p. 21). The rate of profit does not depend on foreign trade, but 'if by foreign commerce, or the discovery of machinery, the commodities consumed by the labourer should become much cheaper, wages would fall; and this, as we have before observed, would raise the profits of the farmer, *and therefore all other profits*' (vol. 4, footnote, p. 26—the italics are mine).

In Ricardo's *Principles*, published two years later, we find him still adhering to the same doctrine. On page 22(35) he tells us that if the farmer's profit falls from 10 per cent to 9 per cent the manufacturer's profit will fall from 10 per cent to 9 per cent. On page 69(117) he says that when the farmer's profit falls owing to the rise of wages, the profits of manufacture 'would conform to the altered rate of those of the farmer'. On page 76(126) he tells us that 'in all countries, and all times, profits depend on the quantity of labour requisite to provide necessaries for the labourers on that land or with that capital which yields no rent'. On page 80(133) we have: 'Foreign trade, then, though highly beneficial to a country . . . has no tendency to raise the profits of stock unless the commodities imported are of that description on which the wages of labour are expended.' In 1820 he said: 'The rate of profits does not depend on foreign trade, but on the returns for labour on the land last cultivated at home, and the distribution of the produce' (vol. 2, p. 363).

These sayings, I think, leave one with the impression that there will be no fall in the general rate of profit until the farmer's profits have fallen, no fall in the farmer's profit until agricultural wages have risen, no rise of wages until the price of corn has risen, and no rise in the price of corn until poorer land is cultivated. The cultivation of inferior land appears to come first; the rise in the price of corn follows in consequence of the increased quantity of labour required for its production; the rise in the price of corn necessitates a rise of wages in all lines of industry, and a consequent fall in the rate of profit in all industries.

Now let us contrast these passages with the following, which appears on page 103(163):

> When a high price of corn is the effect of an increasing demand, it is always preceded by an increase of wages, for demand cannot increase without an increase of means in the people to pay for that which they desire. An accumulation of capital naturally produces an increased competition among the employers of labour, and a consequent rise in its price.[1] The increased wages are not always immediately expended on food, but are first made to contribute to the other enjoyments of the labourer. His improved condition however induces and enables him to marry, and then the demand for food for the support of his family naturally supersedes that of those other enjoyments on which his wages were temporarily expended. Corn rises then because the demand for it increases, because there are those in the society who have improved means of paying for it; and the profits of the farmer will be raised above the general level of profits till the requisite quantity of capital has been employed on its production. Whether, after this has taken place, corn shall again fall to its former price, or shall continue permanently higher, will depend on the quality of the land from which the increased quantity of corn has been supplied. If it be obtained from land of the same fertility as that which was last in cultivation, and with no greater cost of

[1] I.e. in the price of labour.

> labour, the price will fall to its former state; if from poorer land, it will continue permanently higher. The high wages in the first instance proceeded from an increase in the demand for labour; inasmuch as it encouraged marriage, and supported children, it produced the effect of increasing the supply of labour. But when the supply is obtained, wages will again fall to their former price if corn has fallen to its former price; to a higher than the former price if the increased supply of corn has been produced from land of an inferior quality.

Here we have a picture of wages rising before any poorer land is cultivated; it is, in fact, the rise of wages that leads to inferior land being cultivated when there is no more of the good land available. . . . The succession of events here sketched is, first an increase of capital (wages fund) which causes wages to rise because the number of labourers cannot be immediately increased. The labourers are the principal consumers of corn, and with increased wages they increase their demand for corn; and as the quantity cannot be immediately increased, the price of corn rises. The rise of wages diminishes the general rate of profit; but there is nothing to suggest that the farmer's profit is the first to fall, and that profits in other industries follow suit. On the contrary, the rise in the price of corn, which causes the general rate of profit to fall, at the same time raises the farmer's profits higher than it was before. Ricardo himself says: 'The profits of the farmer may, for an interval of some little duration, be above the former level' (70/119). Ultimately, however, agricultural profit will fall to conform with the general rate. Because the price of corn has risen and the general rate of profit fallen, it will now pay to cultivate inferior land which formerly would not have yielded the general rate of profit. So long as the ordinary rate of profit can be obtained in agriculture more and more capital will flow into that industry; 'this is in fact', says Ricardo, 'the mode in which the cultivation of corn is always extended, and the increased wants of the market supplied' (205/306). This inflow of capital will only continue 'till the requisite quantity of capital' has flowed into agriculture (103/163). Ricardo makes it quite plain that additional capital will not be employed in agriculture when the result of increasing the supply of corn would be to depress the price below the remunerative level. On page 220(328) he says that the farmer who employs £10,000 will not employ an additional £1000 unless he can obtain upon it the general rate of profit. And on page 278(407) he asks what motive the farmer could have for increasing his output if the result would be to reduce his profit below the general level?

Although on page 103(163) it is owing to the capitalists increasing their wages fund that wages rise 'in the first instance',[1] Ricardo, taking the long view, feels justified in regarding the law of diminishing returns as responsible for the 'tendency of profit to fall'; it is the increased cost of obtaining food that prevents profit returning to its former level after capital has been increased. If every equal addition to capital could always produce an equal addition to the quantity of food and necessaries there would be no permanent rise of wages, and consequently no permanent fall in the rate of profit. So long as wages are kept down to a minimum by the philoprogenitive habits of the labourers, wages will always be regulated in the long run by the cost of producing 'subsistence'. Improved facilities for the production of manufactured necessaries tend to lower money wages (page 9/16 and page 260/382). If England would import cheap corn from abroad (which Ricardo strongly advocated) the rise of wages might be postponed for many years (76/126). But the rate of money wages depends mainly on the price of food, and if this continuously rises, profits must continuously fall. In the long run, the general rate of wages, and therefore of profits, must depend upon the price it is necessary to pay for food.

The fall in the rate of profit cannot continue indefinitely. If less and less fertile land is cultivated there must come a point, Ricardo tells us on page 71(120), when the whole receipts of the marginal farmer would be swallowed up in wages, and consequently 'there must be an end of accumulation, for no capital can then yield any profit whatever'.

> I have already said [he writes on page 72(122)] that long before this state of prices was become permanent, there would be no motive

---

[1] The first sentence of the passage on page 103 shows that Ricardo is describing what happens *when* wages are raised before the price of corn has risen, which does not mean that the rise of wages *always* comes first. On page 70(118) he says: 'Under ordinary circumstances, no permanent rise takes place in the price of necessaries without occasioning, or having been preceded by, a rise in wages.' The price of corn, he tells us, may be raised by a tax, and then a rise of wages will follow. His demonstration of this on page 105(166) was discussed in our 8th chapter (page 129).

for accumulation; for no one accumulates but with a view to make his accumulation productive. . . . Without a motive there could be no accumulation. . . . The farmer and manufacturer can no more live without profit than the labourer without wages. Their motive for accumulation will diminish with every diminution of profit, and will cease altogether when their profits are so low as not to afford them an adequate compensation for their trouble, and the risk which they must necessarily encounter in employing their capital productively.

Ricardo does not speculate as to how low the rate of profit would have to fall before it ceased to attract new capital to industry, but he expresses the view that not only will the rate of profit continuously fall with the increase of capital, but after accumulation has reached a certain point, further additions made to the total of capital will have the result of diminishing the total quantity of profit instead of increasing it. Hence, when Malthus in his *Principles* (page 199 in first edition, page 190 in second) thought it 'probable' that in the course of time the total profits of the capitalists would outstrip the total rents of the landlords, Ricardo disagreed (vol. 2, p. 182). Let us examine the grounds upon which Ricardo based his conclusion in his *Principles* (73/123):

We should also expect that, however the rate of the profits of stock might diminish in consequence of the accumulation of capital on the land and the rise of wages, yet that the aggregate amount of profits would increase. Thus supposing that, with repeated accumulations of £100,000, the rate of profit should fall from 20 to 19, to 18, to 17 per cent, a constantly diminishing rate, we should expect that the whole amount of profits received by those successive owners of capital would be always progressive; that it would be greater when the capital was £200,000 than when £100,000; still greater when £300,000; and so on, increasing, though at a diminishing rate, with every increase of capital. This progression, however, is only true for a certain time; thus 19 per cent on £200,000 is more than 20 per cent on £100,000; again 18 per cent on £300,000 is more than 19 per cent on £200,000; but after capital has accumulated to a large amount, and profits have fallen, the further accumulation diminishes the aggregate of profits. Thus, suppose the accumulation should be £1,000,000 and profits 7 per cent, the whole amount of profits will be £70,000; now if an addition of £100,000 capital be made to the million, and profits should fall to 6 per cent—£66,000, or a diminution of £4000 will be received by the owners of the stock, although the whole amount of stock will be increased from £1,000,000 to £1,100,000.[1]

This perhaps sounds more like arithmetic than economics (and arithmetic in which a couple of *ifs* play an important part), but Ricardo apparently takes the proposition seriously, for he proceeds to examine what the position of the farmers will be when this situation develops. He begins with his usual assumption that when only one quality of land is cultivated there is no rent to pay. If the quality of the land is such that every farmer with a capital of £3000, employing ten men, can produce 180 quarters of wheat worth £720, then with a hundred thousand times as much capital and labour, and a hundred thousand times as much land of the same quality, the product of the community will be as follows:

Capital employed	£300,000,000
Labour	1,000,000 men
Product	18,000,000 qrs.
Wages £24 per man	£24,000,000
Profit 16 per cent	£48,000,000
Product at £4 per quarter	£72,000,000

These are the figures with which Ricardo starts off on page 75(125). We are now to suppose that the community has reached the limit of its first-class land, and can only increase its supply of wheat by extending cultivation to an inferior quality of soil. On

[1] If Ricardo had kept to the scale with which he commenced the paragraph we should have had the following figures:

£ 900,000	at	12	per cent	earns	£108,000
£1,000,000	,,	11	,,	,,	£110,000
£1,100,000	,,	10	,,	,,	£110,000
£1,200,000	,,	9	,,	,,	£108,000

On the new scale introduced at the end of the paragraph the full figures would be:

£ 600,000	at	11	per cent	earns	£66,000
£ 700,000	,,	10	,,	,,	£70,000
£ 800,000	,,	9	,,	,,	£72,000
£ 900,000	,,	8	,,	,,	£72,000
£1,000,000	,,	7	,,	,,	£70,000
£1,100,000	,,	6	,,	,,	£66,000

The capitalist was better off with £800,000 at 9 per cent than with a million at 7 per cent.

page 68(116) his assumption was that the second-grade land would be so little inferior that the price of wheat would only rise from £4 a quarter to £4 4*s*. 8*d*., and the rise of wages would only be from £24 per annum to £24 14*s*. But he requires a 'strong case' to make clear the principle he is now endeavouring to establish, and his assumption accordingly is that if an additional 5 per cent of capital is to be employed by the farmers it will necessitate the cultivation of such a quality of land as will involve the price of corn rising from £4 a quarter to £6 a quarter, which means that wages must rise from £24 to £30 to enable the labourer to consume the same quantity of provisions as before, and no more. The result will be that the farmers who formerly derived an income of £48 millions from their capital of £300 millions, now only get £44,100,000 from their capital of £315 millions. Let me tabulate Ricardo's figures:

TABLE D

	On the old land	*On the new land*	*Total*
Capital employed	£300,000,000	£15,000,000	£315,000,000
Men employed	1,000,000 men	50,000 men	1,050,000 men
Product	18,000,000 qrs.	600,000 qrs.	18,600,000 qrs.
	£	£	£
Wages £30 per man	30,000,000	1,500,000	31,500,000
Profit 14 per cent	42,000,000	2,100,000	44,100,000
Wages and Profit	72,000,000	3,600,000	75,600,000
Rent	36,000,000	—	36,000,000
Product at £6 per qr.	108,000,000	3,600,000	111,600,000

These figures illustrate Ricardo's statement on page 74(123) that:

> There can, however, be no accumulation of capital, so long as stock yields any profit at all, without its yielding not only an increase of produce, but an increase of value. By employing . . . additional capital, no part of the former capital will be rendered less productive. The produce of the land and labour of the country must increase, and its value will be raised, not only by the value of the addition which is made to the former quantity of productions, but by the new value which is given to the whole produce of the land by the increased difficulty of producing the last portion of it. When the accumulation of capital, however, becomes very great, notwithstanding this increased value, it will be so distributed that a less value than

before will be appropriated to profits, while that which is devoted to rent and wages will be increased.[1]

How low, then, may profits fall before there ceases to be any motive for further accumulation of capital? Obviously, if there were only one capitalist, he would not continue to add to his capital when he found that by doing so he diminished his total income. But in a community where every man is free to save and embark his savings in industry, a newcomer who has accumulated £100,000 will not keep that capital idle for fear that by entering into competition with other capitalists he may reduce the rate of profit from 7 to 6 per cent. Not only will he invest his £100,000 at 6 per cent if he cannot get 7, but when he has saved a further £100,000 he will increase his investment to £200,000 even if it should cause the rate to fall to 5 per cent, because 5 per cent on £200,000 is more than 6 per cent on £100,000.

[1] I confess I am unable to perceive the meaning of Ricardo's remark on page 75(125) that: 'Wages would rise because more labourers would be employed in proportion to capital'; I think this must be a slip.

10

Ricardo's doctrine that if Wages rise, Profits fall, while the Price of the product is not affected

THE ordinary business man, in reading our last chapter, may have said to himself, 'If I had to raise the wages of my labourers on account of a rise in the cost of living, I should consider myself justified in raising the price of my product. I cannot see why it is taken for granted that the whole addition to wages will come out of my profits, leaving the price of the product unaffected.'

Such, however, is Ricardo's doctrine, as set forth in the heading of the very first section of his first chapter; and that he never wavered in this doctrine will be seen from the following extracts taken from all parts of his book.

> The proportion which might be paid for wages is of the utmost importance in the question of profits; for it must at once be seen that profits would be high or low exactly in proportion as wages were low or high; but it could not in the least affect the relative value of fish and game, as wages would be high or low at the same time in both occupations (16/27).
>
> There can be no rise in the value of labour[1] without a fall of profits. If the corn is to be divided between the farmer and the labourer, the larger the proportion that is given to the latter the less will remain for the former. So if cloth or cotton goods be divided between the workman and his employer, the larger the proportion given to the former the less remains for the latter (21/35).
>
> A rise of wages from the circumstances of the labourer being more liberally rewarded, or from a difficulty of procuring the necessaries

[1] I.e. the price that the employer must pay for it.

on which wages are expended, does not, except in some instances,[1] produce the effect of raising price, but has a great effect in lowering profits (31/48).

In all cases, commodities rise because more labour is expended on them, and not because the labour which is expended on them is at a higher value (69/118).

Whatever increases wages necessarily reduces profits . . . nothing can affect profits but a rise in wages (70/118).

I have endeavoured to show, first, that a rise of wages would not raise the price of commodities, but would invariably lower profits . . . (76/127).

The rate of profits can never be increased but by a fall in wages (80/132).

Every diminution in the wages of labour raises profits but produces no effect on the price of commodities (81/133).[2]

Whatever raises the wages of labour, lowers the profits of stoc (132/205).

[He has, he thinks] succeeded in showing that it is not the rise in the money wages of labour which raises the price of commodities, but that such rise always affects profits (202/303).

—profits being at all times raised as wages fall, and lowered as wages rise (223/333).

I have endeavoured to show that whatever facility or difficulty there may be in the production of corn, wages and profits together will be of the same value. When wages rise it is always at the expense of profits, and when they fall, profits always rise (276/404).[3]

Probably there are no dicta of Ricardo's that at first sight appear more at variance with actual experience. It is, in fact, almost an axiom in Economics that if wages rise the price of the product will rise. But before condemning Ricardo's dicta we must ask what he understood by a rise of wages?[4]

[1] The words 'except in some instances' did not appear in either of the first two editions, as pointed out by Cannan.

[2] In saying that prices are unaffected, Ricardo ignores his own 'modification' that a change in the rate of wages will alter the ratio of exchange between an article produced with little fixed capital and another produced with little labour.

[3] The reference given by Ricardo is incorrect, as pointed out by Sraffa; the passage Ricardo intended to refer to will be found on page 67/115.

[4] We have already noted Ricardo's habit of giving to current expressions (such as 'real value', 'circulating capital', 'natural rate') a meaning of his own —a habit which called forth the following remark of Malthus: 'It is specifically this unusual application of common terms which has rendered Mr.

When the ordinary man speaks of wages rising his meaning may be either that the labourer's money income is increased (which Adam Smith called a rise of nominal wages) or that his commodity income is increased (which Smith called a rise of real wages).[1] But Ricardo regards wages as having risen if the labourer receives a larger percentage of the product than he received before (31/49). This proposition would offer little difficulty if the product itself never varied in quantity. If, for instance, the work of a farm labourer, assisted by an unchanging quantity of capital, always produced 18 quarters of wheat in a year, and if the labourer always received one-third of this as wages, then his wage would always be 6 quarters and the farmer's profit 12 quarters. Any increase in the proportion given to the labourer would be an increase in the quantity of wheat received by him. But what will be the position if, owing to the law of diminishing returns, the product falls from 18 to 16 quarters? If the labourer still receives 6 quarters of wheat Ricardo would say that his wages have risen; they have risen from one-third to more than one-third (vol. 2, pp. 61 and 196). Indeed, if the quantity of wheat given to the labourer should be reduced from 6 quarters to $5\frac{1}{2}$ he would still say that wages have risen, because $5\frac{1}{2}$ is more than one-third of 16. It was perhaps lucky for Ricardo that his seat in Parliament did not depend upon popular election,[2] for if, on the hustings, he had tried to persuade an audience of labourers that their wages had *risen* from 6 to $5\frac{1}{2}$, he

---

Ricardo's work so difficult to be understood by many people. It requires a constant and laborious effort of the mind to recollect at all times what is meant by high and low rents, and high or low wages' (footnote to page 214 in the first edition of Malthus' *Principles*; page 202 in his second edition).

[1] Economists have followed Adam Smith, but in this book I use the term 'commodity wages' to avoid confusion with the different sense in which Ricardo uses the word 'real'. In the *Notes on Malthus* (vol. 2, p. 371) he himself refers to 'a low commodity price of labour, if I may be allowed the expression'.

[2] Ricardo entered Parliament in 1819 as Member for Portarlington in Ireland, a seat previously held by a gentleman well known in London society as 'Conversation Sharp'. For the privilege of sharing in the government of his country Ricardo seems to have paid the 'owner' of the seat about £1000 per annum (vol. 8, p. 327). Ricardo appears never to have visited his constituency. He was not singular in that respect; when Lord Palmerston was given a seat in the Isle of Wight the 'proprietor' made it a condition that he should never set foot in the constituency (Guedalla, *Palmerston*, page 55).

might have found it difficult to dodge a shower of unpleasant missiles.

While Malthus was the last person likely to approve the pelting of Political Economists (for he was one himself),[1] he was quite as much opposed as the labourers to Ricardo's method of assessing a rise of wages. He held that improvements in the technique of production might result in an increase of both wages and profits. Ricardo rejected this; in the *Notes on Malthus* he made the following comment on his friend's doctrine:

> He, for example, says that profits and wages may, and frequently do, rise at the same time. This, I say, never can be true. Why? Because value is measured by proportions, and a high value means a large proportion of the whole produce. As one proportion of a whole increases, the other must diminish (vol. 2, p. 267).

Let us try to understand Ricardo's point of view. His doctrine was that if two articles are produced at the same cost they will have the same value. If, with a given quantity of labour and capital, you can produce either 180 quarters of wheat or 720 yards of cloth, then 720 yards of cloth will have the same value as 180 quarters of wheat; if the cloth sells at £1 a yard the wheat will sell at £4 a quarter, and the total value in each case will be £720. Now if the law of diminishing returns reduces the quantity of wheat that can be produced at this cost to 160 quarters, while there is no alteration in the cost of producing cloth, then 160 quarters of wheat will be worth 720 yards of cloth; the price of cloth will remain at £1 a yard while the price of a quarter of wheat will rise to £4 10*s*., the total remaining in each case £720.[2]

What follows from this? Formerly the labourers produced 180 quarters and received 60; now they produce only 160 quarters, and if they still receive 60, their wages have risen. Formerly they received one-third of the product, one-third of £720; now they

[1] Malthus, in fact, was the first 'Professor of Political Economy' ever appointed in England. This was at Haileybury College in Hertfordshire, where the students had a playful habit which Principal Le Bas dignified by the name of lithobolizing. Hence, when the philosopher Mackintosh received an appointment at that seat of culture, Sydney Smith wrote: 'Poor Mackintosh, I am heartily sorry for him . . . He should stipulate for *pebble money* as it is there technically called, or an annual pension in case he is disabled by the pelting of the students' (see *The Pope of Holland House*, page 313).

[2] He assumes that there is no alteration in the value of money.

receive more than one-third of the product, more than one-third of £720. The wage bill has risen from £240 to £270. Even if the labourers now receive only 56·6 quarters, or the equivalent in money, their wages have risen. Reckoned in Ricardo's way they have risen because 56·6 is more than one-third of 160; reckoned as the ordinary man in the street reckons, they have risen because £255 (56·6 quarters at £4 10*s.*) is more than £240 (60 quarters at £4) (68/116).

Looked at in this light Ricardo's proposition loses its air of paradox; it does not conflict with the ordinary man's method of assessing a rise or fall of wages. True, it is a rise of money wages only, not of commodity wages. Ricardo did not overlook this. In his *Notes on Malthus* (vol. 2, pp. 136–7) he observes: 'The unfortunate labourer, however, finds when he goes to market with his increased wages, he can obtain a less quantity of one of the chief necessaries of life.' Hence he tells us in a later note (vol. 2, p. 250) that in order to know what the condition of the labourer is—'I should first enquire what the labourer's money wages were, and should estimate his condition by the abundance of necessaries which those money wages would procure him.' But the sayings of Ricardo quoted at the beginning of this chapter are not concerned with the condition of the labourer. What they assert is that profits fall when wages rise. If the farmer, by employing a capital of £3000, can obtain a product that realises £720, his profit depends on the proportion of that amount that remains after payment of wages. If wages rise from £240 to £255, profit falls from £480 to £465; if wages rise to £274 5*s.*, profit sinks to £445 15*s.* 'Whatever facility or difficulty there may be in the production of corn, wages and profits together will be of the same value' (276/404).

It is Ricardo's view that this decline in the rate of profit is an inevitable consequence of the law of diminishing returns. The commodity wage of the labourers is so low that it cannot be substantially reduced without starving the labourers out of existence; hence, with a diminished product, the reduction necessarily falls on the capitalist's share.

The decline in profit, as pointed out in our last chapter, is not confined to agriculture; it affects the manufacturer just as much as the farmer. In manufacture, it is true, increase of knowledge and experience has resulted, and continues to result, in an increase of product and a cheapening of commodities, but this does not make the position of the manufacturer as regards profit any different from that of the farmer. Although the physical product of capital and labour diminishes in the one case and increases in the other, the *value* of what is produced by a given quantity of labour and capital remains constant in both cases, and in both cases an increasing proportion of this value is absorbed by wages, since labourers in all branches of industry are equally affected by the rise in the price of food. Ricardo leaves us in no doubt as to his teaching on this point. The increase in the labourer's money wage, he says, 'would necessarily diminish the profits of the manufacturer; for his goods would sell at no higher price and yet the expense of producing them would be increased' (58/102). Referring to the manufacturer, on page 69(117) he says: 'If his commodities sold before for £720, they would continue to sell at the same price; but the wages of labour, which were before £240, would rise, when corn was at £5 2*s.* 10*d.*, to £274 5*s.*' Probably this assumption that after wages have risen the capitalist will continue to sell his product for the same quantity of money as before, is one that the reader will find it hard to accept. No capitalist is pleased to see the rate of profit diminish, and if he can prevent this by raising the price of his product he will not hesitate to do so. But Ricardo's doctrine is that it is impossible for prices to be raised when wages rise, and that even if the capitalist could raise his price, he would gain nothing by doing so. We will examine each of these arguments in turn.

Ricardo's contention that the capitalists cannot raise prices when wages rise is set forth on page 60(104–5). In reading this passage it is necessary to keep in mind Ricardo's invariable assumption that there is one universal rate of wages, so that, if a rise of wages caused prices to rise, the rise of prices would apply to everything; and his argument is that it would be impossible for all prices to rise unless there were an increase in the quantity of money. Here is what he says:

> When wages rise it is generally because the increase of wealth and capital have occasioned a new demand for labour, which will infallibly be attended with an increased production of commodities. To circulate these additional commodities, even at the same prices as before, more money is required, more of this foreign commodity from which money is made, and which can only be obtained by

importation.[1] Whenever a commodity is required in greater abundance than before, its relative value rises comparatively with those commodities with which its purchase is made. If more hats were wanted, their price would rise, and more gold would be given for them. If more gold were required, gold would rise, and hats would fall in price, as a greater quantity of hats and of all other things would then be necessary to purchase the same quantity of gold. But in the case supposed, to say that commodities will rise because wages rise, is to affirm a positive contradiction; for we first say that gold will rise in relative value in consequence of demand, and secondly, that it will fall in relative value because prices will rise, two effects which are totally incompatible with each other. To say that commodities are raised in price is the same thing as to say that money is lowered in relative value; for it is by commodities that the relative value of gold is estimated. If, then, all commodities rose in price, gold could not come from abroad to purchase those dear commodities, but it would go from home to be employed with advantage in purchasing the comparatively cheaper foreign commodities. It appears, then, that the rise of wages will not raise the prices of commodities, whether the metal from which money is made be produced at home or in a foreign country. All commodities cannot rise at the same time without an addition to the quantity of money. This addition could not be obtained at home, as we have already shown[2] nor could it be imported from abroad. To purchase any additional quantity of gold from abroad, commodities at home must be cheap, not dear. The importation of gold, and a rise in the price of all home-made commodities with which gold is purchased or paid for, are effects absolutely incompatible.

This is a good argument within its limits. It is, indeed, one of the chief recommendations of gold as money that it opposes just such an obstacle to the manipulation of prices, and thus gives some degree of stability to the standard of value. But since Ricardo's purpose on page 60(104) was merely to prove his contention on page 58(102) repeated on page 69(117) that after wages have risen the manufacturer will continue to sell his product at the same price as before, it might have been better had he contented himself with

[1] Ricardo is not here arguing on the assumption of a money unvarying in value. On the contrary, he assumes the British sovereign to be in circulation, as it had been for a hundred years, though at the time of his writing the circulation was suspended by the Bank Restriction Act.

[2] This was presumably a reference to the passage on page 28 of his first edition, which was left out in third edition (see vol. 1, p. 55).

pointing out that all prices cannot rise unless there is an increase in the supply of money, and that a rise of prices would drive some of the money out of the country instead of attracting an additional supply. But Ricardo wanders away from this point, and tells us that the new demand for labour, caused by the increase of capital (or wages fund), 'will infallibly be attended with an increase of commodities'. This is presumably an instance of what De Quincey called Ricardo's 'elliptical thinking'. If we try to insert the missing links the argument might be that the rise of wages will lead, first, to an increase of population, and then to an increase in the quantity of labour, which will have for one effect a lowering of wages, and for another an increase in the quantity of goods produced. When the quantity of goods to be 'circulated' is thus increased, prices must infallibly fall if the quantity of money is not increased. But since the fall in prices will attract money from abroad, prices will rise again. At each stage in this series of events there will be readjustments; in short, Ricardo's argument opens up a vista of changes which by no means leads to the conclusion that the money price of what is produced by a given quantity of capital and labour will always be the same. That conclusion, in fact, is based on the assumption of an imaginary money that never alters in value.

The argument on page 60(104) reappears in two of Ricardo's chapters on Taxation. If the farmer is called upon to pay a tax upon his produce, says Ricardo, the price of produce will be raised; but, he adds on page 107(168), 'corn and *all* home commodities could not be materially raised in price without an influx of the precious metals; for the same quantity of money could not circulate the same quantity of commodities at high as at low prices, and the precious metals never could be purchased with dear commodities'. Hence:

> The probable effect of a tax on raw produce [1] would be to raise the price of raw produce, and of all commodities in which raw produce entered, but not in any degree proportioned to the tax;

[1] 'Raw produce' here means crops only, such as corn or cotton; metals and earths are raw materials, but not 'produce'. But Ricardo does not always make this distinction; on page 126(196) for example, he refers to 'the produce of gold mines'; and when in his Preface and in chapter 26 he speaks of the whole produce of land, labour and capital being divided between three classes, he presumably means the whole product of industry.

> while other commodities in which no raw produce entered, such as articles made of the metals and the earths, would fall in price; so that the same quantity of money as before would be adequate to the whole circulation (107/169).

In other words, when some prices rise, others must fall if the same quantity of money is to circulate the same quantity of goods as before.

In a later chapter, however, Ricardo confronts the question what would happen if, not one commodity only, but every commodity were taxed? On page 138(213) he writes:

> If it be agreed that, by taxing the profits of one manufacturer only, the price of his goods would rise to put him on an equality with all other manufacturers, and that by taxing the profits of two manufacturers the prices of two descriptions of goods must rise, I do not see how it can be disputed that by taxing the profits of all manufacturers the prices of all goods would rise, provided the mine which supplied us with money were in this country and continued untaxed.[1] But as money, or the standard of money, is a commodity imported from abroad, the prices of all goods could not rise; for such an effect could not take place without an additional quantity of money, which could not be obtained in exchange for dear goods, as was shown on page 60(104). If, however, such a rise could take place, it could not be permanent, for . . .

We need not concern ourselves, I think, with Ricardo's further remarks on the situation which would thus be created because, 'on further consideration', he came to the conclusion that a rise of prices caused by taxation would not necessitate the employment of an increased quantity of money, and accordingly, although he did not modify the text, he inserted in his third edition a footnote to the above passage, as well as to the passage on page 107. The note on page 107(169) reads as follows: 'It may be doubted whether commodities, raised in price merely by taxation, would require any more money for their circulation. I believe they would not.' His reason for believing that no additional money would be required is explained in the new note on page 138(213). His argument is to the effect that if the farmer is called upon to pay a tax of 8*s*. per quarter on his corn, he will add 8*s*. to his selling price. In doing so he merely serves as tax-collector for the government.

[1] Ricardo's chapter on the Taxation of Profits is discussed in our 16th chapter.

Each time that a tax of 8*s*. is taken from the pocket of the consumer, he is left with 8*s*. less to spend on commodities, while the government has 8*s*. more. Taxes collected by the government, like bets made on a race course, represent a mere transfer of purchasing power; there is no alteration in the ratio between the total quantity of money and the total of commodities to be exchanged for money.[1]

Ricardo, then, gives up his contention that it is impossible under any circumstances for all prices to rise without an increase in the nation's stock of money; but this does not imply abandonment of the doctrine that, if the quantity of money remains unaltered, a general rise of wages must involve a general fall in the rate of profit. The problem, in fact, is not in reality a monetary one at all. If a community is made up of three classes, *a* labourers, *b* capitalists, and *c* government employees, then if more is taken from *a* and *b*, and bestowed on *c*, it is obvious that less of the product will remain for division between *a* and *b*; and if the consumption of the labourers cannot be reduced, then the whole of the diminution must fall upon the capitalists.

This, I think, rather than the doctrine on page 60(104) is the real basis of Ricardo's contention that if wages rise it is not the value of the product, but the proportions in which it is divided between capital and labour that will be affected. His idea is that what is produced by a given quantity of capital and labour always represents the same value; 'Wages and profit together will be of the same value' (footnote, 276/404); not only will the value be always the same, but the money price of the product will be always the same provided money itself never varies in value. It is of a perfect measure, a money with an invariable value, that Ricardo is thinking when he tells us that if the product of a given quantity of capital and labour shrinks from 180 to 160 quarters, owing to the law of diminishing returns, its value will still be the

[1] The two footnotes in Ricardo's third edition appear to have been suggested by a discussion with his friend Trower (see vol. 4, p. 321). Why did Ricardo need this discussion? In 1811 he had himself said that an increase of money would not be needed when prices rose in consequence of a tax (vol. 3, 243). In his *Notes on Trotter* he had said: 'Taxation does not require any addition to money, or if any, so little as not to be worth computing' (vol. 3, p. 385). I think his meaning must have been the same when he said in his *Notes on Bentham* (vol. 3, p. 301): 'The mass of prices might remain the same though each individual article has risen in consequence of taxation.'

same, namely £720, and that if wages rise from £240 to £255, profit necessarily falls from £480 to £465. Fundamentally, his 'law' has nothing to do with the quantity of money, and would be the same if no such thing as money existed, and the labourer received as wages a share of the actual product. His proportion of the product cannot increase without the capitalist's proportion being diminished.

That this is what Ricardo had in mind will become plain, I think, if we now turn to his second argument, namely, his contention that even if the capitalists could raise their prices when wages rose, they would gain nothing by doing so. This argument is used in several places. It first appears on page 76(126), where he writes:

> In the chapter on wages we have endeavoured to show that the money price of commodities would not be raised by a rise of wages, either on the supposition that gold, the standard of money, was the produce of this country, or that it was imported from abroad. But if it were otherwise, if the prices of commodities were permanently raised by high wages, the proposition would not be less true which asserts that high wages invariably affect the employers of labour by depriving them of a portion of their real profits. Supposing the hatter, the hosier, and the shoemaker each paid £10 more wages in the manufacture of a particular quantity of their commodities, and that the price of hats, stockings, and shoes rose by a sum sufficient to repay the manufacturer the £10; their situation would be no better than if no such rise took place. If the hosier sold his stockings for £110 instead of £100, his profits would be precisely the same money amount as before; but as he would obtain in exchange for this equal sum one tenth less of hats, shoes, and every other commodity . . . he would be in no better situation than if his money profits had been really diminished in amount and everything had remained at its former price. Thus, then, I have endeavoured to show, first, that a rise of wages would not raise the price of commodities, but would invariably lower profits; and secondly, that if the prices of all commodities could be raised, still the effect on profits would be the same; and that, in fact, the value of the medium only in which prices and profits are estimated would be lowered.[1]

[1] A similar argument is used on pages 147/8(226) where he says: 'If taxes press unequally on the farmer, he will be enabled to raise the price of raw produce, to place himself on a level with those who carry on other trades; but a tax on wages, which would not affect him more than it would affect any other trade, could not be removed or compensated by a high price of raw produce; for the same reason which should induce him to raise the price of

This argument does not seem to be a very good one. If the capitalist originally paid £80 in wages and sold his product for £100, his profit was £20, or one-fifth of the product. If wages rise to £90 while the price remains unaltered, his profit sinks to £10; he will get just half as much as before, whereas by raising his price to £110 his share of the product sinks only from two-tenths to two-elevenths. If wages were originally £90 and profit £10, a rise of £10 in wages would extinguish profit altogether if the price were not raised.

Quite a small increase of wages may suffice to extinguish profit. Ricardo usually assumes that the capitalist begins the year with a twelve-month wages fund in hand, and must wait till the end of the year before he sells his product and gets his advances back. But he knew this was not so, and on page 19(31) he tells us that the baker's circulating capital may return to him afresh every week. Suppose this capital to amount to £100, which the baker pays out every week in wages, selling each week's product for £105. By the end of the year he has paid out £5200, and has received £5460. The difference, £260, is his profit, and if his fixed capital is small it may be a high rate; but it is obvious that if his weekly wages bill rises from £100 to £105 his entire profit will be wiped out, and it will be impossible for him to carry on business without raising the price of bread.[1]

On page 133(206) Ricardo brings forward a somewhat similar argument. He tells us that if a tax of 10 per cent reduces the capitalist's profit from £1000 to £900, he may restore his money income to its original figure by adding £100 to the price of his product; but, he says, 'he will not obtain more for his £1000 than

corn, namely to remunerate himself for the tax, would induce the clothier to raise the price of cloth, the shoemaker, hatter, and upholsterer, to raise the price of shoes, hats and furniture. If they could all raise the price of their goods, so as to remunerate themselves, with a profit, for the tax; as they are all consumers of each other's commodities, it is obvious that the tax could never be paid; for who would be the contributors if all were compensated?' The assumption that if prices are raised, all would rise by the same percentage, ignores his own demonstration on pages 22(35) and 134(208) that they would not do so owing to the different proportions in which labour and fixed capital are combined in different products. On the question whether prices would rise or not, see page 132(205–6).

[1] This was pointed out by Malthus in his *Principles*, page 93 in first edition, page 90 in second edition.

he before obtained for £910'. What Ricardo apparently had in mind was that if a man's income is diminished by 10 per cent, his consumption of goods will be reduced to nine-tenths of its former amount, whereas if his income is not reduced but prices rise by 10 per cent, he will be able to obtain ten-elevenths of the former amount, which is more, but very little more, than nine-tenths. This is an improvement on page 76(126), since it is no longer stated that the capitalist will gain nothing at all by keeping the same money income.

Ricardo's idea that the capitalist would gain nothing by raising the price of his product arose, I think, partly from his habit of treating the product of industry as being divided into two parts only, one the wages of labour and the other the profit of the capitalist (64/110), and partly from his assumption that the share given to the labourers is never more than the minimum that just suffices for their continued existence. From these assumptions it follows that if a third party, namely the government, demands a portion of the product, that portion must come out of the capitalist's share. The government may tax profits or it may tax wages, but the latter comes to the same thing, because the tax inevitably comes out of the capitalist's share. 'This principle of the division of the produce of labour and capital between wages and profits, which I have endeavoured to establish', says Ricardo, 'appears to me so certain that, excepting in the immediate effects, I should think it of little importance whether the profits of stock or the wages of labour were taxed' (148/226).[1]

[1] On page 140(215) Ricardo had said that the 'ultimate effects' are the same, whether the tax is placed on profits or on wages; here he suggests that the 'immediate effects' may be different. He explains why; but his language is not very clear. I suppose him to mean that if the tax is placed on wages, it is the labourers who will suffer in the first instance. Wages will be 'too low', and therefore the labourers will be unable to maintain their numbers; the consequent diminution in the supply of labour will ultimately raise wages, and so diminish the rate of profit. If on the other hand the tax is levied directly on the capitalists, profit will be diminished at once while the labourers will not be immediately affected. But since the capitalists, with diminished profit, will not be able to save so much, the increase of the wages fund will not keep pace with the growth of population; the fund will not be large enough to pay the same rate of wages to an increased number of labourers; wages will be 'too high' in proportion to the fund, and must fall. Wages will again be too low for the labourers' needs, and their numbers must diminish until wages rise again, and the proper proportion is restored between the fund and the quantity of labour.

The capitalist, then, must pay the tax. Now let us suppose that he endeavours to recoup himself for this additional expense by raising the price of the product, what will happen? He will still have to pay part of the tax in the shape of higher prices for the goods he buys for his own consumption; and not only so, but since the labourers were only just able to survive on their wages before prices rose, they will no longer be able to survive unless their wages are raised; and if this rise of wages is followed by a further rise of prices, and this in turn by another rise of wages, we have an endless spiral as futile as a cat chasing its own tail. On page 147(225) Ricardo writes:

> This rise in the price of goods will again operate on wages, and the action and reaction, first of wages on goods, and then of goods on wages, will be extended without any assignable limits. The arguments by which this theory is supported lead to such absurd conclusions that it may at once be seen that the principle is wholly indefensible.

Thus, on the assumption that the labourers can neither pay taxes nor higher prices, it is impossible for the capitalist to saddle them permanently with any portion of the tax; and if there are no consumers except himself and his men, it follows that 'he must himself wholly and without compensation pay such a tax' (148/226).

But why did Ricardo assume in all his illustrations (see Table A in our third chapter) that the whole product is consumed by the capitalist and his men? When he said (21/35) that the corn is divided between the farmer and the labourers, and when he told us (64/110) that the whole product consists of wages and profit, he was dealing with the marginal producer, who pays no rent. He held that it is the marginal producer's cost of production that determines the price of corn. The farmer of better land, it is true, pays rent, but he does not charge either more or less for a bushel of corn than the marginal farmer. Rent then, according to Ricardo, does not enter into the problem of price, and he thinks it can be left out of consideration. He writes to McCulloch (vol. 8, p. 194):

> By getting rid of rent, which we may do on the corn produced with the capital last employed, and on all commodities produced by labour in manufactures, the distribution between capitalist and labourer becomes a much more simple consideration. The greater the portion of the result of labour that is given to the labourer, the smaller must be the rate of profit and *vice versa*.

The question we are now dealing with, however, is not whether, if the employer is taxed on the wages of his labourers, he can recover the tax by charging his labourers more for what they consume; the question is whether there are not other consumers, such as wealthy landlords, to whom the capitalist can pass on at least a part of the tax in the shape of higher prices. In the industrial microcosm depicted in Ricardo on page 265(388) there are no landlords; the only consumers are the capitalist and his men; but we cannot afford to get rid of rent in studying the problem we have now before us.

If the capitalist continues to sell his product at the same price after the expense of production has risen, the whole loss comes out of his profit, whereas by raising his price he is able to distribute the burden over the whole body of consumers, himself being one. The labourers (or some of them) may have to be 'compensated', but if the price were not raised, those consumers who enjoy rents would contribute nothing towards the tax, whereas by raising the price of the product they may be compelled to bear a portion of the burden. Nor are the landlords the only consumers who may be made to contribute. In every old country there are many persons entitled to fixed amounts of money income from investments in government or municipal loans, from debentures, from pensions they have earned or annuities they have purchased. All these will escape the tax levied on industry if prices are not raised; all may be made to contribute by increased prices (as Ricardo recognised, page 138(213)). It is of the pensioner or annuitant, rather than the capitalist, that it can be said that 'he must himself wholly and without compensation' pay whatever tax the government impose upon him, or which may be transferred to his shoulders through the medium of higher prices.

Ricardo's assumption that the whole product is consumed by the capitalist and his men was erroneous; equally erroneous was his other assumption that the consumption of the labourers is at an irreducible minimum. In his third edition he admitted that 'perhaps this is expressed too strongly' (234/348). He had, in fact, known all along, and admitted in section 2 of his first chapter, that although some labourers are paid very little, others are paid more; and in his article on the Funding System in the *Encyclopaedia Britannica* published in 1820, while he contended that large taxes necessarily came out of the pockets of property-owners, he admitted that some taxes were paid by people who owned no property, such as wage-earners, salaried men, and professional men living on fees (vol. 4, p. 188). The capitalist, then, whose cost of production is increased by a tax, can, by raising the price of his product, recover most of it in small amounts from his numerous customers.

In this connection it may be well to notice Ricardo's comments on the teaching of Adam Smith. Ricardo's view is, as we have seen, that 'towards a tax on wages, consequently neither the stockholder, the landlord, nor any other class but the employers of labour will contribute' (140/215). Smith, on the other hand, thinks that some labourers are well enough off to pay the tax themselves; and while it may be necessary to raise the wages of 'the inferior classes of workmen', the employers will succeed in shifting at least a portion of the burden onto other shoulders. The final payment of the tax, says Smith:

> would in different cases fall upon different persons. The rise which such a tax might occasion in the wages of manufacturing labour would be advanced by the master manufacturer, who would both be entitled and obliged to charge it, with a profit, upon the price of his goods. The final payment of this rise of wages, therefore, together with the additional profit of the master manufacturer, would fall upon the consumer. The rise which such a tax might occasion in the wages of country labour would be advanced by the farmer, who . . . would . . . pay less rent to the landlord. The final payment of this rise of wages, therefore, would in this case fall upon the landlord.[1]

Ricardo quotes this passage, and makes the following comment:

> In this passage it is asserted that the additional wages paid by farmers will ultimately fall on the landlords, who will receive a diminished rent; but that the additional wages paid by manufacturers will occasion a rise in the price of manufactured goods, and will therefore fall on the consumers of those commodities. Now

[1] *Wealth of Nations*, Bk. 5, chap. 2, article 3 (2nd paragraph). In the 2nd paragraph of article 2 (and again in the last paragraph but five) Adam Smith gives his reason for differentiating between agricultural products and manufactured goods. If the manufacturer finds that the demand diminishes when the price is raised he can quickly diminish the quantity of his output, whereas the farmer has not the same facility for reducing supply and therefore cannot raise his price. In this connection see the comments made in our eighth chapter on Ricardo's teaching on page 105(166).

suppose a society to consist of landlords, manufacturers, farmers, and labourers; the labourers, it is agreed, would be recompensed for the tax; but by whom?—who would pay that portion which did not fall on the landlords? The manufacturers could pay no part of it; for if the price of their commodities should rise in proportion to the additional wages they paid, they would be in a better position after than before the tax. . . . If the clothier paid more for his hats and shoes, he would receive more for his cloth; and if the hatter paid more for his cloth and shoes, he would receive more for his hats. All manufactured commodities, then, would be bought by them with as much advantage as before, and inasmuch as corn would not be raised in price, which is Dr. Smith's supposition, whilst they had an additional sum to lay out upon its purchase, they would be benefited and[1] not injured by such a tax. If, then, neither the labourers nor the manufacturers would contribute towards such a tax—if the farmers would be also recompensed by a fall of rent—landlords alone must not only bear its whole weight, but they must also contribute to the increased gains of the manufacturers (146/223).

This attempt to reduce Adam Smith's argument to absurdity is hardly fair to Smith, whose reasoning does not imply that the whole burden of the tax falls on the landlords. True, he represents the landlord as twice hit, once by the decrease of rent, and again by the higher prices he must pay for manufactured goods. If the marginal farmer pays no rent, he too will be twice hit, for his profit will be smaller, while he must pay more for the manufactured goods that he consumes. Does the manufacturer escape the tax? Not so; it was Ricardo's own argument on page 133(206) that though keeping the same money income he would get fewer goods for it. The same argument applies to the rent-paying farmer, who keeps the same income but can get less goods for it. As to the 'labourers', these include many highly paid professional men, and Adam Smith's idea was that only the 'inferior' class of workmen would have their wages raised, while the rest, with the same incomes as before, would contribute to the tax in higher prices and reduced consumption. In short, if the government decides to obtain a share of the product that results annually from the co-operation of land, labour and capital, there is no class of consumers who may not be made to contribute by a diminished consumption.

According to Adam Smith, if the manufacturer raises his price

[1] *Everyman* edition erroneously prints *but* instead of *and*.

to preserve his profit, he will nevertheless find that the increased price causes some diminution of his sales. 'The increase in the wages of labour', he says, 'necessarily increases the price of many commodities, by increasing that part of it which resolves itself into wages, and so far tends to diminish their consumption both at home and abroad.'[1] Now the capitalist is not going to submit to a loss of profit if he can help it. On the contrary, he is always on the look-out, says Smith, for some means 'to make a smaller quantity of labour produce a greater quantity of work'. The higher wages rise, the keener will be his search for 'labour-saving' devices as a means of reducing his cost of production. Ricardo himself, by the time he published his third edition, had come to recognise that high wages are a direct incentive to the employment of machinery.[2] His cost of production being reduced by this or other improvements in the technique of production, he will in all probability be able to offer his goods at lower prices than before; and in arriving at a new scale of prices it may well happen that he is able to restore the rate of profit he enjoyed before wages rose. Malthus, as mentioned earlier in this chapter, saw no reason why the capitalist should not get a better return on his capital and the labourer a better reward for his labour.

Ricardo, to the end of his life, clung to the idea that a rise of wages, whether due to taxation or anything else, did not raise prices. In his pamphlet on *Protection to Agriculture*, which was the last thing he published (1822; he died in 1823), he forgets or treats as negligible all admissions or modifications he had made, and reiterates the old doctrine that a tax on wages comes entirely out of the profit of the capitalist, and leaves the price of the product unaffected. He says:

> In all cases the rise of wages, when general, diminishes profits, and does not raise the prices of commodities. If the prices of commodities rose, no producer would be benefited; for of what consequence could it be to him to sell his commodity at an advance of 25 per cent if he in his turn were obliged to give 25 per cent more for every commodity which he purchased? He would be precisely in the same condition whether he sold his corn for 25 per cent advance and gave

[1] *Wealth of Nations*, Bk. 1, chap. 8, last paragraph. See also the last paragraph but two in the Introduction to Bk. 2.

[2] This will be dealt with when we come to consider the modifications introduced by Ricardo in his third edition.

> an additional 25 per cent in the price of his hats, shoes, clothes, etc., etc., as if he sold his corn at the usual price and bought all the commodities which he consumed at the prices which he had before given for them. No one class of producers, then, is entitled to protection on account of a rise of wages, because a rise of wages equally affects all producers; it does not raise the prices of commodities because it diminishes profits; and if it did raise the price of commodities, it would raise them all in the same proportion, and would not, therefore, alter their exchangeable value (vol. 4, p. 215).

Thus Ricardo reiterates that a rise of wages will not alter prices or relative values, forgetting, or treating as negligible, his admission (22/35) that even if there were only one rate of wages, yet when those wages rose, some prices would rise more than others, while some would actually fall.

11

Controversy with Malthus regarding Redundant Capital or Deficient Demand

We have seen in a previous chapter that Ricardo regards the rate of profit as entirely dependent upon the rate of wages. 'No accumulation of capital', he says, 'will permanently lower profits unless there be some permanent cause for the rise of wages' (192/289). Again: 'There is no other adequate reason for a fall of profit but a rise of wages', and 'the only adequate and permanent cause for the rise of wages is the increasing difficulty of providing food and necessaries for the increasing number of workmen' (197/296). Hence he disagrees with the following passage in Adam Smith:

> When the stocks of many rich merchants are turned into the same trade, their mutual competition naturally tends to lower its profit; and when there is a like increase of stock in all the different trades carried on in the same society, the same competition must produce the same effect in them all.[1]

Ricardo rejects this doctrine; Adam Smith, he says, 'uniformly ascribes the fall of profits to accumulation of capital, and to the competition which will result from it, without ever adverting to the increasing difficulty of providing food for the additional number of labourers which the additional capital will employ' (192/289).[2]

[1] *Wealth of Nations*, Bk. 1, chap. 9, 2nd paragraph.

[2] Smith did not refer to 'increasing difficulty' in providing food because he did not believe that there was any increased difficulty in the case of corn, the labourer's main sustenance (see footnote in our sixth chapter, page 63).

Ricardo does not deny that if capital increases faster than population there will be increased competition among capitalists for labour, with consequent rise of wages and fall of profits; but this condition will be temporary. Encouraged by the high wages, an increase of population will overtake the increase of capital, and the rate of wages will fall again. If the additional food required by the increased population could be produced at the same cost as before, both wages and profits would return to the old figure. If they do not return to the old figure it is because, owing to the law of diminishing returns, food is now dearer; the labourer's subsistence absorbs a larger proportion of the product than was formerly the case, and the capitalist must content himself with less profit. Profit falls, not because the competition of capitalists has increased, but because the labourer's subsistence has risen in price (103/163).

In thinking that the growth of capital creates keener competition, says Ricardo (192/290), Adam Smith 'does not appear to see that at the same time that capital is increased, the work to be effected by capital is increased in the same proportion. M. Say has, however, most satisfactorily shown that there is no amount of capital which may not be employed in a country, because demand is only limited by production.'[1]

What does this mean? It means that buying and selling are but exchanging, and the goods produced by one man pay for those produced by the other. Every man who has something to sell wants something in exchange for it. Each is in turn a seller and a buyer; the more sellers there are, the more buyers there are. Increase of supply, therefore, is increase of demand.[2] The idea that supply may exceed demand, and cause a fall of price and loss of

[1] This was Ricardo's teaching from the first (1817). In 1819 he twice reconfirmed his faith in the doctrine—once in his article on the Funding System (published in the following year, vol. 4, p. 178), and once in his evidence before the House of Lords (vol. 5, p. 435, in answer to question 63), when he said: 'There can be no production without occasioning an equal consumption', by which their lordships no doubt understood, and were meant to understand, a corresponding effective demand.

[2] To adopt the language of a later writer, aggregate supply and aggregate demand are the same thing seen from different angles—they are 'different faces of the same facts . . . consequently, neither can increase nor diminish without a corresponding increase or diminution of the other' (J. E. Cairnes, *Some Leading Principles*, chap. 2, sections 2 and 4).

profit, is therefore groundless. 'There cannot then, be accumulated in a country any amount of capital which cannot be employed productively[1] until wages rise so high in consequence of the rise of necessaries, and so little consequently remains for the profit of stock, that the motive for accumulation ceases' (193/290).[2]

If Adam Smith had confined himself to stating that there may be too much capital engaged in the production of some particular commodity, and that profits in that industry would consequently decline, both Say and Ricardo would have agreed with him; but Smith says this condition may prevail in all industries simultaneously, and here we have a doctrine that Say and Ricardo refuse to accept. On page 195(293) Ricardo quotes Smith himself in support of the view that there is no limit to the desire for commodities:

> Adam Smith has justly observed 'that the desire of food is limited in every man by the narrow capacity of the human stomach, but the desire of the conveniences and ornaments of building, dress, equipage, and household furniture, seems to have no limit or certain boundary.[3]

And Ricardo then goes on to say:

> Nature then has necessarily limited the amount of capital which can at any one time be profitably engaged in agriculture, but she has placed no limits to the amount of capital that may be employed in procuring 'the conveniences and ornaments' of life . . . and while there is no limit to the desire of 'conveniences, ornaments of building, dress, equipage, and household furniture', there can be no limit to the capital that may be employed in procuring them, except that which bounds our power to maintain the workmen who are to produce them.

Thus there is no limit to human wants, and supply can never exceed demand. 'No man produces but with a view to consume or sell, and he never sells but with an intention to purchase some other commodity which may be immediately useful to him, or which may contribute to future production' (192/290).

This view did not pass unchallenged. It found a vigorous

[1] Presumably he uses the word *productive* here in the sense often given to it by Adam Smith, i.e. productive of profit.

[2] Ricardo adds a footnote here, suggesting that some of M. Say's dicta are inconsistent with his own doctrine.

[3] *Wealth of Nations*, Bk. 1, chap. 11, 7th paragraph in Part 2.

opponent where perhaps one would have been least expected, in the author of the famous *Essay on the Principle of Population.* The reader will not have forgotten 'the barbourous and impious Malthus' whom Cobbett so cordially hated—'the check-population parson' who had made a name for himself a generation earlier by his picturesque representation of niggardly nature banging the dining-room door in the face of would-be gate-crashers for whom there was no room at the table. He had furnished the public with an easily remembered formula in the 'algebraical' increase of mouths compared with the 'arithmetical' increase of food. According to this doctrine, if the labouring classes were ill-fed, ill-housed, and scantily clothed, it was not the fault of the capitalists, nor yet of the landlords; the blame must be placed either upon niggardly nature, which provided so little, or on the poor themselves, who failed to restrict their numbers to correspond with that little. Ricardo had faithfully followed Malthus in this explanation of the chronic poverty of the bulk of mankind, and he was not disposed to change his opinion. But twenty years of reflection had brought Malthus to the conclusion that the fault was not wholly with nature or the working classes. 'In a former work', he said, 'I endeavoured to trace the causes which practically keep down the population of a country to the level of its actual supplies. It is now my object to show what are the causes which chiefly influence these supplies, or call the powers of production forth into the shape of increasing wealth.'[1] So far from the growth of population having been slowed down by nature's grudging response to human effort, Malthus now finds that man's powers of production have never been exerted to the full; he now believes that if the structure of society had permitted the hungry multitudes to avail themselves fully of the facilities offered by bounteous Nature 'the earth would probably before this period have contained, at the very least, ten times as many inhabitants as are supported on its surface at present'.[2]

Production, in short, is restricted by Man, not by nature. 'It is scarcely possible', says Malthus, 'to cast our eyes on any nation of the world without seeing a striking confirmation of what has been advanced. Almost universally, the actual wealth of all the

[1] Malthus' *Principles of Political Economy* (1820), page 345 in first edition; page 309 in second edition.

[2] Ibid., page 348 in first edition; page 311 in second.

states with which we are acquainted is very far short of their powers of production.'[1] The smallness of production, compared with what it might be, is not due to lack of capital or shortage of labourers; nor does it arise from the reluctance of nature to yield up her treasures, for in fact it often occurs 'long before there is any real difficulty in procuring the means of subsistence'.[2] The key to the situation is the fact that if production were pushed to the limit of capacity, the result would be over-production—over-production, that is to say, in the sense that the capitalists could not sell all they produced at a remunerative price. Instead of the quantity of production determining the quantity of demand, as Say and Ricardo taught, it is the quantity of effectual demand that determines how much shall be produced.[3]

In saying just now that this vigorous attack came from what seemed an unlikely quarter, I meant that such views, coming from Malthus, must have taken the public by surprise. It can have been no surprise to Ricardo himself, who had long been familiar with the views of his friend. As far back as January, 1817, Malthus had written him: 'I am quite of opinion that *practically* the actual check to produce and population arises more from want of stimulus than want of power to produce' (vol. 7, p. 123). Since then they had had many a discussion. Shortly before Malthus published his *Principles* Ricardo wrote to McCulloch: 'Mr. Malthus continues stoutly to deny that demand is only limited by production—he thinks that capital might be very mischievously augmented in a country, and he intends in his new publication to make some remarks on this' (vol. 8, p. 159). When the book appeared Ricardo was kept busy for some time writing notes on the various points with which he disagreed. These notes he never published, but they were found and given to the world a hundred

[1] Malthus' *Principles*, page 350 in first edition, page 313 in second.

[2] Ibid., page 469 in first edition, page 402 in second.

[3] In *Das Kapital* (page 574 in *Everyman* translation) Karl Marx says of Malthus: 'Naturally, it was far more convenient to himself, and far more accordant with the interests of the ruling classes (whom Malthus idolised with all the fervour which was fitting in a parson) for him to explain this "over-population" as due to the eternal laws of nature, instead of explaining it as the outcome of nothing more than the natural history of capitalist production.' From this uncalled-for sneer at a singularly honest, earnest, and thoughtful man one can only infer that the wide reading of Marx did not include a careful perusal of Malthus' *Political Economy*.

years after his death, and they now form volume 2 in Mr. Sraffa's collected edition of Ricardo's Works.

The mere notion that there might be a difficulty in finding consumers was utterly at variance with Ricardo's ideas. Everybody wishes to consume. A country can consume little if its producers are few, or lack energy. 'It requires an exertion of some magnitude', says Ricardo, 'to apply one's body and mind to productive labour for ten or twelve hours of the day, but no exertion at all to consume what one has before been at the pains of producing' (vol. 2, p. 364). It is then ridiculous to suppose that more can be produced than the producers care to consume. Every producer, says Ricardo (192/290) 'necessarily becomes either the consumer of his own goods, or the purchaser and consumer of the goods of some other person'. There may be a limit to demand in the sense that we are not willing to pay the price exacted by nature; we may prefer more ease and leisure to more goods. Indolence, says Ricardo, 'might be a reason for commodities not being produced abundantly, but it can be no reason, when they are produced, for their not being exchanged against each other. We all like to buy and consume; the difficulty is in the production. One product is bought by another; every man will buy if he has a product to give in exchange, and does not value that higher than the commodity offered' (vol. 2, p. 240).

To no one was the heresy of Malthus more repugnant than to M. Say, who had 'most satisfactorily shown' that products create their own market; and in a series of open letters addressed to Malthus[1] he sought to refute the new doctrine. Ricardo (quite rightly) did not think that Say made a very good job of it (vol. 8, p. 276); nevertheless, he did not himself publicly enter the lists, but contented himself with compiling those *Notes* already mentioned which he circulated among his friends, including Malthus. In these *Notes* he was even more severe than Say on 'the great and fundamental error of Mr. Malthus, who contends that there may be at one and the same time a glut of all commodities, and that it may arise from a want of demand for all' (vol. 8, p. 257).

Let us see by what line of reasoning Malthus reaches the conclusion that appears so fantastic to Say and Ricardo. He begins in his Introduction by suggesting that Adam Smith's praise of

[1] *Letters to Thomas Robert Malthus on Political Economy and Stagnation of Commerce*, by Jean-Baptiste Say, 1821 (published in both French and English).

thrift requires some qualification.[1] It is by parsimony, or saving, says Smith, that capital is accumulated, and it is by increasing capital, or the means of production, that the annual revenue of the community is augmented.[2] Quite true, says Malthus; nevertheless, parsimony, or the cutting down of present consumption, must not be carried too far. If we reduce our present consumption to a minimum in order that we may increase our capital, we shall be rewarded in due course with an increased power of consumption. But if we continue to content ourselves with a minimum of consumption—if saving becomes so much a habit that we refuse to consume the larger product now made possible—we defeat the very purpose for which capital was increased. 'The principle of saving', says Malthus, 'pushed to excess, would destroy the motive to production.'[3] If demand and consumption do not increase in the necessary proportion, the result must be over-capitalisation; either some capital will be thrown out of employment, or there will be over-production, making it impossible to sell the whole product at a profit. Production will be discouraged if sales at a profit do not result from the employment of capital, and many labourers will be without work and without wages. It is when demand is expanding that capital can be economically and profitably increased. 'When the capital of a country is deficient compared with the demand for its products', says Malthus, 'a temporary economy of consumption is required in order to provide that supply of capital which can alone furnish the means of an increased consumption in future.'[4] Larger production and stationary consumption are incompatible. 'On the supposition indeed of a *given* consumption the accumulation of capital beyond a certain point must appear at once to be perfectly futile.'[5]

Capital and production may be increased provided consumption

[1] Malthus' *Principles*, page 8.

[2] *Wealth of Nations*, Bk. 2, chap. 3, 14th and following paragraphs.

[3] Malthus' *Principles*, page 8.

[4] Ibid., page 369 in first edition; page 326 in second.

[5] Ibid., page 370 in first edition. Malthus was not the first to contend that capital may increase too fast, nor the first to advocate free spending by landlords. In 1807 William Spence had published his *Britain Independent of Commerce*, in which these ideas appeared; James Mill replied with his *Commerce Defended*, in which, like Say, he 'most satisfactorily showed' that supply can never exceed demand. I have not seen these pamphlets, but use the information given in an article by R. L. Meek in the *Economic Journal* of March, 1951.

keeps pace with the increase. 'Unquestionably', says Malthus, 'any country has the power of consuming all that it produces.'[1] It is not the power, but the will, that he thinks is lacking. We may view the country's total output of commodities during the year as the nation's commodity income, but it is not in fact the product of the whole nation, nor is every citizen entitled to a share of it. According to Adam Smith, the annual product of the land, labour and capital of the country belongs exclusively, in the first instance, to those who own the land, labour and capital employed in producing it; it belongs, that is to say, and is shared among, the landlords, the labourers, and the capitalists.[2] This view is also implicit in Ricardo's Preface. So far as the labourers are concerned, Ricardo may be right in assuming that the will to consume is always equal to the power to consume; they would consume more if they had the power. But in the case of the capitalists, Malthus holds, the opposite is the case—their power to consume exceeds their will to do so. Of them it does not appear to be true that, in Adam Smith's phrase, the desire for the conveniences and ornaments of life has no limit or certain boundary. 'That it has no *certain* boundary', says Malthus, 'is unquestionably true; that it has no limit must be allowed to be too strong an expression, when we consider how it will be practically limited . . . by the general desire of mankind to better their condition, and make a provision for a family, a principle which, as Adam Smith himself states, is on the whole stronger than the principle which prompts to expense.'[3] The capitalists, says Malthus, 'have certainly the power of

[1] Malthus' *Principles*, page 411 in first edition. In the second edition (page 359) this is changed to 'any country is entitled to consume'.

[2] 'The whole annual produce of the land and labour of every country . . . naturally divides itself . . . into three parts; the rent of land, the wages of labour, and the profits of stock; and constitutes a revenue of three different orders of people. . . . These are the three great, original and constituent orders of every civilised society, from whose revenue that of every other order is ultimately derived' (*Wealth of Nations*, Bk. 1, chap. 11, paragraph 7 in section headed 'Conclusion of the Chapter').

[3] Malthus' *Principles*, page 468 in first edition (page 402 in second). Ricardo had read these remarks of Malthus when, in October, 1820, he wrote to his friend Trower: 'The demand for commodities such as luxuries; or for services, such as are performed by gardeners, menial servants, builders, etc., etc., is unlimited, or rather it is only limited by the means of the demanders' (vol. 8, p. 272). Surely Malthus was correct in saying that this could not be true in the case of those who saved part of their incomes?

consuming their profits. . . . But such consumption is not consistent with the actual habits of the generality of capitalists. The great object of their lives is to save a fortune. . . . But if this be true of them as a body, taken one with another, it is quite obvious that, with their actual habits, they could not afford an adequate market to each other by exchanging their several products'.[1]

Malthus thinks that in a society where one section of the community regularly produces more than it consumes, production and consumption cannot balance—producers cannot find sufficient consumers—unless another section of the community regularly demands and consumes more than it produces, or consumes without producing at all. It is here that the landlords sprout a halo. As they consume a great deal, while producing nothing, they contribute substantially towards making demand equal to supply. But, alas, no class of human beings is perfect; despite their halo the landlords are tainted with the same failing as the capitalists, namely, the habit of saving a considerable portion of their income instead of consuming the whole of it. Something might be done to reduce this evil, Malthus thinks, by breaking down large estates into smaller holdings. He writes:

> A very large proprietor, surrounded by very poor peasants, presents a distribution of property most unfavourable to effective demand.[2]
>
> Thirty or forty proprietors, with incomes answering to between one thousand and five thousand a year, would create a much more effective demand for wheaten bread, good meat, and manufactured products, than a single proprietor possessing a hundred thousand a year.[3]
>
> Practically it has always been found that the excessive wealth of the few is in no respect equivalent, with regard to effective demand, to the more moderate wealth of the many.[4]

But even the splitting up of large estates would not suffice to make demand equal to supply in a highly capitalised country. Still other non-producing consumers must be found before the capitalist can sell the whole of his product and make a profit on the whole of his capital. Luckily, there are in every wealthy country a great many other consumers who are not producers of

---

[1] Malthus' *Principles*, page 465 in first edition; page 399 in second.

[2] Ibid., first edition, page 429; second, page 373.

[3] Ibid., pages 430 and 374.

[4] Ibid., pages 431 and 375.

commodities. Neither capitalist nor landlord could derive much enjoyment from his vast possessions without footmen to wait upon him, housemaids to do the housework, coachmen and stable-boys to look after the horses and carriages, gardeners to keep the grounds in order, and so forth.[1] Large possessions would mean drudgery instead of ease if the owners had to do all their own work. Hence in addition to the consumption of commodities by landlords and capitalists, there is also a large consumption of commodities by their 'dependants'. Nor are these household servants the only retainers of the wealthy. Those who can afford it, employ the services of doctors, dentists, nurses, teachers and preachers, singers, actors, and numerous other consumers who do not produce commodities. And in addition to all these, armies and navies, policemen, magistrates, and a host of civil servants are furnished through the medium of taxation with the power to demand and consume.[2] In this way much is done to make the demand for commodities balance, or nearly balance, the quantity of supply. Every addition to the number of non-producing consumers helps to offset the deficiency of demand created by the saving habits of the capitalists. A falling off in non-producer demand would lead promptly to the closing down of many factories and the dismissal of many productive labourers. On the other hand, that an increase of non-producer demand results in increased industrial activity and production is exemplified whenever war breaks out; employment is then plentiful, profits are easy to earn, and production expands.

To Ricardo, all this appears to be sheer nonsense. He writes politely to Malthus: 'I can see no soundness in the reasons you give for the usefulness of demand on the part of unproductive consumers. How their consuming, without reproduction, can be beneficial to a country, in any possible state of it, I confess I cannot discover' (vol. 8, p. 301). But in the *Notes on Malthus*, presumably intended at the time of writing for his own private eye only, though subsequently communicated to Malthus and others, he

[1] Malthus' *Principles*, page 408 in second edition. Compare page 479 in first edition.

[2] 'With regard to these latter classes, such as statesmen, soldiers, sailors, and those who live upon the interest of a national debt, it cannot be denied that they contribute powerfully to distribution and demand,' says Malthus (page 479 in first edition; page 409 in second).

expresses a degree of amusement and contempt which must surely have wounded the feelings of his friend.[1] 'Mr. Malthus' peculiar theory is that supplies may be so abundant that they may not find a market,' says Ricardo (vol. 2, p. 240), and on page 307 he follows this up by saying that we must

> petition the King to dismiss his present economical ministers, and to replace them by others who would more effectually promote the best interests of the country by promoting public extravagance and expenditure. We are, it seems, a nation of producers, and have few consumers amongst us, and the evil has at last become of that magnitude that we shall be irretrievably miserable if the parliament or the ministers do not immediately adopt an efficient plan of expenditure.

In the same ironic vein he writes (vol. 2, p. 450): 'If the people will not expend enough themselves, what can be more expedient than to call upon the state to spend for them? What could be more wise, if Mr. Malthus' doctrine be true, than to increase the army and double the salaries of all the officers of the government?' Scarcely less biting is the remark on page 421: 'A body of unproductive labourers are just as necessary and as useful, with a view to future production, as a fire which should consume in the manufacturer's warehouse the goods which those unproductive labourers would otherwise consume.' And on page 425 he asks: 'Will the taking of 100 pieces of cloth from a clothier's manufactory, and clothing soldiers and sailors with it, add to his profits? Will it stimulate him to produce? Yes, in the same way as a fire would.'

Ricardo, however, does not confine himself to ridicule; he seeks to rebut the contentions of Malthus by argument. He rejects entirely the idea that saving reduces the demand for commodities, 'I deny that the wants of the consumers generally are diminished by parsimony', he said; 'they are transferred, with the power to

[1] Malthus, although a mild man, was hardened by long experience to public controversy, and it probably did not occur to him that his friend could be wounded by public criticism of his doctrines. Ricardo, however, himself the most courteous of controversialists, thought Malthus had not dealt fairly with him in his book (see his letter to Trower, vol. 8, p. 349). Nevertheless, he was quite incapable of deliberately hurting any man's feelings, and we must suppose that in circulating his *Notes* he had forgotten how freely he had expressed himself in them.

consume, to another set of consumers' (vol. 2, p. 309). Possibly he had in mind Adam Smith's statement: 'What is annually saved is as regularly consumed as what is annually spent, and nearly in the same time too; but it is consumed by a different set of people.'[1] Smith goes on to say:

> By what a frugal man annually saves, he not only affords maintenance to an additional number of productive hands for that or the ensuing year, but . . . he establishes, as it were, a perpetual fund for the maintenance of an equal number in all times to come.

In other words, the labourers employed by this capital continually reproduce what they consume, and therefore they continually furnish the means of sustaining the same number of men. This is also the doctrine of Ricardo; hence he regards it as absurd to suggest that saving creates unemployment, which is what Malthus does when he writes:

> If in the process of saving, all that was lost by the capitalist was gained by the labourer, the check to the progress of wealth would be but temporary, as stated by Mr. Ricardo; and the consequences need not be apprehended. But if the conversion of revenue into capital pushed beyond a certain point must, by diminishing the effectual demand for produce, throw the labouring classes out of employment, it is obvious that the adoption of parsimonious habits in too great a degree may be accompanied by the most distressing effects at first, and by a marked depression of wealth and population permanently.[2]

Upon which Ricardo remarks: 'Here the difference between Mr. Malthus and me is fairly stated. The reader must judge on which side truth lies' (vol. 2, p. 325).

Malthus does not dispute that by adding to his wages fund the capitalist affords subsistence to productive labourers, but he contends that the capitalist will not voluntarily increase the amount

[1] *Wealth of Nations*, Bk. 2, chap. 3, 18th paragraph. See also Bk. 5, chap. 2, article 4th, 43rd paragraph in the section headed 'taxes upon consumable commodities': 'Almost the whole capital of every country is annually distributed among the inferior ranks of people as the wages of productive labour.'

[2] Malthus' *Principles*, page 369 in first edition; in the second edition the last sentence is slightly modified (page 326).

he pays in wages unless he can thereby increase his profit; he says:

> No productive labour will ever be in demand[1] unless the produce when obtained is of greater value than the labour which obtained it. No fresh hands can be employed in any sort of industry merely in consequence of the demand for its produce occasioned by the persons employed.

The position, then, is that if the labourer can produce no more than he consumes the capitalist has no motive to employ him; on the other hand, if the labourer can produce in a physical sense more than he consumes, yet if there is no buyer for this surplus product, and the capitalist does not wish to consume it himself, then there is still no profit for the capitalist.

Ricardo is ready to meet this objection; if the capitalist does not desire to make any increase in his consumption at the present time, he can always reinvest the surplus without losing his power to consume the equivalent at a future time together with an increment as a reward for waiting. Ricardo writes:

> The consumption and demand occasioned by the persons employed in producing any particular quantity of wealth can never be a sufficient motive for producing it, if they are to have the whole of the commodities produced, and are to give for it only the labour which produced it. But suppose they take seven-eighths of it, and their employer retains one-eighth, with which he can again employ five or ten additional men, who again take seven-eighths of the commodities they produce, leaving the employer the power to employ additional labour the following year; cannot such accumulations go on while the land last cultivated will yield more food than is consumed by the cultivator? When it will not do that, there is an end on every system to all accumulation. . . . Accumulation could go on to this point, provided only that the population increased fast enough (vol. 2, p. 302; see also p. 318 and p. 429).

Thus, in Ricardo's view, the demand of the labourers and the capitalists, taken together, always increases at the same pace as production. There is never any deficiency of demand, and the capitalist may continue to increase his capital without causing 'over-production', fall of prices, or diminution in the rate of profit.

[1] In the second edition (page 312) this is followed by the words 'with a view to profit'. See first edition, page 348.

Were it not for the law of diminishing returns, this might continue indefinitely, but that law will necessarily some day put an end to accumulation. Even then there will be no deficiency of demand for what is produced, as the capitalists will naturally consume as much as they can purchase with their incomes, since additional investment would yield them no additional profit.

> When in the course of things profits shall be so low from a great accumulation of capital and a want of means of providing food for an increasing population [Ricardo writes to Malthus], all motive for further savings will cease; but there will be no stagnation; all that is produced will be at its fair relative price, and will be freely exchanged. Surely the word stagnation is improperly applied to such a state of things, for there will not be a general glut, nor will any particular commodity be necessarily produced in greater abundance than the demand shall warrant (vol. 9, p. 25).

Malthus, however, does not accept Ricardo's view that the investment of additional capital always is, and always will be, productive of profit until the time is reached when nature makes it impossible for additional labourers to produce more than they consume. He writes:

> It has been fully stated and allowed that a period of stagnation must finally arrive in every country from the difficulty of procuring subsistence. But an indisposition to consume in large quantities the goods produced . . . may occasion, and has often occasioned, a similar stagnation at a very early period of a nation's progress.[1]

Again, he writes:

> It appears to me perfectly clear in theory, and universally confirmed by experience, that the employment of a capital too rapidly increased by parsimonious habits may find a limit, and does in fact often find a limit, long before there is any real difficulty in procuring the means of subsistence; and that both capital and population may be at the same time, and for a period of great length, redundant, compared with the effective demand for produce.[2]

---

[1] Malthus' *Principles*, page 448 in first edition; page 388 in second.

[2] Ibid., page 469 in first edition; page 402 in reprint. See also footnote on page 512 of first edition: 'if capital be abundant compared with the demand for commodities, profits may be low. . . .' This footnote was omitted in the second edition.

Ricardo's comment on this is as follows:

> How capital and population should be both redundant while you can increase the supply of necessaries, I am at a loss to conceive. It is a contradiction in terms; it is saying there is a capital unemployed because its owner cannot find labourers, and there are people unemployed because there is no one having a capital to employ them (vol. 2, p. 426).

These remarks do not reflect much credit on Ricardo as a commentator. Malthus did not say that capital and labour might be redundant compared with one another, but that both might be redundant compared with the demand for their products.[1] The factory may be shut down and the labourers condemned to idleness because more goods have already been produced than can be sold at a remunerative price. But the idea of deficient demand is so foreign to Ricardo's thought that, incredible as it might seem, he entirely misses the point. Ricardo, in fact, was one of those men who, though gifted with keen reasoning powers, nevertheless lack the ability to grasp the meaning of anyone whose mind follows a different train of thought. Ricardo recognised his own weakness in this respect, for he wrote to Malthus:

> Knowing as I do how much we are influenced by taking a particular view of a subject, and how difficult it is to destroy a train of ideas which have long followed each other in the mind, I will not say I am right . . . and therefore it is possible that five years hence, I may think as you do. . . .[2]

Let us try to follow the train of ideas which made Ricardo's mind inaccessible to the argument of Malthus.

While Malthus wrestles with the complexities and perplexities of a society developed, organised, and controlled under a monetary system, Ricardo believes that the best approach to the study of the subject is to leave money out of account and endeavour to see how things would work out under a system of barter. Whatever problem he tackles, Ricardo seeks the fundamental, the primitive form of the problem, stripped of the complications of

[1] Malthus himself, in his second edition, pointed out this mistake of Ricardo (see footnote page 414).

[2] Vol. 8, p. 311. In a later letter (vol. 9, p. 95) Ricardo notes that his inability to understand Malthus 'may arise, as you say, from my being too much prepossessed in favour of my own views'.

modern life. Even barter is not his starting point; he seems to imagine a primitive savage—or shall we say a Robinson Crusoe?—dependent entirely on his own efforts for the satisfaction of his wants. He is both producer and consumer, both demander and supplier. He produces because he desires to consume, and what he does not desire to consume he does not put himself to the trouble of producing. The price he pays for his enjoyments is the labour of obtaining them.

The next step is to imagine two men instead of one. Exchange, and therefore division of labour, now becomes possible[1]—to the advantage of both parties, as it results in an increase of the total product.

> Whoever has commodities [says Ricardo] has the power to consume, and as it suits mankind to divide their employments, individuals will produce one commodity with a view to purchase another; these exchanges are mutually beneficial; but they are not absolutely necessary, for every man might employ his funds, and the labour at his command, in producing the very commodities he and his workmen intended to consume; in which case there would be no market, and consequently there could be no glut (vol. 2, p. 306).

Thus does Ricardo demolish the doctrine of Malthus that goods may be unsold because nobody is prepared to give for them what they cost to produce; thus does he prove the contention of Say that demand is always equal to supply.[2] Demand and supply must

[1] 'As it is the power of exchanging that gives occasion to the division of labour . . .' (*Wealth of Nations*, Bk. 1, chap. 3, 1st paragraph). Those who prefer Ruskin to Adam Smith as an economist may recall that some unfortunate spouter at a Social Science meeting in Glasgow brought the following down upon him: 'The ineffable blockhead who wrote the paper forgot that the principle of division of labour *underlies* that of exchange, and does not arise out of it, but is the only reason for it' (*Fors Clavigera*, 2nd Aug., 1874).

[2] Say has a still more remarkable way of showing that the demand for products is necessarily equal to the supply. In the Epitome to his *Treatise* he defines 'To produce' as 'To give to a thing a recognised value susceptible of procuring in exchange another thing of equal value'. Hence, a product is not a product if it cannot be sold at its natural price; all products can be sold at a remunerative price, because if they cannot be sold at a remunerative price they are not products! See also Say's public *Letters to Thomas Robert Malthus*, page 28 in the 1936 reprint of the English edition. Writing to Say in 1827, Malthus protested against this reasoning (see his letter on page 508 of Say's *Œuvres Diverses*, 1848 edition). Say's defence was practically this, that to spend 5 in producing 4 is not production but consumption.

balance because every man who produces 'necessarily becomes either the consumer of his own goods, or the purchaser and consumer of the goods of some other person' (192/290).

This is an argument that one might expect from Robinson Crusoe rather than from a citizen of London in the nineteenth century. Once the system of divided labour has become universal, exchange is no longer optional, as Ricardo represents it, but absolutely essential if the efforts of the producer are to benefit either himself or anyone else. We have burnt our boats. The capitalist who has sunk £10,000 or £20,000 in a plant for the manufacture of wash-tubs or kettles cannot consume his own products; he cannot, on his wife's birthday, switch a portion of his capital and labour from the production of tubs to the production of gowns or necklaces. He must find purchasers for what he produces before he can himself become a purchaser of other people's products. If his goods are left on his hands, he will become bankrupt. His products, if unsold, will be mere junk, without utility and without value.[1]

However much labour may be bestowed upon a product, and however well qualified it may be to afford service or pleasure to a consumer, it will represent so much wasted effort and expense unless it reaches the consumer. Malthus illustrates this point when he says:

> If the roads and canals of England were suddenly broken up and destroyed, so as to prevent all passage and interchange of goods, there would at first be no diminution of commodities, but there would be immediately a most alarming diminution both of value and wealth. A great quantity of goods would at once lose their value by becoming utterly useless.[2]

Instead of saying that the goods that are left unsold on the shelves of the maker lose their utility and value, Malthus should perhaps rather have said that they lose their chance of *acquiring*

[1] Professor Hollander, in the Introduction to his edition of the *Notes on Malthus* (page lxxix), quotes from Mercier de la Rivière (1797): 'Productions which should remain unconsumed would degenerate into superfluity, without utility, without value, and thenceforward no one would go to the expense of producing them.' For an excellent article by R. G. Hawtrey on the importance of finding consumers see the *Economic Journal* of September, 1951. Mr. Hawtrey, however, does not mention Malthus.

[2] Malthus' *Principles*, page 340 in first edition; page 301 in second.

utility and value. For such is his theory; it is by passing from the hands of the maker, who cannot use them, into the hands of consumers whose wants they will satisfy, that products acquire utility. For the consumers they have a value, whereas they would never have acquired a value if condemned to remain in the hands of the man who could not use them. Any utility they may be supposed to possess while still in the hands of the maker or his agent is merely an anticipation of the use to which they will one day be put if all goes well; and any value that is ascribed to them is a prospective one, based on the expectation that they will in due course be purchased by someone to whom they are worth as much as or more than they cost to produce.

Hence, in a world of divided labour production must be followed by exchange, or sale to consumers. Not only does exchange, or distribution (as Malthus often calls it), give birth to utility, it also, according to Malthus, imparts value to what perhaps had no value in the hands of the seller, or enhances any value the commodity previously possessed. He writes:

> Every exchange which takes place in a country effects a distribution of its produce better adapted to the wants of the society. It is, with regard to both parties concerned, an exchange of what is wanted less for what is wanted more, and must therefore raise the value of both the products.[1]

Now Ricardo agrees that both parties make a gain in utility; he admits that the aggregate of utility enjoyed by the society is increased; but in his opinion the quantity of value is not affected by the exchange. While it may be true that each party 'values' what he obtains more than he valued the article parted with, yet this is something that concerns nobody but himself. These personal valuations or subjective values are, he thinks, quite outside the domain of Political Economy. 'One set of necessaries and conveniences', he writes on the last page of his book, 'admits of no comparison with any other set; value in use cannot be measured by any known standard; it is differently estimated[2] by different persons.' In one of his pamphlets (vol. 4, p. 61) Ricardo wrote: 'If we say that value should be measured by the enjoyments which

[1] Malthus' *Principles*, page 440 in first edition; page 382 in second. Malthus was apparently a reader of Condillac, from whom we shall quote in our chapter on Say.

[2] Some copies of Ricardo's third edition read 'variously estimated'.

the exchange of the commodity can procure for its owner, we are still as much at a loss as ever to estimate value, because two persons may derive very different degrees of enjoyment from the possession of the same commodity.'

In Ricardo's opinion, the economist is not concerned with what Adam Smith called 'value in use',[1] but with value in exchange only, and individual estimates of utility have little or nothing to do with the ratio in which products exchange for one another in the market. This ratio is decided by cost of production. Equal values, not equal utilities (of which there can be no common measure), exchange for one another. The exchange may add to the sum of utility, but can add nothing to the sum of value. Ricardo accordingly commenced his chapter on Foreign Trade with the following words: 'No extension of foreign trade will immediately increase the amount of value in a country, although it will very powerfully contribute to increase the mass of commodities, and therefore the sum of enjoyments' (77/128). On a later page (214/319) Ricardo confirms this: 'In the seventh chapter of this work I have endeavoured to show that all trade, whether foreign or domestic, is beneficial, by increasing the quantity and not by increasing the value of productions.'[2]

Incidentally it may be noted (though it has little bearing on the point we are discussing) that in both these passages Ricardo represents the gain of utility arising from trade (i.e. from exchange) as taking the form of an increase in the quantity of product. When different men or different nations specialise in different products the result is an increase in the aggregate product to be shared between them by exchange. Malthus commented on this: 'Mr. Ricardo', he says, 'always views foreign trade in the light of means of obtaining *cheaper* commodities',[3] and he goes on to point out that the principal advantage of foreign commerce is that it enables us to obtain *different* commodities, i.e. goods of a kind that we cannot produce at home. In his third edition Ricardo did not think it worth while to modify either of the passages quoted

[1] Say, a great admirer of Adam Smith, thought Smith did wrong to speak of value in use instead of quantity or degree of utility.

[2] In 1819 Ricardo told a Committee of the House of Lords that 'Foreign Trade may alter the description of commodities produced, but cannot increase their aggregate value' (vol. 5, p. 435).

[3] Malthus' *Principles*, page 461 in his first edition, page 396 in second.

above; nor did he alter the statement that 'we manufacture commodities, and with them we buy goods abroad, because we can obtain a greater quantity than we could make at home' (196/295). Nevertheless he seems to have accepted this small correction from Malthus, though he continued to reject the latter's view that exchange increases value. In his *Notes on Malthus* he remarked: 'By foreign trade, then, we have got a more desirable commodity, but not a more valuable commodity' (vol. 2, p. 405), while in a footnote to his third edition he said, 'the whole benefits of commerce resolve themselves into the means which it gives us of acquiring, not more valuable objects, but more useful ones' (176/264).

On this point, the views of the two men were irreconcilable. In his *Principles* Malthus wrote:

> It will readily be allowed that an increase in the *quantity* of commodities is one of the most desirable effects of foreign commerce; but I wish particularly to press on the attention of the reader that in almost all cases another most important effect accompanies it, expressly rejected by Mr. Ricardo, namely, an increase in the amount of exchangeable value. And that this latter effect is so necessary, in order to create a continued stimulus to productive industry, and keep up an abundant supply of commodities, that in the few cases in which it does not take place, a stagnation in the demand for labour is immediately perceptible, and the progress of wealth is checked.[1]

This passage, isolated from its context, might seem to suggest that the increase of value, as a result of exchange, is something peculiar to foreign trade; but such is not the meaning of Malthus. His theory is that every exchange, whether domestic or foreign, adds to the value as well as the utility of the commodities transferred. And by this he does not mean merely that there is an increase of subjective value, an increase in the eyes of the individual who acquires what he wants; his doctrine is that the distribution of commodities, their transfer from producer to consumer, is what gives them an objective value, a value which is reflected in the market price and therefore becomes a reality for the vendor as well as the purchaser. Bananas, coconuts, pineapples, which would rot on Robinson Crusoe's island, will, if sent to Europe, acquire a value, not derived from the cost of carriage, but from an

[1] Malthus' *Principles*, pages 454/5 in first edition; in the second edition (page 393) the words 'expressly rejected by Mr. Ricardo' are left out.

eagerness to consume which justifies the cost of transport. Needles produced in Birmingham in quantity sufficient to supply a million each to every inhabitant within a mile of her famous Town Hall will create a mere glut if the market is restricted to that locality, but if there are facilities for their distribution throughout the length and breadth of the country they find countless buyers who value them and return a value to the producer. 'It has never, I believe, occurred', writes Malthus in his second edition, 'that the better distribution of the commodities of a country, occasioned by improved facilities of communication, has failed to increase the value as well as the quantity of the whole produce.'[1] One advantage of foreign trade is that it extends the opportunities of producers to find consumers for their products, and to increase the value of the materials they work on.

If a schoolboy whose aunt has given him *Our Village*, swops it for *Ivanhoe*, each boy gets what he values more for what he values less, but the market prices of the two books may be identical. That is barter; but it is not a picture of modern 'exchange' if by this term we mean the distribution of new products. It may be true in a very real sense that goods are bought with goods, and that he who sells in his turn becomes a buyer; but the process is very different from barter. Underlying the doctrine of Malthus that exchange, or distribution, enhances the value of products, is the notion that the real essence of exchange under a system of divided labour is the transfer of goods from the producer to the consumer; whether producer and consumer are citizens of the same or different countries makes no difference to the nature of the transaction. The gain in value comes from the utility acquired by the article when it passes from one who does not wish to use it to one who does wish to use it, or from one who values it little to one who values it much. If Robinson Crusoe destroys one thing to make another, he values what he aims to acquire more than he values what he is content to sacrifice. The increase of value may in this case be called subjective; or it may be called a gain in utility only; but in a world of divided labour, operating under a monetary system, this enhancement of value must be reflected in an increase of price. For the producer the cost of production is represented by a certain sum of money. What he

[1] Malthus' *Principles*, page 362. This sentence does not appear in the corresponding paragraph of the first edition, page 415.

produces he cannot consume; it is imperative that he shall be able to sell it, and it is also imperative that the sum for which he sells it shall exceed the sum of his outlay. Unless it does so, he cannot continue producing.

If exchange, or rather the sale of commodities to consumers, did not result in producers and merchants receiving for the product more money than they had spent in obtaining it, modern industry would be paralysed. Increase of value is at once the incentive to industry, and the compass by which industry is guided. Utility, or enjoyment, is the ultimate object of all production, but under modern conditions the producer does not produce what he desires to consume, and is not concerned with the utility of what he produces except as it affects the value of his product in the market. His immediate aim is to create value. 'Even those who pass their lives in the production of the most useful objects', wrote one of Ricardo's own disciples many years later, 'acquire the habit of regarding those objects as chiefly important by their capacity of being exchanged for money.'[1] Adam Smith said that the merchant who carries goods from one country to another has nothing to consider but their money price, or the difference between the quantity of silver for which he buys them and that for which he is likely to sell them.[2] When Malthus quotes this saying, Ricardo comments: 'I cannot agree with Adam Smith, or with Mr. Malthus, that it is the nominal value of goods, or their prices only, which enter into the consideration of the merchant' (vol. 2, p. 26). What Ricardo meant by this is not at all clear, and is the more puzzling because he himself had said something very like it in his chapter on Foreign Trade: 'Cloth cannot be imported into Portugal unless it sell there for more gold than it cost in the country from which it was imported' (84/137). In another passage (vol. 3, p. 409) he asks what inducement there would be for a merchant to import wheat 'if he cannot sell it for more money than he has purchased it for?'[3] Neither the producer nor the distributor, in fact, can have any way of measuring the increase of utility due to his efforts, but under a monetary system it is easy for him to ascertain whether his work is or is not productive of an increase of value. It is the increase of value that tells

[1] J. S. Mill's *Principles*, Bk. 3, chap. 7, section 3.

[2] *Wealth of Nations*, Bk. 1, chap. 5, paragraph 20.

[3] He makes a similar remark in vol. 6, p. 27.

the manufacturer and the merchant what is wanted and where it is wanted. And it is the same increase of value—that is to say, the difference between their money outlay and their money receipts—that enables them in their turn to become the purchasers and consumers of other people's products.

Increase of value, then, is indispensable to industry as actually carried on. 'I am inclined to think', says Malthus, 'that no single instance can be produced of a country engaged in a successful commerce, and exhibiting an increasing plenty of commodities, where the value of the whole produce . . . was retrograde or even stationary.'[1]

While Malthus recognises (as Ricardo himself did) that rising prices are a great encouragement to production, it is not of rising prices that he is thinking when he says that what is necessary to secure increasing production is an increase in 'the value of the whole produce'. What he means is that if more labour and capital are to be employed in production, they must result in an increased value as well as an increased product, otherwise the additional capital will go unrewarded. In the *Notes on Malthus* Ricardo seems to miss this point; he appears sometimes to be under the impression that Malthus is rejecting the proposition that improvements in the method of production often make it possible to increase output without an increase of expense, in which case the larger output can be sold at the same total price as before without any sacrifice of profit. 'What we should desire', writes Ricardo, 'is to increase the quantity of commodities without increasing their value' (vol. 2, p. 373).

> Mr. Malthus' error [he remarks a few pages later] is in supposing that cheap corn and cheap commodities necessarily imply a glut of corn and commodities. We agree that a glut is an evil. It generally implies production without profit, and sometimes without even the return of the capital employed. It arises always, I think, from a bad selection in the object produced. But cheapness from facility of production, which I think is the only legitimate cheapness, never fails of being attended with the happiest effects, and is as different from glut as light is from darkness (vol. 2, pp. 412–13).

It is astonishing that Ricardo should have imagined that Malthus needed this lesson; even more astonishing, I think, that

[1] Malthus' *Principles*, page 459 in first edition; page 395 in reprint.

Ricardo should have allowed himself to forward such a criticism to Malthus for perusal, seeing that Malthus had made his meaning so clear that even Ricardo's office-boy could scarcely have been excused for not understanding it. He tells us that a reduction of prices, an increase of production, an increase of sales, and an increase of total profit, are normal results of an increase of capital when the additional capital takes the form of machinery. When much machinery is employed, he says:

> it almost always happens . . . not only that the quantity of manufactures is very greatly increased, but that the value of the whole mass is augmented, from the great extension of the demand for them both abroad and at home, occasioned by their cheapness.[1]

On a later page he gives an instance; he says:

> The consumption of cotton goods has been so greatly extended both at home and abroad, on account of their cheapness, that the value of the whole of the cotton goods and twist now made exceeds beyond comparison the former value.[2]

Once more:

> The reader will be fully aware that a great fall in the price of particular commodities, either from improved machinery or foreign commerce, is perfectly compatible with a continued and great increase, not only in the exchangeable value of the whole produce of the country, but even in the exchangeable value of the whole produce of these particular articles themselves. It has been repeatedly stated that the whole value of the cottons produced in this country has been prodigiously increased, notwithstanding the great fall in their price.[3]

In view of such plain statements, Ricardo's remark that Mr. Malthus' error is in supposing that cheap commodities necessarily imply glut, absence of profit, and perhaps loss of capital, exhibits him as a very poor critic.

The doctrine of Malthus as to increase in the value as well as in the quantity of the total product contained nothing that should have proved a stumbling-block to Ricardo, for he himself said in his *Notes* (vol. 2, p. 416): 'If a nation saves, and employs more labour in production, it will increase the quantity and value of its produce.' The only difference between the two men is that Ricardo

[1] Malthus' *Principles*, page 170 in first edition; 166 in second.
[2] Ibid., page 402 in first edition; 352 in second.
[3] Ibid., page 456 in first edition; 394 in second.

assumes the increase of value as something that cannot fail to occur, whereas Malthus says increased outlay *should* produce increased value, but may fail to do so owing to the product not being of the kind, or being in excess of the quantity, for which there is an effectual demand. Ricardo agrees with this too, but regards it as applicable only to particular commodities, not to production in the aggregate. 'Men err in their productions', he says; 'there is no deficiency of demand' (vol. 8, p. 277). Glut is due to 'bad selection' of the object to be produced. 'If the commodities produced be suited to the wants of the purchasers', he says, 'they cannot exist in such abundance as not to find a market' (vol. 2, p. 304); 'if they were suited to the wants of those who would have the power to purchase them, they could not fail to find purchasers, and that without any fall of price' (vol. 2, p. 303). While Malthus thinks that, for manufacturers, production is comparatively simple and certain, but sale often difficult and subject to ruinous competition, Ricardo regards production as difficult but thinks the exchange of what has been produced is and must be easy, simple and certain. 'I think that demand depends only on supply' (vol. 2, p. 365). Ricardo in fact followed Say, who had 'most satisfactorily shown that . . . demand is only limited by production' (192/290), and a note of scorn is discernible in his remark: 'Mr. Malthus, it will be observed, loses no occasion of insisting on the importance of demand in stimulating countries to exertion, and is always fearful of a deficiency of this invigorating force' (vol. 2, p. 370).

Yes, Malthus regards keen demand as exercising an invigorating influence upon industry; for this view he could have quoted Ricardo's own statement in his *Principles* (283/414):

> It is the rise in the market price of corn which alone encourages its production; for it may be laid down as a principle uniformly true that the only great encouragement to the increased production of a commodity is its market value exceeding its natural or necessary value.

If this is 'uniformly true' in the case of each commodity taken separately, Malthus cannot see why it is not true of production taken as a whole; he writes:

> In individual cases, the power of producing particular commodities is called into action in proportion to the effective demand

for them; and the greatest stimulus to their production is a high market price, or an increase of their exchangeable value before more capital and labour have been employed upon them. In the same manner, the greatest stimulus to the continued production of commodities, taken all together, is an increase in the exchangeable value of the whole mass before more labour and capital have been employed upon them.[1]

This puzzles Ricardo; in the *Notes* (vol. 2, p. 367) he writes:

> What is meant by 'an increase in the exchangeable value of the whole mass of commodities before more labour and capital have been employed upon them'? If it be meant that they are more valuable as compared with labour, it is a roundabout way of saying that labour has fallen in value.

What Malthus meant seems clear enough; he meant what Ricardo meant when he said (283/415) that production is stimulated when increase of demand causes the market price to rise above the natural price. And, in the opinion of Malthus, if capitalists did not increase their capital until a rise of market price indicated that demand had increased, and if they then only increased their capital to the extent required to satisfy the increased demand, the progress of industry, employment, and production would be smooth and uninterrupted. But while it may be true that the only *great* encouragement to increase of production is a rise of price, the fact is, in the opinion of Malthus, that capitalists do not wait for this encouragement before increasing their capital. They do not even wait until there seems a likelihood that prices may rise in the near future. Each capitalist is eager to increase his capital, and does not trouble himself overmuch as to whether his goods are bought by new consumers or by purchasers he has attracted from other capitalists; provided he can increase his own sales he can earn a profit on an increased capital. Capitalists are always saving, and additions are constantly made to capital; the tendency is for increase of capital to run ahead of increase of demand. It becomes difficult or impossible for all producers to find sufficient consumers. A cut-throat competition develops in which the weaker or the smaller man is driven out of business. He not only loses profit on his capital, but perhaps also his capital itself. On the

[1] Malthus' *Principles*, page 414. In the second edition (or at all events in the reprint, page 361) 'taken all together' is misprinted 'taken altogether'.

other hand, his competitor, although successful, nevertheless finds his profit reduced by the enormous sums he has to spend upon advertising and display in order to attract and retain his customers.

Thus Malthus concludes that industry is in a healthy state if demand runs ahead of production; whereas if production continually runs ahead of demand, there will always be difficulty in finding sufficient customers, and therefore in finding value. If Malthus 'loses no occasion of insisting on the importance of demand', if he is 'always fearful of a deficiency of this invigorating force', it is because he thinks the tendency is towards too much saving, and he sees in saving or parsimony a force which tends to hold consumption in check at the same time that it promotes production. He recognises, however, that we cannot do without saving. In this dilemma, he brings forward his formula for continuous progress. This makes its first appearance unobtrusively in a brief footnote reading as follows: 'Parsimony, or the conversion of revenue into capital, may take place without any diminution of consumption, if the revenue increases first.'[1] This makes Ricardo lose patience; he exclaims:

> I say it always takes place without any diminution of consumption. Mr. Malthus clogs the proposition with a condition—'if the revenue increases first'. I do not understand what Mr. M. means—if the revenue increases first. Before what? (vol. 2, p. 326).

'Mr. M.' must have smiled, or shrugged his shoulders, when he read this outburst, for it appears highly probable that what he had in his mind was Ricardo's own dictum on page 79(131) of his *Principles*:—

> There are two ways in which capital may be accumulated; it may be saved either in consequence of increased revenue, or of diminished consumption. If my profits are raised from £1000 to £1200 while my expenditure continues the same, I accumulate annually £200 more than I did before. If I save £200 out of my expenditure, while my profits continue the same, the same effect will be produced; £200 per annum will be added to my capital.[2]

---

[1] Malthus' *Principles*, page 369 in first edition; page 326 in second.

[2] On page 459 of his first edition Malthus again refers to 'the two ways in which capital may be accumulated, as stated by Mr. Ricardo'. In the second edition (or at all events in the reprint, page 396) he quotes the number of Ricardo's page incorrectly.

There seems no reason, then, why Ricardo should have found the meaning of Malthus so elusive. If a man's income rises from £1000 to £1200 he can both consume more and invest more if he so chooses, and if the community's income increases from £10,000,000 to £12,000,000 it also can add to its consumption at the same time that it adds to its capital. Malthus thinks that marketing difficulties must necessarily occur if capital is increased when there is no increase of demand, still more if there is a diminution of demand. But if, despite saving, there is a net increase of demand, so that the total product, now increased, sells for a larger total price than before, then the additional capital is rewarded.

The footnote of Malthus which Ricardo found so incomprehensible is expanded by Malthus on a later page, where he writes:

> It has already been shown that this value cannot be maintained in the case of a rapid accumulation of capital occasioned by an actual and continued diminution in the expenditure of the higher classes of society. Yet it will be most readily allowed that the saving from revenue to add to capital is an absolutely necessary step in the progress of wealth. How then is saving to take place without producing the diminution of value apprehended?
>
> It may take place, and practically almost always does take place, in consequence of a previous increase of value, or of revenue, in which case a saving may be effected, not only without any diminution of demand and consumption, but under an actual increase of demand, consumption and value during every part of the process. And it is in fact this previous increase of value and revenue which both gives the great stimulus to accumulation, and makes that accumulation effective in the continued production of wealth.[1]

Here there appears to be a somewhat puzzling inconsistency. His complaint is that wealth-production, and continuous employment for capital and labour, are impeded by excessive saving, whereas what is required is that increase of demand shall always be a little ahead of increase of supply. Yet he tells us not only that increase of revenue and demand may take place, but that it 'practically almost always does take place'; and he goes on to say that 'many a merchant has made a large fortune although, during the acquisition of this fortune, there was perhaps hardly a single year in which he did not rather increase than diminish his

[1] Malthus' *Principles*, page 419 in first edition; page 365 in second.

expenditure in objects of luxury, enjoyment, and liberality'.[1] The same inconsistency is shown at the end of the section. 'In general', he says, 'an increase of produce and an increase of value go on together; and this is that natural and healthy state of things, which is most favourable to the progress of wealth',[2] but he finishes the paragraph with the remark that if production and distribution are *not* in the proper proportions, they 'produce only, after the lapse of many thousand years, the scanty riches and scanty population which are at present scattered over the face of the globe'. We must infer, then, that, whatever may be the case at certain periods, the history of mankind does not justify the conclusion that 'practically almost always' distribution keeps pace with production; if this natural and healthy state of things had been the rule instead of the exception 'the earth would probably before this period have contained, at the very least, ten times as many inhabitants as are supported on its surface at present'.[3] As for the position in England at the time when he wrote, he remarks near the end of his book: 'What is now wanted in this country is an increased national revenue—an increase in the exchangeable value of the whole produce, estimated in bullion.'[4]

This might seem to indicate that Malthus had come to the conclusion that the failure of demand to keep pace with increasing production had a monetary origin, and required a monetary remedy. What is required he says, is that revenue[5] shall increase first. If the income of the individual rises from £1000 to £1200, and the national revenue from ten million to twelve million, the larger product can be sold for a larger total price, and there need be no fall of prices or reduction in the rate of profit. But if increase of money income lags behind increase of production, there must be a more or less chronic difficulty in selling all that is produced at a remunerative price.

Something of this sort seems to have been in Malthus' mind, but without taking definite shape. He did express the view that it is a mistake to treat trade as mere barter and to leave out of

[1] Malthus' *Principles*, page 421 in first edition; page 367 in second.

[2] Ibid., page 426 in first edition; page 371 in second.

[3] Ibid., page 348 in first edition, as quoted earlier in this chapter; page 311 in reprint.

[4] Ibid., page 505 in first edition; page 424 in reprint.

[5] Malthus defines national revenue as 'the sum of rents, profits, and wages' (page 454 in first edition, page 392 in second edition).

account the part played by money; 'we are much more likely to obscure our reasonings', he says, 'than to render them clearer, by throwing it out of our consideration'.[1] Nevertheless, although he wants to see the nation's output worth more 'bullion', he does not attribute the deficiency of demand to an inadequate supply of gold. It is interesting to speculate as to what course their discussions might have taken if Malthus and Ricardo had sat down together to consider the implications of the latter's remarks on page 60 of his *Principles* where he tells us that as a nation advances, more and more capital is saved, more and more labour is employed, and the process 'will infallibly be attended with an increased production of commodities. To circulate these commodities,' says Ricardo, 'even at the same price as before, more money is required, more of this foreign commodity from which money is made, and which can only be obtained by importation.'[2] Here, Malthus might have said, we are furnished with a monetary explanation of those recurring periods of depression which too often interrupt the process of production in a world of divided labour using gold as a medium of exchange. The capitalists keep on adding to capital in the hope of selling a larger total output at a larger total price, and this is not possible until the quantity of money is increased. But the quantity of money will not increase until prices have fallen and attracted more gold from abroad. A periodical fall of prices, therefore, is an inevitable accompaniment of the increase of capital. The fall will in due course automatically bring about its own remedy, namely, an influx of gold and a rise of prices, but nevertheless the period during which prices are falling may be of considerable duration, and it will be a period of depression, when profits are diminishing and employment is becoming scarcer. The revival of trade, the invigorating demand so necessary for the capitalist and for the man who depends on wages, will come, as already suggested, when additional money comes from oversea and enters into circulation.

After discussing Ricardo's page 60(104), the two men might

[1] Malthus' *Principles*, page 444 in first edition; page 385 in reprint.

[2] In following the arguments of Malthus and Ricardo which we are about to examine it is very necessary for the reader to keep in mind that British money consisted of the 'foreign commodity' gold throughout the eighteenth and nineteenth centuries (apart from a temporary suspension).

well have gone on to consider the arguments put forward by David Hume in his famous essay on Money (1752).

In that essay Hume expressed the view that the discovery of rich mines in America, and the consequent inflow of the precious metals into Europe, was responsible for a great increase in industry, productivity, and prosperity. Owing to these metals being used as money, their importation was on a different footing from the importation of corn or iron; it was practically an importation of additional money. 'We find', says Hume, 'that in every kingdom into which money begins to flow in greater abundance than formerly, everything takes a new face; labour and industry gain life; the merchant becomes more enterprising, the manufacturer more diligent, and even the farmer follows his plough with greater alacrity and attention.'[1]

> From the whole of this reasoning we may conclude that it is of no manner of consequence, with regard to the domestic happiness of a state, whether money be in a greater or less quantity. The good policy of the magistrate[2] consists only in keeping it, if possible, still increasing; because by that means he keeps alive a spirit of industry in the nation, and increases the stock of labour, in which consists all real power and riches.[3]

It is surprising that Malthus makes no mention of Hume's essay. Even if he differed from Hume in some particulars, one would have thought that he would see in Hume's theory a powerful support for his own doctrine that industry flourishes when revenue increases first. Ricardo is equally silent, but his silence is easier to understand. He regarded Hume's argument as fallacious.[4] He agreed with Hume that it is of no consequence

[1] Sixth paragraph in Hume's essay on Money. Compare with chap. 6 in Part 2 of Cantillon's *Essay on the Nature of Commerce*. As this essay existed only in manuscript at the time when Hume wrote, it is, I suppose, unlikely that he was acquainted with it.

[2] I.e. the policy of the government.

[3] Ninth paragraph in Hume's essay. In the same paragraph Hume also paints the reverse of this picture; when the quantity of money is diminishing, this diminution is just as pernicious to industry as an increasing supply is beneficial—'the farmer cannot dispose of his corn and cattle, though he must pay the same rent to his landlord. The poverty, beggary, and sloth, which must ensue, are easily foreseen.'

[4] See his reference to 'an erroneous view of Mr. Hume', page 524 in vol. 5. In his notes on Bentham he wrote: 'Why should the mere increase of money have any other effect than to lower its value? How would it cause any increase

'whether money be in greater or less quantity'; he makes the same statement himself on page 124(194): 'No more advantage results from using twenty millions than from using ten millions of currency'; but there is no reason to suppose that Ricardo ever troubled himself very much to consider the condition of things likely to prevail in a country while the quantity of money is increasing from ten millions to twenty millions. Money is only the medium by which the exchange is effected (194/291). If the quantity of money is increased when there is no corresponding increase in the quantity of goods to be circulated, all prices will be higher, including the price of labour, and the quantity of commodities the labourer will get for his money will not be affected (104/164). Nor will the increase of money affect the rate of profit, for 'if the manufacturer has more to pay for wages, he will receive more for his manufactured goods' (90/146). In his *Notes on Malthus* (vol. 2, p. 396) Ricardo wrote: 'An alteration in the value of money has no effect on the relative value of commodities, for it raises or sinks their price in the same proportion.' In a letter to Malthus he said: 'Nothing is to me so little important as the fall and rise of commodities in money' (vol. 9, p. 83). And a fortnight later: 'I say again that too much importance is attached to money; facility of production is the great and interesting point' (vol. 9, p. 100).

Thus we see that, unlike Hume, and unlike Malthus, Ricardo shuts his eyes to the invigorating effect which is felt in every branch of industry when there is a progressive increase in the flow of money from consumers to producers. A letter which Ricardo wrote to Malthus in 1817 throws some light upon his attitude; he said:

> It appears to me that one great cause of our difference in opinion on the subjects which we have so often discussed is that you have always in your mind the immediate and temporary effects of particular changes, whereas I put these immediate and temporary effects quite aside, and fix my whole attention on the permanent state of things which will result from them (vol. 7, p. 120).

---

in the production of commodities?' (vol. 3, p. 298). Another note reads: 'Is it not to be doubted whether the augmentation of money in any way accelerates the prosperity of a country; for the reasons I have given I think it retards it.' Other references to Hume's doctrine will be found on page 90 in vol. 3 and page 36 in vol. 4.

The 'permanent state of things' that Ricardo sees as resulting from an increase of money is a higher price-level; if the quantity of money in circulation rises from ten to twenty million, the only result will be that everybody will receive double the quantity of money for what he sells, and will have to pay double the quantity for everything he buys. Ricardo's 'whole attention' is fixed on the ultimate result, and the intermediate period, when prices are rising, is ignored.[1] On page 88(143) he writes: 'No effect will be produced on the rate of profits either from the influx or efflux of money.' That is to say, there will be no permanent effect; immediate and temporary effects are disregarded; he looks only at what the position will be after influx or efflux has run its course. When prices have had time to adjust themselves to the changed money-flow, he assumes, relative values will be the same as before.

This is not the view of Malthus. Costs and prices 'never all rise at the same time, or even finally in the same proportion'.[2] Moreover, while Ricardo looks only at the ultimate result, Malthus pays attention to the immediate and temporary effect of rising prices. 'A period of some continuance can scarcely fail to occur', he remarks, 'when the difference between the price of produce and the cost of production is so increased as to give a great stimulus to agriculture'.[3] A page or two earlier he said: 'A fall in the value of the precious metals . . . has a strong tendency, while it lasts,[4] to encourage the cultivation of fresh land.'[5] Thus Malthus stresses the importance of these intervals of rising price, whereas Ricardo, if he mentions them at all, does so to belittle them; he says (the italics are mine): 'It is, then, *only* during the interval after the rise in the market price of commodities, and till the additional supply is obtained, that the manufacturers will

[1] In January, 1811, Ricardo had admitted that a period of increasing money and rising prices would result in temporary increase of profits at the expense of the labourer, owing to the wage-lag. See vol. 3, pp. 318–19, and vol. 6, pp. 16–17.

[2] Malthus' *Principles*, page 172 in first edition; page 167 in second.

[3] He refers here (page 172) to agriculture because it is with the rent of land that he is dealing; but the principle applies also to other industries.

[4] Presumably he means while the value of money continues to fall, i.e. while prices continue to rise.

[5] Malthus' *Principles*, page 170 in first edition; page 166 in second.

enjoy high profits' (209/313).[1] On page 283(415), it is true, he attaches importance to a temporary rise of price and profit; the only great encouragement to increased production, he says, is the market price exceeding the natural price; but this remark refers to a particular commodity, and Ricardo disagrees when Malthus assumes that the same thing holds good of a general rise of prices. Says Malthus:

> Whenever there is a general demand for commodities . . . there is the same kind of reason for expecting a general increase of commodities as there is for expecting an increase of particular commodities when their market prices rise.[2]

Ricardo does not look upon a general rise of prices, caused by an increase in the supply of money, as indicating an increase in the demand for commodities. What it indicates, in his view, is that money has fallen in value. It will not be long before the price of labour catches up to the new level of commodity prices, and once more costs and prices will correspond. Hence he writes to Malthus (as already partly quoted):

> Nothing is to me so little important as the fall and rise of commodities in money; the great enquiries on which to fix our attention are the rise or fall of corn, labour, and commodities in real value, that is to say the increase or diminution of the quantity of labour necessary to raise corn and to manufacture commodities. It may be curious to develop the effect of an alteration of real value on money price; but mankind are only really interested in making labour productive, and in the enjoyment of abundance, and in a good distribution of the produce obtained by capital and industry. I cannot help thinking that in your speculation you suppose these much too closely connected with money price (vol. 9, p. 83).

Ricardo did not see any close connection between money and prosperity because he thought that 'all trade is in fact a trade of barter' (vol. 2, p. 146). In his *Principles* he observed: 'Productions are always bought by productions or by services; money is only the medium by which exchange is effected' (194/291). Hume himself said that money is 'only the instrument which men have agreed upon to facilitate the exchange of one commodity for

[1] Ricardo writes to Malthus: 'I acknowledge the intervals on which you so exclusively dwell, but still they are only intervals' (vol. 8, p. 302).

[2] Malthus' *Principles*, page 417 in first edition; page 363 in second. For Ricardo's comment see vol. 2, p. 372.

another'.[1] Many years later Ricardo's disciple, J. S. Mill, wrote in the same strain; he said:

> There cannot, in short, be intrinsically a more insignificant thing in the economy of society than money; except in the character of a contrivance for sparing time and labour. It is a machine for doing quickly and commodiously what would be done, though less quickly and commodiously, without it.[2]

One may doubt Mill's conclusion that everything that money enables us to do could be done without it. It is difficult, for instance, to conceive a great ocean liner being built, or being operated, under a system of barter. At all events, the world has outgrown barter; the shoemaker no longer offers his shoes in exchange for bread;[3] it is not the offer of goods but the offer of money that constitutes effective demand; and so far from thinking that Malthus saw too close a connection between money and industry, we must agree with him that 'in civilised countries we may be quite sure that if the farmer or manufacturer cannot sell his products so as to give him a profit estimated in money, his industry will immediately slacken'.[4] As early as 1814 Malthus appears to have had the idea that unless the money income of consumers increases before the increase of production there will be trouble in selling products at remunerative prices; the question, he writes to Ricardo, is not whether people would gladly consume more if more can be produced, 'but whether you can furnish to persons of the same incomes a great additional quantity of commodities without lowering their price so much compared with the price of production as to destroy the effective demand for such a supply, and consequently check its continuance to the same extent'.[5] It is no answer to this to say that buying and selling are

[1] It is curious that Hume begins his essay with this remark, seeing that the very purpose of his essay is to show what a vital influence money exercises upon national prosperity. [2] J. S. Mill's *Principles*, Bk. 3, chap. 7, section 3.

[3] As suggested by Ricardo in an early letter to Malthus (vol. 6, p. 164).

[4] Footnote, pages 361–2 in first edition, page 324 in second (where there are slight alterations). Ricardo himself (1822) said in Parliament: 'In no case would production go on, for any considerable length of time, without remunerating prices' (vol. 5, p. 213).

[5] Vol. 6, p. 142. This is not very well expressed, but his remarks at the top of the previous page make it clear that, by 'destroying' the effective demand, he means that the demand will not be effective if the money price obtainable for the product 'compared with the money expense of production' does not afford a sufficient margin to make the production profitable.

only a form of barter, and that 'accumulation necessarily increases production, and as necessarily increases consumption' (vol. 6, p. 164). Ricardo's own doctrine on page 60(104) implies that with growth in the production of commodities there must be a growth of money income, or prices will necessarily fall. And Ricardo also said (279/409) that 'in the usual and ordinary course of things the demand for all commodities precedes their supply', and how, under a monetary system, can increased production of commodities be preceded by an increased effective demand unless it is preceded by an increase in the total of money income? Revenue, said Malthus, must increase first.

In view of the importance that Malthus attaches to increase of money-spending on the part of consumers we might have expected him to devote a good deal of attention to Hume's essay on money, but as already remarked, he makes no reference to it in his *Principles*, and we have to ask why? The reason appears to be that he thinks the flow of money through the consumer market can increase, and in fact does increase, without any addition to the stock of money, whenever there is an increased desire to consume on the part of those who at present save a large part of their incomes. 'It is quite certain', he says, 'that an adequate passion for consumption may fully keep up the proper proportion between supply and demand, whatever may be the powers of production.'[1] Clearly, he does not accept Ricardo's doctrine on page 60(104) that if we want to circulate a larger quantity of commodities at the same prices as before we must first obtain a larger supply of money—must import more gold from abroad. His idea appears to be that the same object can be achieved by a more rapid circulation of money; £1 circulating twice will purchase as much as £2 circulating once.

If Malthus had believed that an increase in the quantity of money was necessary to prevent prices falling when a community is continuously adding to its capital and production, he would have attached special importance to foreign trade as the only means by which a country such as England, without gold mines, could add to its stock of money. That such additions, when they occur, give 'a considerable stimulus' to industry by raising prices, was one of his contentions,[2] and he remarked: 'A successful

[1] Malthus' *Principles*, page 365 in first edition; page 325 in second.

[2] Ibid., page 170 in first edition; page 166 in second.

extension of foreign trade is exactly that state of things which most directly leads to the importation of bullion.'[1] But he regarded this as quite a subordinate advantage in foreign trade. The remark, in fact, was a mere dig at Ricardo who maintained that foreign trade adds to utility but not to value, and apart from this solitary sally Malthus makes no distinction between domestic and foreign trade as a means of giving value to products and affording profit to producers. 'There is no magic in foreign markets,' he says.[2] It is exchange, or rather, it is the transfer of goods from producer to consumer, that confers value on commodities; and if all classes were as eager to consume as they are to produce—if they were as eager to spend their money incomes as they are to acquire them—everything produced would be quickly exchanged, and producers would enjoy the necessary encouragement to produce more. It is slow sales—sluggish buying—that prevents labour and capital being always kept busy to their fullest capacity. The difficulty is not in producing, but in finding consumers; and it is here that Malthus sees an advantage in foreign trade. From the producer's point of view, a world-wide market is superior to a market which is purely local because it increases his chance of finding consumers. Wants and tastes being more numerous, more diversified, there is a greater probability that every kind of article offered for sale will answer to the need or suit the taste of someone. In a large market, it is true, there will be more producers as well as more consumers, but on the other hand the greater variety of goods for sale increases the likelihood that every man with money in his pocket will discover a number of things that he would like to possess. When only local products are offered for sale the British consumer soon has enough, but when such tempting articles as tea, sugar, coffee, wine, tobacco, rice, oranges, pineapples, ostrich feathers, furs, silk, diamonds, marble, are brought to his very door, every man, and every man's wife, desires to become a large-scale consumer, and there is some approach to Ricardo's assumption that all who have the power to consume *will* consume as much as they can pay for. This, rather than the importation of money, is the advantage that Malthus sees in foreign trade as a means of increasing the total value as well as the total quantity of what is produced.

[1] Malthus' *Principles*, page 453 in first edition; page 391 in second.

[2] Ibid., page 411 in first edition; page 359 in second.

> If goods could be produced at home [he says], which would . . . communicate the same enjoyments, and create a consumption of the same *value*, foreign markets would be useless. We know, however, from experience, that very few countries are capable of producing commodities of the same efficacy, in this respect, as those which may be obtained by a trade to various climates and soils.[1]

Thus Malthus believes that foreign trade increases value because he believes that all trade, all exchange, increases value; products acquire utility and value by being transferred from producers to consumers. He writes:

> A great increase of productions may immediately find an adequate market, and experience consequently a great increase of exchangeable value, if they are so well distributed and so well adapted to the tastes and wants of the society as to excite the desire of making an adequate sacrifice in order to procure and consume them.[2]

In the second edition the passage continues as follows:

> In fact, such an increase of value always really takes place on occasion of an increased foreign demand for commodities; and unquestionably a similar increase of value would take place in the case of such a production and distribution of domestic commodities as better to suit the tastes and desires of the domestic consumers.[3]

Obviously, then, as already stated, Malthus does not regard an addition to the stock of money as necessary to enable the nation's annual product to grow in money value as well as in quantity. So

[1] Malthus' *Principles*, pages 411–12 in first edition; page 359 in second.

[2] Ibid., page 421 in first edition; page 366 in second. It will be noted that Malthus uses the word 'distribution' in more than one sense. Here the word obviously refers to that geographical dispersal of the goods (without any *necessary* change of ownership) which brings them to the notice of potential consumers in various places, whereas when he tells us on page 479 (409 in second) that soldiers, sailors, and annuitants, contribute powerfully to distribution, he means that they create a large effective demand. Purchase by consumers is the kind of 'distribution' on which he counts to confer value upon products. He uses 'distribution' in a third sense when he tells us on page 429 (373 in second) that if a few are rich while most are poor, it is a distribution of property, or purchasing power, very unfavourable to effective demand. Effective demand is the only 'distribution' that confers value. (When Ricardo speaks of 'a more just distribution of the produce' in a letter to Malthus (vol. 9, p. 26), he uses the word to mean the proportions in which the product is divided between capital and labour.)

[3] See also the passage on page 510 quoted later in this chapter.

far as increase of value is concerned, he sees no difference between sales at home and sales abroad. Although he knew that if a country develops a great superiority to other countries in the manufacture of cotton goods the result may be that the demand of foreign countries for these products grows more largely than the local demand for foreign goods, which is 'exactly that state of things which most directly leads to the importation of bullion', he nevertheless regards a brisk local demand as having the same effect in increasing the total money price. He quite recognises that some people (Ricardo, for instance) take a different view. It will perhaps be said, he remarks on page 451 of the first edition, that the value of the whole produce, estimated in money, cannot be increased if the quantity of money is not increased.[1] He proceeds on the next page to combat this view.

> With regard to money [he says] this most useful measure of value would perform its functions very indifferently if it could in no respect accommodate itself to cases of this kind. . . . But this is far from being the case, even if we do not suppose any fresh importation of the precious metals. The occurrence of such an event is precisely the period when a greater velocity is given to the circulation of the money actually in use, and when fresh paper may be issued without a fall in the rate of foreign exchanges, or a rise in the price of bullion and of goods.[2]

These words, it is true, are not to be found in his second edition because the whole page is omitted; but Malthus did not abandon the doctrine, for it reappears in his second edition in the shape of a new footnote to his chapter on Measures of Value, where he says:

> Repeated experience appears to have shown us that in the case of a brisk demand, no difficulty is ever found in furnishing the means of a considerable rise in price in some classes of commodities, without any tendency to fall in others. Currency is always at hand.[3]

And for what it may be worth as reflecting the opinion of Malthus it may be pointed out that the friend who edited the second edition of Malthus' *Principles* (published after his death) adds a

[1] In his second edition Malthus made some alterations, but he repeats this remark (page 391): 'It may perhaps be thought that the money value of the whole produce cannot be increased without an importation of money.'

[2] I.e. bank paper may be issued without causing depreciation.

[3] Page 128 in second edition. And in a new footnote to his chapter on Rent (page 174), the same doctrine appears, but viewed in reverse.

footnote of his own, commencing: 'The importation of bullion is not necessary to a rise of prices; for there is no necessary connection between a given quantity of money and a given scale of prices.'[1]

No one disputes that £1 circulating twice does as much work as £2 circulating once; but was Malthus justified in assuming that an increase in the rapidity of circulation automatically results from an increased desire on the part of the public to spend their money on consumption?

What are the factors that decide the rapidity of circulation? The most important of these in a modern society would appear to be the practice of the community with regard to the payment of wages. If wages are paid weekly, they are spent weekly; the money leaves the bank at the end of the week for distribution to the wage-earners, and after being spent in the shops, is back in the bank before next weekend and is available for payment of another week's wages. Thus one million sovereigns circulating weekly enable the capitalists to pay their employees £52,000,000 in the course of the year, and to sell them £52,000,000 worth of goods. On the other hand, if wages are paid once a fortnight the bank must supply two million sovereigns on every fourteenth day to enable the labourers to receive and the capitalists to sell them £52,000,000 worth of goods in the course of twelve months. It is true, then, that there is no fixed relationship between the quantity of money and the quantity of payments that can be made with it during the year; one million sovereigns circulating 52 times do as much work as two million sovereigns circulating 26 times.

A quicker circulation, then, can be secured—the same aggregate of payments can be achieved in a year with a smaller quantity of money—by changing monthly or fortnightly distributions of wages to weekly, quarterly payments to monthly, half-yearly payments to quarterly, and so on. But there appears no reason to suppose that changes such as these will come about as a natural consequence of an increased eagerness to consume commodities. Nor, I think, had Malthus anything of this sort in his mind. His idea was that the man of small means creates as much demand for

[1] Page 391 in second edition. For Ricardo's opinion as to when prices can be raised without importing additional bullion, see his footnotes to pages 107/169 and 138/213 of his *Principles*.

commodities as it is in his power to create with his scanty income, whereas people with much larger purchasing power commonly exercise only a portion of that purchasing power, preferring to save the rest as a provision for the future. Unlike the labourers these people could, if they chose, increase their demand for goods without any increase of money income, and without its being necessary to add a single pound or a single penny to the community's stock of money. All that is necessary is that they shall spend a larger proportion of the money they receive, and save a smaller proportion. Malthus did not accept the view of Ricardo that what the wealthy do not spend upon themselves they turn over to the labourers in the form of wages; he appears to reject[1] the dictum of Adam Smith that 'what is annually saved is as regularly consumed as what is annually spent, and nearly in the same time too'.[2]

Did Malthus, then, believe that money 'saved' is withdrawn from circulation—hoarded? He expressly repudiated that idea; he said: 'No Political Economist of the present day can by saving mean mere hoarding.'[3] But if the money saved is not hoarded—if it is all spent in one way or another—it is not clear in what manner he supposed that greater eagerness on the part of the wealthy to consume would result in a quicker circulation of money.

No doubt wealthy people accumulate bank balances which, to the extent that they remain undrawn upon, are neither invested nor spent, and may be looked upon as hoarded purchasing power; everybody, in fact, who can do so, finds it convenient to keep a certain quantity of purchasing power in reserve. No doubt, too, there are periods of considerable length when a tendency to tighten the purse strings becomes very general, and other periods when it becomes equally general to spend more freely. These fluctuations are important; nevertheless they *are* fluctuations, and do not represent a progressive and permanent shrinkage, or a progressive and permanent growth, of demand. The real question to

[1] He might be supposed to *accept* this dictum when he says (page 31 of his first edition): 'It is stated by Adam Smith, and it must be allowed to be stated justly', etc., but this seeming approval is whittled away by qualifications, and in the second edition (page 38 of reprint), the approving phrase disappears.

[2] *Wealth of Nations*, Bk. 2, chap. 3, 18th paragraph.

[3] Malthus' *Principles*, page 32 in first edition; page 38 in second.

be asked is whether a steady and progessive increase in the quantity of the nation's money income can be made to accompany a continuous growth in capital, in population, and in production, merely by increasing the rapidity with which money circulates? In other words, can the community's total money income rise progressively from ten to twelve millions, from twelve to twenty, thirty, fifty millions, always keeping pace with the expanding production of commodities, without an increase in the quantity of money? Our conclusion must be, I think, that while something might be done by shortening the period for wage payments, etc., there is a limit to this device, and Ricardo was right in holding that in a country whose currency is gold, prices must fall when the quantity of goods is increased unless the quantity of gold in circulation is also increased.

Malthus, however, does not rely upon increased rapidity alone as a means of increasing the aggregate of money payments; he refers also to the issue of 'fresh paper'.

It must have been of ordinary bank-notes, redeemable on demand in gold, or perhaps of bank credits which also entitle the customer or his transferee to receive actual cash on demand, that Malthus was thinking when he said that 'fresh paper may be issued without a fall in the rate of foreign exchanges or a rise in the price of bullion and of goods'. These bank promises, circulating as freely as money, give elasticity to the currency, and enable it to expand when there is 'more work' to be done. When there is an increasing demand for commodities the banker is always ready to help the producer; he is always glad to increase his loans, and thus earn interest, when the customer can satisfy him of his ability to repay the loan punctually.

Opinions may differ as to whether these loans should be regarded as a temporary increase in the quantity of money, or as a temporary increase in the rapidity of circulation, but in any case they can be brought about without importing more gold; and it is clear that the banker increases the customer's immediate purchasing power without diminishing the purchasing power of any other member of the community. Thus a larger quantity can change hands without any fall in price. Malthus apparently regards this as a refutation of Ricardo's dictum (60/104) that if we wish to circulate more commodities at the same prices we must import more gold.

Malthus, however, does not seem to have thought out carefully the part played by bank-notes when their issue is governed and circumscribed by the necessity of redeeming them in gold on demand.

Let us look into this matter. On page 60(104) Ricardo speaks of the quantity of money required to circulate commodities, but 'circulate' is not a very good word to employ in reference to the distribution of goods to consumers. Money circulates without being consumed, but goods are produced to be consumed. Money goes round and round, from hand to hand, but goods, after a short journey, reach the consumer, and there is no more any question of 'circulation'. It is true that under a system of divided labour a product may change hands many times during its progress from raw material to finished article, but the course it follows, though it may sometimes appear circuitous, is in reality a continuous forward journey which comes to an end when the finished product reaches its destination, the consumer. Perhaps it would be better to say that there are two markets, the Producers' market where materials and goods move from one capitalist to another without being consumed, and the Consumers' market where completed products make their final appearance before being consumed, or at any rate bought 'for keeps'. In the Producers' market the manufacturer buys the materials that he intends to transform, and the merchant buys the stocks that he intends to split up and distribute to retailers. Neither manufacturer nor merchant nor retailer consumes the goods he handles; he buys to sell again; and it is in this market, where goods may be said to circulate or pass from hand to hand without being consumed, that credit is largely employed as a means of purchase; or rather, as a means of securing the passage of the goods through all the different stages of production under a system where many changes of place may be necessary, and many changes of ownership, before the product emerges in a form ready for, and accessible to, the consumer. What we see in the Producers' market it not an exchange of money income for commodity income, but a circulation of capital. The banker plays a very useful part in facilitating these successive transfers. Bank paper and trade credit affords a means by which raw materials pass through all the stages of production without the necessity of withdrawing any money from the consumers until the producers are ready to hand over the completed items of commodity income in exchange for money income.

It is in the Producers' market that 'currency is always at hand'. The banks give elasticity to the medium of exchange. The quantity of currency is increased temporarily, not because the borrower wishes to increase his consumption, but because he has a new asset which will serve as guarantee for the prompt repayment of the advance. But the conditions are not the same in the Consumers' market. It is not the proper function of the banker to enable his customers to consume more than they can pay for, and so long as banks are obliged to give gold in exchange for their paper there is little danger of their lending any considerable sum to consumers. I do not know what may be the policy of the banks under the system of inconvertible paper money that at present prevails (1956), but throughout the 19th century it was held that mortgages on land or other non-liquid assets were unsuitable security for a bank-loan. No doubt there was some lending to consumers on a restricted scale, but even this could not be regarded as a means for a sustained growth of money income such as Malthus had in view, since the borrower must always repay his loan, and if he increases his consumption today he must correspondingly reduce it tomorrow.

I may be told that even if banks lend to producers only, their loans necessarily increase consumer-demand. A manufacturer may borrow £1000 from the bank to buy raw material; the owner of the raw material thus receives money which he can spend upon consumption. The manufacturer also hires labour with the money borrowed, and the labourers spend their wages upon consumption. And when the manufacturer has completed his product a merchant buys it from him with paper he has borrowed from the bank, and the price received by the manufacturer enables him to repay his loan with interest, while at the same time it enables him to pocket his profit and to spend it upon consumption. All this is true, but it does not show that the nation's money income can grow from ten to twenty, thirty, forty million pounds by a gradual growth of bank advances. The increase of bank advances will follow close on the heels of growing consumer money income, but the banker never advances to the producer the full amount which the latter expects to get for his product when he sells it. This price will have to exceed the banker's loan by the amount required to pay the bank's interest and the amount required to afford the producer his profit. The whole process of financing production is dependent for its success on the consumer being able to pay, from his money income, sufficient to recoup the whole expense of production. Let money income 'increase first', and increase of production, facilitated by increase of bank-loans, will follow in its wake.

Of course, if a country abandons the precious metals as its measure of value and medium of exchange, and adopts inconvertible paper money for the latter purpose (as most countries have been forced to do in this twentieth century) it is easy enough to make prices rise; it is not only easy to increase money incomes, but easy to make revenue increase *first*. With the assistance of the printing-press money income can be kept constantly increasing, and industry may receive a continuous stimulus. Theoretically at least, it becomes possible to prevent Depressions and Unemployment being caused by a general fall of prices. In the opinion of many, this feature of 'managed money' more than compensates for all the disadvantages attendant on a fiat money unanchored to gold or any other standard of value.[1]

But it was certainly not of inconvertible paper money that Malthus was thinking when he said that the issue of fresh paper would not cause a rise in the price of goods or bullion. On the other hand, it *was* of such inconvertible paper that he was thinking when he wrote:

> It is, I believe, the opinion of many persons, particularly among the mercantile classes, that nothing would so soon and so effectively increase the revenue and consumption of the country as a free issue of paper. But in holding this opinion they have mistaken the nature of the great advantage which the national wealth may sometimes unquestionably derive from a fall in the value of the currency.[2]

A fall in the value of the currency is the same thing as a rise in the general price level, and what Malthus had in mind when he penned this passage must have been, I think, the rise of prices which occurred in his own day when for the first time England had a taste of inconvertible paper currency.

[1] See Paul Einzig's *How Money is Managed* (a Pelican Book), particularly the last chapter.

[2] Malthus' *Principles*, pages 513–15 in first edition; pages 430–2 in second.

It may be worth while to interrupt our argument for a few paragraphs for a brief review of the monetary situation in England at the time when Malthus and Ricardo wrote.

Up to 1797 gold coins circulated freely throughout the country, and all bank-notes were payable on demand in gold. In that year, however, there was a run on the Bank of England, and the stock of gold fell so low that the Directors feared they could not continue much longer to cash their notes; hence Parliament, to avert what would have been a national calamity, passed the Bank Restriction Act, whereby the redemption of notes in gold was prohibited.[1]

Thus by a stroke of the pen the Bank of England note was transmuted into what was practically paper money. I use the word transmuted instead of transformed because the *form* of the note remained the same; but while it continued to 'lift its lying head' (as Pope said of the Monument[2])—while it continued to masquerade as a promise to pay gold on demand—it ceased to be an undertaking to pay anything, and itself became, for the time being, England's 'pound sterling'.

The government did not deliberately adopt paper money. It did not repudiate the liability to pay in gold; it merely suspended or postponed the performance of the promise to a more convenient season and ultimately the convertibility of the note was restored, but not until 1821. For nearly a quarter of a century England was off the gold standard; the sovereign disappeared from circulation and was replaced by the one-pound note.[3] The change from gold to paper was hardly felt. At first there was no rise of prices; and when, with increasing issues, goods began to rise in price, there were plenty of people to argue that it was not the value of the paper pound that had fallen but the value of goods that had risen.

[1] On page 243(359) (quoting his own pamphlet of 1816) Ricardo says: 'If the Bank had continued paying in cash, probably the panic would have subsided before the coin had been exhausted.' In 1822 he remained of the same opinion (see vol. 5, pp. 166 and 208). In Clapham's history of the Bank of England we are told that the Bank was willing to resume cash payments in 1797, but was not encouraged to do so.

[2] Pope's allusion was to the inscription which figured on the Monument for many years ascribing the Fire of London to the Catholics.

[3] To enable the Bank of England note to supply the place of the sovereign in domestic circulation, the issue of £1 notes was authorised by Parliament. Previously the lowest denomination permitted was £5.

Ricardo was to the fore in correcting this error. In his pamphlet on the *High Price of Bullion* (1810) he declared that so long as bank-notes 'were payable in specie on demand' the Bank 'could never issue more notes than the value of the coin which would have circulated had there been no bank. If they attempted to exceed this amount, the excess would be immediately returned to them for specie' (vol. 3, p. 57). Again: 'If, whilst the Bank paid their notes on demand in specie, they were to increase the quantity, they would produce little permanent effect on the value of the currency, because nearly an equal quantity of the coin would be withdrawn from circulation and exported' (vol. 3, p. 90). Thus the issue of 'fresh paper', so long as it is redeemable in gold, does not raise prices, because it drives abroad part of the gold in circulation, leaving the total purchasing power in circulation much the same as it was before. His reason for coming to this conclusion was that if the same amount of coin remained in circulation after the issue of the notes, the result would be an increase in the total of purchasing power, and prices would rise, with the twofold consequence that, our products being dearer, our exports would diminish, and foreign goods being comparatively cheaper, our imports would increase, and therefore gold would have to be sent abroad in payment of the shortage. The exodus of gold would continue until prices at home and abroad were once more in harmony.[1]

Thus Ricardo and Malthus are agreed that the employment of bank paper does not raise prices, provided it is always exchangeable for gold on demand. And they are also agreed that when notes are made inconvertible it is no longer true that the Bank cannot issue more than the amount required to circulate increasing quantities of goods at the same prices as before. Ricardo, in fact, is even more emphatic than Malthus in his warning against the danger of depreciation when bank-notes are made inconvertible—

[1] It is on this principle that, on page 60(105) of his *Principles*, Ricardo says: 'The extensive use of paper money does not alter this question, for paper money conforms, or ought to conform, to the value of gold, and therefore its value is influenced by such causes only as influence the value of the metal.' This dictum is not very carefully worded. It is not very logical to say that paper has, because it ought to have, the same value as gold. And if paper is money (which is what he calls it), it is not logical to say that the quantity of money can only be increased by importing more from abroad.

that is to say, when they cease to be engagements to pay money and become for all practical purposes paper money.

He had no theoretical objection to paper money[1] if the quantity were properly controlled. He said in his *Principles* (244/361): 'A currency is in its most perfect state when it consists wholly of paper money, but of paper money of an equal value with the gold which it professes to represent. The use of paper instead of gold substitutes the cheapest in place of the most expensive medium.' On page 239(354) he said: 'It is not necessary that paper money should be payable in specie to secure its value, it is only necessary that its quantity should be regulated according to the value of the metal which is declared to be the standard.' But, alas, theory and practice are two very different things.

> Experience, however, shows [says Ricardo on page 241(356)] that neither a State nor a Bank ever have had the unrestricted power of issuing paper money without abusing that power; in all States therefore the issue of paper money ought to be under some check and control; and none seems so proper for that purpose as that of subjecting the issuers of paper money to the obligation of paying their notes either in gold coin or bullion.

Without this obligation to cash the notes in coin, or at all events to give bullion for export whenever demanded, there is no guarantee, and indeed little likelihood, of the paper not depreciating. Even if the right to increase the quantity of money by the printing-press were reserved strictly to the government, and the quantity kept within rigid bounds, the government would be powerless to prevent paper money depreciating in value, if holders of notes were not entitled to obtain gold for export. This is stated by Ricardo on page 239(354) as follows:

> After the establishment of Banks, the State has not the sole power of coining or issuing money. The currency may as effectually be increased by paper as by coin; so that if a State were to debase its money, and limit its quantity, it could not support its value, because the Banks would have an equal power of adding to the whole quantity of circulation.

Although Ricardo here seems somewhat vague in his employ-

[1] On the contrary, he seems to have preferred it; in his diary in 1822 he writes: 'If we must have metallic money, then give me such money as that of England' (vol. 10, p. 201).

ment of the word 'money', his line of thought appears clear enough. The government 'debases' the pound sterling by making it of paper instead of gold. But although the issue of these pounds is a government monopoly, the private banks would still supply a large part of the circulating medium in the form of bank credit, and (unless prohibited) bank-notes. Now Ricardo maintained, as we have seen, that when paper is redeemable in gold, bank-loans and bank-notes do not increase the circulation or raise prices, because 'an equal quantity of coin would be withdrawn from circulation and exported'. But you cannot export paper money and therefore the injection by the banks of fresh purchasing power into the circulation would not provoke a corresponding diminution in the amount of paper pounds in circulation; the fresh paper would not displace part of the existing medium, but would be wholly an addition to it. True, the banks would be obliged to redeem their notes or credits in paper pounds if demanded; but they would seldom be asked to do so, since their notes would be just as good as paper pounds for domestic payments and purchases and the paper pounds could no more be exported than the bank-notes for the purpose of making purchases abroad. Under these circumstances, a steady growth in the quantity of currency must be expected. The banks, it is true, although running little risk of being called upon to redeem a large portion of their notes in paper pounds, would not grant loans unless assured of repayment; but they would no longer be so particular as to early repayment; they might even prefer long loans to short ones. They might, too, be tempted by a high rate of interest to grant loans to consumers on the mortgage of their property; but even if this type of loan continued to be regarded as outside the sphere of legitimate banking, the circulation would be continually swollen by larger and larger loans to manufacturers and merchants. No doubt the banks would be as careful as ever to have a good margin of security, but each addition to the currency would tend to raise prices, each rise of prices would give additional 'value' to the commodities offered as security for repayment of the debt, and each increase of value would furnish the basis for a larger loan. The Directors of the Bank of England do not seem to have understood this;[1] they apparently thought the

[1] Ricardo said of them: 'They are indeed a very ignorant set' (vol. 9, p. 15). Nevertheless, he remarked: 'The danger, however, is that this power would

issue of notes could never be excessive, and could never cause depreciation, so long as the Bank observed the 'banking principle' of lending only for short periods and to those only who could furnish easily realisable security for repayment. It did not occur to them that what might be true enough so long as notes were redeemable on demand in gold which could be exported, might no longer be true when this overflow pipe was abolished.

This digression concerning paper money will, I hope, be pardoned by the reader. Admittedly, it has little bearing on the subject of this chapter except as explaining why Malthus, despite his reference to 'the great advantage which the national wealth may sometimes unquestionably derive from a fall in the value of the currency', was as strongly opposed as Ricardo to the employment of inconvertible paper. Neither of them looked upon paper money as an instrument 'to achieve the highest degree of welfare for the largest possible number, if necessary even at the cost of sacrificing stability'.[1] On the contrary, to both men the maintenance of the utmost attainable stability in the standard or measure of value appeared to be a matter of prime importance.

Malthus, it is true, desired to see the revenue 'increase first'. But he did not think it was essential for this purpose to obtain more money from abroad; he therefore ignored Hume's theory at the same time that he rejected inconvertible paper. He appears to have thought that if all the citizens of the country were as eager to increase their commodity consumption as they are to increase their money incomes the monetary circulation would somehow adapt itself to this increase in 'the propensity to consume' and producers would have no difficulty in selling everything produced at a profit, no matter how great or how rapid the growth in the quantity of goods produced. The one source of trouble that Malthus diagnosed in the situation was that people did not buy and consume as much as they had the power to buy and consume. In his *Principles* he wrote:

> The causes of an increase in effective demand for particular commodities are of very easy explanation; but it has been considered, and with reason, as not very easy to explain the cause of that general

---

be more likely to be abused if in the hands of government than if in the hands of a banking company' (245/362).

[1] Einzig's *How Money is Managed*, page 347.

> briskness of demand which is sometimes so very sensibly felt throughout a whole country, and is so strikingly contrasted with the feeling which gives rise to the expression of trade being universally very dead. As the specific and immediate cause of this general increase of effective demand, I should decidedly point to such a distribution of the produce, and such an adaptation of it to the wants and tastes of the society as will give the money price for which it sells an increased command of domestic and foreign labour.[1]

Again, he writes:

> As I have attempted to show in the 8th section of this chapter, the natural and permanent tendency of all extension of trade, both domestic and foreign, is to increase the exchangeable value of the whole produce. . . . This better distribution of the produce of the country, this better adaptation of it to the wants and tastes of the consumers, will at once give it a greater market value, and at once increase the national revenue, the rate of steady profits, and the wages of labour.[2]

Not a word of any need for additional money. If the growth of consumption lags behind the growth of production it is not due to a shortage of money, but to the fact that people with large money incomes habitually spend only part of what they receive upon consumption. After stating that 'what is now wanted in this country is an increased national revenue—an increase in the exchangeable value of the whole produce estimated in bullion',[3] Malthus goes on to ask: 'How . . . are we to obtain this increase of revenue? What steps are we to take in order to raise the exchangeable value of the whole produce?' In the answer which he proceeds to give to his own question there is no reference whatever to importation of bullion, to increase of money, nor even to the issue of fresh paper. He says:

> The three causes which, by favouring distribution, tend most to keep up and increase the exchangeable value of the whole produce, are the division of landed property, the extension of domestic and foreign trade, and the maintenance of unproductive labourers.[4]

---

[1] Malthus' *Principles*, page 458 in first edition; page 395 in second.

[2] Ibid., page 510 in first edition; page 429 in second.

[3] Ibid., page 505 in first edition; page 424 in second.

[4] Ibid., pages 505–6 in first edition. In the second edition, page 425, the last clause reads: 'and the maintenance of such a proportion of unproductive consumers as is best adapted to the powers of production'. In his first edition (page 464) he had written: 'What the proportion is between the productive

Large estates must be subdivided because landlords with huge rent rolls save a substantial portion of their incomes; the same income spread among more numerous landlords would result in more spending on consumption. Trade between different parts of the country and different regions of the world is also favourable to consumption, because it places before the recipients of large incomes a tempting array of luxuries which they find it difficult to resist. And the more people there are who receive money incomes for services that add nothing to the quantity of commodities, the larger will be the demand for commodities in proportion to the supply.

Seeing that the division of landed property is the first of the three 'steps' proposed by Malthus for the purpose of increasing the value of the national product and the amount of the national revenue, one might have supposed that he would urge strongly that something should be done in the matter; but he presently observes: 'I have given my reasons for thinking that, in the actual and peculiar state of this country, the abolition of the law of primogeniture would produce more evil than good.'[1] On reading this we can scarcely know whether to adopt the view of Professor Cannan, who declared that Malthus was seldom blessed with a clear opinion on any subject,[2] or to liken him to the Prince of Denmark, who saw so many pros and cons that the native hue of resolution was sicklied o'er with the pale cast of thought.

Since the landlords are not to be interfered with, let us turn to the capitalists, who are even greater sinners than the landlords, for 'the great object of their lives is to save a fortune'.[3] But it appears that the capitalists are not to be interfered with either. The

---

and unproductive classes of a society which affords the greatest encouragement to the continued increase of wealth, it has before been said that the resources of political economy are unequal to determine.' In the second edition (page 399) 'unproductive classes' is changed to 'those engaged in personal services'.

[1] Malthus' *Principles*, page 507 in first edition; page 426 in second. If Malthus was a sycophant, as suggested by Karl Marx, then so was that old Tory Dr. Johnson, who remarked (when breakfasting at Streatham on Saturday, 16th March, 1776): 'Entails are good, because it is good to preserve in a country a series of men to whom the people are accustomed to look up to as their leaders.'

[2] *Theories of Production*, page 7.

[3] Malthus' *Principles*, page 465 in first edition; page 400 in second.

reader might be pardoned for supposing that the following words were penned by Ricardo, not Malthus:

> Whenever capital increases too fast, the motive to accumulation diminishes, and there will be a natural tendency to spend more and save less. When profits rise, the motive to accumulation will increase, and there will be a tendency to spend a smaller proportion of the gains, and to save a greater. These tendencies, operating on individuals, direct them towards the just mean, which they would more frequently attain if they were not interrupted by bad laws or unwise exhortations.[1]

Precisely what laws Malthus had in mind I do not know; but what he meant by unwise exhortations he proceeds to explain. Although a fall in the rate of profit may be relied upon to check saving to some extent, yet according to his teaching there is always the likelihood that too much rather than too little will be saved, and it is therefore unfortunate that economists from Adam Smith onwards should encourage parsimony by representing it as a virtue. Saving, up to a point, he admits, is necessary:

> there is no reason, however, for giving an additional sanction to it by calling it a public duty. The market for national capital will be supplied, like other markets, without the aid of patriotism. And in leaving the whole question of saving to the uninfluenced operation of individual interest and individual feelings[2] we shall best conform to that great principle of political economy laid down by Adam Smith, which teaches us a general maxim, liable to very few exceptions, that the wealth of nations is best secured by allowing every person, as long as he adheres to the rules of justice, to pursue his own interest in his own way.[3]

So although, in a world 'where the right of private property is established', a man may starve if there is no demand for his labour 'by those who have the disposal of produce';[4] although 'it is scarcely possible to cast our eyes on any nation of the world without seeing' that 'almost universally, the actual wealth of all the states with which we are acquainted is very far short of their

[1] Malthus' *Principles*, page 516 in first edition; page 433 in second.

[2] 'Who has ever proposed to leave it to any other?' Ricardo asks (vol. 2, p. 450).

[3] Malthus' *Principles*, pages 517–18 in first edition; page 434 in second.

[4] Ibid., page 348 in first edition; page 311 in second.

powers of production';[1] nevertheless, *laissez-faire* is still to be our motto. Although Malthus thought and taught that excessive saving limited the demand for products and thereby caused unemployment, yet he apparently did not write his book with the hope of inducing those with large incomes to observe moderation in their saving, for they will do this of their own accord if left alone. The object of Malthus, it would seem here, was to persuade economists to let them alone, and not give an artificial stimulus to saving by patting the savers on the back! It seems a lame and impotent conclusion for a philosopher who, impatient of Ricardo's abstract reasonings, boldly labelled his book: *Principles of Political Economy, considered with a view to their Practical Application.* He might have done better, one feels, to omit the reference to practical application, and replace it with two lines from *Hamlet*—

> The time is out of joint, O cursed spite
> That ever I was born to set it right.

One is not surprised that the working classes have preferred (at second hand) the ponderous and unreadable Marx, with his practical battle-cry of *Down with the Capitalists*, to the honest, able, and acute, but hesitating Malthus.[2]

[1] Malthus' *Principles*, page 350 in first edition; page 313 in second.

[2] It is surprising that Marx did not make more use of Sismondi. Sismondi's *New Principles of Political Economy* was published in 1819, the *Principles* of Malthus not until 1820, but the latter was in no sense inspired by Sismondi's book. Malthus' correspondence with Ricardo shows that for some years he had been turning over in his mind the arguments he used in his *Principles*; and although there are many points of resemblance, his development of his doctrine is quite different from that of Sismondi. Sismondi's book had become very scarce, and it is gratifying that a reprint has recently been published in Geneva.

12

Ricardo's New Chapter on Machinery. His "Change of Opinion"

RICARDO held, as we saw in the last chapter, that increase of capital necessarily increases production, and as necessarily increases demand, while his opponent, Malthus, affirmed that increase in the power of production is by no means always accompanied by a corresponding increase of demand. Malthus recognised, of course, that if production is increased, the power to consume is increased; but this power is vested in the rich; it is not at the command of the needy labourers, who would gladly purchase more if they had the means. The product of industry belongs to the capitalists, who own the capital employed in production, who own or have hired the land, and who have hired and paid for the labour. If the product increases, the capitalists can add to their enjoyments, but Malthus thinks they have already surrounded themselves with so many luxuries that they have little desire to increase their consumption. Ricardo's reply to this is: 'We all wish to add to our enjoyments or to our power. Consumption adds to our enjoyments, accumulation to our power, and they equally promote demand' (vol. 6, pp. 134–5). Hence, if the capitalist does not wish to increase his consumption, he will add to his power by increasing his army of labourers. What the capitalists do not spend upon enjoyments they add to their wages fund, and it is spent by the labourers.

It is curious, I think, that in their discussion of the question whether saving does or does not diminish total demand neither Malthus nor Ricardo ever mentions machinery. One might have thought that Malthus would point out that the capitalist who saves in order to increase his capital does not necessarily add the amount to his wages fund, but may buy a machine with the money. Had he done so, Ricardo might have replied that in buying a machine thc capitalist causes just as much demand as if he spent the same amount on the purchase of a carpet or a suite of furniture. But Ricardo never employs this argument to rebut the contention of Malthus that saving diminishes demand, but always alleges that what the capitalists save they add to their wages fund. He knew very well, of course, that some capital consists of machinery, etc., but he seems always to have carried in his mind the saying of Adam Smith that almost the whole of every country's capital is distributed annually as wages. In 1814, three years before he published his book, he wrote to Malthus: 'The very term accumulation of capital supposes a power somewhere to employ more labour' (vol. 6, p. 148); and again: 'Accumulation of capital has a tendency to lower profits. Why? Because every accumulation is attended with increased difficulty in obtaining food . . .' (vol. 6, p. 162). In his *Principles* he said: 'Population regulates itself by the funds which are to employ it, and therefore always increases or diminishes with the increase or diminution of capital' (41/78); and again: 'In proportion to the increase of capital will be the increase in the demand for labour' (54/95). Two pages later he writes:

> With a population pressing against the means of subsistence, the only remedies are either a reduction of people or a more rapid accumulation of capital. In rich countries, where all the fertile land is already cultivated, the latter remedy is neither very practicable nor very desirable, because its effect[1] would be, if pushed very far, to render all classes equally poor (56/99).

Once more, if we go forward to page 193(291) we find:

> If ten thousand pounds were given to a man having £10,000 per annum, he would not lock it up in a chest, but would either increase his expenses by £10,000; employ it himself productively, or lend it to some other person for that purpose; in either case demand would be increased, although it would be for different objects. If he increased his expenses, his effectual demand might probably be for buildings, furniture, or some such enjoyment. If he employed his £10,000 productively, his effectual demand would be for food,

[1] 'Effect', misprinted 'effort' in *Everyman*. At the beginning of the paragraph 'of capital' is misprinted 'a capital'.

clothing, and raw material, which might set new labourers to work; but still it would be demand.[1]

In all these passages it is taken for granted that every addition to capital is an addition to the wages fund; tools and other aids to production seem completely forgotten. In the last quotation, there is mention of raw materials, but no suggestion that the capitalist might spend his £10,000 on the purchase of a machine instead of in the purchase of food and clothing for additional labourers. This is the more remarkable because this passage appeared in his first edition, and in that edition on an earlier page he had imagined the case of a capitalist who, instead of dispensing £20,000 in wages, devoted the money to the purchases of a machine which would produce commodities, and yield the usual profit, while giving scarcely any employment to labour.

In view of this, it is difficult to understand how Ricardo could maintain that if a man receives a gift of £10,000, and does not want to lock it up in a chest, the only alternatives before him are to spend the money in the purchase of luxuries for his own enjoyment or to employ it in the purchase of food and clothing for labourers.

It was not until after he had read the *Principles* of Malthus more than once that Ricardo came to recognise his own inconsistency. Somewhat belatedly, he realised the necessity of distinguishing sharply between capital devoted to the payment of wages and capital invested in buildings, shipping, wharves, etc. Hitherto he had done his best, one might say, to blur or obliterate the distinction between fixed and circulating capital by lumping them together as a single mass of 'accumulated labour', all of which is regularly consumed and reproduced, some of it slowly, and some of it quickly. What we mean when we call some capital *fixed* and some *circulating*, he tells us (18/31), is that some of the items that constitute capital are quickly perishable and require to be renewed or replaced at short intervals, while other parts are more durable, and do not need replacement so often.[2] Food, for instance, perishes quickly, while the labourer's shoes and clothing may last quite a long time, although not so long as ships and machinery.

[1] Malthus cited and criticised this passage, page 360 in first edition of his *Principles*, page 322 in second.

[2] On page 133(207) Ricardo refers to 'the division of capital into fixed and circulating, or rather into durable and perishable capital'.

Thus the question whether this or that article is circulating or fixed capital depends upon its durability; in his second edition he added a footnote to emphasise that the distinction between fixed and circulating is 'not essential', and no line of demarcation can be 'accurately drawn'.

This dictum still appears in Ricardo's third edition, together with other statements quoted above which imply that every increase of capital is an increase of the wages fund. Yet there is no doubt that before that edition was published Ricardo's opinion had undergone a change. It is only natural that we should examine the *Notes on Malthus* for the earliest indications of this change; but I venture to think that up to the time when Ricardo finished these notes (16 November, 1820, as he advised Mill—see vol. 8, p. 296) his doctrine had undergone no change whatever. Mr. Sraffa is perfectly correct in saying (vol. 1, p. lix) that Note No. 149 (vol. 2, p. 234) marks a transition stage in Ricardo's thinking on the subject; but I think it is quite clear that this note must have been inserted at a later date. Mr. Sraffa himself gives a reason for thinking that Ricardo's opinion had not changed by the 29th November, when the writing of the *Notes* was already 'finished'; but there are independent reasons for concluding that this note was not among those sent to McCulloch for perusal. If, then, we decide for the time being to ignore Note 149, we find that from end to end of the *Notes on Malthus* Ricardo continues to maintain his old doctrine which practically identifies capital with a fund for the maintenance of labour. Let me cite a few notes, all subsequent to No. 149.

Note 155: 'I must repeat here what I have often said elsewhere, that capital and labour could not both be abundant at the same time, for the one will always purchase the other, however they may be multiplied. To say that I have a very abundant capital is to say that I have a great demand for labour' (vol. 2, p. 241).

Note 178: 'Under every increase of capital, if population increases still faster, and labour falls, population is redundant as compared with capital; and if population increases at a slower rate than capital, capital is relatively redundant to population. This is again another way of stating that profits will be high or low according as wages are low or high' (page 277).

In Note 196, as we saw in our last chapter, the capitalist who receives one-eighth of the product as profit either consumes it himself or adds it to his fund for the employment of labourers (page 302).

Note 201: 'The will to consume exists wherever the power to consume is. Mr. Malthus proves that this power is not annihilated, but transferred to the labourer' (page 311).

Note 209: 'I am desirous to accumulate capital from my revenue—if I employ my revenue as capital, I shall want labour' (page 322).

Note 215: 'By accumulation of capital from revenue is meant an increase of consumption by productive labourers instead of unproductive' (page 326). He followed this up when he published the third edition of his *Principles* by adding a new footnote which says: 'When we say that revenue is saved and added to capital, what we mean is that the portion of revenue so said to be added to capital, is consumed by productive instead of unproductive labourers' (94/151).

Note 291. And almost at the end of the *Notes on Malthus* (vol. 2, p. 426) occurs the passage quoted in our last chapter in which he affirms that it is a contradiction in terms to say that labour and capital are both redundant—a contradiction, because he interprets it to mean that there is more food than there are mouths to eat it, and more people than there is food for.

In all these passages an increase of capital is viewed as an addition to the wages fund. In the opinion of Malthus, this doctrine was erroneous for two reasons; first, because there may be an increase of fixed capital without any increase in the wages fund; and secondly, because when an addition to capital takes the form of a machine that will produce with the aid of two men what formerly required the labour of ten men, there is always the possibility that eight men will lose their employment. This, of course, does not necessarily occur; for to say that machinery enables the manufacturer to produce the same product with less labour is equivalent to saying that with the same quantity of labour he can produce a larger product. This is recognised by Malthus, who however holds that whether the quantity of labour is reduced, or the quantity of product so much increased that all the labourers formerly employed upon hand-work are needed as machine-tenders, depends on the elasticity of demand; and he cites the cotton industry as one in which the number of men employed has not merely been maintained but enormously increased.[1] But this he regards as an exceptional case. The sensational growth in the demand for English cotton goods which followed the reduction in their price occurred, Malthus thought, because the home demand was supplemented by a flood of orders from foreign

[1] Malthus' *Principles*, page 402 in first edition; page 352 in second.

countries not at that time equipped with the means of supplying themselves with this type of goods so cheaply. 'If', said Malthus, 'we could not export our cottons, it is quite certain that, though we might have the power, we should not have the will to consume them all in kind at home.'[1]

If the sale of a product is confined to the local market the reduction of price that follows the use of machinery is almost certain to occasion an increase of demand, but not necessarily an increase large enough to absorb all the labour formerly employed. Hitherto, it may be, three capitalists, each employing 100 men, supplied the community with the quantity required. The adoption of machinery perhaps leads to such a reduction of price as causes the demand to double; but if one capitalist, with his 100 men and a machine, can supply the whole of this demand, the other two capitalists will have to look round for a new employment for their capital, and the other 200 men will have to seek another market for their labour. Ricardo holds that as long as capital and labourers remain in existence they will co-operate in producing something else, while Malthus thinks both capital and labour may be redundant in proportion to the demand for their services. He says:

> If, in order to try the principle, we were to push it further and to suppose that, without any extension of the foreign market for our goods, we could by means of machinery obtain all the commodities at present in use with one third of the labour now applied, is it in any degree probable that the mass of vacant capitals could be advantageously employed, or that the mass of labourers thrown out of work could find the means of commanding an adequate share of the national produce?[2]

Ricardo has no hesitation in returning an affirmative answer to this question. In the *Notes on Malthus* (vol. 2, p. 355) he writes:

> I answer, Yes. Suppose three men employed ten men each, one in the production of shoes, another in the manufacture of stockings, and the other in the manufacture of cloth, all which commodities were required and consumed in the society. Suppose now that each

[1] Malthus' *Principles*, page 411 in first edition; on page 359 of second edition his words are: 'If we could not export our cottons, it is quite certain that, though we might have the power, we should not have the will to consume them all ourselves at such prices as would pay the producers.'

[2] Ibid., page 404 in first edition; page 354 in second.

> discovers an improved process, by which they can each produce the same quantity of their respective commodities with the labour of five men—will they not, having each the means of employing the labour of ten men, continue to employ the other five; not indeed in the production of cloth, shoes, and stockings, but in the production of some out of the numerous commodities which are useful and desirable to man? Would they not obtain, having it in their power so to do, hats, wine, beer, furniture or any other commodities for which they might have a greater inclination? Mr. Malthus' error appears to me to be in thinking that nothing could be done without the extension of foreign trade. Are we all satiated with our own productions? Would none of us like more and better clothes, an increase of furniture, more carriages and horses, and better and more commodious houses?

This extract differs somewhat from those already cited. While it denies that the employment of machinery will have any effect on the quantity of labour employed, it nevertheless recognises that fixed capital and circulating capital are not to be lumped together as a single homogeneous mass. The employment of machinery may compel some labourers to change their occupation; but they will find other employment. While the quantity of fixed capital has been increased, there has been no diminution in the quantity of circulating capital. . . . The same amount as before is available as wages, the quantity of labour available is the same as before, and there is never any lack of demand for what labour and capital can produce. If any one suffers, it is the capitalist who has to scrap outmoded plant—'the individual may suffer, but the community benefits' (vol. 2, p. 351).

The Notes being finished, Ricardo intended that Malthus, from whom he was expecting a visit, should be the first to see them, and he held them accordingly; but this visit being unexpectedly delayed, Ricardo despatched the Notes to McCulloch, who was eager to see them. McCulloch was no admirer of Malthus. Even before he had seen Malthus' book—before, in fact, it was published—McCulloch had itched for an opportunity to review it unfavourably in the *Edinburgh Review*; he itched, as Macaulay itched some years later, to review Croker in the same journal, and to 'dust the varlet's jacket'. But, unlike Macaulay, McCulloch did not have the opportunity. In December, 1819, he had written to Ricardo: 'You will forgive me for saying that I consider Mr. Malthus' reputation as an economist to be very much over-rated, and were it not that he was a particular friend of Jeffrey,[1] who would most likely oppose his veto, I should attempt to reduce him to his just magnitude' (vol. 8, p. 139). In another letter he said: 'I am anxious to see Mr. Malthus' work. He deserves to be very roughly handled'—and McCulloch felt that he was the man for the job.[2]

Poor McCulloch—he little knew what was in store for him. He devoured Ricardo's Notes with delight, and when returning them wrote: 'If Mr. Malthus can read over your remarks on his work without renouncing many of those positions on which he has laid the greatest stress, he can have but a very slender claim to the character of a candid reasoner or a sincere lover of truth. . . . Nothing remains for him but to surrender unconditionally' (vol. 8, p. 358). His faith in the Ricardian doctrine thus refreshed and fortified, he proceeded to proclaim in the *Edinburgh Review* that machinery neither reduces wages nor diminishes employment, and he wrote to Ricardo: 'When you read over the article in question you will be at no loss to discover the source from whence I have borrowed the greater part of my principles—I have been quite as much indebted to you on this as on other occasions' (vol. 8, p. 351). A fortnight or so later, when sending Ricardo 'the article in question' to read, he said: 'I hope it will have a good effect in counteracting the influence of the poisonous nostrums (for they can be called nothing else) of Messrs. Sismondi and Malthus' (vol. 8, p. 366). Judge, then, of the unfortunate man's dismay when the next thing that happens is that Ricardo issues a new edition of his *Principles* with a new chapter on Machinery which commences with the startling announcement that his opinions 'respecting the influence of machinery on the interests of the different classes of society . . . have on further reflection, undergone a considerable change; . . . I am convinced that the substitution of machinery for human labour is often very injurious to the interests of the class of labourers' (263–4/386–8). More in sorrow than in anger McCulloch wrote to Ricardo: 'Little did I expect, after reading your triumphant answer to the arguments of Mr. Malthus, that you were so soon to shake hands with him, and to give up all' (vol. 8,

[1] Jeffrey was the Editor of the *Edinburgh*. He was the man who, according to Sydney Smith, had been heard to speak disrespectfully of the Equator—but not of his friend Malthus, even though Malthus was a Tory.

[2] Vol. 8, p. 167. In the end, McCulloch reviewed Malthus (but not in the *Edinburgh*) 'with the greatest civility and good humour' (vol. 8, p. 185).

p. 382). Ricardo, unmoved, writes calmly to Malthus: 'McCulloch has specifically and strongly objected to my chapter on machinery; he thinks I have ruined my book' (vol. 9, p. 14).

To understand how Ricardo's change of opinion came about I think we must go back to 1817, when he first published his *Principles*. Among his first readers was a thoughtful young Quaker of 28, named John Barton, who ventured to put his views before Ricardo. His views were not acceptable to our author, but were nevertheless replied to with Ricardo's unfailing courtesy (vol. 7, p. 155). Shortly afterwards Barton published a pamphlet entitled *Observations on the Circumstances which influence the condition of the Labouring Classes of Society*, from which the following is an extract:

> As the doctrine that the progress of population is measured by the increase of wealth does not appear to be true in fact, so on the other hand it seems to me not consistent with sound reasoning. It does not seem that every accession of capital necessarily sets in motion an additional quantity of labour. Let us suppose a case. A manufacturer possesses a capital of £1000 which he employs in maintaining twenty weavers, paying them £50 per annum each. His capital is suddenly increased to £2000. With double means he does however hire double the number of workmen, but lays out £1500 in erecting machinery, by the help of which five men are enabled to perform the same quantity of work as twenty did before. Are there not then fifteen men discharged in consequence of the manufacturer having increased his capital?

Hence Barton concludes that—'the demand for labour depends then on the increase of circulating, and not of fixed capital'.[1]

Whether Ricardo read this pamphlet in 1817 we do not know, but if he did, it made no more impression on him than Hume's essay on Money. Malthus, on the other hand, not only read the pamphlet, but profited by it, and drew attention to it when he published his *Principles* in 1820. In the following remarks Malthus appears to have in mind both Ricardo's machine that produces goods with very little labour and Barton's description of the manner in which the capitalist converts part of his circulating capital into fixed capital:

> If, for instance, a capitalist who employed £20,000 in productive

[1] See pages 16–17 in the reprint of Barton's pamphlet by the Johns Hopkins Press, under the editorship of the late Prof. Hollander.

labour, and had been in the habit of selling his goods for £22,000, making a profit of 10 per cent, were to employ the same quantity of labour in the construction of a machine worth £20,000, which would enable him to carry on his business without labour in future except as his machine might require repair, it is obvious that during the first year[1] the same value of the annual produce and the same demand for labour would exist; but in the next year, as it would only be necessary for the capitalist, in order to obtain the same rate of profits as before, to sell his goods for a little more than £2000 instead of £22,000. . . .[2]

This is the passage on which Ricardo was commenting when he wrote Note No. 149, which I must now quote:

The effective demand for labour must depend upon the increase of that part of capital in which the wages of labour are paid. . . . If I have a revenue of £2000, in the expenditure of that revenue I necessarily employ labour. If I turn this revenue into capital, I at first employ the same labour as before, but productively instead of unproductively. This labour may be employed in making a machine; the machine becomes a capital, and all that it produces is the revenue derived from that capital. Or this labour may be employed on the land, and the corn which it produces may be a capital to enable me to employ an additional quantity of labour. A society does one or the other in proportion to the demand for either objects of men's work, or for objects which are almost exclusively produced by machinery. In general, the capital accumulated will consist of a mixture of both, of fixed and of circulating capital. It appears then that, to the person saving capital, it can be of no importance whether it be employed as fixed or as circulating capital;[3] if profits be 10 per cent, they will equally yield a revenue of £200 on £2000 of capital . . . but it is of the greatest importance to those who live by the wages of labour. . . . If capital is realised in machinery, there will be little demand for an increased quantity of labour (vol. 2, pp. 234–6).

---

[1] I.e. while the men are employed in producing the machine.

[2] I quote from the long-winded Malthus only sufficient to explain Ricardo's remarks. The quotation is from pages 261–2 (Sraffa's vol. 2, p. 235). Malthus altered his text in his second edition.

[3] In his *Principles* Ricardo had said: 'To an individual with a capital of £20,000, whose profits were £2000 per annum, it would be a matter quite indifferent whether his capital would employ a hundred or a thousand men . . . provided in all cases his profits were not diminished below £2000' (234/348).

It seems incredible that after penning these words Ricardo should have gone on to add a whole series of Notes in which it is taken for granted that additions to capital always take the form of additions to the fund distributed as wages. It seems equally incredible that if this Note had formed part of the bunch sent to McCulloch he should have written as he did when returning the Notes, and should have been taken entirely by surprise when he discovered Ricardo's change of view in his new chapter. Both these puzzles appear to be solved if we assume that Note 149 represents a later addition, the result of a change of opinion on Ricardo's part.

I am not suggesting that this Note reflects the full change of opinion to which Ricardo confessed in his new chapter; it indicates, as Mr. Sraffa says, a transition period in his thought. When did this occur? On this point we are reduced to conjecture. My own guess would be some time in February, 1821. It was in July, 1820, while on holiday at Brighton, that Ricardo read Malthus' book carefully for a second time, and commenced making his Notes. From Brighton he went to his own country seat, Gatcomb, where the Notes were finished after some months and sent to McCulloch some time in December, 1820. In January, 1821, Ricardo had to return to town for the Parliamentary Session. On the 14th of that month he wrote that he was returning to London in a few days' time and expected that the printing of his third edition would then begin (vol. 8, p. 333). Now it seems not impossible that, without perhaps attaching much importance to the point, Ricardo had decided that when he got back to his house in London he would dig out of some cupboard that pamphlet of Barton's which he had forgotten, but of which Malthus spoke so highly, and read it again for himself. Might not the first result of this be that Ricardo accepted Barton's conclusion that 'the demand for labour depends on the increase of circulating, and not of fixed capital'? This would account for the composition of Note No. 149. After all, this was no real change of opinion. He had never imagined that fixed capital served as wages fund; his mistake had been in speaking too often as if capital consisted of nothing but wages fund. If he continued to ponder over Barton's proposition he would be led a step further. We have seen that in Note 236 (vol. 2, p. 355) Ricardo admitted that machinery might diminish the demand for labour in some employments, but he argued that there would be no diminution in the total quantity of employment because there was no diminution in the quantity of circulating capital. But this is not the position depicted by Barton. He presents a situation in which circulating capital is *converted* into fixed capital; the result is that fixed capital is increased but circulating capital is diminished. That in these circumstances there should be a diminution of employment was entirely in accordance with his own doctrine. This is the view of the matter adopted by Ricardo in the new chapter.

Exactly when Ricardo adopted this view we do not know. We know it was not later than 12th March, 1821, for on that date his changed attitude towards machinery was mentioned by Malthus in a letter to Sismondi (vol. 8, p. 377). On the other hand the printing of the new edition of his *Principles* began near the end of January, and it seems likely that the change of opinion did not occur until a considerable number of chapters were already in type, so that, while it was still possible to insert an additional chapter, it was too late to bring the old chapters into harmony with the new one. It might be possible here and there to insert a footnote, but many statements in the old text inconsistent with the new theory had to be left standing, to the perpetual bewilderment of the reader.

Let us now examine this new chapter of Ricardo's, which in the opinion of McCulloch ruined his book.

Ricardo begins with a frank confession that formerly he had thought that the only result of using machinery would be to make goods cheaper for everybody, and that everybody would benefit, for 'I thought that no reduction of wages would take place because the capitalist would have the power of demanding and employing the same quantity of labour as before, although he might be under the necessity of employing it in the production of a new, or at any rate of a different commodity' (264/387). This, in fact, is the view set forth in Note 236 (vol. 2, p. 355). The first modification of Ricardo's view came in Note 149, where he admitted that 'if capital is realised in machinery there will be little demand for an increased quantity of labour'; in the new chapter he goes much further; he says that 'the substitution of machinery for human labour is often very injurious to the interests of the class of labourers', and 'the same cause which may increase the net income of the country may at the same time render the population redundant, and deteriorate the condition of the labourer' (264/388).

He then proceeds to show how this may happen. He adopts Barton's explanation of the manner in which circulating capital may be converted into fixed capital. Barton imagined the case of a weaver, but Ricardo wanted to make his illustration more general; so, instead of a weaver producing cloth only, he imagines a capitalist who produces everything necessary for existence. His capitalist carries on 'the joint business of a farmer and a manufacturer of necessaries'. As farmer, or man on the land, he produces both food and materials, and as manufacturer he converts the materials into useful commodities. Thus we have a self-contained community, a microcosm, capable of supplying all its own wants (264/388).

The capitalist, says Ricardo, begins the year with a total capital of £20,000, made up of machinery, buildings, etc., worth £7000 and a store of food and necessaries worth £13,000. Wages are assumed by Barton to be £50 per annum, but for simplicity we will suppose that the capitalist employs 130 men at £100 each. Ricardo, like Barton, assumes that some of the labourers keep the fixed capital constantly new,[1] while the remainder, with the aid of the fixed capital, reproduce the commodities they and their colleagues consume, together with a surplus which rewards the capitalist for the use of his capital. His figures on page 265(389) may be tabulated as follows:

	Capital	*Product*
Fixed capital:	£	£
Kept as good as new	7000	
Circulating capital:		
Consumed annually	13,000	
Annually reproduced		13,000
Surplus annually produced (10 per cent on total capital)		2000
Product, food and necessaries worth		£15,000

If the capitalist each year consumes the whole of his profit, there is of course neither increase nor decrease of capital. Nevertheless,

[1] Barton, I should have mentioned, after showing how the number of weavers is reduced from twenty to five, corrects this by saying that perhaps three men will have to be employed to keep the machine in good repair and to construct a new one to take its place when worn out.

according to Barton, he may increase his fixed capital by converting part of his circulating capital into machinery. Ricardo's capitalist follows this course by diverting half his labour force from the production of food and necessaries to the production of a machine. At the end of the year he again has a product worth £15,000; he again makes a profit of £2000; but the product this time consists of a machine worth £7500 and food and necessaries worth £7500. The capitalist and his family can no more eat machinery as food, nor wear it as clothes than the labourers can, and the capitalist therefore takes his profit in the form of £2000 worth of food and necessaries, leaving only £5500 worth of food and necessaries for the maintenance of labourers in the following year. Hence, instead of employing 130 men, he will only be able to employ 55—'His means of employing labour', says Ricardo (page 265/389), 'would be reduced in the proportion of £13,000 to £5500, and consequently all the labour which was before employed by £7500 would become redundant'. The figures for the following year will be as follows:

	Capital	*Product*
	£	£
Old fixed capital	7000	
New fixed capital (machinery)	7500	
Circulating capital:		
Consumed annually	5500	
Annually reproduced		5500
Surplus annually produced (10 per cent on total capital)		2000
Product, food and necessaries worth		£7500

Such is the nature of the reasoning which, 'on further reflection', convinced Ricardo 'that the substitution of machinery for human labour is often very injurious to the interests of the class of labourers'. In consequence of the action taken by the capitalist 'there will necessarily be a diminution in the demand for labour, population will become redundant and the situation of the labouring classes will be that of distress and poverty' (266/390). On reading this, one cannot help thinking of the dictum of Malthus:

> If want alone, or the desire of the labouring classes to possess the necessaries and conveniences of life, were a sufficient stimulus to production, there is no state in Europe, or in the world, that would have found any other practical limit to its wealth than its power to

produce; and the earth would probably before this period have contained, at the very least, ten times as many inhabitants as are supported on its surface at present.[1]

McCulloch regarded Ricardo's new chapter as a surrender to Malthus. According to Ricardo's original teaching (still left standing in the third edition) the distress and privations of the labouring classes are due to their constant effort to multiply in an algebraical ratio, whereas food can only be increased in an arithmetical ratio. But now he seems, like Malthus, to have come round to the view that it is Man, not niggardly Nature, that bangs the dining-room door in the face of the hungry multitude. If Ricardo had wished to support Malthus, he could hardly have invented a more striking illustration. Above half the population are condemned to perish, not because sufficient food cannot be produced, but because it suits the capitalist equally well, or better, to employ machinery instead of labour; it suits him equally well because his profit of £2000 remains undiminished; it suits him even better because, although his money income is not increased, he will be able to buy more with it, since goods made by machinery are cheaper than goods made by labour alone—see page 266(390) and page 268(392).

But I fancy that surrender to Malthus was no more palatable to Ricardo than to McCulloch.[2] Ricardo's change of opinion was due to 'further reflection'. If my conjectures above are well founded, Ricardo had, in fact, read Malthus twice from end to end without any change of opinion, and it was his reading of Barton that converted him, or at all events put him on the scent of an explanation of unemployment not due to over-production. In the new chapter he quotes Barton, and gives him a pat on the back (270/396), but there is nowhere any mention of Malthus. In the hypothetical case presented by Ricardo on page 265(389) neither new saving, nor fall in the rate of profit, nor unwillingness to buy and consume all that is produced, nor anything else that Malthus had suggested, is in any way responsible for the reduction in the demand for labour. The demand for labour shrinks because capital (or at all

[1] Malthus' *Principles*, page 348 in first edition; page 311 in reprint. Abbreviated on page 300 of Sraffa's vol. 2.

[2] In a letter to McCulloch Ricardo strongly repudiates the idea that he has approached a single step towards the doctrine of Malthus (vol. 8, p. 387), and McCulloch apologises for having suggested it.

events circulating capital) has shrunk. And least of all has Malthus' pet bogey, over-production, anything to do with the matter, for not only is there no over-production, but Ricardo, the lover of paradox, tells us that the result is likely to be a shrinkage in the quantity of commodities produced—'All I wish to prove is that the discovery and use of machinery may be attended with a diminution of gross produce' (266/390)—and by gross produce 'I mean always quantity of commodities, and not value' (267/392). The value of the product, in his illustration, falls from £15,000 to £7500; the quantity of the product does not necessarily shrink in the same proportion, but it shrinks, presumably because 55 men with the aid of machinery are not able to produce as much as 130 men without machinery.

Whether Ricardo's new chapter 'ruined the book' or not, it is at all events a pity, I think, that it had to be hurriedly composed to enable the printers to finish their work on the third edition. As it stands, there appears much to criticise. In adopting Barton's explanation of the manner in which circulating capital may be converted into fixed capital, Ricardo presents us on page 265(389) with a community in which there is no way of increasing fixed capital except by withdrawing men from the production of food and necessaries. If this self-contained community is intended to be a picture of the real world, one can only marvel at its distortion of the facts; if, on the other hand, its purpose is merely to show that it would be possible to conceive a case in which the introduction of machinery might render population redundant and deteriorate the condition of the labourer, then we must marvel at his bringing it forward as the ground upon which, on further reflection, he has become 'convinced that the substitution of machinery for human labour *is often* very injurious to the interests of the class of labourers' (264/388, but the italics are mine).

That he should base this conclusion on this reasoning is the more astonishing because, before the end of the chapter, he seems to throw overboard this picture of industrial revolution. After making the tender-hearted reader shiver, shudder, or shed tears, over the plight of labourers turned out of their employment—after making the reader's blood boil at the inhumanity of the capitalist to whom it is of no importance whether his capital is circulating or fixed—he calmly remarks:

> The statements which I have made will not, I hope, lead to the

inference that machinery should not be encouraged. To elucidate the principle I have been supposing that improved machinery is *suddenly* discovered and extensively used; but the truth is that these discoveries are gradual, and rather operate in determining the employment of the capital which is saved and accumulated than in diverting capital from its actual employment (270/395).[1]

Thus, instead of the introduction of machinery involving a catastrophic reduction of the wages fund, there is no reduction —not even a small one; in fact he goes on to say there is a steady increase. Instead of old circulating capital being converted into fixed capital (as depicted on page 265(389)), what happens is that new savings are made from time to time, and these are devoted partly to the increase of fixed and partly to the increase of circulating capital, as depicted in Note 149. 'The demand for labour', says Ricardo on page 270(395), 'will continue to increase with an increase of capital, but not in proportion to its increase; the ratio will necessarily be a diminishing ratio.[2] Barton had said: 'It is easy to conceive that under certain circumstances the whole of the annual savings of an industrious people might be added to fixed capital, in which case they would have no effect in increasing the demand for labour.'[3] Ricardo disagrees. He says: 'It is not easy, I think, to conceive that, under any circumstances, an increase of capital should not be followed by an increased demand for labour' (270/396, footnote). But is this logical? What he had in mind was that even the most ingenious machinery would require some labour for its operation (see page 271(396) and his letter to Barton, vol. 7, p. 157). Moreover, a certain amount of labour is needed to keep the machine in perfect order and replace it in due course. But this is not a reason for concluding that the total labour employed must always increase, for if a machine that only requires

[1] Malthus had said: 'In general, however, the use of fixed capital is extremely favourable to the abundance of circulating capital.' Again: 'In general therefore, there is little to fear that the introduction of fixed capital, as it is likely to take place in practice, will diminish the effective demand for labour; indeed it is to this source that we are to look for the main cause of its future increase' (see page 262 and page 264 in first edition; the second passage will be found on page 238 of Malthus' second edition).

[2] Karl Marx makes much of this 'law', i.e. 'growth in the quantity of the means of production as compared with the quantity of the labour-power' (for these words, see page 687 in *Everyman* translation of *Das Kapital*).

[3] Page 18 in the reprint of Barton's pamphlet.

the labour of five men takes the place of one that required the labour of ten, there is no increase, but a decrease in the demand for labour. In Note 149 Ricardo said that the addition made to capital from new savings would take the form of fixed or circulating capital 'in proportion to the demand for either the objects of men's work, or for objects which are almost exclusively produced by machinery'. But this is not strictly logical either; there may be a demand for an increased supply of both descriptions of goods, yet the whole of the additional capital may go into a machine which with half the labour produces twice as much as the old one—in which case it may satisfy the increased demand for machine-made goods while releasing sufficient labour to satisfy the increased demand for articles produced or procured by 'men's work'.

These are details. The important point is that Ricardo appears to admit that in actual life the state of things imagined on page 265(389) never occurs. The figures were merely intended 'to elucidate the principle' (269–70/395). What principle do they elucidate? Even in this imaginary picture it is not 'the discovery and use of machinery' that causes the supply of food and necessaries to diminish. This happens because 50 per cent of the labourers engaged in producing these commodities are withdrawn from that occupation before there is any machinery to make the labour of the remaining 50 per cent more productive. Precisely the same calamity would have overtaken the community if the labourers withdrawn from agriculture had been drafted into the army or set to work producing guns—as might happen in time of war. On the other hand, the production of machinery would not have involved a diminution in the supply of food if the labourers had been drawn from the ranks of those engaged in the production of luxuries, or from the numerous body of men employed in 'unproductive' pursuits, whether civil or military. Ricardo's figures may be said to illustrate the 'principle' that if a man gives up cultivating the soil with a spade in order to devote his whole time to the production of a plough, he may die of starvation before the plough is ready for use; but the 'principle' that Ricardo had in mind seems to have been that under these circumstances, while the labourer perishes, the capitalist may preserve his profit unimpaired.

The puzzling feature of Ricardo's new chapter is that although on page 270(395) he seems to pass the sponge over the illustration on page 265(389), yet it is on this illustration that he bases the statement with which he opens the chapter: 'I am convinced that the substitution of machinery for human labour is often very injurious to the interests of the class of labourers.' This conclusion he confirms on page 267(392) when he declares, 'that the opinion entertained by the labouring class, that the employment of machinery is frequently detrimental to their interests, is not founded on prejudice and error, but is conformable to the correct principles of political economy'. It is true that he follows this up by telling us that 'if the improved means of production, in consequence of the use of machinery, should increase the net produce of a country in a degree so great as not to diminish the gross produce[1]. . . then the situation of all classes will be improved'.[2] This, however, is all based on 'If', and he perhaps regards it as something unlikely to happen. At all events, soon after the publication of the new chapter these qualifications of the doctrine on page 265(389) seem to be forgotten. On 18th June, 1821, he writes to McCulloch: 'The whole change of my opinion is simply this: I formerly thought that machinery enabled a country to add annually to the gross produce of its commodities, and I now think that the use of it rather tends to the diminution of the gross produce' (vol. 8, p. 387). McCulloch, as we have seen, found Ricardo's new doctrine hard to digest; but Ricardo was hopeful of converting him, and on 8th July he reports to Malthus:

Two or three letters have passed between us on this subject; in

[1] Ricardo seems to think he is stretching a point in allowing that a smaller number of men might, with the aid of machinery, be able to produce *as much* as was produced before. Why might they not produce *more* than before? He himself told Malthus (vol. 8, p. 278) that it is impossible to lay down any law as to the quantity of the physical product that might result from inventions, discoveries, improved methods, increase of knowledge and skill.

[2] The labourers will benefit, says Ricardo, 'from the low price of all articles of consumption on which their wages will be expended'. Did he forget his own dictum on page 9(16) that 'so far is it from being true' that the labourer permanently benefits by a fall in the price of necessaries that 'it is probable his wages would in no long time be adjusted by the effects of competition, and the stimulus to population, to the new value of the necessaries on which they were expended'. See also the dicta quoted in a previous chapter: 'Diminish the cost of subsistence of men . . . and wages will ultimately fall' (260/382), and 'It has been one of the objects of this work to show that with every fall in the real value of necessaries, the wages of labour would fall' (287/420).

> his last he appears to me to acknowledge the effect of the use of machinery may be to diminish the annual quantity and value of gross produce. In yielding this, he gives up the question, for it is impossible to contend that with a diminished quantity of gross produce there would be the same means of employing labour. The truth of my propositions on this subject appear [*sic*] to me absolutely demonstrable (vol. 9, p. 14).

In his reply Malthus remarks:

> . . . practically I think that the cases are very rare in which for any length of time the gross produce is diminished by machinery . . . You said for instance in your letter to me that an increased power of production must be accompanied with an increase of productive or unproductive expenditure, which could not be the case if the gross produce were diminished (vol. 9, p. 18).

To this Ricardo replies:

> I have never said that machinery enables you to get a greater quantity of gross produce; my sole complaint against it is that it sometimes actually diminishes the gross produce (vol. 9, p. 23).

Whether Ricardo continued during the remainder of his life to hold that the tendency of machinery is to diminish output, I do not know; he at all events clung to the conclusion that the use of machinery diminishes the demand for labour. Formerly (1819) he had told the House of Commons that 'it could not be denied, on the whole view of the subject, that machinery did not lessen the demand for labour' (vol. 5, p. 30). Since then he had changed his opinion, as announced in his new chapter, and in May, 1823, he is reported as saying in the same august assembly:

> . . . it was evident that the extensive use of machinery, by throwing a large portion of labour into the market, while on the other hand there might not be a corresponding increase of demand for it, must in some degree operate prejudicially to the working classes . . . his proposition was not that the use of machinery was prejudicial to persons employed in one particular manufacture, but to the working classes generally. It was the means of throwing additional labour into the market, and thus the demand for labour, generally, was diminished (vol. 5, p. 303).

Thus, as I said just now, Ricardo seems to forget his statement of page 270(395) that in practice, despite the increasing employment of machinery, there is never any actual diminution in the quantity of the wages fund or the quantity of employment, and to remember only the conclusion he based on his 'extreme case', that the labouring classes have good reason for thinking that machinery throws them out of employment.

13

The Demand for Labour. Further comments on Ricardo's new Chapter

RICARDO's new chapter 'On Machinery' would have been more appropriately labelled 'On the Demand for Labour'. The manner in which the demand for labour is affected by machinery forms only part of the question discussed; after drawing a line across the page he goes on to consider other influences which may affect the quantity of employment.

Hitherto Ricardo's teaching had been that the demand for labour, and the quantity of population, increases or diminishes in proportion to the increase or decrease of capital. This seemed to imply (although it was never expressly stated) that all capital consists of wages fund, and that capital is the only fund from which wages are paid. Neither of these assumptions is correct, and in his new chapter Ricardo seeks to rectify both errors. Adam Smith had said that some wages are advanced from capital, and some are paid out of income. This view was accepted by Malthus, and Ricardo adopts it in the new chapter.

It would not be correct to represent this as an entirely new opinion of Ricardo's, for he had always recognised that the wages of some workers are paid out of profits and rents. Even in his first edition he had said that a nation's 'power of supporting fleets and armies, and all species of unproductive labour, must be in proportion to its net, and not in proportion to its gross income' (235/348). Nevertheless, in framing his theory of wages and employment (chapter 5) he did not take rents and profits into account as contributing to the supply of wages, and did not take 'unproductive' labourers into account as part of the supply of labour. He balanced against one another the quantity of capital and the quantity of population; labour as a mass exchanged for capital as a mass, and the rate of wages depended on the ratio between these two totals.

Why did Ricardo ignore unproductive labour in his chapter on Wages? This, I think, is easily explained. His aim, as stated in his Preface, was to discover the laws that govern the distribution of the community's annual product amongst the three classes concerned in its production, the productive labourers, the capitalists, and the landlords. He studies this problem in separate chapters devoted respectively to wages, profits, and rent. It is no part of his purpose to enquire what use each class makes of the share that falls to its lot, except to this extent—it is implied that the whole of the labourer's share or wage is inevitably expended on necessaries for himself and his family, and it also seems to be implied that if the other two classes have anything to spare after furnishing themselves with both necessaries and luxuries, they add it to their fund for the maintenance of productive labourers. There is, I think, no hint of the employment of unproductive labourers until chapter 16 (144/220), where there is a passing reference to soldiers supported by taxation,[1] while the passage that I quoted in my last paragraph does not occur until chapter 26. Ricardo may have considered that the proportion of the population employed on unproductive labour was so small that it could be neglected; he may also have thought that the proportion of their incomes which landlords and capitalists chose to devote to the support of domestic servants, actors, singers, etc., was too arbitrary to allow of its being fitted into a scientific law of wages.

Whatever may have been his reason for ignoring unproductive labour in his chapter on Wages, he brings it into account in his new chapter. The reader will have noticed his statement on page 267(392), quoted in our last chapter, that if the smaller number of men employed after the introduction of machinery are able to produce as large a product as was produced before, not only will the landlords and capitalists benefit, but the labourers also will benefit, partly by the lower prices they will pay for the things they buy, and partly by an increased demand for menial servants. It is

[1] In chapter 8 (94/150) there are references to unproductive labour, but these were not inserted until the third edition, and form part of the altered view which we are now considering.

here that Ricardo draws a line across the page[1] and proceeds to develop his proposition as follows:

> Independently of the consideration of the discovery and use of machinery, to which our attention has been just directed, the labouring class have no small interest in the manner in which the net income of the country is expended, although it should in all cases be expended for the gratification and enjoyments of those who are fairly entitled to it.
>
> If a landlord or a capitalist expends his revenue in the manner of an ancient baron in the support of a great number of retainers, or menial servants, he will give employment to much more labour than if he expended it on fine clothes or costly furniture, on carriages, on horses, or in the purchase of any other luxuries.
>
> In both cases the net revenue would be the same, and so would be the gross revenue, but the former would be realised in different commodities. If my revenue were £10,000, the same quantity nearly of productive labour would be employed, whether I realised it in fine clothes and costly furniture, etc., etc., or in a quantity of food and clothing of the same value. If, however, I realised my revenue in the first set of commodities, no more labour would be *consequently* employed; I should enjoy my furniture and my clothes, and there would be an end of them; but if I realised my revenue in food and clothing, and my desire was to employ menial servants, all those whom I could so employ with my revenue of £10,000, or with the food and clothing which it would purchase, would be to be added to the former demand for labourers, and this addition would take place only because I chose this mode of expending my revenue. As the labourers, then, are interested in the demand for labour, they must naturally desire that as much of the revenue as possible should be diverted from expenditure on luxuries to be expended in the support of menial servants (268/393).

Thus Ricardo appears to have abandoned the notion that the one thing the labourers have to pray for is that the capitalists shall spend less and save more because whatever they save becomes wages fund. His view here is that each year the permanent wages fund is temporarily augmented by a varying portion of net revenue

[1] This line across the page is omitted in *Everyman* edition, page 268. The line was apparently intended to indicate that he had finished one argument (at any rate for the time being) and was turning to another. We may infer this, I think, from the fact that where in his third edition we have a new section-heading (section 2 of chap. 1) there was in the first edition merely a horizontal line. See Sraffa's footnote, vol. 1, p. 17.

expended by the receivers of rents and profits on 'unproductive' services. Thus there are two demands for labour competing in the market. If all the labour in the market is already employed it would seem that the quantity of unproductive labour cannot be increased without a diminution of productive labour. If the demand for luxuries diminishes while the demand for services increases, it would seem that the only way to meet the situation would be for the labourers who have hitherto produced luxuries to quit that trade and perform personal services instead. Ricardo, however, appears to assume that formerly there was some labour unemployed, for he tells us that when the baron hires unproductive labour instead of buying luxuries he will give employment to much more labour. He says the same quantity nearly of productive labour will be employed; it is apparently assumed that the labourers who formerly produced luxuries for the baron will now produce food and necessaries for his servants, and these servants will form an addition to the total quantity of labour employed.

Ricardo goes on to apply his argument to the condition that arises in time of war, when the baron, whether he likes it or not, is compelled to reduce his consumption of luxuries because a portion of his income is taken from him by the government, and expended on the employment of such unproductive labourers as soldiers. So long as the war lasts the baron must forego his consumption of 'furniture, clothes, books, etc., etc.'; but, says Ricardo, 'there would be the same quantity of labour employed in production, for the food and clothing of the soldier and sailor would require the same amount of industry to produce it as the more luxurious commodities; but in the case of the war there would be the additional demand for men as soldiers and sailors; and consequently, a war which is supported out of the revenue, and not from the capital of a country, is favourable to the increase of population' (269/394).

I think Ricardo's love of paradox must have been tickled[1] when he penned the last few words. Those who imagine that a long war may reduce the numbers of the people are mistaken. In time of war there is an increased demand for men; this leads to a rise of

[1] Ricardo was conscious of his propensity to paradox, but denied a liking for it; he wrote to Malthus: 'I want an able pen on my side to put my opinions in a clear light, and to divest them of that appearance of paradox which they now wear' (vol. 7, p. 222).

wages; the rise of wages encourages early marriages and larger families; despite the slaughter of the fighting men, the population, and therefore the supply of labour, will be larger at the end of the war than it was at the beginning.[1] But what will be the position when the war ends and the country no longer needs these armies of unproductive labourers? 'A country engaged in war, and which is under the necessity of maintaining large fleets and armies', says Ricardo, 'employs a great many more men than will be employed when the war terminates' (268/393). After telling us that war is favourable to increase of population he goes on to say (269/394):

> At the termination of the war, when part of my revenue reverts to me, and is employed as before in the purchase of wine, furniture, or other luxuries, the population which it before supported, and which the war called into existence, will become redundant, and by its effect on the rest of the population, and its competition with it for employment, will sink the value of wages, and very materially deteriorate the condition of the labouring classes.[2]

Hitherto Ricardo's teaching had been that if the labourers suffered from unemployment or low wages they had themselves to blame; their distress arose because they made no attempt to restrict the increase in the supply of labour to correspond with the increase in the demand for labour. The labourers had the remedy in their own hands, and could not hold the capitalists responsible for their distresses. This view Ricardo apparently abandoned on page 265(389), where labour becomes redundant, not because labourers have multiplied excessively, but because the capitalist has suddenly converted a large part of his circulating capital into

[1] Perhaps Ricardo would have altered his view had he lived in this age when science has provided belligerents with the means of raining death from the skies over wide areas.

[2] Ricardo does not go any further into the situation described, but abruptly returns to the question he was discussing before he drew a line across the page, namely, the effect upon employment when the capitalist substitutes fixed capital for human labour; this time the fixed capital is a stock of horses that displaces a team of men. I think it likely that Ricardo intended another line to be drawn across the page here to mark the end of his digression. To me it seems highly probable that these six paragraphs concerning the baron and the country at war were a last-minute interpolation in the new chapter, which was itself a last-minute addition to his third edition. If this is so, it may explain why the chapter is headed 'On Machinery' instead of 'On the Demand for Labuor'.

fixed capital. He cannot support the same number of labourers as before because the same quantity of food and necessaries has not been produced. But in his remarks concerning the baron and the country at war he seems to have come round to the view of Malthus that there may be distress and unemployment, not because the power to support labourers is lacking, but because the will to do so has diminished. At the termination of the war population suddenly becomes redundant; it is redundant, not in comparison with the means of subsistence, but compared with the demand for labour of one sort and another. If the war had not stopped, the soldiers would have continued to be supplied with food and clothing, to say nothing of arms and ammunition. The war, however, being over, the services of the soldiers are no longer needed. The makers of arms and ammunition will perhaps be set to work producing fine clothes and furniture; but the soldiers are no longer required either for military or civil employment. Called into existence by the war, they constitute 'redundant population' when the war is over, and like the labourers on page 265(389) when machinery made their labour superfluous, they must emigrate either to another country, or to another world.

That there was no lack of means of subsistence at the termination of the war with Napoleon is testified by Malthus, who says:

> From the harvest of 1815 to the harvest of 1816, there cannot be a doubt that the funds for the maintenance of labour in this country were unusually abundant. Corn was particularly plentiful, and no other necessaries were deficient; yet it is an acknowledged fact that great numbers were thrown out of employment.[1]

After the war, according to Malthus, both capital and labour were redundant. While the superfluous labourers were tramping the country in search of work and wages, the barns were bulging with corn, and warehouse shelves were groaning beneath the weight of shoes and clothing, all of which would have been bought and distributed had the war continued, but which could not now be sold at a remunerative price because so many labourers had no wages wherewith to buy them. 'The failure of home demand', says Malthus, 'filled the warehouses of the manufacturers with unsold goods, which urged them to export more largely at all risks. But this excessive exportation glutted all the

[1] Malthus' *Principles*, page 444 in first edition; page 386 in second.

foreign markets, and prevented the merchants from receiving adequate returns.'[1] Thus the slump in the demand for services caused a slump in the demand for commodities, and the slump in the demand for commodities caused a slump in the demand for productive labour. Ricardo himself says the competition of the ex-soldiers for employment 'will sink the value of wages' (269/394). Wages are low at the same time that profit is low, a state of things which Ricardo had said was impossible.

The stagnation of trade that followed the 'outbreak of Peace' in 1815 must, of course, have been as well known to Ricardo as to Malthus; but prior to the composition of his new chapter he had been in the habit of regarding war as one of those disturbances of equilibrium which he was content to leave out of account as merely a temporary interruption in the progress of the nation. He did not ignore war completely, however. He devoted a chapter to 'Sudden Changes in the Channels of Trade', and in this he said (176/265):

> The commencement of war after a long peace, or of peace after a long war, generally produces considerable distress in trade. It changes in a great degree the nature of the employments to which the respective capitals of countries were before devoted; and during the interval while they are settling in the situations which new circumstances have made the most beneficial, much fixed capital is unemployed, perhaps wholly lost, and labourers are without full employment. . . . When, however, such distress immediately accompanies a change from war to peace, our knowledge of the existence of such a cause will make it reasonable to believe that the funds for the maintenance of labour have rather been diverted from their usual channel than materially impaired, and that, after temporary suffering, the nation will again advance in prosperity.[2]

Ricardo sees no difference between the transition from peace to war, and the transition from war to peace. In both cases there is need for a readjustment, because there is a sudden change in the

[1] Malthus' *Principles*, page 494 in first edition; page 416 in second.

[2] Malthus probably had this passage in mind when he wrote the paragraphs (too long to quote) commencing: 'That the transition from war to peace', and ending with the statement that the countries having the greatest powers of production are likely to be the greatest sufferers when peace returns—'They suffered the least by the war, or rather were enriched by it, and they are now suffering the most by the peace' (pages 498–501 in first edition of Malthus' *Principles*, pages 420–2 in second).

nature of demand. Both capitalist and labourer will suffer loss until industry is placed on a new footing. But the point Ricardo wishes to emphasise is that the distress which accompanies the transition from war to peace is merely temporary; he is anxious to allay the fears of those who think that there is perhaps a permanent shrinkage in the demand for labour. His language seems to indicate that the need for adjustment when peace follows war hits the capitalist harder than it hits the labourer, because it is easier for the labourer to change his occupation[1] than for the capitalist to change the nature of his fixed capital; capital, in fact, may be 'wholly lost', whereas the labourer suffers nothing more than temporary unemployment (176/265).

Such was Ricardo's teaching before he wrote his new chapter. When that chapter was written, the printing of the third edition had already gone so far that it was no longer possible to bring the old chapters into harmony with the new one. What alterations Ricardo would have made if a fourth edition had been called for during the brief remainder of his lifetime we have no means of knowing, but he seems himself to have thought his teaching in the old chapters was not substantially modified by anything he said in his new chapter. Had he thought otherwise he would surely have inserted the new chapter at the end of the book by way of postscript or 'second thoughts', whereas it is sandwiched in between two other chapters as though it were a mere digression. Even in the new chapter itself, on page 270(395), as already pointed out, he seems more or less to pass a sponge over what he has just written, or perhaps I should rather say he seems to treat his remarks as having theoretical interest rather than practical importance. The wholesale unemployment depicted on page 265(389) is an extreme case, imagined to illustrate the danger of mechanising industry too rapidly—a condition which, he tells us, happily does not actually occur. The widespread suffering and starvation at the end of the war is another extreme case, which illustrates the danger of stimulating an increase of population beyond the

[1] It must be borne in mind that Ricardo uniformly treats all labourers as having the same natural and acquired abilities, so that a scarcity of watchmakers with a plethora of bricklayers will be adjusted by a transfer of some labour from bricklaying to watchmaking. The serious errors flowing from the assumption of a uniform rate of pay for all kinds and qualities of labour will be touched upon in our next chapter.

normal requirements of peace time; and if this case, unfortunately, cannot be set aside as imaginary, yet Ricardo may have felt that it was altogether abnormal, and that as Political Economy deals with the ordinary processes of peace-time industry the economist is not called upon to make his theories fit into the conditions that may arise when all ordinary economic forces are overwhelmed by some great national catastrophe such as war, earthquake, flood or pestilence.

But in the opinion of Malthus the trouble that occurred at the end of the war with Napoleon, although admittedly an extreme case, arose from a cause which is continually in operation, even in peace time. Even when there is no war, there are great fluctuations in the quantity of unemployment. There are periods of good trade and periods of bad trade; periods when both capital and labour are kept busy, when goods are sold at a profit as fast as they can be produced, and other periods when demand seems to fall away, goods remain unsold in the hands of the producers, and many labourers are dismissed; both wages and profits are low at the same time.

This was a doctrine that Ricardo would never accept. He had always maintained that wages and profits could not both be low at the same time. And whatever might be the position at the end of the war, he had regarded general over-production or glut in peace time as an impossibility. Nothing in the new chapter changed his view on these points. He continued to believe, with Say, that demand increases to precisely the same extent that production increases; see his letter to Mill, in which he complains that Malthus attacks himself and Say, 'because we have said that, when produced, commodities would always find a market, and some consumers would be found for them who had an equivalent to give for them' (vol. 9, p. 13). This was written some months after the publication of the new chapter, and on the same day (9th July, 1821) he wrote to Malthus that he understood his contention to be that more goods have been produced than there is a demand for,

> and that we are now suffering the consequences of it in a stagnation of trade, in want of employment for our labourers, etc., etc.; and the remedy you propose is an increase of consumption. It is against this latter doctrine that I protest, and give my decided opposition. I acknowledge that there may not be adequate motives for production,

> and therefore things will not be produced, but I cannot allow, first that with these inadequate motives commodities will be produced,[1] and secondly that if their production is attended with loss to the producer, it is for any other reason than because too great a proportion is given to the labourers employed. Increase their number, and the evil is remedied. Let the employer consume more himself, and there will be no diminution of demand for labour, but the pay of the labourer, which was before extravagantly high, will be reduced (vol. 9, p. 16).

In his next letter he repeats this opinion; if production does not yield a profit to the capitalist

> it is only because it is attended with disproportionate and unusual benefits to the labourers. The remedy therefore, and the sole remedy, is a more just distribution of the produce; and this can be brought about only, as I said in my last letter, by an increase of workmen, or by a more liberal unproductive expenditure on the part of the capitalist (vol. 9, p. 26).

Thus Ricardo commences by opposing an increase of unproductive consumption and apparently finishes by recommending the very thing he opposes. He seems to adopt the view of Malthus, who held that if the receivers of rents and profits spent all their income (as the labourers do) on consumable commodities, there would never be over-production; there would never be unemployment for either capital or labour, but on the contrary, both would be kept perpetually busy, and no matter how much production might increase, there would always be a ready sale for it. It was only because Malthus was convinced that there was no hope of inducing the wealthy to diminish their saving that he came to look upon a large body of unproductive consumers as a necessary condition to full-time employment for capital and labour.

In the *Notes on Malthus*, as we have seen, Ricardo poured ridicule on unproductive consumption as a method of promoting the prosperity of industry; and if he now recommends that the capitalists shall spend more and save less, it is not with any idea that this will increase total consumption or demand. He had steadily maintained that the total quantity of demand is not affected by saving; 'I deny that the wants of consumers generally are

[1] Ricardo errs in suggesting that there is no adequate motive for production. The motive is the *expectation* of selling the product at a profit.

diminished by parsimony; they are transferred with the power to consume, to another set of consumers' (vol. 2, p. 309). In recommending that capitalists should spend more and save less Ricardo is not counting on an increase of total demand; what he is counting on to cure the trouble is a fall of wages which will result from less saving. The labourers are always increasing in number; let the capitalists discontinue making regular additions to their wages fund and presently wages will fall and the rate of profit will rise.

Here is the fundamental difference between Malthus and Ricardo. Malthus did not believe in the doctrine of Say, Mill and Ricardo, that to increase production is to increase demand to the same extent. If that were true there could never be any widespread hitch in production and exchange. That these hitches did occur —that from time to time there were periods of bad trade when both wages and profits were low—Malthus considered a matter of common experience, and the business of the economist was to trace the cause of these hitches. But Ricardo apparently did not believe that such hitches occurred. He appears to have little respect for 'experience' when it suggests a state of things which logical theory shows to be impossible. There is a curious passage in his letter of 21st July, 1821, which throws light on his attitude in this respect. He writes to Malthus (vol. 9, p. 25):

> You say we know from repeated experience that the money price of labour never falls till many workmen have been for some time out of work. I know no such thing, and if wages were previously high, I can see no reason whatever why they should not fall before many labourers were thrown out of work. All general reasoning, I apprehend, is in favour of my view of this question, for why should some agree to go without any wages while others were most liberally rewarded? Once more I must say that a sudden and diminished demand for labour in this case must mean a diminished reward to the labourer, and not a diminished employment of him—he will work at least as much as before, but will have a less proportion of the produce of his work. . . .[1]

[1] How does this agree with Ricardo's picture on page 265(389) of the capitalist who gets rid of more than half his men when he starts to use machinery? With regard to this case Ricardo himself wrote to McCulloch that if it should suit the purpose of the capitalist 'to substitute a fixed capital of an equal value for this circulating capital, it will be inevitably followed by a necessity for dismissing a part of his workmen' (vol. 8, p. 390).

Thus Ricardo rejects the evidence of 'repeated experience' and prefers to rely on abstract reasoning.[1] Malthus is satisfied that experience affords abundant proof that from time to time there are periods of over-production, as a consequence of which both wages and profits are low at the same time, which in turn makes demand all the smaller. Ricardo, like Mr. Podsnap in *Our Mutual Friend* (with or without a sweep of the arm), brushes all this aside and proceeds to prescribe for the 'sufferings of which we have lately had to complain' on the assumption that profits are abnormally low because wages are abnormally high. He will not admit that there is any over-production:

> such and such evils may exist, but the question is do they exist now? I think not; none of the symptoms indicate that they do, and in my opinion increased savings would alleviate rather than aggravate the suffering of which we have lately had to complain. Stagnation is a derangement of the system, and not too much general production, arising from too great an accumulation of capital (vol. 9, pp. 26–7).

Ricardo allows nothing to shake his faith in his old doctrines, the truth of which he considers 'demonstrable'. Wages and profits cannot both be high, or both low, at the same time. If profit on capital is low, it is because capital (i.e. wages fund) is too abundant in proportion to the number of men among whom it is distributed. If, on the other hand, wages are low, it is because capital (wages fund) is too small compared with the quantity of labour, and the distresses of the labourers will be alleviated by increased savings.

He also adheres to his old idea that the labourers have only themselves to blame if they choose to propagate in excess of the demand for labour. In this chapter, as we have seen, he spoke of many labourers losing their jobs because the capitalist found it

[1] Ricardo rejects 'experience' because he thinks (with Hume on Miracles) that 'facts' may be inaccurately reported or misinterpreted. He prefers to rely on 'general reasoning'; which reminds one of Dr. Johnson's remark when told of a machine which went without horses—'a man who sat in it turned a handle, which worked a spring that drove it forward'. 'Then, sir,' said Johnson, 'what is gained is, the man has the choice whether he will move himself alone, or himself and the machine too' (Boswell's *Life*, 26th Oct., 1769). Bernard Shaw followed this line of logic when he wrote (in *An Unsocial Socialist*): 'I think the most ridiculous sight in the world is a man on a bicycle, working away with his feet as hard as he possibly can and believing that his horse is carrying him—instead of, as anyone can see, he carrying the horse.'

suited him to convert part of his circulating capital into fixed capital. He also told us that many labourers would lose their employment if the community decided that it did not require the same quantity of personal services as before. One would have thought this would compel him to abandon the idea that the labourers need never suffer distresses if only they would regulate their habits of propagation to suit the demand for labour. But apparently this lesson was not among the things that he carried in his mind when, two years after the publication of his new chapter, he addressed the House of Commons on the labour troubles caused by machinery. After the remarks quoted at the end of our last chapter he continued as follows:

> But still, he would not tolerate any law to prevent the use of machinery. The question was—if they gave up a system which enabled them to undersell in the foreign market, would other nations refrain from pursuing it? Certainly not. They were therefore bound, for their own interest, to continue it.[1] Gentlemen ought, however, to inculcate this truth on the minds of the working classes—that the value of labour, like the value of other things, depended on the relative proportion of supply to demand. If the supply of labourers were greater than could be employed, then the people must be miserable. But the people had the remedy in their own hands. A little forethought, a little prudence (which probably they would exert if they were not made such machines of by the poor-laws), a little of that caution which the better educated felt it necessary to use, would enable them to improve their situation (vol. 5, p. 303).[2]

[1] Ricardo made this point in his new chapter, page 271(396).

[2] Sismondi pointed out that those classes of society so situated that they can form a reasonably correct estimate of future income for themselves and their future offspring naturally take these prospects into account before marrying and rearing children; but this caution and prudence is inevitably replaced by a careless reliance on luck in the case of labourers who have no means of guessing how long they will themselves obtain employment, and still less of estimating the prospects for the next generation (see pages 175–6 in vol. 2 of the 1953 reprint of his *Nouveaux Principes*).

14

Ricardo versus Say. Cost or Utility the foundation of Value?

Sir E. C. K. Gonner, in the Introduction to his edition of Ricardo's *Principles*, remarks: 'At times, indeed, Ricardo seems about to make a great mistake. He nearly calls cost of production the cause of value; he does call it the foundation.'[1]

Say, on the other hand, declares that utility is the foundation of value; and at least upon one occasion he obtained from Ricardo a qualified assent to this proposition. In August, 1815, Ricardo wrote to Say:

> Utility is certainly the foundation of value, but the degree of utility can never be the measure by which to estimate value. A commodity difficult of production will always be more valuable than one which is easily produced, although all men should agree that the latter is more useful than the former. A commodity must be useful to have value, but the difficulty of its production is the true measure of its value. For this reason Iron, though more useful, is of less value than gold (vol. 6, p. 247).

On thinking over the matter, however, Ricardo seems to have felt that, even with this qualification, it is wrong to call utility the foundation of value, and accordingly in his *Principles*, published about two years later, we find that while he admits on his first page that utility is essential to value, he refrains from calling it the foundation; on the contrary, as remarked by Gonner, he describes cost of production as the foundation. He does so, for example, at

[1] In one of his notes Ricardo wrote (1810): 'I like the distinction which Adam Smith makes between value in use and value in exchange. According to that opinion utility is not the source of value.' But he struck out *source* and substituted *measure* (vol. 3, p. 284).

the beginning of section 2 of his first chapter, while on his first page he refers to the labour required for production as a 'source' from which value is 'derived'. In view of the letter quoted above, one would have expected Ricardo to say that it is human needs or desires that give value to things, but that the price that has to be paid for them depends on the cost of production. Why did he not say so? What made him withdraw the statement that utility is the foundation of value, and 'nearly call' cost of production the cause of value?

The explanation appears to be that he regarded value and price as practically equivalent expressions, the only difference being that when we speak of the quantity of money for which a thing will exchange we use the term price, whereas when we examine the ratio in which commodities exchange for one another we use the expression relative values.[1] Relative values and relative prices are the same thing, and any attempt to account for differences of price or value by differences in the quantity or degree of utility is foredoomed to failure. Despite the great utility of water it seldom has any value in exchange; when a price must be paid for it, it is only because labour has been necessary to bring it to the spot where it is required. What causes a thing to have a price is that it cannot be obtained without labour, and the amount of the price depends on the amount of labour. Adam Smith described labour as the original price of all things,[2] and it is the business of the economist to account for differences of price and for changes of price.

That the quantity or degree of utility cannot explain prices Ricardo thinks must be evident to anyone who remembers that in the market the price of a commodity is the same for all buyers, whereas 'two persons may derive very different degrees of enjoyment from the possession of the same commodity' (vol. 4, p. 61). In a letter to Malthus (vol. 8, p. 276) which the reader will find quoted at the end of our second chapter Ricardo accused Say of holding that 'a commodity is valuable in proportion to its utility',

[1] 'The price of a commodity is its exchangeable value in money only. The value of a commodity is estimated by the quantity of other things generally for which it will exchange' (vol. 4, p. 60). 'If price be estimated in a medium unvarying in value, price and value mean the same thing' (vol. 2, p. 242).

[2] *Wealth of Nations*, Bk. 1, chap. 5, 2nd paragraph quoted by Ricardo, page 6(13).

whereas, says Ricardo, its value, or price in the market, is determined by its cost of production. And he criticised Malthus for the same reason that he criticised Say. In the *Notes on Malthus* (vol. 2, p. 24) he wrote:

> In all that Mr. M. has yet said about exchangeable value, it appears to depend a great deal on the wants of mankind and the relative estimation in which they hold commodities. This would be true if men from various countries were to meet in a fair, with a variety of productions, and each with a separate commodity, undisturbed by the competition of any other seller. Commodities under such circumstances would be bought and sold according to the relative wants of those attending the fair—but when the wants of society are well known, when there are hundreds of competitors who are willing to satisfy those wants on the condition only that they shall have the known and usual profits, there can be no such rule regulating the value of commodities. In such a fair as I have supposed a man might be willing to give a pound of gold for a pound of iron, knowing the uses of the latter metal; but when competition freely operated, he could not give[1] that value for iron, and why?—because iron would infallibly sink to its cost of production—cost of production being the pivot about which all market price moves.[2]

Thus, according to Ricardo, it is cost of production that regulates prices; he, however, warns his reader at the outset (on his second page) that there are some exceptions to this rule. With regard to old masterpieces, and wines of special vintage, he says: 'No labour can increase the quantity of such goods, and therefore their value cannot be lowered by an increased supply.' Their prices accordingly are fixed by the competition of buyers. 'These commodities, however,' says Ricardo, 'form a very small part of the mass of commodities daily exchanged in the market', and he is therefore content to leave such goods outside the scope of his 'law' of value. He also leaves outside products that are controlled by monopoly. He apparently prefers a clear and simple law which is not quite universal to a universal law which is not so clear and simple. He likes to make sweeping generalisations, and it is the reader's own fault if he forgets the admitted exceptions or 'modifications' of which he was warned at the outset. With regard to commodities which can be multiplied 'almost without any assign-

[1] This should rather be, 'the seller could not obtain'.

[2] See also (vol. 2, p. 38) and page 188(283) in his *Principles*.

able limit' (6/12) he affirms that 'the real and ultimate[1] regulator of the relative value of any two commodities is the cost of their production, and not the respective quantities which may be produced, nor the competition amongst the purchasers' (231/344). Thus Ricardo introduces a new law which he apparently regards as superseding or overriding the law of demand and supply by which both Say and Malthus, followers of Adam Smith, sought to explain prices. 'The opinion that the price of commodities depends solely on the proportion of supply to demand, or demand to supply,' says Ricardo, 'has become almost an axiom in political economy, and has been the source of much error in that science' (260/382). His chapter 'On the influence of demand and supply on prices' opens with the following paragraph:

> It is the cost of production which must ultimately regulate the price of commodities, and not, as has been often said, the proportion between the supply and demand; the proportion between supply and demand may, indeed, for a time, affect the market value of a commodity, until it is supplied in greater or less abundance, according as the demand may have increased or diminished; but this effect will be only of temporary duration.

Thus Ricardo appears to think that he has got rid of demand as an active influence upon price, except as a disturbing factor which from time to time ruffles the level upon which it can make no permanent impression. All that supply and demand can do in the market is to make the price oscillate about the cost of production; cost of production remains the permanent 'pivot' about which these oscillations take place. Nevertheless, the very language that he uses admits that the cost of production does not affect the price unless or until it affects the ratio between supply and demand. And Ricardo had to recognise the significance of this when Malthus pointed it out. If, said Malthus, despite the fall in the cost of production, the commodity were only brought to market in the same quantity as before, there would be no need for the producer to lower his price. To which Ricardo replies as follows in the *Notes on Malthus* (vol. 2, p. 48):

> Mr. Malthus mistakes the question—I do not say that the value of a commodity will always conform to its natural price without an

[1] Note the word *ultimate*.

additional supply, but I say that the cost of production regulates the supply, and therefore regulates the price.[1]

Thus Ricardo is driven into a new line of defence; in order to prove that price is not determined by supply and demand, but by cost of production, he avers that the latter regulates the quantity of supply, which is the exact opposite of his dictum on page 285(415) of his *Principles*, where he says: 'It is not the price at which corn can be produced that has any influence on the quantity produced, but the price at which it can be sold.'

Another of the Notes (vol. 2, p. 45) reads as follows: 'It is admitted by everybody that demand and supply govern market price, but what is it determines supply at a particular price? Cost of production.' If this is what Ricardo had in mind in his Note on page 48, he must have got fogged, for it is quite a different proposition. This Note on page 45 supports the dictum in the *Principles* that it is the price at which corn can be sold that determines whether the supply shall be large or small. If the price in the market is 4*s.* a bushel, there will be a certain supply; if the competition of buyers raises the price to 5*s.* the supply will be larger, because more farmers can make a profit at the higher price than at the lower.

A similar fog must have obscured Ricardo's usually clear thinking when he penned the following note:

> A hatter can produce 10,000 hats at the same rate of charge that he can produce 1000; their natural price, whether he produces the one quantity or the other, is therefore the same;[2] but their market price will depend on supply and demand—the supply will be finally determined by the natural price—that is to say, by the cost of production (vol. 2, pp. 46–7).

Surely Ricardo has here lost his bearings completely. How can the quantity of supply be 'finally determined' by the cost of production if the cost per unit is the same whether the quantity supplied

[1] The reader will have noted the same dictum in his letter to Malthus (vol. 8, p. 277) quoted in our second chapter. The same dictum appears in a letter to Say (vol. 9, p. 172).

[2] In a letter to Trower Ricardo wrote: 'The terms on which a commodity can be produced, so as to remunerate the producer, will remain the same although the demand should be for 5 times the quantity produced' (vol. 8, p. 207). This seems a strange assumption.

be 1000 or 10,000? Ricardo himself observes in a later Note (vol. 2, pp. 224–5) that 'while a commodity will sell in the market for its natural price, or above it, it will be supplied', i.e. it is the demand that determines the quantity of supply. But having made this just observation, Ricardo adds: 'Mr. Malthus says the demand compared to the supply regulates price, and the cost of producing the commodity regulates the supply. This is a dispute about words —whatever regulates the supply, regulates the price.' A dispute about words? It is Ricardo's own contention (vol. 2, p. 45) that demand and supply determine market price, and that the quantity of supply at that price is determined by the cost of production.

Such are Ricardo's *Notes on Malthus*, which McCulloch so much admired, and found so convincing.

Not only in the case of hats, but with regard to manufactures of all kinds, Ricardo's usual assumption is that the cost of production is the same for all producers,[1] and as they compete with one another, the price is kept down to this minimum. Consumers have no say in the matter. By their demand they can determine what goods shall be produced, and in what quantities, but they cannot influence the price. Such is Ricardo's doctrine. He admits that where the supply is restricted by monopoly the competition of consumers may raise the price above the level of cost (164/249), but where there is no monopoly, the cost of production regulates the price.

While Ricardo admits that this law does not apply to everything, he tries to bring as many things as possible within its scope. Since the production of corn is not a monopoly, he maintains that its price is fixed by the competition of producers and, like the price of manufactures, is determined by the cost of production. 'Raw produce', he says, 'is not at a monopoly price, because the market price of barley and wheat is as much regulated by their cost of production as the market price of cloth and linen' (165/250); and when he catches Malthus saying that circumstances 'might reduce the price of raw produce, like the price of manufactures, to the cost of production', he exclaims (278/408): 'Might reduce the price

[1] In a footnote to chapter 5 I have already pointed out that, apart from a paragraph on page 37(73), Ricardo appears everywhere to assume that 'in the production of manufactured commodities every portion of capital is employed with the same result'.

of raw produce to the cost of production? Is it ever for any length of time either above or below this price?'[1]

To the plain man this appears somewhat casuistical. The theory of rent, as expounded by Ricardo, is based on the assumption that different farmers have different costs of production, yet all obtain the same price for their products. It follows that some receive for their product more than it cost to produce; the fact that there are others whose costs are so high that they can pay no rent hardly justifies the generalisation that barley and wheat are sold for what they cost to produce.

Ricardo's doctrine that demand exercises no permanent influence on price appears reasonable enough when applied to commodities that anyone can produce in unlimited quantity at a uniform cost of production. What made him think that the same held good in the case of barley and wheat? He does not deny that buyers exercise a temporary influence. If the price of corn rises, he says, it does so 'in the first instance through the comparative state of demand and supply' (71/119). 'With every increased demand for corn', he goes on, its price 'may rise so high as to afford more than the general profits to the farmer'. But his idea is that the competition of consumers only regulates the price until supply is augmented, and then it is the competition of producers that dictates the price.[2] 'If there be plenty of fertile land', he says, 'the price of corn will again fall to its former standard . . . but if there be not plenty of fertile land—if to produce this additional quantity more than the usual quantity of capital and labour be required—corn will not fall to its former level. Its natural price will be raised' (71/120. See also 103/162).

[1] I have restored the first question-mark, which was omitted in Ricardo's third edition. Perhaps he intended to substitute an exclamation mark. As to Malthus, he very rightly contested the proposition that wheat and barley are sold at their natural price, if by this is meant their cost of production. He would prefer to use the term 'necessary price' to indicate the lowest price which will result in these commodities being brought to market in quantity sufficient to satisfy the demand. See page 83 in first edition of Malthus' *Principles*, altered in second edition, page 77.

[2] He writes to Malthus (as already quoted in our second chapter): 'I do not dispute, either, the influence of demand on the price of corn or on the price of all other things; but supply follows close at its heels and soon takes the power of regulating price in his [*sic*] own hands, and in regulating it he is determined by cost of production' (vol. 8, p. 302).

By natural price, Ricardo always means cost of production. If something had happened to cause a universal increase in the cost of producing corn, then indeed its natural price would be raised. But in the above passage it is only the additional quantity of corn that is assumed to be produced at a higher cost. We may, if we choose, say that it is the producers who fix the price, but only in the sense that they will not sell their produce at 4*s*. a bushel if they can get 5*s*. for it. If we adopted the language used by Ricardo in reference to the price of iron, we might say that although the producers on the better lands might be willing to sell their corn at its cost of production, 'they could not', because the competition of buyers would inevitably raise the price above that level. After all, it is only competition on the part of producers that keeps price down to the cost of production, and producers on the good lands will not compete to keep the price down to 4*s*. when the marginal producer is able to sell his corn for 5*s*. It is the pressure of demand that keeps the price at a level that enables the farmers of the better lands to pay rent, and it is only because it keeps price at a high level that the marginal producer is able to make a profit by cultivating inferior land.

When the total quantity of corn for sale is increased by the marginal producer's product, this must tend to lower price; but it does not necessarily reduce it (as Ricardo assumes) to a level with the marginal producer's cost of production; it may happen that even with this additional supply the price remains at a level which gives the marginal producer 'rent' as well as ordinary profit, because the next-best land is so inferior that it will not pay to cultivate it until the pressure of demand has raised the market price still higher.

It follows, then, that where there is a uniform price for a commodity, but not a uniform cost of production, it is an error to assume that demand only influences price 'in the first instance', and that 'buyers have the least in the world to do in regulating price'. It is the buyers who regulate the price by their competition, and the cost of production that can be profitably incurred is determined by this price. Should the market price fall the cost of production will fall, because the producer with the highest cost will have to leave production to those whose cost is lower.

But this is by no means the full extent of the error into which Ricardo was led by turning his back on demand or desire as the source of value, and trying to explain almost all prices by cost of production. He failed to see that cost of production itself is largely affected by demand. On this point Say (and Malthus too) laboured in vain to open his eyes. He professed to agree with Say's 'doctrine of services', but there is ample evidence that he had not the faintest comprehension of that doctrine.

Let us examine Say's teaching, beginning at the beginning. As already stated, Say bases his theory of value on utility, not cost of production. He commences with the statement that:

> The value that men attach to things has its original foundation in the use they can make of them. Some serve as food, others as clothing; others, such as houses, defend us from the inclemency of the weather; others, such as ornaments and decorations, satisfy our tastes, which are a species of want, or merely our vanity, which is also a want. The fact always is that if men attach value to a thing, it is on account of its uses; what is good for nothing, they do not value. This capacity possessed by certain things to satisfy the various wants of men, I venture to call Utility.[1]

Say proceeds to point out that man cannot create matter; all he can do is to impart utility to various materials provided by Nature. This can be done in two ways—(1) by changing their form, as when iron is converted into pots and pans, sheep's wool into coats and blankets, timber into furniture, clay into bricks and bricks into houses; or (2) by merely changing their place, i.e. transporting things from where they benefit nobody to where they can be made to contribute to human happiness. As instances of the latter, he refers to coal which may exist in the earth, and to fish which may exist in the sea, but which while they remain where Nature put them are of no use to anyone. Bring the coal to the surface, catch the fish and place it on the fishmonger's slab, and both have a value—a value derived, not from the labour expended upon them, but from the wants and desires for whose satisfaction they

[1] Say's *Treatise on Political Economy*, vol. 1, pages 3–4. All my quotations (unless otherwise stated) are from the fourth edition, which was the last published in Ricardo's lifetime. Ricardo, in chapters 17 and 20 of his last edition (1821), comments on Say's fourth edition; but all his other references to Say are left standing as they were, and probably refer to Say's second edition (1814). Say apparently claimed to be the originator of the definition of utility as the faculty of satisfying a desire, whether good or bad, and in a letter to Malthus (July, 1827) he defended his choice as follows: 'If I had found a word more perfectly suitable both for corn and diamonds, I would gladly have employed it; but I know of none such.'

are now available. 'They have acquired a utility, a value, which they did not before possess' (vol. 1, p. 16).

The man who brings cotton from Brazil, where it exists in far greater abundance than can be utilised locally, to Europe, where they have none and are eager for it, increases its utility and therefore its value in precisely the same manner as the fisherman and the coal-miner increase the utility and therefore the value of fish and coal.

> Commercial industry co-operates in production, as well as manufacturing industry, in raising the value of a product by its transport from one place to another. A quintal of Brazilian cotton has acquired an additional use, and is worth more, in a European warehouse than in a warehouse in Pernambuco (Say's vol. 1, page 12).

It is interesting to recall Ricardo's comments on this doctrine in the footnote on page 176(264) of his *Principles*.[1] First, he quotes Say as follows:

> Commerce enables us to obtain a commodity in the place where it is to be found, and to convey it to another where it is to be consumed; it therefore gives us the power of increasing the value of the commodity by the whole difference between its price in the first of these places and its price in the second.

Ricardo's comment on this is as follows:

> True, but how is this additional value given to it? By adding to the cost of production, first, the expenses of conveyance; secondly, the profit on the advances of capital made by the merchant. The commodity is only more valuable for the same reason that every other commodity may become more valuable, because more labour is expended on its production and conveyance before it is purchased by the consumer.

Here we have the two theories side by side. Say attributes the increase of value to the increase of utility; Ricardo attributes it to the increased cost. Say thinks that but for the increase of utility there would be no increase of value, despite the increased cost; Ricardo contends that but for the increased cost there would be no increase of price, despite the augmented utility. Say holds that

[1] This footnote made its first appearance in Ricardo's third edition; the words he quotes are a somewhat free translation from Say's Epitome, page 458 in vol. 2.

the increase of cost is not the cause but the consequence of the increased value, in the sense that the cost of transport would not have been incurred had the merchant not perceived that the value of the cotton would be so much greater in Europe than in Brazil as to more than cover the cost of transport.[1] Ricardo admits that so long as cotton is scarce in Europe compared with the demand for it, the value will be high; but he asserts that it will not for long be much higher in Europe than in Brazil unless the cost of transport is high; for, so long as more than the ordinary rate of profit can be obtained by importing cotton, the supply will go on increasing and the price falling. When at length only the ordinary rate of profit can be gained, supply and demand will no longer govern the price; it will be governed by the cost of production.

Ricardo claims that there are times when Say himself acknowledges the truth of this proposition. Say remarks, for example: 'The market price of every product, owing to free competition, constantly tends to approximate to the market price of the services employed in its production; that is to say, it approximates to its cost of production, or natural price as Adam Smith calls it' (Say, vol. 2, p. 486). Accordingly, Ricardo charges Say with inconsistency. 'M. Say acknowledges', he says (231/344), 'that the cost of production is the foundation of price, and yet in various parts of his book he maintains that price is regulated by the proportion which demand bears to supply.'

This remark shows that Ricardo did not understand Say's doctrine of services. Say, as already mentioned, believed that the law of supply and demand not only regulates prices in the market where entrepreneurs sell their products, but also in the market where they purchase the various items which make up their cost of production. 'The market value of the productive factors', says Say, 'is established on the same principles as the value of all other things, that is to say, in proportion to the supply and demand' (Say, vol. 2, p. 24). Malthus adopted this view, and when he published his *Principles* he expounded at considerable length the manner in which 'the great principle of demand and supply is called into action to determine what Adam Smith calls

[1] 'A thing does not have a value because it *costs*; but it *costs* because it has a value.' Condillac's *Commerce and Government*, published in 1776 (page 253 in the 1847 reprint of the *Principal Economists*).

natural prices, as well as market prices'.[1] Whereupon Ricardo remarks:

> The author forgets Adam Smith's definition of natural price, or he would not say that demand and supply could determine natural price. Natural price is only another name for cost of production. When any commodity sells for that price which will repay the wages for labour expended on it, will also afford rent and profit at their then current rate, Adam Smith would say that commodity was at its natural price. Now these charges would remain the same whether commodities were much or little demanded, whether they sold at high or low market price. The hatter can produce 10,000 hats at the same rate of charge that, etc. (vol. 2, p. 46).[2]

Thus Ricardo does not forget Smith's definition of natural price, but while he has got Smith's words by heart, the most junior copyist in his employ could not have more completely missed their meaning. He thinks that Smith's definition excludes demand and supply from exercising any influence on natural price, or cost of production, whereas the fact is Smith expressly states that the services of land, capital and labour have to be purchased by the entrepreneur in the market at their current prices, and elsewhere he dwells on the different prices that have to be paid for different kinds and qualities of labour.

Seeing that Ricardo had such a hazy idea of Smith's teaching, and found Say's doctrines so incomprehensible and inconsistent, let us study the latter in more detail.

Products, Say maintains, derive their value from their utility, or the fact that they are desired.[3] Ricardo himself admits that utility is essential to value; what no one wants can have no value, whatever its cost. But Ricardo goes no further along this line, whereas Say continues by telling us that because desire confers value on products, it confers value on the means of producing

[1] Malthus' *Principles*, page 75 in first edition; page 71 in second.

[2] Ricardo criticised Say for including rent in cost of production, yet here he appears to see no objection to Adam Smith doing so. But what can he mean by the statement that rent would be the same whether the product fetched a high price or a low price? We can hardly suppose he meant that if the market price of wheat rose from 5*s*. a bushel to 10*s*. the rent would remain unaltered.

[3] 'The utility of a thing, that is to say, one's need of it' (Say's *Treatise*, vol. 2, p. 17). He does not actually use the word *desire*, although some of his sayings, as will be seen later, imply it.

them. If golden eggs have a value, the goose that lays the golden eggs will have a value. If shoes are valued for the comfort they afford, then the leather of which shoes are made will have a value; and the hides, which are the raw material of the leather, acquire a value from the value of leather; ultimately, the value of the hides is derived from the value of the shoes and other goods into whose composition they enter. As the Austrian school of economists put it, value is transmitted backwards from the article that is desired 'for its own sake' to the various constituents of which it is composed. But these constituents do not consist of materials only. The labour 'bestowed' upon and 'realised in' the product (to use Ricardo's expressions) is also a constituent which has a value because the product of that labour has a use and value to the consumer. And capital as well as labour contributes to the product. 'A field or a factory', says Say, 'does not furnish directly any appreciable enjoyment to its possessor'; such things are not valued 'for their own sake', but nevertheless have a value 'derived from the value of the product which may be obtained from them; and the value of the product is founded on the use that can be made of it, and the enjoyment that can be got from it' (Say, vol. 2, p. 24). In another place he observes: 'As it is the utility of the product that causes it to be in demand, and gives it value, so it is the capacity to create this utility that causes the productive services to be in demand, and gives them a value' (Say, vol. 2, p. 9).

There is, then, a demand for productive services—the services of the worker, the services of capital, and the services of land.[1] 'Those who possess one or other of these three sources of production', Say remarks, 'are sellers of what we here call productive

[1] Say makes a useful distinction between labour, or work, which is a productive service, and the labourer himself, who is the owner of the labour-power; and a similar distinction between the productive service of land and the land itself; and between the productive service of capital and the capital itself. Selling land and selling capital are quite a different matter from selling their services, and it is the sale of services only that Say has in mind when he says: 'In exchanging one product for another all that is exchanged is the productive services by which they were created' (Say's vol. 2, page 504, quoted by Ricardo with approval on page 187(282) in the paragraph numbered 1). It is necessary to recollect, however, that the owner of a mine or quarry really sells part of his asset with each ton of mineral taken away. And the purchaser of a machine-made article must also pay for wear and tear of the machine as well as for the service of the machine.

services; the consumers of the products are the buyers.[1] The value of the services, like that of everything else, always rises directly with demand, and inversely with supply' (Say, vol. 2, p. 67). In another place he observes: 'The market value of the factors of production is determined on the same principles as the value of all other things, that is to say, in proportion to supply and demand' (Say, vol. 2, p. 24), and 'the result is that there comes to be a market value, or current price, for productive services as well as for products . . . each kind of productive service, even, has a market price peculiar to itself' (Say, vol. 2, pp. 8–9).

Here, then, we have an explanation of the 'inconsistency' that Ricardo thought he detected in the teaching of Say, who 'acknowledges that the cost of production is the foundation of price, and yet in various parts of his book he maintains that price is regulated by the proportion which demand bears to supply' (231/344). In the sale of products, Ricardo sees only the competition of sellers, which keeps the price down to the cost of production. Say recognises this, but also sees competition among those who buy productive services, the sum total of which constitutes the cost of production. Whether it is labour, or materials, or anything else that you buy, you must pay the current market price. Leather, we said just now, derives a value from the value which utility confers upon shoes. But leather serves as material for many other products—travel-trunks, handbags, purses, pocket-books, saddles, harness, belts, gloves—and the demand for each of these articles is a source of value, swelling the aggregate demand for leather and tending to raise its price in the market, and therefore to raise the cost of producing leather goods of every description.

What applies to materials applies also to labour. If you call in a carpenter to put up some shelves in your pantry, the price of the carpenter's labour will not be determined by the value that you individually place upon this particular job, nor yet by 'higgling' between the two of you. You must pay him what he can get from other people who also value his services because they value his products; in other words, you must buy his labour at the market price, or go without it. For labour of different kinds and qualities there are different prices, determined by demand and supply, and the manufacturer must pay these rates, and therefore his cost of

[1] The immediate buyer is the entrepreneur engaged in production; but he buys to sell again; the ultimate buyer is the consumer who 'buys for keeps'.

production depends not merely on the quantity of labour he employs, but also on the price he must pay for it.[1]

To Say it must have appeared strange that Ricardo could not understand what he had made so plain; on the other hand, Ricardo considered that his own doctrine was misunderstood and misrepresented by Say.[2] In his *Treatise* Say had said that it is the value of products that gives value to the productive services, and not the value of productive services that gives value to the products 'as some authors have contended', and he added a footnote naming Ricardo as the author he had in mind (Say, vol. 2, p. 9). In a letter to Say Ricardo disowns the teaching attributed to him; he writes (vol. 8, p. 149): 'I do not say that it is the value of labour which regulates the value of commodities, for that is an opinion I do all in my power to overthrow; but I say that it is the comparative quantity of labour necessary to the production of commodities which regulates their relative value'. To which the puzzled Frenchman replies:

> I acknowledge that I do not understand very well the distinction which you lay down between *the value of the work which does not determine the value of the products*, and the *quantity of work necessary to their production which does determine the value of the products*. It seems to me that you cannot determine the quantity and the quality of the work except by the price paid to obtain it. This at least is what I have always understood by the quantity of that productive service which

---

[1] In this connection I cannot resist the temptation to quote from the Autobiography of dear old George Arliss, who (heaven be thanked) did not devote his talents to the dry-as-dust study of economics, but who nevertheless teaches better economics than Ricardo in the following passage: 'In the entertainment world, where people pay money for admission, the value of the one who entertains cannot be gauged by his deserts, or his brainpower, or even by his ability; it is bound to depend on how much money he draws to the box-office. Whatever the cause—it may be a woman's charm, or a man's unusual personality, or five babies all born together—but whatever it is, if it draws money to the box-office competition arises between managers, and the salary is bound to go up.'

[2] 'I am not convinced by anything Say says of me,' he writes to Malthus; 'he does not understand me' (vol. 8, p. 228). Again, after a visit to Paris he reports that neither Garnier 'nor Say have succeeded in at all understanding what my opinions are' (vol. 9, p. 249). To his friend Trower he makes a similar complaint (always good-humoured) of Malthus, who 'has, I am sure without intending it, misrepresented me in many important particulars' (vol. 8, p. 349).

I have called *industrial service*. Its price makes part of the costs of production, and you yourself very justly lay down that the aggregate of the costs of production regulates the value of the product (vol. 8, p. 161).

Ricardo seems to have had no perception that his idea of cost of production differed from that of Adam Smith and Say. Since Say agreed that the competition of entrepreneurs with one another results in price being kept down to cost of production, he appears to have been satisfied that on this point Say was teaching the same thing as himself, and was therefore inconsistent in regarding utility as the foundation of value. In a letter to Malthus, after condemning Say's doctrine that value depends upon utility, or demand, he adds: 'I think more may be said in defence of his doctrine of services; they are, I think, the regulators of value, and if he would give up rent, he and I should not differ very materially on that subject' (vol. 8, p. 277). And in due course this view was incorporated in the new (the third and last) edition of his *Principles*. In revising his chapter on Values and Riches Ricardo summarised in a series of numbered paragraphs what he regarded as Say's inconsistencies,[1] and he proceeded to remark:

> In No. 4 M. Say maintains, with scarcely any variation, the doctrine which I hold concerning value. In his productive services he includes the services rendered by land, capital, and labour; in mine I include only capital and labour, and wholly exclude land. Our difference proceeds from the different view which we take of rent (189/283).

Thus their *only* difference is on the question whether rent is to be included in the cost of production; apparently he has entirely

[1] Ricardo arranged these paragraphs in parallel columns thus:

No. 1	opposite	No. 5
2	,,	6
3	,,	7
4	,,	8, 9, 10, 11, 12

the doctrines on the right being in Ricardo's opinion inconsistent with those on the left. Unfortunately, in the *Everyman* edition (pages 187–8) the 12 paragraphs are printed as a continuous series. (For paragraphs 4 and 5 Ricardo gives no reference. All the references actually given are to Say's fourth edition, and all except two are to pages in the Epitome at the end of the second volume; but the reference for the second paragraph should apparently be page 457, not 497. The other two references are given as 'vol. 2, p. 4', but the reference for paragraph 6 should apparently be vol. 1, page 4).

overlooked, or attaches no importance to, the fact that Say reckons that the amount of wages that enters into the cost of production depends on the quality as well as the quantity of labour employed, and that the price of this labour is determined by the law of supply and demand.

Ricardo, while he thinks he is in agreement with Say in other respects, refuses to include rent as a cost of production. Some writers have gone further, and refused to regard wages and profits as a cost of production.[1] Products are obtained, they argue, by the co-operation of land, labour, and capital. Wages, profits, and rents are not productive services; they are shares in the product allotted respectively to labourers, capitalists, and the owners of land.[2] This is true enough, but does not alter the fact that what is remuneration to one man for his services, or the services of something that he owns, is a cost to the man who employs those services and must pay for them. If an entrepreneur hires labour of various qualities, he must pay out various amounts in wages. To the total thus paid he must add interest due to the owner of the capital as a reward for his 'waiting',[3] as well as an amount to compensate for the wear and tear of tools, machines, etc. If he pays a tax, Ricardo himself admits this as a cost of production.[4] And if he pays rent either for a field or a factory site, one cannot see how he can arrive at his cost of production, or estimate the price that will yield him a profit, if he neglects to include this item along with the other disbursements that his undertaking has imposed upon him.

Ricardo's reason for excluding rent from the cost of production had no connection with that put forward by Cairnes, otherwise he would have excluded wages and profits, whereas he said in the *Notes on Malthus* (vol. 2, p. 42): 'By cost of production I invariably mean wages and profits.' And he would not have included taxes,

[1] J. E. Cairnes, *Some Leading Principles of Political Economy*, chap. 3, sec. 3. J. S. Mill had already made this point in his essays on *Some Unsettled Questions of Political Economy*.

[2] To regard these shares in the product as *cost*, said Cairnes, is to confound cost with its antithesis, reward. This is practically the same criticism that Malthus made when he said that Ricardo confounded 'the very important distinction between cost and value' (see footnote on page 30(47) of Ricardo's *Principles*).

[3] Admitted as a cost by Ricardo on page 23(37).

[4] 'Any tax which may be imposed on the cultivator . . . will increase the cost of production . . .' (98/156. See also 132/205 and 160/243).

which cannot even claim to be a reward for assisting in the creation of the product. He included taxes and excluded rents because the tax adds to the price that the consumer must pay, whilst the price paid by the consumer for wheat and barley is the same whether the cultivator pays a high rent, a low rent, or no rent at all. But if rent does not affect the price, the logical conclusion would seem to be that prices are not determined by cost of production. The contention that barley and wheat are sold for what they cost to produce can only be justified by supposing that the rent paid by the farmer of good land brings his cost up to the same level as the marginal farmer's, as suggested by Anderson, the father of the rent theory. But Ricardo excluded this view by holding that rent does not form part of the cost of production.

The entrepreneur must reckon up his costs in money, since it is for money that he sells his goods. According to Say: 'The farmer, the manufacturer, or the merchant, is continually comparing the price the consumer is willing and able to pay for this or that commodity with the cost at which it can be produced.'[1] Ricardo does not dispute this; on the contrary, he writes to Trower: 'What all producers look steadily at is market price, and its relation to natural price' (vol. 8, p. 256). To the same correspondent he wrote: 'If any man wishes to increase his capital' (he might have said, if any man wishes to make a profit), 'he produces that which he has good reason to think he can sell at a remunerative price. It is with money he has to pay labour, and it is money which he seeks to obtain' (vol. 8, p. 235). There is no difference between Ricardo and Say on this point; in fact, a month or two after puzzling Say by the statement that it is not the value of labour but the quantity of it that regulates the value of the product, we find him writing to Malthus: 'Cost of production, in money, means the value of labour as well as profits' (vol. 8, p. 279).

Despite this apparent agreement with Say, the doctrines of the two men were poles apart. Ricardo thought it made no difference whether you reckoned labour-cost by the quantity of labour or by the price paid for it because, notwithstanding his admission of different rates of pay in section 2 of his first chapter, he continued always to treat all labour as remunerated at the same rate. He also continued to assume that demand and supply, though they might

[1] Say's *Treatise*, vol. 2, p. 68.

cause fluctuations in the market price of commodities, exercised no influence whatever on the cost of production. After reading Malthus' *Principles* he wrote to Trower:

> I have not met with many persons who have yet read Malthus' book. I am pleased however with the observations you make on what he has said respecting my doctrine of price being ultimately regulated by cost of production. By the very definition of natural price, it is wholly dependent on cost of production, and has nothing to do with demand and supply. The terms on which a commodity can be produced, so as to remunerate the producer, will remain the same although the demand should be for five times the quantity produced. We all acknowledge the effect of such a demand on market price (vol. 8, p. 207).

There seems good reason to suppose that, at the back of Ricardo's mind, natural price was the same thing as Nature's price. According to Adam Smith (whom he quotes on his second page), labour was the original price paid for all things. This may be called Nature's price, for although Nature makes no charge for the materials and forces she places at the disposal of mankind, man nevertheless pays a price, since he must exert himself to gather what he wants, and in most cases must further exert himself to transform what he has collected into the shape that answers to his needs and desires.

Ricardo recognised also that labour, though the principal, is not the only price that man must pay for the satisfaction of his wants; the element of time must not be overlooked. The farmer must wait for the seed to root and ripen; the pastoralist must tend his flocks and herds in patience while they grow flesh and wool and hides; there will be more waiting, as well as work, while the wool is converted into clothing, the hides into leather, and the leather into shoes and harness. Accordingly, in Ricardo's account of the cost of production the reward of waiting (interest or profit) figures along with the reward of labour (wages) as part of the natural price or cost of production.

So long, therefore, as competition among labourers keeps wages down to the minimum necessary for continued existence, and competition amongst capitalists keeps the charge for waiting to the minimum which induces people to save in the quantity required, Ricardo regards both wages and profits as at their natural rate; and so long as products are sold at a price that only covers these expenses, the purchaser obtains them for the lowest price that Nature makes possible.

But this was certainly not what Adam Smith had in mind when he introduced the term *natural price* to express the price that yields to the producers wages, profits, and rent, at the ordinary rates current in the market. Smith was not defining Nature's price. He was dealing with the terms upon which men exchange with one another their services or the things they possess in a world where one man has land and another is landless, where one has capital and another has none, where one possesses natural or acquired skill, which another lacks. Ricardo, even more than Smith, should have followed this course, seeing that his object, as explained in his Preface, was not to discuss the most effective means of wealth-production, but to investigate the 'laws' or forces which, in a growing community, gradually change the proportions in which the wealth produced is shared between labourers, capitalists, and landlords. In a letter to Malthus he said: 'Political Economy, you think, is an enquiry into the nature and causes of wealth; I think it should rather be called an enquiry into the laws which determine the division of the produce of industry amongst the classes who concur in its formation' (vol. 8, p. 278).

Although Adam Smith's immortal work had for its subject the 'nature and causes of wealth', he too had something to say about changes that occur in the division of that wealth amongst the different classes of the community. In the eighth paragraph of his sixth chapter he said:

> As soon as the land of any country has all become private property, the landlords, like all other men, love to reap where they never sowed, and demand a rent even for its natural produce. The wood of the forest, the grass of the field, and all the natural fruits of the earth, which, when the land was in common, cost the labourer only the trouble of gathering them, come even to him to have an additional price fixed upon them.[1] He must give up to the landlord a portion of what his labour either collects or produces. This portion, or what comes to the same thing, the price of this portion, constitutes the rent of land, and in the price of the greater part of commodities makes a third component part.

[1] Later (in the 3rd paragraph of chapter 11) Smith mentions that landlords whose property borders the sea charge a rent for permission to gather sea-weed on the rocks.

Thus Nature's gifts are no longer free; raw materials are no longer to be had in exchange for the mere labour of collecting them, or extracting them from the earth. Smith's remarks seem to have made no impression on Ricardo; according to him, labour is the only price paid. He begins his chapter on the Rent of Mines as follows:

> The metals, like other things, are obtained by labour. Nature, indeed, produces them; but it is the labour of man which extracts them from the bowels of the earth and prepares them for our service... It will be sufficient to remark that the same general rule which regulates the value of raw produce and manufactured commodities is applicable also to the metals; their value depending not on the rate of profits, nor on the rate of wages, nor on the rent paid for mines, but on the total quantity of labour necessary to obtain the metal and to bring it to market (46/85).

And his 27th chapter commences with the statement that:

> Gold and silver, like all other commodities, are valuable only in proportion to the quantity of labour necessary to produce them and bring them to market. Gold is about fifteen times dearer than silver, not because there is a greater demand for it, nor because the supply of silver is fifteen times greater than that of gold, but solely because fifteen times the quantity of labour is necessary to procure a given quantity of it (238/352).

Thus, according to Ricardo, the consumer pays nothing for the materials provided by Nature; he pays only for the labour of extracting them, conveying them, or converting them.

This view was defended by McCulloch, the same valiant henchman who justified Ricardo's doctrine that value is in proportion to the *quantity* of labour by suggesting that if the clever labourer is paid twice as much as the less clever, he must be regarded as two labourers. In his *Principles of Political Economy* (published after Ricardo's death) McCulloch rebukes a writer in the *Quarterly Review* who 'contends that the earth is a source of wealth because it supplies us with the matter of commodities. . . . It would in truth be just as correct to say that the earth is a source of pictures and statues because it supplies the materials made use of by painters and statuaries.' He quotes Locke's *Civil Government* to the effect that nine-tenths, perhaps ninety-nine hundredths, of the utility or wealth enjoyed by man is attributable to the labour bestowed by him upon Nature's gifts. But McCulloch goes further than this; apparently he will not give Nature credit even for one-tenth or one-hundredth of the utility enjoyed by man from the commodities with which his labour is rewarded. He says:

> Labour . . . is the only source of wealth. Nature spontaneously furnishes the matter of which all commodities are made; but until labour has been expended in appropriating matter, or in adapting it to our use, it is wholly destitute of value, and is not, nor ever has been, considered as forming wealth.[1]

Thus Adam Smith is unjust to the landlords in accusing them of reaping where they have not sown; have not they, or their ancestors, given a utility and value to the land by taking the trouble to appropriate it, including the seaweed on the shore?

That the minerals or metals lying buried in the earth have a value not conferred upon them by labour is sufficiently shown by the fact that those who desire to undertake the labour of extracting them are willing to pay the owner of the land for the privilege of doing so. And those who desire to consume what is extracted must repay to the capitalist not merely the cost of extraction, but also what he has been compelled to pay for the privilege of extracting. It is strange that Ricardo should have assumed that manufactures are usually sold to the public at a price which consists exclusively of wages and profit (64/110). Nature may make no charge for materials beyond the labour of extracting them, but the landlord has stepped into Nature's shoes, and 'as long as society is constituted as it now is',[2] the manufacturer will find few materials that can be had without payment of rent or royalty to the owner of the land whence those materials were taken. Adam Smith therefore was right in saying that in the price charged for most things rent 'makes a third component part'.

Ricardo knew well enough that if the manufacturer must pay more for his materials he must charge more for the manufactured article. In 1815 he had acknowledged to Malthus that in one of his statements he had overlooked this.

> I made no allowance [he said] for the altered value of the raw material in all manufactured goods; they would, I think, be subject

[1] See first paragraph in Part 2 of McCulloch's *Principles*.

[2] I borrow this expression from Ricardo's pamphlet *On Protection to Agriculture* (vol. 4, p. 222).

> to a variation in price, not on account of increased or diminished wages, but on account of the rise or fall in the price of the raw produce which enters into their composition, and which in some commodities cannot be inconsiderable (vol. 6, p. 179).

Accordingly, in his *Principles* (59/104) he tells us that linen, shoes, and cloth would rise in price if the price of raw materials rose; and on page 69(117) he said:

> There are few commodities which are not more or less affected in their price by the rise of raw produce, because some raw material from the land enters into the composition of most commodities. Cotton goods, linen, and cloth will all rise in price with the rise of wheat;[1] but they rise on account of the greater quantity of labour expended on the raw material from which they are made, and not because more was paid by the manufacturer to the labourers whom he employed on those commodities.

Yet between these two statements we have the dictum on page 64(110) that the owner of the land from which the materials were taken has no share in the price of manufactured commodities, the whole of which is divided exclusively between the manufacturer and his men. Ricardo sees nothing contradictory in these statements because he attributes every permanent rise of price to increase in the quantity of labour employed on production. More labour than before is required to produce wheat, more labour than before to produce metals and minerals, therefore their price rises; the fact that it is only part of the supply that requires more labour than before is ignored, and he is blind to the fact that it is only because increase of demand has raised the price, and keeps it at a high level, that the marginal producer is able to make a profit despite his high costs.

You cannot explain the value of land, the value of raw materials, or the value of products—you cannot explain prices—unless, like

[1] Although in writing to Malthus Ricardo spoke of the material used in *all* manufactured goods, it is curious that he apparently only applies the principle to materials grown on the surface of the earth, and not to metals or minerals. The passage on page 69(118) continues as follows: 'In all cases commodities rise because more labour is expended on them . . . articles of jewellery, of iron, of plate, and of copper, would not rise, because none of the raw produce from the surface of the earth enters into their composition.' So a rise in the price of coal or iron ore will not affect the costs of the manufacturer!

Say, you recognise that desire, demand, is the source of value. Recognise this, and you are able to explain everything. You do not need one law for scarce goods and another for goods that can be multiplied without assignable limit; one law for monopoly and another for competition. You do not need, after framing your law, to set about making exceptions. There is, however, or was before the theory of utility had been carefully worked out, some difficulty in tracing exactly how desire affects price under a variety of different circumstances, and Ricardo was not alone in failing to obtain clear ideas on the subject. Others, both before and after Ricardo, seem to have found something elusive, something that evaded their grasp, in the notion of value; and strangely enough, Say himself, despite his admirable account of the manner in which prices are determined, got out of his depth and floundered badly when he dealt with value as distinct from price.

In this book we are concerned with Ricardo, not Say; but since we have accused Ricardo of failing to understand his French contemporary, it is only fair to admit that there was considerable ground for Ricardo's criticism that Say 'is frequently at variance with himself when value is the subject he treats of' (vol. 8, p. 228), and: 'In Say's works generally there is a great mixture of profound thinking and of egregious blundering' (vol. 8, p. 302). Let us investigate the charge.

On page 4 of his first volume Say remarks:

> The mass of matter of which the world is composed can neither increase nor diminish. All we can do is to reproduce these materials in another form which makes them suitable for a use for which they were not suitable in their original form; or it may be we merely add to the utility they already possessed. Hence there is a creation, not of matter, but of utility; there is a production of wealth. It is thus that the word production must be understood in political economy and throughout the course of this work. Production is not a creation of matter, but a creation of utility. It is not measured by the length, bulk or weight of the product, but by its utility.

It would have been well if Say had contented himself with this definition of production. But in the paragraph which immediately precedes this passage he says that to create articles that have utility 'is to create wealth, since the utility of these articles is the original foundation of their value, and since their value is wealth'. Or, as he puts it a few pages later (page 21): 'Wealth consists in the value given to things by human industry with the aid of natural agents.' Thus the things themselves are not wealth; it is their value that is wealth.

Ricardo's chapter on Riches and Value was devoted to a refutation of this error. Wealth consists of useful things—necessaries and luxuries. When the supply of commodities increases there is an increase of wealth, but not necessarily an increase of value. If a given expenditure of labour can be made to produce two pairs of stockings instead of one, wealth or utility is doubled, but the value produced—or rather, the value of what is produced—will be no greater than before, for the price of stockings will have fallen to half. 'Value, then,' says Ricardo (182/273), 'essentially differs from riches, for value depends, not on abundance, but on the difficulty or facility of production.'[1] Diminution of supply, which is diminution of wealth, may result in increase of value. 'A bad harvest will produce a high price' (102/162). On the other hand 'a very abundant crop will be worth less money than a scanty one' (vol. 2, p. 232). Hence fishermen have been known to throw part of their catch back into the sea, and history records cases where the monopolists of rich spices have destroyed part of their crop to keep the price up.

In one of the above quotations Say defines production as the creation of utility; in the other he practically defines it as the creation of value. He was impressed, I think, by the fact that in a world of divided labour the aim of the entrepreneur is to produce value rather than utility. As already pointed out in an earlier chapter of this book, entrepreneurs produce goods which they do not want for their own consumption; the production of utility is with them only a means to an end, their immediate object being to produce a value which will exceed the aggregate of values consumed or destroyed in the process of production. Hence Say may have concluded that production should be defined as the creation of value rather than the creation of utility.[2] It is true that in the

[1] Or on scarcity, see third paragraph in Ricardo's first chapter.

[2] Say could, of course, claim that Adam Smith classifies a labourer as 'productive' if he adds to his employer's money income more than the amount of his wages, whereas the domestic cook, who creates pies, puddings and cakes, is an 'unproductive' labourer.

Epitome at the end of his second volume he tells us (page 490) that 'the utility created constitutes the product; the exchangeable value which results is only the measure of this utility—the measure of the production that has taken place'; but on page 487 we have this: 'To produce is to give to a thing a recognised value capable of procuring by exchange something else of equal value; to increase the recognised value that a thing already has is also production.' This harmonises with the statement in his *Letters to T. R. Malthus*:[1] 'To create a thing, the want of which does not exist, is to create a thing without value; this would not be production.' The essence of production, apparently, is the creation of value, and if the recognised value, or price for which the thing can be sold, is less than the cost of its creation, the thing is not a product. This, as pointed out in an earlier chapter, seems to explain Say's doctrine that every product can be sold at a remunerative price.

On page 487 Say also says: 'Production creates value in giving or increasing the utility of the thing, and in establishing thereby the demand for it, which is the first cause of its having value.' Here we have his theory that demand depends upon supply, but his reasoning seems involved, if not circuitous. The thing created will not have value unless it is in demand, but it is the creation of the thing that creates the demand, and the demand that gives it its value.

These definitions seem to suggest a certain haziness in Say's thinking, not perhaps incompatible with common sense; but what are we to think of the following passage from Say's *Letters to T. R. Malthus*, published in reply to Malthus' *Principles*?—

> We do not create, we do not destroy, a single atom. We confine ourselves to changing the combinations; and everything we put into our products is immaterial; it is value; and it is this value, also immaterial, that we consume daily, annually, and which keeps us alive.[2]

So we are not nourished by substance, but by something immaterial—not by meat and vegetables, but by their value. No one wants to eat a raw potato; it would merely give one indigestion. Cook it (Ricardo would say bestow labour on it), and you not only

[1] Page 28 in the reprint of the English edition.

[2] Page 17 in reprint of English version, but I have tried to keep closer to the original French.

give it utility, but value, which is what keeps us alive. Swallowing value will not give you indigestion, which is not surprising, as it is immaterial; what does surprise is that it gives bone and muscle to the Irish peasant.

In Say's *Treatise* this remarkable doctrine is insisted upon again and again. He commences his third chapter by enumerating some products of previous industry indispensable to the creation of value, such as tools, food to sustain the labourer while at work, and materials to work upon, and he finishes (vol. 1, p. 24) not by telling us that these things constitute capital, but by saying 'the value of all these things constitutes what we call productive capital'. At the beginning of the next chapter he seems about to revert to the language of common sense when he speaks of the 'aid that industry receives from capital, that is to say, from products that it has already created', but he immediately proceeds to remark (page 28):

> Thus when a field is ploughed and sown, besides the labour and knowledge employed in this operation, besides the already-created values brought into use—such as the value of the plough, the barrow, the seed-corn, the food and clothing consumed by the labourers during the process of production—there is a work performed by the soil, by the air, by water, and by the sun, in which man bears no part, but which nevertheless co-operate in the creation of a new product that will be gathered at the time of the harvest.

While the object of this passage is to point out that Nature's contribution must not be overlooked, I quote it here because it suggests that the cultivator is not assisted by the plough, but by its value; and the value of the garments worn by the labourers co-operates with sun, soil, air, and water in the germination of the seed.

Other passages are to the same effect. On pages 29–30 we are informed that 'in the work done by machines, by means of which man adds so much to his power, a part of the product obtained is due to the capital value of the machine'. On page 116 he observes: 'The faculty of amassing capital, or maintaining values is, it seems to me, one of the causes of the very great superiority of man over the animals.' And again, on page 193, we have the remark: 'It is not matter, but the value of matter, that is wealth.' Even utility, it will be noticed, has dropped out, and value is everything. It would seem that the plough is not valuable because it is useful, but is useful because it has value.

In view of these strange utterances it is not surprising that Ricardo regarded Say's 'deep thinking' as mingled with a good deal of 'blundering'. I have suggested that Say was led astray by the fact that every entrepreneur is engaged in the task of producing a greater value than the sum of the values consumed or destroyed in the process of production. He was also impressed by the fact that the conservation of capital is the maintenance of value rather than the preservation and accumulation of the particular things in which that value resides. Food and necessaries are consumed by the workman, who does not necessarily reproduce food and necessaries, but does reproduce the value of what he consumes. In the manufacture of steel there is a destruction of coal and iron, but the value of the steel replaces the values that have been destroyed. Machinery is gradually worn out, but none of its value is lost to the capitalist, who lays aside year by year a portion of the product—or rather, a portion of its value—as a fund for replacement. Thus Say came to look upon capital as consisting, not of things which are destroyed, but of value which survives. 'What it is important to conserve', he says, 'is the value of the capital, not any particular material object. The value of the capital is perpetuated in spite of frequent changes in the material forms in which the value resides' (Say, vol. 1, p. 203). In most cases it is quite impossible to measure the product against the things destroyed—the reward against the sacrifice—by comparison of number, weight, length, bulk, or even of utility; they can only be measured by value. Hence Say's identification of capital with its value. He commences his eleventh chapter with the following remarks:

> The preceding chapter has shown how productive capitals, constantly busy, tossed this way and that and subjected to wear and tear in the process of production, emerge, when the product is complete, with their value intact. Now as it is the value of matter, and not matter itself, that constitutes wealth, it will be understood, I hope, how productive capital, despite several changes of form, remains nevertheless always the same capital (Say, vol. 1, p. 99).

Now all this, properly handled, might have been very illuminating; but handled as Say handles it, the result is only to obscure much of his teaching which would otherwise have been quite clear.

Say is on firmer ground when he regards value-in-use (as Adam Smith called it) as the sole source of value-in-exchange; but he goes too far when he says that price measures the value of things, and their value is the measure of their utility (Say's vol. 1, p. 4). Ricardo regards this as one of Say's worst 'blunders'. I have already quoted his remark that Say 'certainly has not a correct notion of what is meant by value when he contends that a commodity is valuable in proportion to its utility' (vol. 8, p. 276). In this dictum of Say's he does not distinguish between the two different senses of the word *value* pointed out by Adam Smith. He must have been thinking of value in exchange when he said that price measures the value of things; but when he followed this up with the statement that their value is the measure of their utility what he had in mind was presumably value in use—the value or importance which each individual consumer attributes to the thing he wants. In the opening lines of his first chapter Ricardo quotes the words of Adam Smith, including his remark that 'the things which have the greatest value in use have frequently little or no value in exchange'; and Ricardo comments: 'Utility, then, is not the measure of exchangeable value.' The price in the market, which is usually the same for all buyers, does not and cannot correspond with the personal valuation of each individual purchaser, since value in use 'is differently estimated by different persons' (292/429).[1]

Ricardo holds that differences in the degree of utility seldom play any part in the determination of price. His view is that, where there are competing producers, goods are sold at a price that covers their cost of production, and differences of price accordingly reflect or measure differences in the cost of production, not differences in the degree of utility. If the price of a watch is £25 while the charge for a pair of shoelaces is no more than sixpence, it is because the one costs 1000 times as much as the other to produce.

But cost of production only determines the lowest price that the producer can afford to accept. It explains why he is willing to

[1] See also page 159(241): 'Every man has some standard in his own mind by which he estimates the value of his enjoyments, but that standard is as various as the human character.'

take less for the laces than for the watch; it does not explain why the buyer is willing to give so much more for the one than for the other. 'Does the purchaser of a commodity ever enquire', said Ricardo in one of his pamphlets, 'concerning the terms on which the producer can afford to raise or make it?' (vol. 4, p. 248). If the consumer is willing to give a thousand times as much for a watch as for a pair of laces it must be because he reckons that the service or utility he will derive from the former over a long series of years will enormously exceed that of a single pair of laces.

But while this is true, it does not justify the conclusion that the prices paid measure, either exactly or approximately, the purchaser's estimate of the difference in the degree of utility. Whatever may be the consumer's estimate of utility, he does not pay more than the seller asks. If he pays what, in proportion to his income, is a high price, we are entitled to infer that he attaches a high importance to the thing purchased; but we cannot similarly conclude that when he pays a low price, it is because the commodity has little importance in his eyes. What he acquires at a low price may be something for which he would be prepared to pay a much higher price rather than go without it.[1] Nor, when he pays a high price, can we be sure that this price represents the limit to which he would have been prepared to go. All that we can safely infer, whether the price paid is high or low, is that the purchaser considers that the article he buys is worth to him at least what he gives for it.

I say *at least*, because the whole object of exchange, whether by individual barter or through the medium of the market, is an increase of utility or enjoyment. Ricardo admitted that trade or exchange increases utility, although he repudiated Malthus' contention that there is an increase of value. On this point Say appears to share Ricardo's view. 'In all commerce which is not swindling', he says, 'the exchange is of things which at the time and place of the exchange are worth one another' (Say's vol. 1, p. 13). This, however, seems inconsistent with his dictum that price measures value and value measures utility. Ricardo's view is that there is no correspondence between price and degree of utility. His theory

[1] It is because the consumer's estimate of use-value is higher than the producer's price that the government is able to step in and collect a tax on many commodities.

assumes that the cost of producing a watch is the same for all producers and the price paid for a watch is the same for all purchasers. To one man a watch may have a particularly high utility, but he does not on that account pay more for it than other consumers. Exchange-value and use-value are not to be measured by one scale. If the market value or price of a watch is £25, the price of two watches will be double that. But if a consumer pays £25 for a watch because he estimates its use-value to be at least equal to that, the acquisition of a second watch will not add to his sum of utility anything like the same amount; in fact, he may have no use for it at all; and certainly, unless he is a very rich man, he will know of a great many other ways of spending his second £25 that will yield him far more utility than he would derive from the acquisition of a second watch.

When a man goes shopping it is for the purpose of satisfying his wants or desires. What he wishes to obtain is something that he does not already possess, or does not possess in as large a quantity as he desires. If he already has a watch he is not very likely to buy a second one; a second watch would not supply a lack or minister to an unsatisfied craving; it, at all events, would not add to his stock of utility nearly as much as could be added by spending his money on something else. With such things as a watch, a pair of spectacles, a bicycle, or a microscope, a man is usually content with a single specimen; the want is completely satisfied. But there are numerous other things of which a large supply is much more useful, and affords much more satisfaction, than a small supply. It is with goods of this kind more particularly that the modern theory of 'diminishing utility' and 'marginal utility' helps us to understand the relationship between value-in-use and value-in-exchange.

This theory was not developed until many years after both Say and Ricardo were dead. It is not necessary for us to go into it here. The main point is that, as already remarked, value-in-use is the sole source and the only explanation of value-in-exchange, and that the whole purpose of exchange is to create or increase utility. Malthus held that this increase of utility was reflected in an increase of value. Ricardo denied this. We should have expected Say to side with Malthus on this point, but I have already quoted his remark that in every exchange the things exchanged are of equal value. Let me now give this passage in full:

> Genovesi,[1] who lectured on Political Economy at Naples, defines commerce as the exchange of the superfluous for the necessary. The reason he gives is that in an exchange the article that each party desires to acquire is, for each of them, more necessary than the one he offers. This is a subtlety; I mention it because it is often repeated. It would be difficult to prove that a poor workman who goes on Sunday to the tavern,[2] there parts with his superfluity in exchange for what he needs. In all commerce which is not swindling the exchange is of things which at the time and place of the exchange are worth one another. Commercial production, that is to say the value added to the goods exchanged, does not arise from the exchange, but from the commercial operations which were responsible for bringing the goods to the market (Say's vol. 1, p. 13).

If Ricardo had written this, we could understand it, for he admitted that both parties to an exchange gain in utility, but thought that subjective values had no influence upon objective values. But Say's doctrine was that utility is the foundation of all value, that value is the measure of utility, that it is by increasing utility that you increase value, and that cotton which in Brazil exists in greater quantities than can be used, and is therefore largely superfluous, acquires both utility and value by being carried to Europe; and the Brazilians are accordingly able to exchange their superfluity for things which are necessary, or at all events more useful and more valuable to them than the superfluous cotton that they part with. This is what Genovesi says, yet Say pooh-poohs it.

Equally strange, coming from Say, is the criticism of Genovesi's reference to the manner in which the poor workman spends his wages. Say seems to forget that according to his own teaching whatever a man desires has 'utility' in the economic sense of the word,[3] and that each individual is the sole judge of what is more and what less desirable. 'The consumption of individuals', he tells us, 'is constantly influenced by the character and the passions of men. At one time the noblest, at another the vilest, propensities

[1] 1712–69.

[2] English readers need to recollect that in France Sunday is (or was, when I knew the country) the labourer's only weekly holiday. Good Catholics discharge their religious duties early in the morning, and give the remainder of the day to enjoyment.

[3] 'For an object to have utility', says Palgrave's Dictionary, 'it must be desired; it need not be desirable.'

exert their influence; they are excited by love of sensual pleasure, by vanity, generosity, revenge, cupidity itself' (Say's vol. 1, p. 244). If the workman's choice falls on beer or gin in preference to food and clothing for his children it is because, at the time and place of the exchange, 'the vilest propensities of our nature' are sometimes allowed to decide what is most 'useful'.

If Say got no light from the Italian Genovesi, we might at least have expected him to profit by the writings of his distinguished countryman Condillac, whose *Commerce and Government* was published in the same year as *The Wealth of Nations* (1776).[1] Condillac adopts from the start the psychological or subjective basis for his theory of value. Value reflects the different degrees of estimation in which we hold various articles or commodities, or quantities of commodities, owing to the greatness of our real or fancied need of them. He tells us that if we have no more of a commodity than we want, and still more if we have less than we want, we attach a value to it; but if we have so much of it that we cannot use it all, the excess, the superfluous or superabundant part, is useless to us. Here, then, we have a theory of diminishing utility and diminishing value; value is graded, being high when the supply is small and falling to nothing when the supply is more than sufficient for every purpose. True, he does not put forward a theory that between these two extremes there is a gradual diminution by almost imperceptible degrees; but the idea of diminishing utility seems to be implicit in the argument; and it is interesting to note that the concept of tiny increments is actually presented to us in connection with cost. He tells us (page 254)[2] that if you engage a gardener for a day, and after he has driven his spade into the earth you change your mind and discontinue the work, nevertheless some work has been done, although it is very little. And he goes on to say that while it is commonly said that water costs nothing, it should rather be said that it often costs very little, since even a man who lives on the brink of a stream must stoop to get the water. But although he thus pictures in detail the tiny increments of cost, in the case of utility he contents himself with broader outlines—'a thing is scarce when we judge that we have

[1] Adam Smith's failure to profit by this book in his subsequent editions is as much a mystery as his neglect of Anderson's theory of rent.

[2] My references to Condillac are to the pages in the edition published by Guillaume and Co. in 1847, in the Collection of *Principal Economists*.

not sufficient for our purposes, it is abundant when we judge that we have all that we require, and it is superabundant when we judge that we have more than enough'.

If we have more than enough, the superabundant part is useless to us; but it may be that another man has insufficient, and what is of no use or value to us will have a utility and value to him. At the same time, the other man may have a superabundance of something we lack and desire; hence there is a mutual advantage in exchange. What was useless becomes useful; what had no value acquires a value. This applies as much to exchanges between nations as to exchanges between individuals. The doctrine, however, is not to be interpreted as meaning that we only part with things that are useless to us; it means that what we acquire is worth more to us than what we part with. Condillac makes this plain. 'It is true', he says (pages 263–4), 'that I might sell a thing that I wanted; but as I would not do so except to procure one that I wanted still more, it is evident that I regard the first as useless to me in comparison with the one that I acquire.' As a matter of fact, this qualification is hardly necessary, for to a very large extent it is literally true that men are engaged in exchanging a positively useless superabundance for other things, of which they have not enough. The manufacturers of hats, shoes, cisterns, saucepans, etc., possess many thousands of these articles of which they could personally make no possible use; each of them, by means of exchange, obtains a variety of things useful to him. It is true that the superabundance in these cases is deliberately produced with a view to exchange; but this does not alter the principle; it shows, on the contrary, that men recognise the increase of utility and value that exchange makes possible. And it brings into prominence another point in Condillac's teaching, namely, that the possibility of increasing wealth by exchange results in a greater aggregate production of useful things than would be the case if exchange were not possible. On page 268 he writes:

> The superabundance of the cultivators forms the basis of commerce. This superabundance is wealth so long as it can be exchanged; for the cultivators procure the thing which has a value for them, while they give up one which has a value for others. If they could make no exchanges, their superabundance would remain in their hands, and would have no value for them. In fact, the superabundant corn which I keep in my granary, and which I cannot exchange, is

> no more wealth for me than the corn which I have not yet produced from the earth. Hence next year I shall sow less, and with a smaller crop I shall be no worse off.

Thus merchants and shopkeepers do a useful work in attending to the transport and distribution of products which would be useless if they did not reach the hands of the persons who desire them, and these traders get their remuneration out of the added value that is brought about by this distribution. Besides this, as Condillac's last remark points out, the activities of the traders not merely give additional value to what is produced, but they result in much being produced that would not be produced at all if it could not be distributed amongst people able and willing to make an acceptable return.

I suggested in an earlier chapter that Malthus appears to have been a reader of Condillac; the following remarks in his *Principles* bear trace of this:

> Every exchange which takes place in a country effects a distribution of its produce better adapted to the wants of the society. It is, with regard to both parties concerned, an exchange of what is wanted less for what is wanted more, and must therefore raise the value of both products. . . . It is impossible to doubt for a moment the direct tendency of all internal trade to increase both the quantity and value of the national produce. If indeed it did not tend to increase the value of the national produce, it would not be carried on. It is out of this increase that the merchants concerned are paid, etc.[1]

The principle is the same whether we are considering the 'society' as consisting of a single nation or of the whole world as a single entity.

But when we turn from Malthus to Say, what do we find? Condillac's teaching, one might have thought, would be welcomed by the man who said that cotton brought from Brazil to Europe gains in value because it gains in utility by being made accessible to the persons who want it; indeed, one would have imagined that Say was as much the disciple of Condillac as he was of Adam Smith.[2] But he is even more severe upon Condillac than upon Genovesi. In the *Preliminary Discourse* to his *Treatise* (page xlv) he

[1] Malthus' *Principles*, pages 440–2 in first edition; pages 382–3 in second.

[2] Even Say's definition of Utility, which he seems to claim as his own, is really the same as Condillac's.

accuses Condillac of undertaking to expound a science which he did not understand. He concedes that amid Condillac's ingenious twaddle (*babil*) there are some good ideas to be found, but his theory that exchange increases value was not one of them. Say refuses to admit that either party makes a gain of value by exchange.[1] He agrees with Condillac that Commerce increases value, but considers that Condillac gives a wrong explanation of the fact. 'He maintains', says Say, 'that commodities, which are worth less to the seller than to the buyer, increase in value by passing from one to the other'; and he continues:

> When one buys Spanish wine in Paris, one gives and receives equal value; the money paid by the buyer and the wine he receives are worth one another; but the wine was not worth so much before leaving Alicante. A real increase of value has taken place in the hands of the merchant, but it does not occur at the moment of handing over the wine to the consumer, but comes from the transport. The seller is not a professional cheat, nor the buyer a dupe, and Condillac is not justified in saying that if the values exchanged were always equal neither party would gain anything by exchange (Say, vol. 1, pp. 14–15).

Lord, how these economists do misunderstand one another! Condillac does not suggest that the wine merchant is a rogue and the customer a fool; he does not suggest that the merchant robs either the consumer or the producer; his doctrine is that products increase in utility and value by being transferred from the producer to the consumer, and that both parties benefit by the intervention of the merchant who brings about the exchange. To the producer the merchant is a consumer-finder; to the consumer he is a commodity-finder; with the merchant as medium of exchange, the producer gets a better price for his product and the buyer better value for his money.

Say denies that the increase of value is due to the 'handing over of the wine to the consumer'; he attributes it to the expense of transport. In reality, the transfer to the consumer is the essence of the transaction; the long transport is subsidiary to this purpose; the change of locality is merely a means to this end, and would not have been necessary if consumers willing to buy the same

[1] Karl Marx also rejects the teaching of Condillac. See *Das Kapital*, page 145 in *Everyman* edition.

quantity and pay the same price could have been found on the spot. In his *Treatise* Say himself wrote:

> The productive power of the soil has no value when its products are not in demand. Travellers come across tracts of fertile land in the interior of America and many other parts of the world which might produce rich harvests, which however produce nothing useful or valuable. But the moment that a colony is established in the neighbourhood, or that for any other reason the products of the soil can be sold at a price which will yield the ordinary rate of interest current in the country on the advances necessary to bring the land under cultivation, the land will be brought under cultivation (Say, vol. 2, page 163).

In this case the goods are not called upon to make a long journey before acquiring value, and their value would not be increased by export. But some goods may be produced for which there is little demand locally, but a great demand abroad, and in this case the change of locality is essential to the acquisition of value. The transport from the place of production to the place where consumers are waiting is undertaken because (to use Say's own words as quoted by Ricardo (176/264)) this gives us the power of increasing the value of the commodity 'by the whole difference between its price in the first of these places and its price in the second'.

At first, the whole of this difference, less the expense of transport, may be profit to the merchant, but after a time the rate of profit will be reduced by the competition of merchants, and the difference between the two prices will be limited to the cost of transport. It is of this that Say is thinking when he remarks that the Spanish wine sold in Paris 'was not worth so much before leaving Alicante'; but this does not justify him in concluding, as he apparently does, that the desire of the consumer has no influence on the price. What he overlooks in this dictum is that the price of Spanish wines in Alicante itself is now high because there is an insistent demand for them, not in Spain only, nor in Spain and France only, but all over the world. The value of high-class wines, to use Ricardo's words, 'is wholly independent of the quantity of labour originally necessary to produce them, and varies with the varying wealth and inclinations of those who are desirous to possess them' (6/12).

15

The Value of Money and of Gold

OUR examination of Ricardo's theory of value, as applied to commodities in general, may now be regarded as closed. He holds that the value of metals such as tin, iron, silver, gold, as well as the value of hats, shoes, and cloth, depends upon the cost of producing them; and it seemed to him to follow that if we make gold our standard money, it will exchange for other metals and other commodities in proportion to their respective costs of production. Yet Ricardo was one of the principal upholders and exponents of what is called the Quantity Theory of Money. As the two theories appear to be incompatible, it is necessary to devote a special chapter to this subject.

To understand Ricardo's arguments regarding the value of money it is necessary to keep in mind the close connection that existed in the nineteenth century between the supply of gold and the supply of money. Prior to 1914 gold moved freely from country to country, and the Mint was always willing to convert into sovereigns (or 'pounds sterling') all the gold that was brought to it. As no charge was made for minting, there was practically no difference between the value of coined and uncoined gold.

It is true that when Ricardo wrote, sovereigns were not in circulation; owing to the Bank Restriction Act the medium of exchange consisted at that time of inconvertible bank-notes. But this ban on the circulation of sovereigns, though it lasted for many years (1797–1821), was always intended to be temporary, and Ricardo seldom paid much attention to temporary conditions. His aim at all times was to deal with 'permanent' or long-term conditions. He did not regard Bank of England notes as money. If a £5 note was not worth five sovereigns, it was not money that had altered in value; it was the notes which, owing to over-issue, had fallen below par with the sovereigns they were supposed to represent. That he thought of British money as gold is shown by many of his sayings; see for instance page 60(104) in his *Principles* where he tells us that the only way to increase our supply of money is to import more of the money-metal from abroad.

Such being Ricardo's view of what constitutes money, let us now study his teaching as to the forces which automatically regulated the quantity of money in circulation and the value of each unit.

Our first step must be to obtain a clear notion of what is meant by the 'value' of money. In economics the expression is commonly used in the same sense as when applied to ordinary commodities, that is, in the sense of relative value, or value-in-exchange; the value of money means its purchasing power, or the ratio in which it exchanges for other things.[1] The value of the pound sterling is higher today than a year ago if it will now exchange for, or purchase, more than it did at that time—in other words, if prices in general have fallen; it is lower than it formerly was if prices have risen, and less can be had in exchange for a pound sterling, or sovereign. 'To say that commodities are raised in price', says Ricardo (60/105), 'is the same thing as to say that money is lowered in relative value; for it is by commodities that the relative value of gold is estimated.' Again (230/342) he says: 'The advance in the value of money is the same thing as the decline in the price of commodities.' And on page 107(169) he remarks: 'When gold is cheap, commodities are dear; and when gold is dear, commodities are cheap.' Similar expressions are to be found in his pamphlet *The High Price of Bullion*. 'For if gold be dearer in France than in England goods must be cheaper' (vol. 3, p. 57); 'commodities measure the value of money in the same manner as money measures the value of goods' (vol. 3, p. 104).

Such being what is meant by the value of money, we now have to ask upon what depends this relative value, or purchasing power; what is it that decides whether a unit of money will purchase much or purchase little?

[1] Financial writers in the newspapers frequently speak of the value or price of money when they mean the rate of interest charged for the loan of money. Money is 'dear' when the rate charged for loans is high, and 'cheap' when money can be borrowed at a low rate. We have nothing to do with this terminology here.

Now here Ricardo endeavours to hold at one and the same time two conflicting opinions; he holds, on the one hand, that the purchasing power of a sovereign depends upon the number of sovereigns in circulation relatively to the things to be bought, and on the other hand he teaches that the ratio in which sovereigns will exchange for other things depends on the cost of producing gold compared with the cost of producing the other things for which it is exchanged. He makes no attempt to reconcile these two explanations, and does not appear to be conscious that the one conflicts with the other.

To make Ricardo's position clear, I will submit samples of his statement. (A) that the value of the money unit depends upon the quantity of money in circulation, (B) that the quantity of money in circulation depends upon the value of the money unit, and (C) that when the precious metals are used as money, the value, or purchasing power, of each unit is determined by the value of the metal it is made of, which value, like that of tin or iron, is determined by the quantity of labour required for its production.[1] Although the first and second propositions may appear mutually contradictory, we shall find that here the contradiction is rather in language than in meaning; it is the third proposition that cannot be reconciled with the other two.

It was as a monetary theorist that Ricardo first came before the public, and established a firm and durable reputation by the publication of his pamphlet *The High Price of Bullion*.[2] As already mentioned, Bank of England notes were at that time inconvertible, and, as generally happens in such cases, sooner or later the quantity in circulation had been increased, with the result that prices rose, including the price of gold reckoned in paper. This is another way of saying that the paper was depreciated compared with the gold it was supposed to represent. A £5 note was no longer worth five sovereigns, and £3 17*s*. 10½*d*. of paper currency would no longer purchase an ounce of standard gold.[3] Ricardo

[1] Perhaps I ought to add a fourth proposition (D) that 'the value of gold as a commodity must be regulated by the quantity of goods which must be given to foreigners in exchange for it' (107/169).

[2] First published in 1809 as a series of letters in the *Morning Chronicle*.

[3] 'Standard gold' in England means gold eleven-twelfths fine, or 22 carat. In the United States, France, and some other countries it means gold nine-tenths fine.

attributed the rise in the price of gold, or rather the fall in the value of paper substitutes, to the excessive quantity of notes issued by the Bank. To discover the cause was to discover the remedy—'If we diminish the quantity of currency, we give an additional value to it' (vol. 3, p. 62), i.e. an additional value to each unit. Accordingly, Ricardo wrote:

> The remedy which I propose for all the evils in our currency, is that the Bank should gradually decrease the amount of their notes in circulation until they shall have rendered the remainder of equal value with the coins which they represent, or in other words, till the prices of gold and silver bullion shall be brought down to their mint price (vol. 3, p. 94).

By diminishing the number of the notes, the value or purchasing power of each paper 'pound' would be raised, for the purchasing power of the money unit depends upon the quantity in circulation. 'That commodities would rise or fall in price in proportion to the increase or diminution of money, I assume, as a fact which is incontrovertible' (vol. 3, p. 193; see also p. 311). Ricardo was satisfied that this applies to gold as well as to paper money. On page 238(353) of his *Principles* he tells us that 'by limiting the quantity of coin, it can be raised to any conceivable value'.[1] He adds:

> It is on this principle that paper money circulates; the whole charge for paper money may be considered as seignorage. Though it has no intrinsic value, yet, by limiting its quantity, its value in exchange is as great as an equal denomination of coin, or of bullion in that coin. On the same principle, too, namely by a limitation of its quantity, a debased coin would circulate at the value it should bear if it were of the legal weight and fineness, and not at the value of the quantity of metal which it actually contained.

In one of his pamphlets he says:

> It appears, then, that although a given weight of bullion can never exceed in value a given weight of coin, a given weight of coin may exceed in value a given weight of bullion by the whole expense of seignorage, however great that seignorage may be (vol. 3, p. 222).

---

[1] This is an exaggeration. If the quantity were diminished beyond a certain point the result would be that the coins would no longer serve as a circulating medium.

But while, by limiting the number of sovereigns, the government may give to each of them a value which exceeds its value as a piece of gold, any attempt to depress the value of the sovereign below the value of its metal content would be defeated. It is here that gold money differs from paper money. Paper money cannot be melted down, nor can it be exported; the quantity of it therefore can be continually increased, and there is no limit to the extent to which its purchasing power may be reduced. But if the quantity of gold money circulating in a country is increased to such an extent that the sovereign, as a coin, has less value than it possesses as a piece of metal, either it will be melted down by jewellers and dentists, who find this the cheapest way of obtaining their raw material, or it will be exported to a country where its purchasing power has not been reduced by an excess of circulation. In this manner the number of sovereigns circulating at home would be reduced, and their purchasing power would automatically rise. 'The exportation of money would gradually lessen the quantity and raise its value in this country, while the importation of it into other countries would have a contrary effect in them' (vol. 4, p. 215).

Ricardo's whole theory of foreign trade and the distribution of the precious metals is based on the assumption that if there is an increase in the quantity of money in a country, prices in that country will rise; if there is a diminution, prices will fall; the rise in one country and the fall in the other restores equilibrium, and the movement of money from one country to another ceases, while goods continue to exchange for goods.[1]

These quotations illustrate the proposition which I labelled (A), that the value of the money unit falls with the increase and rises with the decrease in the quantity of money in circulation, provided of course there is no change in the quantity of goods to be 'circulated'. Let us now turn to proposition (B) which asserts that the quantity of money in circulation depends upon the value of the money unit. I affix numbers to the following extracts for convenience in discussing them afterwards:

> (1) A circulation can never be so abundant as to overflow; for by diminishing its value, in the same proportion you will increase its quantity, and by increasing its value, diminish its quantity (238/352).

[1] See Ricardo's chapter on Foreign Trade in his *Principles*.

(2) The demand for money is regulated entirely by its value, and its value by its quantity. If gold were of double the value, half the quantity would perform the same functions in circulation, and if it were of half the value, double the quantity would be required (123/193).

(3) If the mines cease to supply the annual consumption of the precious metals, money will become more valuable, and a smaller quantity will be employed as a circulating medium. The diminution in the quantity will be proportioned to the increase in its value. In like manner, if new mines be discovered, the value of the precious metals will be reduced, and an increased quantity used in the circulation (vol. 3, p. 90).

These statements do not appear to harmonise very well with those previously quoted. Instead of saying that by increasing the quantity you diminish the value of each unit, his statement in No. 1 is that by diminishing the value you increase the quantity. In No. 2 the first sentence tells us that the value of money is regulated by its quantity, while the second seems to suggest that the increase or decrease in value is the cause, and not the consequence, of the decreased or increased quantity in circulation. And finally, in No 3 we are told that if money becomes more valuable, a smaller quantity will be employed as a circulating medium. He says 'the diminution in the quantity will be proportioned to the increase of its value'—not (as we should have expected) that the increase of its value will be in proportion to the diminution in the quantity.

And what does Ricardo mean, in No. 2, by the statement that 'the demand for money is regulated entirely by its value'? We can understand that the demand for gold rings and bangles, like the demand for watches, knives, forks, fire-irons, is influenced very largely by their price, decreasing if the price rises, increasing if the price falls; and however low the price may fall, we can understand that there may be a limit to demand—a limit to the quantity that people will wish to acquire at any figure. But money is the one thing for which there is no limit to demand. It is the one thing of which it is literally true that demand increases exactly to the same extent as supply. This is practically admitted by Ricardo himself in this very paragraph, for he tells us that 'the demand for money is not for a definite quantity, as is the demand for clothes, or for food'. And the paragraph ends with the statement that if the supply of money is doubled or trebled, everyone will be 'obliged to employ' twice or thrice as much money to purchase the same quantity of goods. The whole supply of money therefore, however large, will always be absorbed; the demand for it will always be precisely equal to the supply; 'while money is the general medium of exchange, the demand for it is never a matter of choice, but always of necessity; you must take it in exchange for your goods, and therefore there are no limits to the quantity which may be forced on you by foreign trade if it fall in value' (124/194).

No producer of gold, then, need trouble his head about finding a market; no matter how much he produces, his fellow-men will be 'obliged to employ' it, and they will be 'forced' to give him goods in exchange. What, then, does Ricardo mean when he tells us that the demand for money is regulated entirely by its value and at the same time states that there are no limits to the quantity that may be forced on a country by foreign trade 'if it fall in value'?

His meaning appears to be this. If a country employs inconvertible paper, it can control the quantity and thereby make the price-level whatever it chooses to make it. But when a number of countries adopt gold as a common medium of exchange, it is not possible for each country to please itself either as to the quantity of money it will employ, or as to the price-level it will maintain. The price-levels of all the countries (assuming that trade is perfectly free) will be automatically kept in harmony with one another by an automatic adjustment of the quantity of money circulating in each country. For if a deficiency of money in one country should lead to a fall in its prices, gold would flow to that country to take advantage of those low prices; if on the other hand an excess of money led to a rise in its price-level, money would be exported from that country to others where goods were cheaper. In this way any temporary departure from equilibrium would be quickly righted. And in view of this, each country's 'demand for money' may be said to be regulated by its value. Its effective demand is not an unlimited demand; it is not a demand for an indefinite quantity of money, but for the quantity necessary to keep its price-level in harmony or equilibrium with other price-levels. The world as a whole may have an unlimited demand for gold; and if the total quantity is increased, each country will require a share in that increase; but each country's effective demand is for that proportion of the total supply which suffices to keep its price-level in equilibrium with the price-levels of other countries.[1]

Such is Ricardo's meaning, as set forth in his chapter on Foreign Trade and elsewhere; and thus there is no real conflict between proposition (A) that the value of the money unit depends on the quantity in circulation, and proposition (B) that the quantity of money in circulation in any particular country depends upon the value of the money unit.

> If a mine of gold [says Ricardo] were discovered in either of these countries, the currency of that country would be lowered in value in consequence of the increased quantity of the precious metals brought into circulation, and would therefore no longer be of the same value as that of other countries. Gold and silver, whether in coin or in bullion obeying the law which regulates all other commodities, would immediately become articles of exportation; they would leave the country where they were cheap, for those countries where they were dear, etc. (vol. 3, p. 54).

And while the countries where gold has fallen in value thus become exporters of the metal, others where it has not yet fallen necessarily become importers. This is the meaning of the statement that gold 'may be forced on you by foreign trade if it falls in value'.

Curiously enough, on page 238(352) (extract No. 1 above) we find Ricardo stating that 'a circulation can never be so abundant as to overflow'. This would be true enough of an inconvertible paper currency; 'such a currency is necessarily confined to the country where it is issued; it cannot, when too abundant, diffuse itself generally amongst other countries' (91/147). But on page 238/352 he is speaking of gold currency, and it is incomprehensible that he should state that it cannot overflow, since the very essence of his theory of the distribution of the precious metals is that such an overflow will always occur when the value of gold is lower in one country than another. One can only conjecture that the assertion on page 238(352) may be a slip of the pen, and that what he meant to say was what he actually said in his *High Price of Bullion*: 'The circulation can never be over full. If it be one of gold

[1] The demand for gold here referred to is merely the monetary demand. There has always been a demand for gold in the arts, and India has always been a great hoarder.

and silver, any increase in its quantity will be spread over the world' (vol. 3, pp. 91–2).

While Ricardo held that the value of gold will thus be equalised in the different countries, he did not contend that prices would be everywhere exactly the same. If goods of all descriptions could be transported with the same facility as gold, this would doubtless be the case; but some products cannot be exported at all, and others only at varying degrees of expense. On page 91(147) Ricardo writes: 'When each country has precisely the quantity of money which it ought to have, money will not indeed be of the same value in each, for with respect to many commodities it may differ 5, 10, or even 20 per cent, but the exchange will be at par.' In other words, whatever differences may exist in prices, they are not sufficient to provoke a flow of gold in one direction or the other. The countries exchange goods, and the goods exchanged pay for one another.

> Gold and silver having been chosen for the general medium of circulation, they are, by the competition of commerce, distributed in such proportions amongst the different countries of the world as to accommodate themselves to the natural traffic which would take place if no such metals existed, and the trade between countries were purely a trade of barter (83/137).

While the proposition, that the flow of gold from one country to another results in its value or purchasing power being everywhere the same, is thus subject to some qualification, the other doctrine, that the quantity of gold needed or demanded by each country is 'regulated entirely' (123/193) by its value, is also subject to some qualification, as Ricardo himself explains. Even if, in two countries, all prices were exactly the same, and if both transacted the same amount of business, the two countries would not necessarily each require the same quantity of gold to keep their prices equal. In his *High Price of Bullion* (vol. 3, p. 90) Ricardo wrote:

> The value of the circulating medium of every country bears some proportion to the value of the commodities which it circulates. In some countries this proportion is much greater than in others, and varies, on some occasions, in the same country. It depends upon the rapidity of circulation, upon the degree of confidence and credit existing between traders, and above all, on the judicious operations

> of banking. In England, so many means of economising the use of circulating medium have been adopted, that its value, compared with the value of the commodities which it circulates, is probably (during a period of confidence) reduced to as small a proportion as is practicable.

A country's demand for gold for use as currency depends, then, partly on the volume of its transactions, and partly on the extent and efficiency of its devices for economising the use of gold.

Thus, as already remarked on page 304, propositions (A) and (B), when rightly interpreted, are not in conflict, but represent the reactions of quantity on value and of value on quantity. It is, as already stated, proposition (C) that is irreconcilable with the quantity theory of money. This doctrine is that the value of money depends (not on the quantity in circulation, but) on the cost of its production.

Ricardo, of course, did not imagine that in the case of paper money, the cost of its production had anything to do with the determination of its value. In connection with money of this description he recognised that the value, or purchasing power, of the 'pound' depended solely on the quantity of such pounds put into circulation. Moreover, he said that in the case of metallic money the government could, by restricting the quantity, give to each coin a higher value than was possessed by the metal of which it was made. But in England there was no such restriction. On page 238(353) of his *Principles* he says: 'While the State coins money and charges no seignorage, money will be of the same value as any other piece of the same metal of equal weight and fineness.'[1] If we purchase tin or copper with gold, it is the same thing as purchasing gold with copper or tin. It is merely the exchange of a large portion of a cheap metal for a small portion of a dear metal, and according to Ricardo's theory of value, whether a metal or other commodity is cheap or dear depends upon whether it requires little or much labour to produce it.

[1] The equality of value would be exact if, when you took gold to the Mint, they immediately gave you sovereigns in exchange. But the fact that you must wait until the gold is coined makes coined gold slightly more valuable than uncoined. Ricardo pointed this out more than once; see vol. 3, pp. 174–5 and 289, and vol. 5, p. 61. In a memorandum Ricardo discussed the advantages and disadvantages which would arise if the Mint kept a stock of sovereigns ready for immediate exchange (vol. 5, p. 401).

This view, as applied to the value of gold, is expounded again and again. Ricardo writes:

> When I give 2000 times more cloth for a pound of gold than I give for a pound of iron . . . it proves only . . . that the cost of production of gold is 2000 times greater than the cost of production of iron. If the cost of production of the two metals were the same, I should give the same price for them (188/283). Gold and silver, like all other commodities, are valuable only in proportion to the quantity of labour necessary to produce them and bring them to market. Gold is about fifteen times dearer than silver, not because there is a greater demand for it, nor because the supply of silver is fifteen times greater than that of gold, but solely because fifteen times the quantity of labour is necessary to procure a given quantity of it (238/352).

Thus when we buy or sell something, what happens is merely that one commodity is exchanged for another. Gold becomes the medium of exchange because it is a commodity that everybody is glad to acquire. For our own convenience we carry in our pockets small ingots of gold, as we know that anyone will accept them in exchange for other commodities. For our convenience also, the government undertakes to convert any quantity of gold that we take to the Mint into pieces of a definite size and weight, and to put a stamp on them which guarantees their fineness. If the government converted our gold into ingots weighing an ounce, a half-ounce, or a quarter-ounce, we should no doubt reckon values in terms of weight; we should say, for example, 'this piece of cloth is worth an ounce of standard gold'. Parliament decreed, however, that 1000 pounds troy-weight of standard gold shall be divided into 46,725 pieces (commonly called pounds sterling or sovereigns), and the result is that instead of having a sovereign a quarter of an ounce, or 120 grains, we have a sovereign that is a fraction under 123 grains; and instead of saying—'this piece of cloth is worth an ounce of standard gold', we say it is worth £3 17*s.* 10½*d.*, which means the same thing.[1]

In buying iron or tin, therefore, we merely exchange one piece of metal for another, and according to Ricardo's theory of value,

[1] It cannot, I think, be necessary to remind the reader that throughout this chapter we are dealing with gold and money on the basis of nineteenth-century conditions.

the ratio of exchange depends upon the respective costs of production. 'Any improvement in the facility of working the mines, by which the precious metals may be produced with a less quantity of labour, will sink the value of money generally. It will then exchange for fewer commodities in all countries' (90/146). And similarly, any increase in the cost of producing the precious metals will raise their value in comparison with that of other metals, and other commodities of all kinds, whose cost of production has remained the same.

The fact that, under the circumstances described, the value of the sovereign could never for long be above or below that of its metal content, led some writers to think that the quantity theory of money must be abandoned as incompatible with the general theory of value.[1] Without admitting this, it must at all events be conceded that Ricardo's particular brand of the general theory of value is irreconcilable with the quantity theory of money, although he appears to have been strangely unconscious of the fact. He explained the value of gold and of most other commodities by the cost of production, but in reality, even if this theory were true in the case of ordinary commodities such as tin or cloth, it is inapplicable to the money-metal, as can be shown from his own admissions.

It will be remembered that Ricardo himself does not contend that the cost of production governs value in all cases. At the beginning of his *Principles*, he limits the application of this 'law' to 'such commodities only as can be increased in quantity by the exertion of human industry, and on the production of which competition operates without restraint' (6/12). And the reason he gives why, in the case of these commodities, the price of each article will coincide with its cost of production is that if the market value of a commodity rises above its cost of production (including the ordinary rate of profit), there will soon be such an increase of supply as will force the price down again; while, if the market value falls below the cost of production, the commodity will become so scarce that the price will rise again. Hence, as the price cannot remain either above or below the cost of production, it will be identical with it, or will oscillate about it. When therefore Ricardo states that goods exchange for one another in the ratio of their respective costs, he means provided the supply can be so

[1] See J. L. Laughlin's able book *The Principles of Money*, 1903.

adjusted to demand as to bring about this result. Does this apply in the case of gold? Hear what Ricardo himself has to say on this point:

> The agreement of the market and natural prices of all commodities depends at all times on the facility with which the supply can be increased or diminished. In the case of gold, houses, and labour, as well as many other things, this effect cannot, under some circumstances, be speedily produced. But it is different with those commodities which are consumed and reproduced from year to year, such as hats, shoes, corn, and cloth; they may be reduced, if necessary, and the interval cannot be long before the supply is contracted in proportion to the increased charge of producing them (126/196).

The position of gold, then, is 'different' from that of hats, shoes, etc. Whereas a rise in the cost of producing these will be speedily followed by a rise of price, there may be a long interval before there is a sufficient contraction in the supply of gold to raise its value to the level of the new cost of production. On page 124(193) Ricardo writes:

> The metal gold, like all other commodities, has its value in the market ultimately regulated by the comparative facility or difficulty of producing it; and although, from its durable nature, and from the difficulty of reducing its quantity, it does not readily bend to variations in its market value, yet that difficulty is much increased from the circumstance of its being used as money. If the quantity of gold in the market for the purpose of commerce only were 10,000 ounces, and the consumption in our manufactures were 2000 ounces annually, it might be raised one-fourth or 25 per cent in its value in one year by withholding the annual supply; but if, in consequence of its being used as money, the quantity employed were 100,000 ounces, it would not be raised one-fourth in value in less than ten years.

Thus, if the cost of producing hats increases by 25 per cent, the value of hats will rise promptly to the new cost of production, for a cessation of production would soon make hats exceedingly scarce. But this is not so with the money-metal; a total stoppage of gold-mining would not denude the market of money, although it would result in a gradual reduction of the quantity in circulation if 2000 ounces continued to be absorbed annually in the arts. If, to begin with, the quantity in circulation as money were 10,000 ounces, the circulation would be reduced at the end of twelve months to 8000. These 8000 ounces, Ricardo considers, would then have the same purchasing power that 10,000 had a year earlier. But if, at the beginning, the quantity in circulation were 100,000 ounces, it would be ten years before the annual withdrawals of 2000 reduced the circulation to 80,000 and raised the value by 25 per cent. Hence, instead of the value rising 'speedily' when production ceases, as in the case of hats, it is only 'ultimately' that the value of the money-metal will be raised to a level with the new cost of production.

Unfortunately, whenever Ricardo concludes that price must ultimately conform to cost he is apt to argue on the assumption that such conformity exists continuously, or with little interruption. There is no reference to 'ultimately' in the statement (238/352) that 'gold and silver, like all other commodities, are valuable in proportion to the quantity of labour necessary to produce them'. Gold, says Ricardo, is worth fifteen times as much as silver because it costs fifteen times as much to produce. If an ounce of gold will exchange for 2000 ounces of iron, it 'proves', he says, that its cost of production is 2000 times as great. Having reached the conclusion that taxes increase the cost of production and so raise the value (or price) of the product, he applies this not only to hats, shoes, corn, and cloth, but also to the money-metal. In the following passage he remembers to insert the word 'ultimately' but proceeds to argue as though the effect were immediate:

> If, then, the King of Spain, supposing him to be in exclusive possession of the mines,[1] and gold alone to be used for money, were to lay a considerable tax on gold, he would very much raise its natural value; and as its market value in Europe is ultimately regulated by its natural value in Spanish America, more commodities would be given by Europe for a given quantity of gold. But the same quantity of gold would not be produced in America, as its value would only be increased in proportion to the diminution of quantity consequent on its increased cost of production. . . . If in consequence of the tax only one-tenth of the present quantity of gold were obtained from the mines, that tenth would be of equal value with the ten tenths now produced (125/195).

This, I think, is the most extraordinary passage to be found anywhere in Ricardo's writings. Professor Cole[2] refers to 'two extraordinarily muddled chapters' of Ricardo's, but there is nothing

[1] In Ricardo's day, Spanish America was still the principal source of gold.

[2] In his Introduction to Karl Marx's *Capital*, page xxiv (*Everyman* edition).

anywhere, I think, as muddled as this. If the King of Spain had possessed a monopoly of corn instead of gold, there is no saying to what height he might raise the price by reducing production to one-tenth, because people will become desperate if sufficient food is not annually produced. Ricardo assumes that the position will be similar if the production of new gold is reduced; the doctrine appears to ignore entirely the fact that the contraction of current production to one-tenth would not result in the supply of money being reduced to one-tenth.[1] This is the more remarkable because the passage quoted is sandwiched in between the statement on page 124(193) that the value of gold can only be altered slowly and the statement on page 126(196) that gold is not on the same footing as hats, shoes, corn, and cloth.

In the case of hats, shoes, corn, and cloth there is a continuous demand for newly produced supplies. These commodities are 'consumed from year to year', and therefore require to be 'reproduced from year to year'. Therein lies the secret of the producers' power to influence the price in the market. Supply being practically synonymous with current production, the value of the commodity can be varied by varying the quantity produced. If production is open to all upon the same footing, competition will go on increasing the supply until the price falls to equality with the cost of production (including the ordinary rate of profit). If on the other hand the production of a commodity is in the hands of a monopolist, he can raise the value by diminishing the production. By halving the production he halves the supply in the market; by reducing production to one-tenth he reduces the supply to one-tenth. But it is precisely here that the money-metal differs from other commodities. The current production of gold is not synonymous with the quantity of gold in the market. Producers cannot reduce the supply of money to a half or a tenth by reducing their output in that proportion. Moreover, Ricardo's own statement is that 'the demand for money is not for a definite quantity, as is the demand for clothes or for food' (123/193); 'money is a commodity which no country has any wish or necessity to increase; no more advantage results from using twenty millions than from using ten

[1] He also appears to overlook his own statement that if gold becomes an article of export, which other countries will be 'forced' to accept in exchange for their goods, it is because its abundance in the exporting country makes it of less value there than elsewhere.

millions' (124/194). Hence in the case of corn, reduced production would cause a sharp change of values, whereas a reduction in the quantity of new gold produced might be scarcely noticed.

It would not be correct to say that Ricardo is unconscious of this difference between gold and corn; on the contrary, he seems anxious to emphasise it; yet the fact appears to be that his notion of what constitutes the 'supply' of gold was vague and fluctuating. He appears sometimes to think of it as consisting of the annual output from the mines, while at other times he thinks of it as being the total quantity held by the community in the form of money. The King of Spain's power to raise the value of gold by reducing production is obviously based on the conception that, as in the case of shoes and corn, the 'supply' available for exchange in the market will be great or small according as current production is great or small. On the other hand, the statement on the previous page that if the current production of new gold is not sufficient to make good the current absorption of gold in manufactures, the reduction of 'supply' will be very slow, is just as clearly based on recognition of the fact that the 'supply' includes all the money already in the market.

Even if we neglect the King of Spain absurdity, and confine ourselves to the more intelligible doctrine of pages 124 and 126(193 and 196) we still find a vagueness in Ricardo's thinking. On page 124 he tells us that the slowness with which the value of the money-metal conforms to changes in its current cost of production arises 'from its durable nature, and from the difficulty of reducing its quantity'. What has its durable nature to do with the matter? If the value of iron, copper, tin, stone, or bricks conforms quickly to changes in the cost of production, while the value of gold does not, this difference of behaviour cannot be attributed to the greater durability of gold. The difference of behaviour is due to the fact that in the one case society is dependent upon current production for the satisfaction of its current wants, while in the other it is not. If 'durability' is to be regarded as a deciding factor, it is not the physical durability or permanence of the goods offered for exchange, but the permanence of the supply in the market—in the sense that such things as iron and bricks, when exchanged for money, are taken away and no longer form part of the 'supply' available to those who are seeking them, whereas money, while constantly exchanged for commodities, is as constantly returned to the market, where it remains as a permanent or durable supply at the service of an endless succession of purchasers.

That Ricardo's notion of what constitutes 'supply' was hazy is further shown (126/196) by his bracketing together gold and houses as commodities the supply of which is so large that neither an increase nor a decrease of current production can make much impression on the total supply. He does not appear to realise that, while money remains in the market, houses that are sold or let are withdrawn from the market, and cease to be part of the supply available for satisfying the wants of those people who are still looking for houses. In a growing population there is a continuous demand for new (i.e. additional) houses, which can only be supplied by current production; and if the cost of building rises, there is no more reason for supposing that the rise of price will lag behind, owing to the large number of houses already in existence, than there is to suppose that the price of iron or bricks will respond slowly to their cost of production because large quantities of these have already been brought into use and, thanks to their durable nature, are still in use.

It results from what has been said above that Ricardo's efforts to explain the exchange value of the sovereign (1) by the quantity of money in circulation, and (2) by the cost of producing the metal, cannot be reconciled. This does not mean that the quantity theory of money is incompatible with a correct theory of value in general, as Laughlin supposes; it implies only that Ricardo's cost-of-production theory of value is erroneous, or at all events is not applicable to the money-metal. Nor does it mean that the value of gold does not correspond with its marginal cost of production; what it does mean is that if marginal cost corresponds with value, it is because marginal cost follows close at the heels of value, and not *vice versa*. The price obtainable for an ounce of standard gold being always £3 17*s*. 10½*d*., the poorest mine that will yield the ordinary rate of profit at this price will be worked, and in that way the marginal cost of production will be the same, or nearly the same, as the value.

It is strange that Ricardo, whose exposition of the quantity theory of money was both perspicuous and perspicacious, should become so foggy in his thinking when he attempts to reconcile the proposition that the value depends upon the quantity in circulation with the proposition that it depends on the cost of production. In illustration of his King of Spain proposition he asks us on page 126(196) to suppose that there are three mines producing gold. The poorest of these mines yields 70 pounds weight of gold per annum, which just covers the expense of production, including the ordinary rate of profit; in other words, cost and value are the same. The yield of the second-best mine is 80 pounds weight, of which 10 go to the owner of the land as rent, while the best mine produces 100 pounds of gold, of which 30 form rent. Ricardo next asks us to suppose that the King of Spain decides to levy a tax of 70 pounds weight of gold per annum upon every mine. As this will swallow up the entire product of the poorest mine, that mine must necessarily close down, and in Ricardo's view the diminution of the annual supply will raise the value of gold in the market. Despite this rise of value, however, the second-best mine must also close down, for the rise in the value of gold would not be sufficient to enable the capitalist to pay his expenses and make a profit when 70 of the 80 pounds of gold that he produces are taken from him as a tax. One would imagine that the best mine would also have to cease operations if 70 of its 100 pounds were taken by the King; but Ricardo says it is not so. His reason is that when the annual output of gold is reduced from 250 pounds weight to 100 pounds weight, 100 pounds will have the same value that 250 had before; it will 'exchange for the same, or very nearly the same, quantity of commodities as before' (127/198). It follows that those who work the best mine will be able to buy as much with the 30 pounds of gold left them after payment of the tax as they could formerly buy with the 70 pounds formerly left in their hands after payment of rent; in fact, 30 pounds of gold will now buy as much as 75 pounds bought before, and therefore the capitalist will still be able to pay a small rent to the owner of the land. The people who suffer are the landlords, whose rents are extinguished or reduced; but the country as a whole will gain, for the capital and labour formerly employed in the mines that are now closed will be 'liberated' for the production of something else just as valuable as what they produced before.[1] On page 127(198) Ricardo

[1] Characteristically, Ricardo seems to make no allowance for the fact that men accustomed to mining may not prove very expert in another employment, nor for the fact that the greater part of the capital employed in mining may be 'fixed' and have to be totally abandoned.

furnishes a Table to illustrate his conclusion that if formerly Spain obtained 10,000 yards of cloth in exchange for its annual product of 250 pounds of gold, it will now obtain 15,600 yards of cloth in exchange for 100 pounds of gold plus the product of the 'liberated' capital and labour.

In his next paragraph Ricardo proceeds to consider what will be the position 'if the tax, instead of being a fixed sum per mine worked, were a certain portion of its produce . . . a half, a fourth, or a third' (127/199). His conclusion is that there might be no reduction in the amount of gold produced, and consequently no rise in the value of gold. How could this be? Unless the value of gold rises, not even the best of Ricardo's three mines could continue working if a tax took one-half or one-third of the product. Only the best could survive if the tax absorbed a quarter of the product. As to the poorest mine, which only just pays its way when there is neither rent nor tax, it would be obliged to close down if there were any tax at all. But half-way through the paragraph Ricardo seems to forget that he is discussing a tax which absorbs a half, a third, or a fourth of the product; he seems to be under the impression that the proposition he has put forward is that a moderate tax on rent-paying mines will have no effect on the quantity of gold produced, for he tells us that the tax 'would fall entirely on the rent of the mine'; and he adds: 'If pushed a little further, indeed, the tax would not only absorb the whole rent, but would deprive the worker of the mine of the common profits of stock, and he would consequently withdraw his capital from the production of gold' (128/199).[1]

A similar obscurity seems to envelope other references by Ricardo to the taxation of gold. In the last paragraph of his chapter headed 'Taxes on Gold' he writes:

> Taxes on gold are of two kinds, one on the actual quantity of gold in circulation, the other on the quantity that is annually produced from the mines. Both have a tendency to reduce the quantity, and

[1] As remarked in our last footnote, a large part of the capital could not be 'withdrawn', but must be abandoned if the mine is shut down. If an old mine still yields the ordinary rate of profit upon the whole of the capital invested in it from time to time, it would not necessarily close down when taxed, because the annual profit after deduction of the tax might still exceed what could be earned upon that part of the capital which could be withdrawn and put to other uses.

> to raise the value of gold; but by neither will its value be raised till the quantity is reduced, and therefore such taxes will fall for a time, until the supply is diminished on the proprietors of money, etc. (128/199).

Let us consider this; or rather, let us study the more detailed exposition of his view which he gives us earlier in the chapter. In a paragraph on page 122(192) he discusses both forms of the tax; I will quote first the part that relates to the taxation of gold-mining:

> If the mines which supply us with gold were in this country, and if gold were taxed, it could not rise in relative value to other things till its quantity were reduced. This would be more particularly the case if gold were used exclusively for money. It is true that the least productive mines, those which paid no rent, could no longer be worked, as they could not afford the general rate of profits till the relative value of gold rose by a sum equal to the tax. The quantity of gold, and therefore the quantity of money, would be slowly reduced; it would be a little diminished in one year, a little more in another, and finally its value would be raised in proportion to the tax; but in the interval the proprietors or holders, as they would pay the tax, would be the sufferers, and not those who used money.

Now gold-mining, whether taxed or not taxed, increases the stock of gold. A tax on gold-mining may slow down the rate of increase by compelling the least profitable mines to close down. But even if it led to the closing of all the mines, the tax would not diminish the quantity already produced and circulating in the country. Ricardo's own teaching is that taxes collected by the government are spent by the government (144/220), and thus return to the circulation. If, then, the quantity of gold in circulation diminishes when the mines are taxed, it is mainly because a certain quantity is withdrawn year by year for use in the arts, and if the loss is not made good by current production from the mines, the total amount in circulation will gradually diminish.

So much for the taxation of gold-mining. Let me now quote the remainder of the paragraph. Ricardo appears to be unconscious of the fact that in his transition from a tax on gold-mining to a tax on the stock of gold already in circulation he is passing to an entirely different situation. The paragraph I have quoted above continues as follows:

> If out of every 1000 quarters of wheat in the country, and every

> 1000 produced in future, Government should exact 100 quarters as a tax, the remaining 900 quarters would exchange for the same quantity of other commodities that 1000 did before; but if the same thing took place with respect to gold, if of every £1000 money now in the country, or in future to be brought into it, Government could exact £100 as a tax, the remaining £900 would purchase very little more than £900 purchased before. The tax would fall upon him whose property consisted of money, and would continue to do so till its quantity were reduced in proportion to the increased cost of its production caused by the tax (123/192).

Here we have two statements, one relating to wheat and the other to money. In both cases Ricardo appears to assume that what the government take as tax represents a diminution in the supply available for the satisfaction of the community's wants. Are we to suppose that, having annexed one-tenth of the wheat, they proceed to burn it, bury it, or dump it in the sea? Perhaps his idea is that they may export it as a subsidy to a foreign country (compare page 144(221)). Or they may withhold it for the purpose of building up a store of food as an insurance against the risk of a future famine. Whatever they do with it, we have to suppose that it is not available for consumption either by the general public or by employees of the government, and under these circumstances we can understand the statement that 'the remaining 900 quarters would exchange for the same quantity of other commodities that 1000 did before'; but while we accept the principle that scarcity raises its value, we cannot accept the percentage of increase indicated by Ricardo, because we accept the view of that old economist, Gregory King, who said that a shortage of one-tenth in the supply required would raise the value of corn, or its price in the market, by much more than one-tenth.

If it is not the quantity of wheat, but the quantity of gold circulating in the country, that is diminished by the tax, we may suppose that this comes about through the government having decided to accumulate a store of gold in their vaults as a provision for the possibility of a sudden and unexpected war. Or we may imagine that in a burst of loyalty Parliament decides to equip the Royal Palace or Palaces not only with spoons, jugs, teapots and soup tureens made of solid gold, but also with fire-irons, coal-scuttles, spades and rakes made of the same precious metal. Unless these or some other effective means of preventing the gold returning into circulation are employed, there will be no reduction in the quantity of money.[1]

Although, in the paragraph we are discussing, Ricardo brackets together wheat and gold as commodities whose value per unit will increase if the supply is reduced, he warns us that a reduction of one-tenth in the quantity will not affect their value equally. His usual teaching is that if the quantity of money is reduced from £1000 to £900, the latter will have as much value as the former formerly had, which is what he now says of wheat; whereas what he now says of money is that after the reduction, £900 will purchase very little more than it formerly did.

Apart from these inconsistencies, there are other puzzles remaining to be solved. Ricardo does not tell us in what manner the tax on the 'actual quantity of gold in circulation' would be levied. He tells us that 'the tax would fall upon him whose property consisted of money'.[2] Are we, then, to suppose that if a man has just parted with 1000 sovereigns in exchange for a building plot he will escape the tax, while the man who has sold the land for 1000 sovereigns will have 100 of them taken from him? This seems fantastic, and can hardly have been his meaning. In the first part of the paragraph, where he is thinking only of a tax on gold-mining, he says that the tax would fall on 'the proprietors or holders' of gold, and 'not on those who use money'. Is the man who exchanges his land for gold a 'holder' of money (who suffers by the tax), or is he a 'user' (who does not suffer by the tax)? When we are dealing only with a tax on gold-mining it may be possible to distinguish between holders or proprietors on the one hand and users of money on the other; but when dealing with a tax on the 'actual quantity of gold in circulation' it is not easy to know what is meant by the man 'whose property consisted of money'.

If the government desire to build up a reserve of gold for use in the event of war, there would seem to be two ways in which

[1] If the quantity of money in a country is reduced, and prices fall, money will flow in from abroad. Ricardo begins the paragraph by assuming that 'the mines which supply us with gold were in this country', and I think it must be part of his assumption in this paragraph that the country is self-contained, with neither importation nor exportation.

[2] Is this consistent with the statement on page 124(194) that a considerable tax might be levied on gold, but 'upon that portion which was used for money, though a large tax might be received, nobody would pay it'?

this may be done without imposing a special burden on any particular individual. One way would be to increase the ordinary tax upon all incomes and to add the additional sovereigns so collected to the war-chest. The other method would be to recall all the gold in circulation and recoin it with one-tenth less gold in the sovereign; and this perhaps was what Ricardo had in mind when he said that the tax would be received although nobody paid it. It may have been this, too, that he was thinking of when he said that £900 would purchase very little more than before. If, in a self-contained country, the quantity of gold in circulation is reduced, but not the quantity of money (the number of sovereigns), then 'prices' would remain unaltered, and £900 should purchase as much as, but no more than, before.

While, in the paragraph on pages 122–3(192), Ricardo appears to assume that both wheat and gold rise in value because the quantity is reduced, in the very next paragraph (123/192) he reverts to the doctrine that value rises, not because supply is diminished, but because a tax has increased the cost of production.[1] He says:—'If the market value of corn be increased by one-tenth by taxation, or by difficulty of production, it is doubtful whether any effect whatever would be produced on the quantity consumed, because every man's want is for a definite quantity. . . .' If the quantity consumed is not affected we must suppose that the quantity produced is not affected, so it cannot be the diminution of supply that has raised the price. On this point we may turn back to his earlier statement (105/166): 'A tax on corn does not necessarily diminish the quantity of corn, it only raises its money price.' He then goes on to say that the quantity of supply will be reduced in the following year unless wages are raised to enable the labourers to buy as much as before at the enhanced price.

[1] In this paragraph Ricardo dwells on the very great difference in the effect of a change in the quantity of goods and a change in the quantity of money. That the money-metal is not on the same footing as ordinary commodities was one of the first things pointed out by Malthus when he became acquainted with Ricardo (vol. 6, p. 21). Ricardo was slow to admit this; two years later he observed that if the quantity of the money-metal increased 'the consumption would increase in consequence of its diminished value, and the fall of its value would be regulated precisely by the same law as the fall in the value of indigo, sugar or coffee' (vol. 6, p. 90). By the time he published his *Principles*, four years later, he admitted many modifications, but I think the old idea continued to lurk at the back of his head.

16

Ricardo's Chapter on Taxes on Profits

RICARDO's thirteenth chapter headed 'Taxes on Gold', which we have just been studying, does not quite cover all he has to say on the subject. His fifteenth chapter is headed 'Taxes on Profits', but I do not think we shall err if we say that in reality it is a discussion of the manner in which prices are affected by a tax on gold-mining. It is a difficult chapter to read, and there is little hope of a present-day reader understanding it (or this examination of it) unless he keeps in mind what was said at the beginning of our last chapter, namely, that Ricardo assumes throughout that the money circulating in the shops and market places of England consists of little ingots of gold called sovereigns, and that any producer of gold who brings 480 troy ounces of standard gold to the Royal Mint may have the mass melted down and converted into 1869 of these sovereigns.[1] We saw in the last chapter that Ricardo sometimes taught that the purchasing power of gold depends upon the cost of producing the money-metal. In the present chapter it is the latter assumption that we have to deal with, his argument being that if gold or any other commodity is taxed its price or value is thereby increased.

In the first paragraph there is nothing that requires comment, unless it is the curious statement 'that taxes on necessaries do not affect the consumers of necessaries in proportion to the quantity that may be consumed by them, but often in a much higher proportion'. This is the very reverse of what we should have expected from a writer who maintains that no taxes at all fall on the labourers, who are the principal consumers of corn and other necessaries. But Ricardo's next sentence makes his meaning clear: 'A tax on

[1] Thus each ounce will make 3·897 sovereigns, or expressed in sterling, £3 17*s.* 10½*d.*

corn, we have observed, not only affects a manufacturer in the proportion that he and his family may consume corn, but it alters the rate of profits of stock, and therefore also his income.' So the capitalist is the 'consumer' who pays the tax upon what he does not consume as well as on what he does consume.

This, however, is merely a piece of careless language; let us pass on to the second and third paragraphs. 'A tax on hats', says Ricardo, 'will raise the price of hats; a tax on shoes, the price of shoes; if this were not the case, the tax would be finally paid by the manufacturer; his profits would be below the general level . . . and he would quit his employment for another.' This we can understand; but he seems to throw this argument overboard when he adds: 'and if a tax in proportion to profits were laid upon all trades, every commodity would rise in price'.[1] If profits in all trades were taxed, no capitalist would gain anything by changing his trade. But when Ricardo refers to all trades being taxed he evidently means all but one, for he immediately adds: 'But if the mine which supplied us with the standard of our money were in this country, and the profits of the miner were also taxed, the price of no commodity would rise.'

The idea here is that if one article is taxed and not another, the price of the taxed article will rise; if both articles are taxed the price of both will rise, but their relative values will not be altered; they will continue to exchange for one another in the same ratio as before. If, before there was any tax, a ton of iron or fifteen ounces of silver exchanged for one ounce of gold, the ratio of exchange will be the same when a tax has raised the cost of producing gold in the same proportion that it has raised the cost of producing all other things. Hence when gold is used as money, and all commodities including gold are equally taxed, prices remain the same as they were before the tax. This does not mean that the government would not get the tax; it means that every producer would give an equal proportion of his income to the government and prices would remain unaltered. There has been an all-round rise in the cost of production, and an all-round diminution of profit, so that no producer would gain anything by changing his trade. Gold exchanges for everything else in the same ratio as before, which means that the prices of other things, expressed in gold, undergo no change at all.

[1] Ricardo repeats this on page 138(213).

Ricardo's mistake here is in regarding the producer of the money-metal as on the same footing as the producers of those commodities which are continuously consumed and therefore require to be continuously produced. Every day the community needs a fresh supply of bread, milk, fish and meat; shoes and clothes wear out, and have to be replaced. If the cost of producing shoes is increased, the shoemaker can raise his price; he can raise it, not because he is entitled to the same rate of profit as other producers but because any diminution in the production of shoes would quickly result in a reduction of the available supply in the market, an increased competition of consumers, and a restoration of the price to a remunerative level. When there is a seasonal falling off of the supply of eggs, eggs rise in price because the supply is reduced while the desire is not. A partial failure of crops may cause the price of corn to sky-rocket. People may be able to do with fewer hats, fewer clothes; nevertheless, a diminution of current production, which means a diminution of current supply, will result in an increased competition of consumers, and prices will rise. Houses last a long time, but in a growing population there is a continuous demand for new houses; even if population does not grow, old houses decay and new ones must be built, and a diminished production of bricks, timber, iron, copper or tin will lead to a rise in the price of these articles, and a rise in the price of houses too.

But the money-metal stands on a different footing from iron, copper and tin; it is not on the same footing as 'those commodities which are consumed and reproduced year by year', as Ricardo himself pointed out on page 126(196). The supply of money is not consumed; it circulates in the market; it is exchanged for other things, but these exchanges do not result in its withdrawal from the market, as is the case with iron and copper and tin. If the cost of producing gold rises, the miner, in common with the hatter and the shoemaker and the producers of base metals, would like to obtain a higher price, but he has no power to diminish the quantity of money in circulation, and therefore cannot raise the value of his product. Whether his cost of production rises or falls, he will obtain neither more nor less than £3 17*s*. 10½*d*. for every ounce of gold he delivers at the Mint. If he diminishes his production, or ceases operations entirely for a time, no doubt the purchasing power of £3 17*s*. 10½*d*. will 'ultimately' rise; it will rise, however, not because the quantity of money diminishes when no new gold is produced, but because in a growing community the quantity of other products to be 'circulated' will gradually increase, and this must result in a gradual fall of prices if the supply of gold does not also increase. A tax on the gold-miner's profit, therefore, as Ricardo himself points out, will not raise the value of gold 'till the quantity is reduced, and therefore such taxes will fall for a time, until supply is diminished, on the proprietors of money' (128/200). He means, of course, that for the value of gold to rise there must be a diminution in the quantity of money *compared* with the quantity of goods to be circulated, and while it may be safe to assume that this will happen 'ultimately', it by no means justifies the conclusion that a tax on the profits of the miner will raise the value of the money-metal as promptly as a tax on shoes will raise the price of shoes.

In his 15th chapter Ricardo seems quite oblivious of these facts; he seems to forget what he has himself said on the subject. He takes for granted throughout the chapter that if the gold-miner's profits are taxed the value of money will rise promptly; so much does he take this for granted that the expression 'If gold is taxed' may be safely taken as another way of saying 'If money rises in value'. Unless this is constantly borne in mind the chapter is very difficult to read and make sense of.

The 4th paragraph commences as follows: 'If money be not taxed, and therefore be permitted to preserve its value, whilst everything else is taxed and is raised in value. . . .' It may seem a little strange to refer to money as preserving its value while at the same time assuming that all prices rise. In this connection we must remember the distinction made by Ricardo between real value and relative value, or value-in-exchange. At the beginning of the sixth section of his first chapter he said that when there is a change in the relative values of two commodities it may be that only one of them has altered in real value (i.e. in cost of production), while the real value of the other has remained unaltered. Thus in paragraph 4 the rise in prices is not due to a fall in the real value of money, but to a rise in the real value of the commodities whose cost of production has been increased by a tax.

Paragraph 5 begins: 'If money be taxed, or if by any other cause its value be altered, and all commodities remain precisely at the same price as before. . . .' Here it is money that alters in value, while prices remain unaffected; and the explanation is that Ricardo is again referring to what he calls real values, or cost of production. Relative values remain the same because, the tax being laid both on the producers of consumable goods and the producers of the money-metal, both kinds of product rise in real value, or cost of production; the one rise offsets the other, and relative values remain the same as before.

I will say nothing at present regarding paragraphs 6, 7, and 8, because they open up a new line of thought, which had better be left for separate attention later in this chapter.

Passing on to paragraph 9 (135/210), this begins: 'If the profits of all trades were taxed, excepting the profits of the farmer. . . .' He evidently means, if all profits were taxed except those of the farmer and gold-miner. Neither farm produce nor gold being taxed, they continue to exchange for one another in the same ratio as before; but all other things rise in value compared with money and farm produce. But if after a time the tax is extended to the gold-miner, then the prices that formerly rose may fall back to their old level, while the product of the farmer, still untaxed, will fall below its old level, and the farmer would have a smaller money income.

In paragraph 10 Ricardo says that the landlord would be precisely in the same situation as the farmer; but I think in this paragraph his language is not quite clear. The landlord, he tells us, would have the same corn rent and the same money rent 'if all commodities rose in price and money remained at the same value'. I take his meaning to be (as in paragraph 9) that the farmer's income and the landlord's rent would not be altered if the prices of all the *taxed* goods rose while farm produce, not being taxed, continued to sell at the same price as before. He then says that money rent would fall 'if all commodities remained at the same price', by which I think he means that, if money is raised in value, the *taxed* goods may fall back to their original price, while the price of untaxed corn, and consequently the farmer's money income and the landlord's money rent, will fall below their former level.

Ricardo's conclusion that the landlord is on the same footing as his tenant is based on the assumption that the landlord's rent consists of a fixed quantity of corn, not a fixed amount of money. His idea is that if at a given expense one piece of land will yield

160 quarters of corn, another 170 quarters, and another 180 quarters, then while the cultivator of the poorest land will pay no rent at all, the farmer who cultivates the medium good land must pay a rent of 10 quarters, and the farmer who cultivates the best quality land must pay a rent of 20 quarters (136/211). Ricardo knew, of course, that rents are usually paid in money, and fixed by lease for a term of years. If corn rises in price, he says, the farmers 'would be benefited during their leases, and afterwards it would go to the landlord in the form of an increase of rent' (137/212). Hence when he says 'a tax on the profits of stock always leaves corn rent unaltered, and therefore money rent varies with the price of corn', we must understand him to mean that in the long run it is the landlord who benefits by the rise in the price of corn. With each new lease rents will be so adjusted that the rate of profit obtainable on capital in agriculture will be the same as that current in other lines of industry.

It was on the assumption that the farmer's rent may be regarded as a fixed quantity of corn that Ricardo concluded in paragraph 10 that if money rose in value and the price of corn consequently fell, this would reduce the landlord's money rent as well as the farmer's money profit. The landlord would get less money for his share of the corn at the same time that the farmer received less money for the corn that remained to him after deducting the landlord's share. On the same principle (that rent is a fixed quantity of corn) Ricardo concludes in paragraph 12 that if the farmer's profits are taxed, and the price of corn consequently rises, the landlord and the farmer will *not* be on the same footing; the landlord will benefit but the farmer will not. The farmer gains nothing by the rise in the price of corn, for although he receives more money, that additional money is taken from him by the government as a tax on profit. But the landlord, who receives the same quantity of corn as rent, sells that corn for a higher price; his money income is increased, and no part of the additional money is taken from him by the government, since the tax is levied on profits only, not on rents.[1] The position is, then, that when all profits are taxed and all prices raised, everybody has to pay a higher price for the goods he consumes. The landlord, however, is compensated for these higher prices, for he receives a higher

[1] It would be different if the tax were levied on the product instead of on the profit of the producer.

money income. The farmers and manufacturers are not compensated, for although they receive more money, that additional money is taken from them as a tax. Hence Ricardo's conclusion that the landlord 'would be benefited by the tax on his tenant's profits' (136/211). This advantage derived by the landlord from the taxation of his tenant's profit would not be lost if a rise in the value of money caused all prices to fall. 'If money should rise in value', says Ricardo, 'and all things should, after a tax on the profits of stock, fall to their former prices, rent also would be the same as before. The landlord would receive the same money rent, and would obtain all the commodities on which it was expended at their former price; so that under all circumstances he would continue untaxed. This circumstance', Ricardo adds, 'is curious. By taxing the profits of the farmer you do not burthen him more than if you exempted his profits from the tax, and the landlord has a decided interest that his tenant's profits should be taxed, as it is only on that condition that he himself continues really untaxed' (137/212–13).

If we now return to the point from which we started, we see that in all these propositions (commencing with paragraph 4) Ricardo assumes that if the profits of the gold-miner are taxed money will rise in value, and prices will fall. Where he erred, as already pointed out, was in assuming that gold, even when adopted as money, is on precisely the same footing as other metals, and other products of all descriptions.

He himself taught that the purchasing power, or exchange value, of the monetary unit depends on the number of units in circulation. Money may be, and often is, made of paper, in which case cost of production practically plays no part whatever in the determination of its value. And Ricardo held that money made of a metal is subject to the same law (238–9/353). He admitted that a tax on the profits of the gold-miner would not raise the value of his product unless it resulted in a diminution of the quantity in circulation (128/200). But he ignores this in chapter 15, and argues on the assumption that if the gold-miner is taxed the value of his product will rise as promptly as the value of hats or shoes will rise when the profits of the hatter or shoemaker are taxed.

That Ricardo, in one paragraph after another, should base his argument on the assumption that gold rises in value when taxed, is strange enough; but what I think is still more astonishing is that, according to paragraph 3, this rise in value only occurs if the mines from which the money-metal is produced are 'in this country'. What becomes, then, of this argument when he tells us towards the end of the chapter (138/213) that the mines are not 'in this country', and that the gold is all imported from abroad? Whether our products are taxed or untaxed, we export many of them to other parts of the world, and in exchange we may obtain other goods, or we may receive gold, some of it perhaps produced in countries where gold-mining is heavily taxed, some in countries where it is only lightly taxed, some perhaps in countries where it is not taxed at all.

Let us now turn to paragraphs 6, 7 and 8, which we passed over without examination. Happily, in the arguments now to be considered, we need not trouble ourselves with the question whether money is or is not taxed.

Ricardo's doctrine in paragraph 6 (133/207) is that if there is no alteration in the value of money when a tax is laid on the profits of all producers of goods, all prices will rise; but, he says, 'they will not rise in the same proportion; they will not, after the tax, bear the same relative value to one another which they did before the tax'. He illustrates this by some figures in which it is assumed that profit is at the rate of 20 per cent, and the tax is 10 per cent. Two capitalists, each employing a capital of £10,000 will each obtain a profit of £2000; each will pay a tax of £200, and each will add £200 to the price of his product in order to keep his money income the same as it was before. But the price of the goods they sell may be very different, owing to the different proportions in which fixed and circulating capital are employed. Thus Ricardo gives us the following figures:

One capitalist pays wages of	£8000
and adds his profit	2000
Before the tax he sells his product for	£10,000
He now adds the tax	200
and sells his product for	£10,200
The other capitalist pays wages of	£2000
adds his profit	2000
Before the tax he sells his product for	4000
He now adds the tax	200
and sells his product for	£4200

Thus, Ricardo points out, although the tax is the same in both cases, one product has risen by 2 per cent and the other by 5 per cent. Relative values are altered.

Ricardo then proceeds to enquire what would happen if money now rose in value, making all prices fall, and he makes this astonishing statement:

> If, under these circumstances, money rose in value, from whatever cause it might proceed, it would not affect the prices in the same proportion. The same cause which would lower the price of one from £10,200 to £10,000, or less than 2 per cent, would lower the price of the other from £4200 to £4000, or 4¾ per cent. If they fell in any different proportion, profits would not be equal (134/208).

This statement is in accord with that in the 9th paragraph, where he says: 'an alteration in the value of money might sink all the taxed commodities to their former price.' The dictum seems to have puzzled Ricardo's friend Trower (as well it might), and Ricardo sought to make the matter clear to him by the following explanation:

> I have looked to the passages in my book to which you refer. I quite agree with you that in most cases of taxes on income, or on profits, no effect would be produced on prices, and the burthen, which in every case would be equal, would fall on the producer, or the man enjoying the income. But I have supposed a case of our having the mines which supplied our standard, in this country, and that the profits of the miner were not taxed, then commodities would rise in price to the amount of the tax, or the miner's business would be more profitable than any other and consequently would draw capital to that concern. If then all commodities rose in price, what would they rise?—not in proportion to their value, but in proportion to the capitals employed in their production, and therefore as commodities selling for £4000 may be the result of the employment of the same amount of capital as commodities which sell for £10,000, these commodities would not rise in proportion to their prices; but if one rose £200 the other would also rise £200. Now in this situation of things, suppose money to rise in value, and the goods which sell for £10,200 to fall to £10,000, the other goods which sell for £4200 will fall to £4000; but if money should continue to rise in value, and consequently the goods which sold for £10,000 should fall to £5000, then those which sold for £4000 would fall to £2000. Up to a certain point, then, they fall in proportion to the capitals employed in their

production, but subsequently in proportion to the value of the goods themselves (vol. 8, p. 153).

Here Ricardo appears to see no difference between the reduction of prices which would follow a repeal of the tax, and a general fall of prices brought about by a rise in the value of money. He seems to credit one and the same cause (a rise in the value of money) with a sort of discriminatory power. It commences by affecting prices unequally, lowering some by one percentage, others by another percentage; having in this way got rid of the difference of price caused by the tax, it thereafter reduces all prices by the same percentage. Apart from the absurdity of this notion, he appears to overlook that if Parliament has not repealed the tax it will continue, after prices have fallen, to make a difference in relative values.

Ricardo's explanation to Trower is, in fact, no explanation at all, but a mere repetition of the puzzle. It looks as though when writing to his friend, he had himself forgotten what was really in his mind when he wrote paragraph 6 of his fifteenth chapter. The mistake made by Ricardo in that paragraph was in using language which seemed to imply that when prices fall as a result of a rise in the value of money, the adjustments necessary to restore equality in the rate of profit occurred automatically. The position would have been clear to Trower if Ricardo had drawn his attention to the concluding words of paragraph 7, where he points out that if the rise in the value of money caused the rate of profit in one industry to be lower than in others, 'capital would be removed from one employment to another till an equilibrium of profits was restored, which could only be after relative prices were altered'.

In paragraphs 6, 7 and 8, as already remarked, we are not troubled with the question whether taxing the gold-miner raises the value of money. Paragraph 8 deals expressly with the paper money that circulated in England during the period when the Bank of England was prohibited from cashing its notes in gold. And in paragraph 7 the rise or fall in the value of money is explicitly attributed to its 'scarcity or abundance', not to a tax affecting its cost of production, while the 'abundance of money' is attributed to an influx of gold from abroad, and 'scarcity' to its exportation (135/209).

17

The Measurement of Value

WHILE we have very fully discussed Ricardo's teaching as to what causes the value of one thing to be more than that of another, or causes the value of one to rise when that of another remains unchanged or falls, something requires to be said regarding the method of measuring these differences or changes of value.

Let us commence by asking what is meant by measurement? On page 189(284) Ricardo himself answers the question as follows:

> I am of the opinion of a very distinguished writer, M. Destutt de Tracy,[1] who says that 'To measure any one thing is to compare it with a determinate quantity of that same thing which we take for a standard of comparison, for unity. To measure, then, to ascertain a length, a weight, a value, is to find how many times they contain metres, grammes, francs, in a word, unities of the same description.'[2]

But, to measure or ascertain a length, a weight, or a value, it is not sufficient to fix upon a unit; we must devise some means of ascertaining how many of these units are contained in the mass of similar units that is to be measured. For some kinds of measurements this is easy; for others considerable ingenuity is required. We all know how to measure length with a yard-stick and weight by means of balances; but a yard-stick is useless for discovering weight, and balances will not assist us to ascertain a length. For

[1] 'One of the most philosophical of all economists', according to Jevons (Preface to 2nd edition of his *Theory of Political Economy*). 'A very agreeable old gentleman', according to Ricardo, who met him in Paris (vol. 9, p. 248).

[2] This definition would have been better had the word 'francs' been omitted, for while a metre is length only, and a gramme is weight only, francs are material things, and we no more expect to find francs in a roll of calico than we expect to find yard-sticks. It is not the franc, but the value of the franc, that forms the unit for measuring value.

different kinds of measurement different kinds of instruments are necessary; for each kind of measurement there is an appropriate technique. The thermometer has been invented for measuring heat; the sphygmomanometer for measuring blood pressure; the speedometer tells us the rate at which a motor-car is travelling; science has done away with the old device of a plumb-line to measure the depth of the sea and substituted radar. Day and night form, for inhabitants of the Earth, a natural unit of time, but not content with this, mankind have long employed ingenious machines for measuring fractions of this unit. For ages the length of the year was guessed at, and because the means of measurement were imperfect, disorder occurred in the calendar, and it was centuries before astronomers succeeded in discovering exactly how many days and nights, and fractions thereof, are contained in a year. Each kind of measurement, then, requires an appropriate technique. What is the technique for measuring value?

Here again our question is answered by Ricardo himself. 'The value of a commodity', he says in one of his pamphlets, 'is estimated by the quantity of other things generally for which it will exchange' (vol. 4, p. 60). In another pamphlet he wrote: 'Commodities measure the value of money in the same manner as money measures the value of commodities' (vol. 3, p. 104). And in his *Principles* he says: 'It is by commodities that the relative value of gold is estimated' (60/105).

Thus Ricardo lays it down that it is by sale or exchange that value is measured. Yet he appears to reject exchange as a method of measurement when he refuses to accept market price as reflecting what he calls real value. If two things are produced at the same cost, he declares, they are of the same value, though he admits that in the market their prices at any particular time may differ.

In the *Notes on Malthus* Ricardo says: 'A commodity is at its natural value when it repays by its price all the expenses that have been bestowed, from first to last, to produce it and bring it to market' (vol. 2, p. 35). The market price may be above the natural price or real value for a time, owing to demand exceeding the supply available at the time; it will fall below the natural price if supply exceeds demand. But these deviations from the natural price are temporary, and will be quickly rectified by increase of supply in the one case or diminished supply in the other. The natural price, says Adam Smith, is 'as it were, the central price to which the prices of all commodities are continually gravitating'.[1] Ricardo's statement is that the naural price, or real value, or cost of production, is the 'pivot' about which the market price fluctuates (vol. 2, p. 25). If the cost of production changes, the pivot about which the market price oscillates will rise or fall, as the case may be. If two commodities are continually produced at the same cost, they will in the long run, or on the average, sell at the same price. 'I have allowed', says Ricardo, 'that their market prices may differ, but I say commodities so situated will have the same natural price, and will therefore have a constant tendency to agree in market value also; for natural price is the great regulator of market price' (vol. 2, p. 299).

It is a pity that Ricardo did not always express himself so clearly as this in his *Principles*. The trouble arises when, having concluded that natural price (or cost of production) represents the real value, he drops the word *real* and tells us that the ratio in which goods exchange for one another corresponds with their respective costs of production. Ricardo is always impatient of any qualification that blurs the clear outline of a general principle; he prefers to ignore the fluctuations that intrude upon and obscure long-term trends, and therefore, instead of saying, with Adam Smith, that prices constantly tend to conform to the natural price, he prefers to say that prices are governed by the cost of production, and therefore what costs two days' labour to produce must be, and is, worth twice as much as, or has double the value of, what can be produced by one day's labour. Even in chapter 4, which is devoted to showing the extremely important role played by the fluctuations of market price in directing the industry of the country into the channels necessary to satisfy the various and varying requirements of the community, he finishes up by treating market influences as mere accidents to be ignored, and says:

> We will leave them entirely out of our consideration whilst we are treating of the laws which regulate natural prices, natural wages, and natural profits, effects, totally independent of these accidental causes. In speaking, then, of the exchangeable value of commodities, or the power of purchasing possessed by any one commodity, I mean always that power which it would possess if not disturbed by any temporary or accidental cause, and which is its natural price (51/92).

[1] *Wealth of Nations*, Book 1, chap. 7, 15th paragraph.

This dictum is one that we must always keep in mind when interpreting the statement that value is in proportion to the quantity of labour 'realised in' each commodity. But whatever may be said in favour of this way of looking at things 'whilst we are treating of the laws which *regulate* natural price', it throws no light upon the method to be adopted for *measuring*, i.e. ascertaining, relative values. Although market prices may seldom correspond exactly with what Ricardo calls real values, there seems no reason for Ricardo's outright rejection of them as a means of measuring natural prices. If Adam Smith was right that the market price constantly tends to gravitate towards the natural price, and if Ricardo's statement is correct that the natural price of commodities 'always ultimately governs their market price' (142/217), then all we have to do to ascertain or measure their respective natural prices is to eliminate the fluctuations by averaging the price of each commodity over a suitable period.

I cannot recollect that Ricardo ever suggests this method of measuring real value, and the explanation appears to be that he had only a vague and fluctuating conception of what is meant by measurement. He does not seem to distinguish clearly between *determining* the value of a commodity in the sense of dictating or fixing its price, and *determining* its value in the sense in which astronomers determine the length of the year or the distance of the Moon from the Earth. Ricardo nearly always uses the word *determine* in the former sense, but he does occasionally use it in the sense of *ascertain*,[1] and it has been suggested[2] that the fact of the word having two different meanings was perhaps responsible for Ricardo's failure to distinguish clearly between what regulates value and what measures it. While this hardly seems likely, it is nevertheless a fact that at times he appears to use the words *regulate* and *measure*[3] as though they meant the same thing. In a

[1] For instance, near the foot of page 7(14) and at the top of page 28(44), near end of 1st paragraph.

[2] See chap. 10 in Samuel Bailey's *Critical Dissertation on the Nature, Measures and Causes of Value* (1825, reprinted in 1931 by the London School of Economics).

[3] The word *measure* also has more than one meaning; for example, we may speak of the measures taken by the government to *regulate* the trade in liquor. Ricardo uses the word carelessly sometimes; in a passage that I shall quote in a moment he speaks of labour as a measure, whereas it is the thing to be measured.

letter to Malthus he refers to 'our old dispute, whether the quantity of labour in a commodity should be the regulator of its value, of whether the value of all things should, under all circumstances, be estimated by the quantity of corn for which they would exchange' (vol. 9, p. 78). On page 188(283) of his *Principles*, when criticising Say, he compares iron with gold, and remarks: 'If utility were the measure of value, it is probable I should give more for the iron.' Well might the astonished Frenchman protest that he had never suggested that 'utility is the measure of value, but that value is the measure of utility'.[1] What Ricardo meant apparently was that if utility *regulated* value (i.e. if greater utility conferred greater value), then iron would be more valuable than gold.

On page 107(169), on the other hand, Ricardo uses the word *regulate* where *measure* would seem more appropriate. He says: 'The value of gold as a commodity must be regulated by the quantity of goods which must be given to foreigners in exchange for it.' If he had said that the quantity of goods that must be given for gold *measures* its value, it would have been in accord with his own dictum that commodities measure the value of money as money measures the value of commodities. As we saw in the last chapter, he sometimes held that the value or purchasing power of gold is regulated by its quantity, and sometimes that it is regulated by its cost of production; but here he says it is regulated by the quantity of goods it will exchange for—which amounts to saying that the ratio of exchange is regulated by the ratio of exchange!

Again, on page 7(13–14) Ricardo refers to Adam Smith as having 'accurately defined the original source of exchangeable value', and then reproaches him with erecting '*another* standard measure of value'—as though source of value and measure of value meant the same thing—which is very like suggesting that because the thermometer measures heat it must also be the source of heat. In the *Notes on Malthus*, we read: 'The objections made

[1] Say wrote to Ricardo on 2nd December, 1815: 'I must have explained myself very badly, since you accuse me of having said that utility was the measure of value; whereas I thought I had always said that the value which men attach to a thing is the measure of the utility which they find in it' (vol. 6, p. 273). This was two years before Ricardo published his first edition, yet here, six years later in his third edition, we find him still using the same incorrect expression.

here to gold as a measure of value . . . are in substance the very same that were made in the last section to labour itself as a regulator of value' (vol. 2, p. 82).

In accusing Ricardo of not distinguishing between cause and measure of value I am not unmindful of his statement that he accepts Destutt de Tracy's definition of measurement (quoted at the beginning of this chapter); my point is that in reality he does not accept the French writer's definition. After saying that he agrees with de Tracy he proceeds to remark:

> A franc is not a measure of value for anything but for a quantity of the same metal of which francs are made, unless francs, and the thing to be measured, can be referred to some other measure which is common to both. This, I think, they can be, for they are both the result of labour; and therefore labour is a common measure by which their real as well as their relative value may be estimated (189/284).

Thus Ricardo has no sooner expressed his agreement with de Tracy's definition than he throws it overboard; he casts away at the same time various dicta of his own—the dictum, for instance, that money measures the value of commodities and commodities the value of money; and the dictum that the value of a commodity is estimated by the quantity of other things generally for which it will exchange. Surely we may apply to Ricardo what he said of Say, that he 'is frequently at variance with himself',[1] for he now

[1] Vol. 8, p. 228. In the *Notes on Malthus* (vol. 2, p. 78) Ricardo wrote as follows in reference to measuring the value of corn: 'How will it exchange for linen, hats, shoes, iron, and every commodity? It will command double the quantity of them; then, according to my view, it has doubled in value.' Shortly after writing this, Ricardo published his third edition, in which he said exactly the opposite: 'I cannot agree with M. Say in estimating the value of a commodity by the abundance of other commodities for which it will exchange' (189/284). The idea that he goes on to develop is that the value of each commodity is governed by the cost of producing it. If its cost of production has not changed, then its real value has not changed, yet its power of commanding other commodities may have increased through a fall in the cost of producing the latter.

The same idea appears to lie behind another enigmatic dictum of Ricardo's. On page 11(19) he remarks: 'If I have to hire a labourer for a week and instead of ten shillings I pay him eight, no variation having taken place in the value of money, the labourer can probably obtain more food and necessaries with his eight shillings than he before obtained for ten', etc. How can it be said, we ask, that there is no variation in the value of money if 8*s.* will now buy more than 10*s.* would buy before? Ricardo's meaning apparently is that if

tells us that you cannot use a franc to measure the value of iron or timber, or anything except the value of silver. This, I fancy, must have made that 'agreeable old gentleman', M. de Tracy, rub his eyes with amazement. Ricardo's idea appears to be this—a franc is a piece of silver; if a piece of uncoined silver has the same weight as a franc it will have the same value;[1] if it weighs ten times as much as a franc it will have ten times as much value. The same principle applies, of course, to two pieces of iron, but not to a piece of iron and a piece of silver; in this case the ratio of weight does not give the ratio of value, and therefore it is necessary to find 'some other measure which is common to both', which seems to mean that it is necessary to find some quality common to both which is neither weight nor bulk, and which can be measured.

The quality common to both that we desire to measure is value. Both silver and iron have value, and if we adopt the value of the franc as our unit of value, measurement consists in ascertaining how many times this unit is contained in the value of the mass of iron that we desire to find the value of. Ricardo himself said in the *Notes on Malthus* (vol. 2, p. 33): 'Length can only be measured by length, capacity by capacity, and value by value', but, as already remarked, he has no sooner accepted this principle than he appears to discard it in favour of the proposition that if we wish to know the ratio of value between two commodities, we must ascertain the quantity of labour 'contained' in the things whose value is to be measured, and the quantity 'contained' in the thing adopted as a unit of measurement. Once more, then, we find him unable to distinguish between what (in his opinion) regulates the value of commodities and what measures their relative values. Not only so, but he seems to have but a hazy idea of what is meant by measurement, for while he tells us that what we must measure is the quantity of labour, he gives us no indication of the method or technique by which the quantity of labour realised in a com-

---

there has been neither increase nor decrease in the cost of producing gold, but there has been a fall in the cost of producing other things, then it is not the value of money that has risen, but the value of other things that has fallen.

[1] France in Ricardo's day was on a silver standard, but coinage was not gratuitous as in England. Ricardo ignores his own statement that the seignorage gives coined metal a higher value than the uncoined metal.

modity can be discovered or ascertained. There may be a few articles with regard to which the quantity of labour bestowed on them can be ascertained, as in the case of nuts gathered on the wayside by Cobbett's vagrants and the shrimps which Malthus and Ricardo sometimes discussed as a 'standard of value' containing labour only; and in that case it is a simple matter to count the nuts and the shrimps gathered by a morning's work, and to determine the quantity of labour realised in one nut compared with the quantity in one shrimp; but Ricardo's own description of the quantities of labour employed from first to last in the production of a pair of stockings (14/25) is sufficient to convince us that this method cannot be applied in many cases. It would be interesting to know on what Ricardo based his statement that the quantity of labour realised in an ounce of gold is fifteen times as great as the labour embodied in an ounce of silver (238/352), and 2000 times as great as the quantity embodied in an ounce of iron (188/283). I strongly suspect that if challenged to reveal the source of his information he would have had to confess that he deduced the cost from the ratio of exchange. In other words, his contention amounts to this—if we know the relative costs of two commodities we know the ratio in which they exchange for one another; and if we know the ratio in which they exchange we know their relative costs of production. As he wrote to Malthus: 'If my commodity is of equal value with yours, its cost of production must be the same' (vol. 8, p. 279).

The fact seems to be that in discussing the measurement of value Ricardo had no very clear conception of what is meant by *measurement* or of what is meant by *value*. As we have seen, he appears to regard *regulating* and *measuring* as almost interchangeable expressions; and similarly, as Malthus remarked, he made no distinction between *cost of production* and *value*.[1] Is there any way of accounting for this confusion, this fog, in the mind of so clear-headed a man as Ricardo?

It arose, I think, from his line of approach to the subject. Although he devoted his first chapter to the theory of value, it was not in the ratio of exchange that he was primarily interested; it was not so much *differences* of value as *changes* of value that he

[1] Malthus' words will be found in vol. 2, p. 31, and Ricardo's comment on page 34. Ricardo quoted Malthus' remark in his *Principles* and replied to it (30/47).

wanted to measure. For evidence of this we have only to turn to his own statement in section 2 of his first chapter. Although in the first section he tells us that the ratio in which commodities exchange for one another depends on the relative quantities of labour necessary for their production 'and not on the greater or less compensation which is paid for that labour' (see section heading), he admits in the second section that a day's labour of a working jeweller may be 'more valuable than a day's labour by a common labourer' (11/20). Now this admission absolutely knocks on the head the theory that the ratio in which goods exchange for one another is governed by the *quantity* of labour realised in them. But Ricardo lightly brushes this aside on the ground that what he is concerned with is not the quantity of labour required for the production of different commodities, but the different quantity of labour required at one period to produce a thing (for instance, corn) compared with the quantity of labour necessary to produce the same thing a hundred, or several hundred, years later.

To understand why Ricardo attached so much importance to comparing past with present values we must bear in mind the purpose for which he wrote his book. I have already quoted his statement to Malthus that Political Economy is not concerned with the production of wealth, but with its distribution (vol. 8, p. 278). In his Preface he had already said: 'To determine the laws which regulate this distribution is the principal problem of Political Economy.' It was this problem that he set out to tackle. In his view, the law of diminishing returns results in a gradual rise in the value of corn (the food of the labourer) and this in turn causes a gradual and continuous fall in the proportion of the product which goes to the capitalists as profit, and a gradual and progressive increase in the share of the product which goes to landlords as rent.

These changes in the cost of production cannot in any case be measured by exchange for the very good reason that, as Malthus remarked (vol. 9, p. 311), there can be no exchange between the producers of one age and those of another. This, however, would not prevent these changes being measured by exchange if only there were some one article whose value never altered—some article which always required, and always had required, an unvarying quantity of labour to produce it. If we had such an article, any permanent change in the ratio in which it exchanged for other things would show which of them had risen or fallen in cost of production, and by how much their cost had risen or fallen. Hence in his first edition (page 11; see footnote, page 17 in vol. 1) Ricardo wrote:

> If any one commodity could be found which now and at all times required precisely the same quantity of labour to produce it, that commodity would be of an unvarying value, and would be eminently useful as a standard by which the variations of other things might be measured. Of such a commodity we have no knowledge, and consequently are unable to fix on any standard of value.

When Ricardo says that we cannot fix on any standard of value, he means an unvarying standard—a standard comparable to that by which we measure length. With a yard-stick[1] a mother can measure the height of her boy when he is six; she can measure it again when he is sixteen, and learn accurately by how much it has increased. Ricardo lamented that we have no such instrument by which we can measure changes of value with the same accuracy.

By the time Ricardo published his third edition, however, he had come to the conclusion that a commodity always produced by the same quantity of labour, even if it existed, would not furnish us with an appropriate instrument for measuring the real values (i.e. the cost of production) of all other things. What brought about this change of view?

Even when he published his first edition Ricardo was aware that other factors besides labour enter into the cost of production. While enunciating the doctrine that the relative values of commodities are determined by the relative quantities of labour embodied in them he admitted certain 'modifications'. He pointed out that when capital is employed as well as labour the price of the product must include remuneration for the use of capital. He also pointed out that apart from the circulating capital advanced as wages a certain quantity of fixed capital is generally employed,

[1] Ricardo says: 'If I have any doubt whether my foot measure is of the same length now that it was of 20 years ago I have only to compare it with some standard afforded by nature—with a portion of the arc of meridian, or with the space through which a pendulum swings in a given portion of time' (vol. 4, p. 380; see also p. 401). For an earlier reference (1816) see vol. 7, p. 43.

and this quantity may be much greater in some employments than in others. He insisted, too, that a rise or fall in the rate of profit would alter the ratios in which various goods exchanged for one another. But these modifications he regarded as 'of no great magnitude' (vol. 2, p. 101). He considered that differences in the quantity of capital, and consequent differences in the quantity of profit, exercised a quite insignificant influence on prices compared with the influence of difference in the quantity of labour, and he was prepared to ignore them in propounding his law of value. He appears to have applied to economic law the legal maxim *de minimis non curat lex*. He no more included trifles in his cost of production than the bus conductor includes babies in arms when counting the number of his passengers. In one of the *Notes on Malthus* (vol. 2, p. 186) Ricardo says: 'A principle is either true or false', but apparently the principle that value is in proportion to the quantity of labour remains true despite 'some deviations'.[1]

This attitude was challenged by Col. Torrens in 1818, soon after Ricardo's first edition was published. So far from regarding the admitted 'deviations' as insignificant qualifications of the proposition that value is in proportion to the quantity of labour, Torrens considered that they amounted to an utter refutation of that doctrine (vol. 4, p. 317). Even if we hold that prices in all cases are governed by cost of production, we must include in the cost of production every outlay of the capitalist, and prices will be so adjusted as to yield in the long run the same rate of profit in all industries. In his Commonplace Book Ricardo copied out some of Torrens' arguments and placed opposite them quotations from his own book as evidence that he did not neglect to take into account the factors to which Torrens drew attention.[2]

The only consequence of this criticism at the time was that in the second edition of his book, which appeared shortly afterwards (February, 1819), Ricardo made a slight addition to his 'modifications'. He neither withdrew nor modified the dictum that a commodity always produced by the same quantity of labour would

[1] 'Cost of production is, with some deviations, in proportion to labour employed' (vol. 8, p. 279).

[2] Vol. 4, pp. 315–18. In a letter to Mill of 28th December, 1818, Ricardo discusses his difference with Torrens, and holds that difference in the quantity of labour is the great regulator of value, and the other factors mentioned by Torrens 'never supersede but only modify' it (vol. 7, p. 377).

serve as a measure for the value of other commodities; the passage on page 11 of his first edition is repeated word for word on page 10 of the second edition. Up to this time, then, Ricardo had not changed his mind.

While Torrens may have been the first to challenge Ricardo's theories in the public Press, Malthus had long disagreed with him in private. The two men had spent years in amicable discussion of their opposing views, and when Ricardo's book appeared in 1817 Malthus lost no time in writing him: 'I still cannot agree with you that labour alone, in the sense you understand it,[1] is either in theory or fact the best measure of exchangeable value' (vol. 7, p. 176). But at that time (August, 1817) the question of an invariable measure of value had not come up for discussion, and Malthus was only thinking of profits, and the influence of demand on price. It is not till September 1819 that Malthus (apparently following up a conversation between them on the subject) writes to Ricardo as follows: 'If we suppose half an ounce of silver on an average to be picked up by a day's search on the sea shore, money[2] would then always retain most completely the same value. It would always on an average both cost and command the same quantity of labour. The money price of labour could never permanently either rise or fall' (vol. 8, pp. 64–5). But Malthus pointed out later that when it comes to using this commodity produced by labour only for measuring the value of other commodities in which labour and capital are both 'embodied' a difficulty would arise from the fact that 'Scarcely any other commodity can reasonably be supposed to have required in its production exactly the same quantity of fixed and circulating capital employed for exactly the same time' (vol. 8, p. 108). These remarks seem to have made no impression on Ricardo, for a couple of months later we find him writing to McCulloch as follows:

> Col. Torrens showed me the paper which is a copy of the one he sent to you. I am more convinced than ever that the great regulator of value is the quantity of labour required to produce the commodity valued. There are many modifications which must be admitted into this doctrine, from the circumstance of the unequal times that commodities require to be brought to market, but this does not

[1] I.e. the quantity of labour embodied in the commodity.

[2] Malthus here assumes that silver is the standard money.

> invalidate the doctrine itself. I am not satisfied with the explanation which I have given of the principles which regulate value. I wish a more able pen would undertake it—the fault is not in the inadequacy of the doctrine to account for all difficulties, but in the inadequacy of him who has attempted to explain it (vol. 8, p. 142).

The last lines, while they do not indicate any weakening in Ricardo's confidence in his theory show that he was not satisfied with his own exposition of the doctrine, but they do not suggest that at this date (December, 1819) he had any intention, or thought himself capable, of improving it.

The next development is the publication in April 1820 of Malthus' book on the *Principles of Political Economy* in which he expounded the views he had long held and long discussed with Ricardo without reaching any agreement. In section V of his second chapter he deals with Ricardo's commodity of unvarying cost as a measure of value. The section opens with the following words:

> Upon the principle that the labour which a commodity has cost in its production is at once a measure of real and relative value, it has been thought that if there were any article to be found which would at all times cost the same quantity of labour in its production, it might be used as an accurate and standard measure of value (page 108 in Malthus' first edition, page 79 in Sraffa's vol. 2).

Malthus proceeds to examine this proposition. He does not, as I understand him, deny that the value of one commodity can be used to measure the value of others (just as one length can be used to measure other lengths); what he contends is that even if we had a money (whether gold or silver) always produced by the same quantity of labour, the ratio in which it exchanged for other things would not indicate the ratio between the quantity of labour embodied in the standard metal and the quantity of labour embodied in the commodity for which it exchanged. Malthus writes:

> Let us suppose, first, that the precious metals required for their production at the mines which yield no rent a certain quantity of fixed and circulating capital employed for a certain time . . . none of the commodities which would exchange for a given quantity of silver would contain the same quantity of labour as that silver except those which had been produced, not only by the same quantity of labour, but by the same quantities of the two kinds of capital em-

> ployed for the same time and in the same proportions; and in the case of a rise in the price of labour, all commodities which still contained the same quantity of labour would alter in price except those very few which were circumstanced exactly in the same manner with regard to the capitals by which they were produced as the precious metals.
>
> Let us suppose, secondly, that the production of the precious metals required no fixed capital, but merely advances in the payment of manual labour for a year . . . upon a rise in the price of labour, almost all commodities would rise or fall in price.
>
> Let us suppose, thirdly, that labour alone, without any advances above the food of a day, were sufficient to obtain the precious metals. . . . In this case it is obvious that every commodity which had required in its production any sort or quantity of capital beyond the advance of necessaries for a day would differ in price from any portion of gold or silver which had cost the same quantity of labour.
>
> On either of the above suppositions . . . we should be as little able as we are at present to infer from these relative prices the relative proportions of labour employed upon each commodity.

The only comment on the above passage made by Ricardo in the *Notes on Malthus* (vol. 2, p. 82) is to the effect that he has admitted that values are not *exactly* in proportion to the quantity of labour. In a letter to McCulloch (May, 1820) he claims that the points made by Malthus are 'all implied in my book, but I have not been sufficiently explicit' (vol. 8, p. 180). By October 9th he had evidently decided to make his treatment of the subject 'more explicit'; he writes to Malthus: 'My first chapter will not be materially altered—in principle I think it will not be altered at all' (vol. 8, p. 280).

Now if you want to convince your opponent that he is wrong, there is nothing like sitting down with pen in hand to put your arguments clearly on paper. The result sometimes is that you discover some error you overlooked in your previous reasoning. This is perhaps what happened to Ricardo, for when his new edition appeared in May, 1821, it contained a very material alteration in his first chapter. The passage in his first two editions stating that a commodity always produced by the same quantity of labour would serve to measure the values of other things was, as already mentioned, entirely withdrawn, and replaced by a new section (section VI) stating that no one commodity, however constant in its cost of production, could serve as a general measure of value. He does not say in his first chapter, as he does in chapter 20, that the value of one quantity of silver can only be used to measure that of another quantity of silver, but he tells us in effect that if there were never any change in the cost of producing silver it could nevertheless be used only to measure alterations in the value of such other commodities (if any) as happened to be produced under precisely the same conditions as itself.

Ricardo's argument in the new section follows closely the line of reasoning in section V of Malthus' second chapter. But Ricardo had a curious propensity to give a twist of his own to any line of thought suggested to him by another writer. We have seen how, in 'agreeing' with de Tracy, he gave a strange twist to that writer's dictum that one value can only be measured by another value; we have again an instance of this propensity in his treatment of Malthus. Malthus' contention was that the ratio in which two commodities exchange for one another cannot be taken as indicating the relative *quantities of labour* embodied in them unless both are produced by labour and capital combined in the same proportions. Ricardo alters this, and asserts that the ratio in which goods exchange for one another cannot be taken as measuring their relative *values* unless they are produced 'under the same circumstances precisely'. He argues that the value of an article produced by labour alone cannot measure the value of an article produced by labour and capital; an article produced by labour in a year with the assistance of circulating capital (wages fund) cannot measure the value of another article produced by labour, circulating capital and fixed capital; and an article produced in a year by labour with circulating and fixed capital, cannot measure the value of another article produced by this combination if the quantity of fixed capital is different in one case from the other; or if the fixed capital, although the same in quantity, is of different durability. These differences in the proportions in which labour and capital co-operate 'disqualify any commodity that can be thought of from being a perfectly accurate measure of value' (28/44). Ricardo stood by this doctrine to the end of his life. The last words in the last letter that he wrote (written on the very day that he took to his bed) were: 'There is not in nature any correct measure of value, nor can any ingenuity suggest one, for what constitutes a correct measure for some things is a reason why it cannot be a correct one for others' (vol. 9, p. 387).

How did Ricardo arrive at this conclusion? I think the explanation is to be found in that same propensity to give a twist of his own to the teachings of other writers. In this instance the principle he took over from de Tracy was that to measure something was to compare it with a determinate quantity (an agreed unit) of that same thing. Now it is easy to fix on a unit for measuring length or weight, but how can we find a unit for measuring cost of production? In the case of two commodities produced by labour alone (if any) we may adopt a day's work as a unit for measuring their respective costs of production. In the case of two commodities produced by capital alone (if any) we might perhaps be able to fix on a certain quantity of capital expenditure as a unit. But if one commodity is produced by labour only, and the other by capital only, these are things quite different in their nature; they cannot be lumped together and weighed in the same scale; you cannot say this quantity of labour is equal to that quantity of capital; they cannot be merged in one uniform aggregate of cost. Even if two articles are both produced by capital and labour, yet the proportion of capital to labour may not be the same in one as in the other. Shortly before his death Ricardo went even further, and suggested that even if two articles were produced by capital only, you could not employ the cost of the one to measure the cost of the other, because two portions of capital may be quite different in their nature—how, he asks, can you compare 'the capital of the clothier consisting of buildings, steam engines, raw materials, etc., with the capital of the sugar baker, consisting of a very different set of commodities'? (vol. 4, p. 393; see also his letter to McCulloch, vol. 9, p. 357).

Thus in Ricardo's view there is no one unit by which you can measure cost of production, and consequently no one unit by which you can measure value.[1] This indicates, as already remarked,

[1] In the absence of an explanation it must strike the reader as strange that while Ricardo in his third edition introduced this doctrine into his first chapter, he also in the same third edition introduced into his twentieth chapter the statement that the only way to measure the value of commodities is by measuring the quantity of labour realised in each. The only possible explanation appears to be that at the time when he wrote the new matter in chapter 20 he had not composed the new section in the first chapter; and that when writing this section, he had forgotten the new matter inserted in chapter

that Ricardo had no true conception of what value really is. He did not perceive that value is precisely the common denominator to which costs of all kinds can be reduced for the purpose of addition or subtraction, or for the purpose of comparing one quantity of cost with another. He failed to appreciate that, as remarked in an earlier chapter, value is, in all the complexities of modern industry, the only light that producers and traders have to guide them in their operations. They are all engaged in sacrificing one value to produce a higher value; they all aim at selling their goods for more money than they have expended in obtaining them. Money supplies the instrument, the yard-stick, the unit whose value is employed by everyone as a standard of measurement and a medium of exchange for articles of the most various descriptions and of the most various composition and origin.

Money, unfortunately, no matter what it is made of, is far from being a yard-stick of unvarying value such as Ricardo longed for. The nearest approach to a money of unvarying value ever reached by mankind was furnished by the gold standard which prevailed before everything went into the melting-pot as a result of our twentieth century wars. With gold as a standard of value and medium of exchange, a man who lent money to the government for twenty or thirty years could count upon being paid an agreed rate of interest year after year in money which underwent little change in purchasing power, and could also count upon repayment of the principal at maturity in money not differing greatly in value from that originally advanced by him. This comparative steadiness in the value of gold from one year's end to another arose from the fact that the mass of the money-metal already employed was so great that the additional supply received from the mines in any one year could have little influence on the purchasing power of the monetary unit, and perhaps none at all when we

20. The point cannot be cleared up by reference to Ricardo's letters. These show, indeed, that on the 4th December, 1820, he sent to McCulloch for perusal the new matter to be inserted in chapter 20 (vol. 8, p. 315), whilst it was not until the 25th of the following month that he wrote: 'I have made some alterations in the first chapter "on value" which I fear from the remarks in your letter will not meet with your approbation. I wish I had sent you the chapter, as it is now printing' (vol. 8, p. 342). On the other hand, as early as June, 1820, Ricardo had expressed himself in a manner (vol. 8, p. 193) which might seem to indicate that he had already adopted the view expounded in the new section of the first chapter; so the puzzle remains.

take into account the normal growth, year by year, in the quantity of goods to be circulated.

Now let us glance again at the new section 'On an invariable measure of value' which Ricardo inserted in his third edition. As we saw in our chapter on Money, Ricardo held two inconsistent theories as to the value of gold, one that its purchasing power depends on the quantity, and the other that its value, like that of other metals, is determined by its cost of production. In the new section it is the latter doctrine that is adopted, but according to that doctrine in its final shape, even if some one particular commodity (gold, for instance) were always throughout the ages produced by precisely the same combination of labour, capital, etc., it could not function as a true measure of the value of other things, because there are no two things both produced by exactly the same combination of factors. When 'agreeing' with de Tracy he said that one quantity of silver could only measure the value of another quantity of silver. For *silver* read *gold* and we have the new doctrine, but with this difference, that when speaking of silver he suggested that both the measure and the thing to be measured might be reduced to a common denomination, namely, the quantity of labour embodied in them, whereas the new section (which appeared in the same edition of his book) tells us that there is no possibility of comparing accurately the quantity of cost (and therefore value) embodied in one thing with the quantity of cost (and therefore value) embodied in a different thing.

Ricardo agrees, however, in regarding gold as the best practicable standard for use in comparing the values of all sorts of different commodities; but he does not arrive at this conclusion on the basis of the quantity theory referred to above; what he says in the new section is:

> May not gold be considered as a commodity produced with such proportions of the two kinds of capital as approach nearest to the average quantity employed in the production of most commodities? May not these proportions be so nearly equally distant from the two extremes, the one where little fixed capital is used, the other where little labour is employed, as to form a just mean between them?[1]

[1] Pages 28–9(45–6). As mentioned in our last footnote, Ricardo had used almost these very words in his letter to McCulloch of June, 1820 (vol. 8, p. 193). He developed the doctrine at length in the essay he was writing at the time of his death (vol. 4, p. 405).

Was Ricardo himself entirely satisfied with his theory of value? I think not. In 1820, when he had already published two editions of his book, he wrote to McCulloch:

> It must be confessed that this subject of value is encompassed with difficulties. . . . After all, the great questions of Rent, Wages, and Profits must be explained by the proportions in which the whole produce is divided between landlords, capitalists, and labourers, and which are not essentially connected with the doctrine of value (vol. 8, p. 194).

The new section in his third edition represented the result of his further thinking on the doctrine of value, but I imagine that he still felt uneasy, and that the essay which he was writing at the time of his death was undertaken quite as much with the hope of clearing up his own doubts as for the purpose of convincing others.

This essay, however, shows that, despite all efforts to make a new approach to the subject, no fresh light had dawned upon him. He is still unable to free himself from the 'train of ideas which have long followed each other in the mind' (see vol. 8, p. 311). Perhaps if he had lived another five or ten years he might have seen things from a different angle, particularly if his Parliamentary duties had diverted his attention from the problem of value and allowed him after an interval to approach the subject with a fresh mind. As it was, he never got rid entirely of the idea with which he started, namely, that labour is the only price exacted by Nature for her gifts. This idea, I fancy, had captured his imagination at an early period of his economic studies. Nature says to man (as she says to every other animal) 'Help yourself', but even the digging up or cutting down and carrying away of what is thus freely given costs labour, and almost invariably further labour must be bestowed on the materials thus gathered to adapt them to human requirements. Labour, then, is the price paid for practically everything. In 1810, which was seven years before he published his *Principles*, he wrote: 'There is no commodity to the production of which the labour of man is not necessary' (vol. 3, p. 270). Three years after the publication of his *Principles* he said: 'All commodities which have value are produced by labour' (vol. 8, p. 192). A year later, as we have seen, he inserted in his 20th chapter the statement that if you wish to compare the value of one thing with that of another it can be done, 'for they are both the result of labour' (189/284). And in the essay which lay on his desk when he died he said: 'All commodities having value are the result either of immediate labour, or of immediate and accumulated labour' (vol. 4, p. 379).

The last dictum, if not the earlier ones, seems to imply that nothing has value unless it is obtained by labour. Thus fish in the sea have no value so long as they remain in the sea uncaught; they acquire value only when caught and made available for consumption, and since there is free competition among producers, the price charged to the consumer covers only the immediate and accumulated labour involved in catching the fish and bringing it to market.[1] Not a penny of the price the consumer pays goes to Dame Nature for her gift; rent, therefore, may be eliminated as a constituent of the price or value.[2]

But does this hold good in the case of coal, iron, or tin? No doubt, on land as at sea, 'Help yourself' is still Nature's motto, but it is not the motto of Nature's Legal Representatives, the landlords. Robinson Crusoe paid Nature's price for the satisfaction of his wants, but what is called Political Economy deals, according to Ricardo's own definition, with the distribution of wealth between labourers, capitalists, and landlords in a world where every acre of habitable land is someone's property. It is not true that in this market nothing has value in exchange until labour has been bestowed upon it. Coal, iron, tin, salt, and numerous other substances which Nature has buried in the earth have a value in exchange before any human hand has touched them—a value which the owner of the land beneath whose surface they lie will require to be recognised before giving the capitalist and his men permission to drive a spade into the ground.

Ricardo seems to overlook this. At the beginning of his first chapter he admits that there are some things whose value in

[1] In the case of shrimps picked up on the sands, the cost is immediate labour only.

[2] In his third edition, when comparing his definition of cost with that of Say, Ricardo said: 'In his productive services he includes the services rendered by land, capital and labour. In mine I include only capital and labour, and wholly exclude land' (189/283).

exchange is not *in proportion* to the quantity of labour bestowed upon them, but he goes on to say:

> By far the greatest part of those goods which are the objects of desire, are produced by labour; and may be multiplied, not in one country alone, but in many, almost without any assignable limit, if we are disposed to bestow the labour necessary to obtain them (6/12).

He appears to think that, provided there is free competition on the part of producers, those commodities are sold to consumers at prices which cover nothing but the immediate and accumulated labour involved in their production. The price must cover all the labour put into the product 'from first to last'; that is to say, if the product is a tin pot, the price must cover the labour of digging up the tin as well as the labour of making a pot of it; the capitalist's profit at the current rate will be added to this, but nothing will be added for the owner of the land. Ricardo is particularly definite in his assumption that of all the vast sums paid by the public for manufactured goods of one sort or another, not a penny goes as rent to landlords. On page 64(110) he tells us that in the case of manufactured goods the whole value of the product 'is divided into two portions only; one constitutes the profits of stock, the other the wages of labour'. In a letter to McCulloch we have the remark that 'by getting rid of rent, which we may do . . . on all commodities produced by labour in manufactures, and distribution between capitalist and labourer becomes a much more simple consideration' (vol. 8, p. 194).

It is true that by far the greatest part of the things which are objects of desire are produced by labour; but labour can produce nothing without materials. Desire gives value to raw materials because desire gives value to what can be made from them. Materials buried in the ground where they are useless often have value because they will have a value when brought to the surface. Ricardo made a great mistake in assuming that demand only exercises an occasional and temporary influence on price. In turning his back on utility or desire as the source of value Ricardo started off on the wrong path from the very beginning, and Jevons did but speak the truth when he said:

> that able but wrong-headed man, David Ricardo, shunted the car of Economic science on to a wrong line, a line, however, on which

> it was further urged towards confusion by his equally able and wrong-headed admirer, John Stuart Mill. There were Economists, such as Malthus and Senior, who had a far better comprehension of the true doctrines (though not free from the Ricardian errors) but they were driven out of the field by the unity and influence of the Ricardo–Mill school.[1]

Thus for about half a century the teaching of Political Economy in England was to a large extent on the wrong path, and it has been worth while, I think, to study the way in which this state of things came about.

There is, of course, a sense in which it is perfectly true that labour is the price, and the only price, that the great bulk of mankind pay for the goods they consume. Whether I earn my living as a blacksmith, a bricklayer, or a writer of detective yarns, whether I be a lawyer, a singer, an acrobat, or a policeman, the price I pay for the commodities I obtain is my labour; and at all times and places, as Adam Smith said, that, to me, is cheap which I can acquire with very little labour, and that dear which costs me much labour. But this does not imply that what I receive in exchange for my exertions 'contains' the same quantity of somebody else's labour. If Nature had endowed me with a beautiful voice—or even if, like the Isle of Man, I had three legs instead of two—I might get a great deal of some people's labour for very little of my own; on the other hand, I may give a great deal of my labour for what perhaps 'contains' no labour at all, such as a piece of unimproved land. You may measure the value of this land by the quantity of labour or other things it will exchange for in the market; but if you measure it by the quantity of labour that 'produced it', you must conclude that it has no value at all. It was for saying this that Ricardo criticised Adam Smith (9/16); it was in rejecting Smith's view that Ricardo shunted his reasoning on to the wrong line.

[1] *Theory of Political Economy*, last page in Preface to second edition.

INDEX OF PASSAGES

in

RICARDO'S *PRINCIPLES*

quoted or referred to in this book

The pages in column E are those in the 'Everyman's' edition of Ricardo's *Principles*. Column S gives the corresponding pages in the annotated edition of the *Principles* which forms volume 1 of Sraffa's edition of Ricardo's Works.

For Product Safety Concerns and Information please contact our EU representative GPSR@taylorandfrancis.com
Taylor & Francis Verlag GmbH, Kaufingerstraße 24, 80331 München, Germany

www.ingramcontent.com/pod-product-compliance
Lightning Source LLC
LaVergne TN
LVHW011108300926
849160LV00008B/305
* 9 7 8 0 4 1 5 6 0 7 2 8 5 *